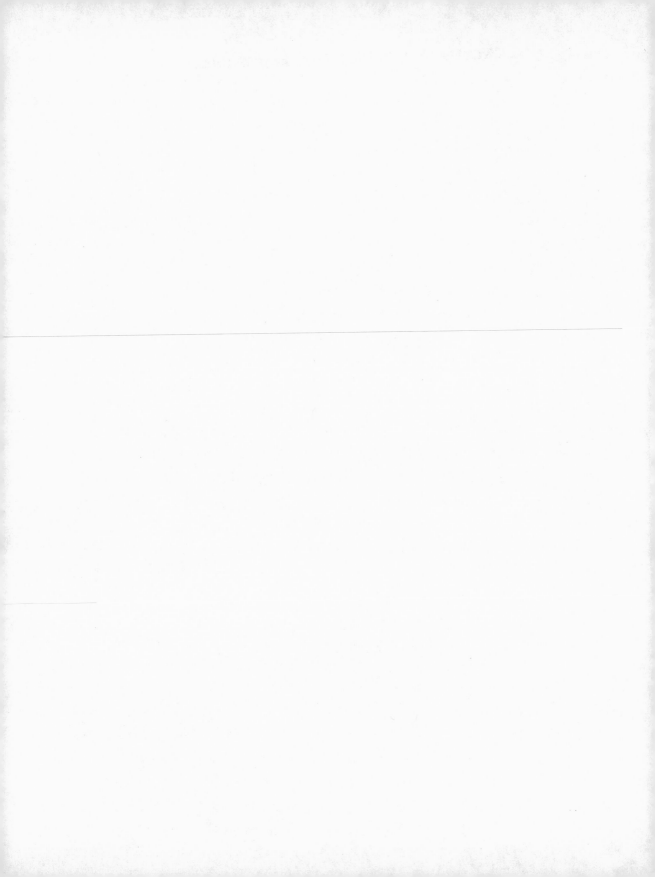

# Dynamics of
# INTERCULTURAL COMMUNICATION

### Fourth Edition

### Carley H. Dodd
*Abilene Christian University*

WCB Brown & Benchmark
PUBLISHERS

Madison, Wisconsin • Dubuque, Iowa

## Book Team

Editor *Stan Stoga*
Developmental Editor *Kassi Radomski*
Production Editor *Robin Storm*
Art Editor *Joseph P. O'Connell*
Visuals/Design Freelance Specialist *Mary L. Christianson*
Marketing Manager *Pamela Cooper*
Production Manager *Beth Kundert*

**Brown &
Benchmark**

A Division of Wm. C. Brown Communications, Inc.

Executive Vice President/General Manager *Thomas E. Doran*
Vice President/Editor in Chief *Edgar J. Laube*
Vice President/Marketing and Sales Systems *Eric Ziegler*
Vice President/Production *Vickie Putman*
Director of Custom and Electronic Publishing *Chris Rogers*
National Sales Manager *Bob McLaughlin*

## Wm. C. Brown Communications, Inc.

President and Chief Executive Officer *G. Franklin Lewis*
Senior Vice President, Operations *James H. Higby*
Corporate Senior Vice President and President of Manufacturing *Roger Meyer*
Corporate Senior Vice President and Chief Financial Officer *Robert Chesterman*

Cover design by Kay Fulton

Cover image © Diana Ong/Superstock, Inc.

Copyedited by Anne Scroggin

Printed in the United States of America by Wm. C. Brown Communications, Inc.,
2460 Kerper Boulevard, Dubuque, IA 52001

10   9   8   7   6   5   4   3   2   1

# Brief Contents

93760

# Contents

# Preface

Intercultural communication has become a truly exciting field of study. From the letters I have received and the meetings I have attended over the years inquiring about the first three editions of this text, I have learned how experts from a variety of places and backgrounds use intercultural communication principles. It is interesting and rewarding to know how many of you are contributing to so many people. Now in its fourth edition, this text represents an ongoing story of how people from diverse cultures communicate. In this edition you will find the usual updates on research and new concepts from the multiple areas associated with intercultural communication.

The examples and user-friendliness of the text continue to be positively evaluated by reviewers, students, and colleagues. Also, this edition contains a significantly increased amount of material about communicating with diverse cultures. Not only are diverse cultures discussed in a unique chapter on heritage cultures, but many cocultures and relevant principles of communication appear throughout the text. At the same time, the text preserves and adds to the theories, principles, and skills needed for dealing with intercultural communication between individuals and groups on a macrocultural level. I have merged chapters that dealt with similar themes, where previously the chapters were split for pedagogical reasons. In addition to the new chapter on heritage cultures, a new chapter on intercultural conflict appears. Furthermore, new data and models on competency, preparation, and development necessary for competency leading to intercultural effectiveness are stressed along with original models and self-evaluation scales. Some of the scales are retained in relevant places in the chapters, while other inventories are placed for general use in the appendix. These measurements are useful for personal growth, for intercultural training, for "people helping" opportunities, and certainly for research.

Finally, the central model for the book is employed throughout the text. The perception of difference or diversity motivates a drive toward intercultural competencies designed to create effectiveness in functional, intercultural communication. In dysfunctional, intercultural communication, the drive to deal with difference leads to distortion, withdrawal, hostility, alienation, and poor relationships. All this is explored in the text, but I think you will like the way the theme is carried in every chapter from the central model in chapter 1.

Overall, this book traces the imprint of cultural communication. This influence ranges widely. Consequently, this text covers a wide range of issues. I try not to overwhelm with research and data, but try to be faithful to the research, illuminating concepts, principles, and skills that you can understand and use.

Also, although a central model and theory are evident, you will notice how I use a number of research perspectives and approaches from the literature to build a topic. The purpose of such variety occurs in order to achieve several perspectives and achieve more comprehensive results for intercultural interaction.

An instructor's manual is available, providing professors with a computer test bank, semester and quarterly daily syllabi, overviews, and numerous skills exercises. In this edition, like the last three editions, I have not hesitated to bring analogies, illustrations, and examples from my students as well as from research and consulting, work that spans twenty-five years that included field work in numerous countries and consultations with small and large groups including Fortune 500 organizations and private organizations. The data and experiences are broad and have taught me many lessons in my growth in attempting successful intercultural outcomes. Fortunately, I am still learning and look forward to exploring together these questions raised in the book. You will observe that sometimes the writing is from a dominant U.S. cultural perspective. I hope you will observe also the desire for cultural sensitivity, awakening, and empathy that we intend for all cocultures communicating in a diverse world.

A number of people have been very helpful in developing various aspects of the book. Cecile Garmon, Richard Paine, Peggy Kirby, Diane Schwalm, and Gary Hughes uncovered a great deal of primary research for me in the first edition for which I am truly grateful. Reviewers of the first edition of the book in 1982 include Bill Gudykunst, Young Kim, Nemi Jain, and Jess Yoder. Second edition manuscript reviews were provided by Mara Adelman, Don Boggs, Carolyn Wilkins Fountenberry, Wallace Schmidt, and Andrew Wolvin. The reviewers for the third edition include Roger Conaway, Paul Lakey, Michael Prosser, and Curt Seimers. Thank you for the very helpful insights you provided and the specific suggestions you offered. The fourth edition reviewers and people with helpful comment include: Val Clark, Spokane Community College; Scherrie Foster, Minneapolis Community College; Janie Fritz, Duquesne University; Paul Frye, Trenton State College; and Sue Pendell, Colorado State University.

The staff at Brown and Benchmark have been fantastic. I appreciate their many hours of work and give special credit to Stan Stoga, Kassi Radomski, Robin Storm, and Peggy Selle. I am sure there are others about whom I do not know whose tireless efforts contributed greatly. Also, I owe thanks to the staff and faculty in the Department of Communication at Abilene Christian University for their support and encouragement. Chris Heard and Lynda Thornton were invaluable in providing line drawings. I gratefully acknowledge the ACU Department of Journalism and Mass Communication for various photographs.

I want to thank my parents, Carlysle and Leota Dodd, for the encouragement they have provided me all these years.

Most of all, I dedicate the book to my wife, Ada, who is my best friend and counselor, and to our children Jeremy, Matthew, Philip, and Jennifer. They sacrificed family time for me to complete this project.

Carley H. Dodd
1994

# Introduction and Background to Intercultural Communication

**Chapter** 1

# Overview to Intercultural Communication

**Objectives**

After completing this chapter, you should be able to

1. Define intercultural communication

2. Describe crucial elements within the intercultural communication process

3. Diagram and explain a model of intercultural communication

4. Identify the general or major variables involved as two persons or a group from differing cultural backgrounds communicate

5. Discuss conditions of intercultural communication among groups, identifying types of cultures

6. Identify intercultural communication effectiveness outcomes

A U.S. government official in a conversation with the Minister of Education from a Latin American country offers aid to assist what the former calls "backward" regions of the nation. The Latin American smiles wistfully and continues to talk in a friendly and positive manner. Upon returning to her office in Washington, D.C., the U.S. official finds a scathing letter from the Latin American condemning her for her paternalistic attitudes. How did communication fail?

The wife of a new foreign service officer in Sierra Leone, a country in West Africa, is just learning to buy in the local marketplaces. She returns from an afternoon of shopping, her feelings hurt, because owners of market booths shouted at her during their bargaining transaction. She considers this behavior insulting. Was there misunderstanding?

An African American third-grade student from an inner-city school lowers his head and casts his eyes downward when his teacher looks at him. The teacher is insulted since the young man "refuses" to look at his teacher. What nonverbal communication aspect has been overlooked?

A top manager from Aramco in Houston goes to work for a branch office in Saudi Arabia. After spending two years of successful work, she returns to Houston but no one seems to listen to her ideas for improvements. She has the feeling she is being passed over for a promotion, also. What has occurred in this case of cultural reentry?

Samuel is joining a management team for a Japanese car company doing business in his native Nigeria. After six months he becomes discouraged with what he considers lack of friendliness and concern among his Japanese supervisors. His management training in the United States encouraged quicker decisions and more rapid policy movement than he feels he is receiving from the Japanese organization. What cultural differences would you consider if Samuel called you for an intercultural communication consultation?

Yuko came to the United States one summer from her native Japan to attend graduate seminars. She liked the courses and decided to stay for a complete graduate degree. What troubled her was classroom informality and a sense of personal inadequacy as she frequently was asked to speak in class. What cultural adjustments would be proactive for Yuko or the classroom environment?

A Vietnam veteran seems withdrawn and distant to his family and old high school friends. They try to talk with him but consistently avoid the subject of the war. One by one, the veteran loses contact with these individuals. What dynamics are occurring?

Although these examples touch varied areas, they highlight a theme of intercultural communication: culture influences communication. Beyond using language, the study of intercultural communication recognizes how culture pervades what we are, how we act, how we think, and how we talk and listen. As Brislin (1993) indicates, not only are we *socialized* into a cultural context but culture continues to influence our interaction, our work, our gender expectations, and even our health.

When cultural variables play a primary part of the communication process, the result is intercultural communication. Not only must we trace culture's socializing patterns on each person, but recognize and respect how culture's imprint accounts for differences in communication style, world view, and personality. All too often, experts find messages and relationships halted, because one or both people in the relationship are not sure how to respond to a person who is perceived as dissimilar. Gudykunst and Kim (1984; also Gudykunst and Nishida 1989) apply the metaphor of *stranger* to these encounters with people perceived as "different from me." Inside our information processing functions is a need to explain the nagging uncertainty that accompanies interaction with someone from a contrasting group. The term *perceived cultural difference* reminds people that in the presence of diversity, such as language, values, thought, customs, and style, we often strive to resolve internal inconsistencies posed by the diversity. Effective intercultural communication occurs when the strive becomes a drive to reduce the uncertainty and anxiety of perceived differences. Adjusting, appealing to commonality, and cultural sensitivity are but a few functional, intercultural coping skills. Reinforcing bigotry, negative stereotyping, denial, and withdrawal illustrate dysfunctional pathways to intercultural communication.

To understand how intercultural communication is a special type of communication, consider another instance. If someone is similar to you, for instance a hometown friend or a family member, understanding is not perfect but accessible and even convenient. However, is a person from another region of the country with a different accent and values quite so comfortable? If a person of color is perceived to be "different" from a white person, how facile is their communication? Are physically disadvantaged individuals usually included in group activities of people who do not have physical disadvantages? The perception of difference affects people in powerful ways, easily revealed in verbal and nonverbal communication. With a close friend, we refer to common experiences, perhaps use jargon that we both understand, talk freely, and feel comfortable. With a person from a group perceived to be different from our own, we must listen and speak with a cultural consciousness. At first, conversing interculturally is awkward. Why? Cultural biases obscure our "certainty" and produce ambiguity leading to psychological discomfort.

The examples opening this chapter vividly demonstrate our need to understand culture and intercultural communication principles. The U.S. government official needs to understand the harm of arrogance toward other groups, for ethnocentrism leaks out in subtle, silent messages and actions.

The foreign service officer's wife has not yet learned that her host culture expects and enjoys intensive bargaining. There is no intent of animosity toward her; she does not yet understand interpersonal communication in that culture in that situation. The third-grade teacher apparently has not recognized cultural reasons for the student's lack of eye contact. The student has been taught that looking away is

Intercultural communication involves building commonality in a world of cultural diversity. (Photo by AP services.)

a sign of respect for authority, while the teacher's culture emphasizes respect by direct eye contact. The Japanese student is performing out of a home cultural fabric, the strands of which involve proper behaviors, roles, and rules. The Vietnam veteran is facing a prolonged cultural reentry adjustment. Unfortunately, his family and friends may lack the knowledge or skills to deal effectively with his condition. These examples point to an intricate balance between culture, interaction, and relationships. The way you nurture a relationship and how you say your message in many cultures are more important than the message itself.

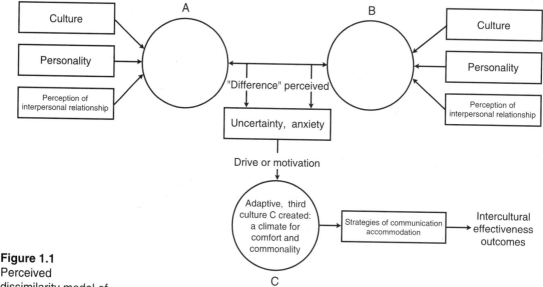

**Figure 1.1**
Perceived dissimilarity model of intercultural communication.

I offer a personal illustration to make the point of how we deal with uncertainty. I was out jogging on a half-moonlit, half-cloudy night and thought the sometimes deserted road was all mine. When two dark figures seemed to come out of nowhere, I confess I felt a slight uncertainty. (Who were these people? I've never seen them before.) An accompanying moderate anxiety developed. (What are they doing out here? Should I be worried?) I quickly moved to the other side of the road, but as I got closer I realized they were husband and wife joggers. When they spoke with an enthusiastic "Good evening," my anxiety disappeared. The uncertainty was reduced, and, smiling, I chugged down my beaten neighborhood path. The dissimilarity I felt (maybe they were muggers) gave way to similarity (I don't know where they are from but who cares—they are fellow joggers into the culture of lowered heart rates and improved HDL ratios. It's okay. They are like me).

## A Model of Intercultural Communication

Messages, perception, and information processing have always been a part of the study of communication, but communication scholars now recognize how culture, and its underlying dimensions, explain communication. When culture plays a critical role between individuals and groups, taking these into account becomes the realm of intercultural communication. The model for this text presented in figure 1.1 portrays this process.

### The Intercultural Communication Model

As the model indicates, we recognize the influence of culture (including group identities), personality (involving communication style), and the perception of an interpersonal relationship on communication outcomes. Intercultural communication emphasizes culture.

Perceived group or cultural differences can create barriers because of our "blind spots," which trap us with biases, misunderstanding, personal arrogance, and negative stereotypes and labels. In the presence of difference the human system motivates communicators into some form of reconciliation. We can speak of this motivation to understand, act, think, and speak appropriately as a drive.

"Perceived difference" means we assess others internally, as if to measure according to a scale of similarity or dissimilarity. This process leads to *social categorizing* whereby individuals supply names, labels, and motives to another person. When social categorization turns negative, it becomes a source of racism, bigotry, intolerance, ethnocentrism, and prejudice. In any case, when faced with difference, there is a "drive" or motivation connected with the encounter. One response is *uncertainty* which is cognitive, leading us to need information to fill in the gaps. A second response possibility is *anxiety,* which is an affective or emotionally based fear. Some people experience only uncertainty, some anxiety, and some experience both.

In other words, the questions and emotions we experience in the presence of "difference" ignite a pivotal beginning in the intercultural communication process, a drive to know another person and do something. In turn, we draw from our cultural and personal identities to estimate something about this new person. If perceived difference results from the "scanning," it calls for reconciliation, without which relationships remain indifferent, warped, or hostile.

One way of solving the uncertainty or anxiety leads to *dysfunctional* strategies, as for instance when the drive leads toward ignoring another person, pretending to like someone, avoiding communication responsibility, or outright hostility. My goal is to lead readers toward *functional* strategies. These approaches are based on competency-based intercultural communication. Competent intercultural communication uses the awareness of cultural variability, an adaptive style, and intercultural communication skills to create effective outcomes for intercultural communicators. Every chapter deals with cultural and group imprint on communication, relationships, and creative ways of developing functional outcomes.

A crucial point of the model in figure 1.1 is the *adaptive culture,* culture C, created as a result of the driving forces at work after differences between A and B are perceived. The entire range of adaptive characteristics are referred to as an adaptive culture. The idea of a third culture is not new; researchers for some time have viewed some form of merging, commonality, or coalescing as an important strategy (Casmir 1978, 1991; Gudykunst, Wiseman, and Hammer 1977; Ouchi and Jaegar 1974; Harris and Moran 1991). In this model, however, we suggest that a new culture created between two individuals or groups results from a drive for communication comfort, is artificially created, and becomes a temporary arena in which interactants adjust to each other within a context striving for balance and equilibrium. Almost everyone develops an adaptive style or set of procedures when faced with uncertainty or anxiety. Unfortunately, some adaptive behaviors coming out of this artificially created "culture" C are dysfunctional. Other adaptive cultural behaviors are functional and lead to positive experiences and effective outcomes.

To make the new culture a healthy place from which to launch outcomes is not automatic. However, it is possible to understand the process and skills needed to be successful.

Striving for a comfortable, adaptive culture between people is one of the human needs most people experience when facing diversity, illustrated by this Russian lawyer conversing with this Chinese student. (Photo by Attitaya Indrakanhang.)

The climate resulting from the development of culture C can turn out positively or negatively depending on changes in three areas. First, there must be a positive *feeling* toward the other person or group (referred to often as the affective level), such as trust, comfort, safety, affirmation, or lowered anxiety. Without this feeling—that one is regarded as worthy and can experience mistakes without being ridiculed or ignored—a person is less likely to communicate well with another who is different. Moreover, adjustment and effectiveness in a new culture may be lessened or prolonged or may never occur at all.

The second area needed to make a successful third cultural climate involves recognizing the *beliefs* we bring to intercultural encounters (frequently called the cognitive level). These include expectations, uncertainties (because of things we do not yet know about a person or a lack of accurate observation), misunderstanding of rules or procedures, a sense of strategy for communication competency, and activation of cues that trigger negative or positive social cognitions (such as stereotypes and attributions). Without accurate understanding a person is less likely to communicate well with another who is different.

A final area needed to build the third culture climate is intercultural communication *competence*. That means developing actions and accompanying skills (called the behavioral level), such as verbal and nonverbal communication performance, survival skills, and interfacing with systems and institutions in a new culture. When Marie, an American student spending a semester in Jerusalem, asked the hotel clerk to change a broken light in her room, she was surprised when he smiled and handed her the replacement bulb. She said later, "I guess I expected the Holiday Inn, where they would fix it for you. I didn't even know where to get a ladder." The light bulb went unchanged. Her expectations and lack of skills led to inefficiency.

In sum, a pattern for climate building is needed. By clearing our feelings positively, by developing good knowledge about the culture and the communication process, and by engaging in communication strategy designed to act competently, we become more successful.

The affective, cognitive, and behavior process in building a successful third culture C is well illustrated in the case of Kaoru (not her real name), a Japanese woman who at twenty-two married an American serviceman. At the time, she felt a need to disengage from her traditional roots. However, she now sees that her marriage was symbolic of her need for autonomy, although she loved her husband. Her parents, steeped in tradition, not only rejected the marriage, they rejected Kaoru. At first, the consequences seemed mild—after all, she was with the man she loved and would find a new life in America. Over time, the consequences were severe.

After some twenty years, Kaoru still knows very little English, engages little with non-Japanese and with only a handful of Japanese, is frequently depressed, and remains secluded from the U.S. culture. At first, it appears that the loss of parental support accounts for her trouble, but deeper examination reveals that she never felt safe in her new culture. Despite efforts by many people, she never developed positive feelings interacting with anyone. Her insecurity was only worsened by negative attitudes she held toward Americans in general. What is more, no one encouraged her development of language skills or of basic survival skills, despite numerous opportunities by Japanese and non-Japanese acquaintances. She never embraced friends, group members, and institutions that would have welcomed her.

From the adaptive culture C positive and effective intercultural outcomes occur when people feel competent and can communicate. If the adaptive culture is dysfunctional or unhealthy, then effectiveness is likely to be illusive or only accidental. If the adaptive culture is functional or healthy, through competent intercultural communication by which we refine adaptation to another culture (that is, adapting communication to cultural factors) effectiveness is more likely.*

---

*This approach is rooted in several rich communication research traditions. Uncertainty reduction theory, discussed by communication scholars (Berger and Calabrese 1975) has been applied to intercultural conditions (Gudykunst and Hammer 1988; Gudykunst and Nishida 1989; Gudykunst and Kim 1984). Third culture building has been a topic in the field, explored by Casmir (1978, 1991), Gudykunst, Wiseman, and Hammer (1977), Ouchi and Jaegar (1974), and Harris and Moran (1991). The concept has elements from what is called coordinated management of meaning (called CMM), where people are said to develop rules and accommodations to the unique social encounters they experience (Pearce and Wiseman 1983; Cronen and Shuter 1983; Cronen, Chen, and Pearce 1988). Research in intercultural accommodation and adjustment has been useful (Kim 1988; Kim 1989; Kim and Gudykunst 1988; Lakey 1988; Norton 1991), as well as research in newly emerging fields of adolescent and family accommodation and development (Lewis, Dodd, and Tippens 1989, 1992). Intercultural competency and effectiveness has been an illuminating area for intercultural communication (Hammer 1989; Wiseman and Abe 1984; Ellingsworth 1983; Koester and Lustig 1993; Kealey 1989). Other communication theory perspectives have been significant as well including homophily theory (Rogers 1983), rhetorical theory (Prosser 1973, 1978; Koester and Holmberg 1983; Monfils 1980; Blackman 1983), constructivism as it relates to perception and social categorization (Applegate and Sypher 1983, 1988; Casmir 1985; Gudykunst and Gumbs 1989; Gallois, Franklyn-Stokes, Giles, and Coupland 1988; Ehrenhaus 1983), face-saving and conflict management (Ting-Toomey 1985, 1989), and what is generally referred to as attribution theory (Dodd and Lewis 1992). This entire model and approach reflects my experience as an intercultural professor, consultant, and researcher.

**Personality and Communicator Style Influencing Intercultural Communication**

Although this text is about cultural communication, the process, by necessity, involves personal style and relationships. Various chapters and sections throughout the text integrate the importance of individual communicator's styles and relationship perception throughout the text. As culture implants its footprints on the communication process, so personal communicator style and relationship development are conditioned by one's culture as well as one uniquely contributing to communication outcomes.

An individual's personal communicator style can be seen as a part of culture and a contributor to intercultural communication outcomes. Consider, for instance, the quiet, nonverbal behavior exhibited by a Japanese person who prefers to go unnoticed in a crowd. Contrast this with a North American who values assertiveness and who believes that self-created recognition may to some extent relate to success. Acceptable personality behaviors in one culture may be offensive in another culture. Cultural types and cultural heroes provide a rich reservoir for learning the ideal types for a culture; often heroes stand as a model for individual personality development. The U.S. dominant cultural person who insists on handshaking and backslapping within a nontouching culture, such as the Laotian culture, may find that his or her personality type is repugnant to Laotians. Each student of intercultural communication must learn as much as possible about ideal roles and cultural expectations.

**Interpersonal Perception Factors Influencing Intercultural Communication**

All of us have "yardsticks" by which we evaluate an interactant in communication. This perception of another person falls into several domains, raising questions. Is this relationship of potential worth? Does this person present risk for me? Power over me? Is there believability? Similarity? Attraction?

In other words, what social or personal attributions do I make about this person? For most people, the attributions color our motivation to interact. For example, you can be an assertive person, but if the other person or group seems to hold little importance or attraction for you, it is unlikely you will feel a motivation to approach, bridge the cultural gap, accommodate, and engage in the process of communicating. Common relationship orientation revolves around interpersonal attraction, group attraction, social network potential, similarity, credibility, and opinion leading relationships.

**Cultural Differences Perceived in Communication**

As we will discuss in chapter 3, culture is the "summation and interrelationship of an identifiable group's beliefs, norms, activities, institutions, and communication patterns." Every culture has themes, expectations, values, modalities, tendencies, procedures, and rules. Culture is like a kaleidoscope with similar shapes but different colors, or at other times, with different shapes but similar colors. One reason to study culture is to be able to recognize its impact on our communication rules, which we bring to intercultural encounters.

How can we examine cultures? When can we recognize cultural differences?

*Macrocultural systems.* Obviously, there are large global regions and national cultures that are structurally and organically bound together into a social system where people have developed a cultural network. Examples include what might be globally described as North American culture, Latin American culture,

Macrocultural differences refer to national and regional cultural factors, illustrated by this Masai tribal man. (Photo by Mike Moore, Kenya.)

African culture, Middle Eastern culture, European culture, and Asian culture. These global differences, marked by geopolitical factors, fit into the study of cultural influence on communication.

*Microcultures and cocultures.* The term microculture, used interchangeably with coculture and diversity culture in this text, is a collectivity with conscious identity and grouping coexisting within a larger culture. Microcultures, or cocultures, often experience common themes regarding image, bonding, and association.

*Microcultures of social identification.* Most people belong to a number of groups, some voluntary, some by birth, adoption, or selection into those groups. Salient groups—the ones we consciously value—provide a source of identity. Structurally, these are microcultures or cocultures within a macroculture. For instance, within the U.S. dominant American culture, we might identify an elderly microculture, a cowboy microculture, an Appalachian microculture, or a volunteer association microculture. Each group exhibits some similarities to the large culture, but also some differences. Within most macrocultures, smaller group cultures are cocultures marked by social class, education, age, and associations.

Microcultures of social identity rely on members' mutual self-perception, but they also are defined by religion, geography, wealth, national origin, age, gender, work, and family. The significance of social identity groups lies in their saliency for any one individual. For instance, your friend might not find much use for a civic club that you enjoy. In this text, heritage cultures refer to those ethnic, racial, adopted, and marital conditions aligning people with a particular group.

*Microcultures of heritage.* Heritage cultures involve common origins, race, or family ties. Ethnic groups are identifiable bodies of people noted for their common heritage and cultural tradition, which are often national. *Interethnic communication* is communication between two or more persons from different ethnic backgrounds. Although any listing of ethnic heritage is certain to omit some significant group, the following exemplify ethnic groups in the United States: Native American, Polish American, Italian American, Irish American, African American, Asian American, Mexican American, and Puerto Rican American.

Race is genetically transmitted involving traits of physical appearance. Therefore, *interracial communication* is communication between two or more persons of differing racial backgrounds. The important concern is that racial differences can trigger negative attributions that cut off potential communication. At one university, an administrator in the office of student affairs argued in a meeting with an African American fraternity leader. Only after a cooling-down period did both men realize and freely admit that their racial differences had produced an immediate and mutually negative response in each, even before either had spoken a word.

The conceptual baggage we often carry with us, such as stereotypes of other racial groups, can easily blind us to the fact that, in many instances, few significant differences exist between two people. Real cultural differences do not always exist beyond ethnicity and race—we simply magnify the immediate through stereotypes.

*Countercultures.* Countercultural communication involves persons of cocultures who in some form oppose a dominant host culture. Prosser (1978) defines it as

> that interaction between members of a subcultural or cultural group whose members largely are alienated from the dominant culture. Members of the group not only reject the values of the dominant culture or society, but may actively work against these values. Conflict is often the result. (p. 69)

Prosser cites an example of the Amish, a coculture whose members have reacted passively, withdrawing from the dominant culture. Consider Polish laborers who, without historical precedent and at risk because of the Soviet Union's anti-strike policies, went on a well-publicized strike to seek to free labor unions from government control. Many of the communication encounters that followed could be considered countercultural types of intercultural communication, at least in terms of rejecting establishment values existing up to that time.

*Demographic group membership communication.* In many instances, social participation and group membership are units marked by their homogeneity on ideological characteristics. Many intergroup differences, fueled by group loyalties, explode into serious concerns for subcultural communication.

The fighting between Protestants and Catholics in Northern Ireland and between Moslems and Christians in Lebanon are examples of the importance of religious group membership as a microculture.

Also, gender, residence, occupation, income, and age exemplify demographic group differences.

*Communication between social classes.*   Some of the differences between people are based on status inferred from income, occupation, and education. Communication between these classes is appropriately labeled social class communication. There is a large gap in many parts of the world between the elite and the masses as well as between the rich and the poor. Often accompanying this gap are significant differences in outlook, customs, and other features. Although these social classes share some aspects of a common culture, their differences become a cultural concern.

*Rural-urban communication.*   Rural and urban life-styles are noted for differences in pace of life, fatalistic tendencies, philosophy, and interpersonal relationship formation among other qualities. These differences represent communication styles and functional differences in communication when rural and urban individuals interact.

*Regional communication.*   People from one region of the United States often have serious communication problems with people from another region. A reserved New Englander is sometimes put off by a syrupy-sweet southern style of communication because he takes it to be a sign of insincerity. On the other hand, a Southerner may interpret the reserved style of her northern friend as a sign of rudeness. Regional cultural styles differ.

*Gender communication.*   Evidence confirms how communication patterns markedly differ between men and women. From examples in management to cases in the family, data remind us that there are male and female cocultures. The different communication styles of males and females can be a source of enormous interpersonal misunderstanding. An understanding of the cultural differences involved can improve intercultural skills.

*Organizational cultural communication.*   Another kind of cultural communication climate in which most of us interact is organizational culture—that is, the culture of an organization that includes its accompanying norms, procedures, and communication patterns. Every organization has its own customs and rules, which along with the mind-set of corporate members, profoundly influences the way organizational members interact among themselves and how they interact with people from other organizational cultures.

The study of corporate culture has shown the need to look at corporations in terms of how they can improve their public image and their business in the international market. For example, an organization that emphasizes task and performance orientation above other factors will likely experience some frustration in communication with or in doing business with an organization that has a more laid-back approach that emphasizes personal relationships, even at the expense of time and productivity. Of course, it is not really the organizations that communicate—it is the people who represent those organizations. One of the discoveries in the field of intercultural relations is that corporate organizational norms vastly influence how organizational members talk to other people, how they feel about themselves, and how successful they are when dealing with someone from a different cultural orientation.

*Family cultures.*   Social research is moving in the direction of how family systems are major agents of social change. For instance, Galvan and Brommel (1986) adapt Olson's family systems model. From the beginning point of cohesion and change as major axes, they develop themes of communication: roles, power, and decision-making as key communication influences. Pearson (1989) relies on a rules perspective to explain not only relational development, but also how families facilitate satisfaction and generate themes of affirmation (Lewis, Dodd, and Tippens 1992).

**Plan for
This Book**

The text is organized around the model presented in this chapter. By nature of its topic, the book elevates *cultural variability* by underscoring the many elements of culture in part 2 (chapters 3–6); linguistic, nonverbal, and information network aspects of culture in part 3 (chapters 7–9); and the numerous ways to adapt to intercultural differences and relationships through intercultural competency skills and strategies in part 4 (chapters 10–14). The multiple topics presented in this text are intended to help the reader account for the dysfunctional and functional adaptive qualities of intercultural communication and to discover what works well in practicing competent intercultural communication.

Each chapter presents material that addresses our central model. In this way, readers can visualize where the data fit into the "big picture" by referring back to chapter 1. Also, to translate the model into parts and chapters, figure 1.2 demonstrates the organizational plan for the book.

The scholarly resources for each chapter are conveniently listed at the end of the book. Each chapter also has exercises planned as pedagogically sound methods of instilling experiences in intercultural communication. Readers in the past editions of this book also have appreciated the skills at the end of each chapter. These are intended as helpful tips that many practitioners have found useful.

**Developing
Skills in
Preparing for
Intercultural
Communication**

1. *Work on developing a theory-oriented mind-set.* This book emphasizes doing and practicing, not just knowing principles of intercultural communication. However, this chapter is a good place for examining assumptions behind an idea. Part of a theory-oriented mind-set includes looking for single and multiple causes and effects, ascertaining social and historical forces behind the origination of a new concept, and creating new concepts. Reasoning, looking for and analyzing facts, synthesizing, and offering critiques are also important skills for the intercultural communication process.

2. *Develop fluency in thought.* Surprisingly, many people find that their communication skills are not weak in what they think but in articulating their thoughts ("I know what I think—I just can't say it"). The ability to develop communication of concept and to express that diversity is important. Especially during intercultural communication, we must explain our meanings in more than one way. Forcing ourselves into multiple ways of describing our feelings, thoughts, and behaviors is a step in initiating improved intercultural communication skills.

Part 1 : Introduction and Background to Intercultural Communication

   1. Overview to Intercultural Communication
   2. Background to Intercultural Communication

Part 2 : Perceiving Cultural and Social Diversity

   3. Elements of Cultural Systems
   4. Microcultures of Heritage and Group Attitudes
   5. Microcultures of Social Identification and Group Relations
   6. Underlying Dimensions of Culture

Part 3 : Understanding Intercultural Information

   7. Cultures of Linguistic Diversity
   8. Intercultural Communication and Nonverbal Messages
   9. Cultures of Networking and Information Flow

Part 4 : Cultural Adaptation and Communication Accommodation:
Applying Intercultural Competencies

  10. Adapting to Culture
  11. Intercultural Competencies and Effectiveness
  12. Intercultural Communication and Conflict
  13. Intercultural Communication and Mass Media as Cultural Influence
  14. Intercultural Communication, Innovation, and Change

Appendix: Self-Report Assessment Applied to Intercultural Communication

**Figure 1.2**
A visual model of
chapter topics.

3. *See success with people as success in task.* Effective intercultural communication begins with a recognition that a focus on task alone is insufficient. Communication relationships must be planted, watered, and cultivated along with our task orientation for successful intercultural communication experiences. Intercultural relationship success is an important ingredient for task success.

4. *Try to be a facilitator with people.* Another skill that can be helpful in intercultural relations is the ability to link persons who have not met. By simple introductions, by emphasis on their commonalities, and by staying with people long enough, we can serve an important liaison role. Sometimes, just knowing the right questions to ask can spotlight others in a positive way. We do not have to be glib or effervescent, just sincere and willing to invest time and energy in others. Then, by sharing our positive insights during an informal introduction to another person, we can build relationships between others that can be exciting for us and helpful to them.

5. *Assume the burden of communication to be yours.* Many people simply avoid the sometimes difficult task of communicating with someone from a culture different from their own. Assuming the burden for making the attempt is an important first step in improving intercultural communication skills. When intercultural "breakdowns" occur, try to take responsibility for finding creative ways of solving the problem.

**This Chapter in Perspective**

Successful intercultural communication converts the drives of perceived dissimilarity (between culture A and B) into applying intercultural competency as part of an adaptive third culture (culture C) leading to communication accommodation strategies ultimately leading to intercultural effectiveness outcomes.

Intercultural communication involves understanding the influence of culture, personal communicator style, and interpersonal relationship attributes as these affect intercultural communication and perception of difference. These factors influence two people in building a third culture or communication climate from which they find commonality, reduce uncertainty and anxiety, and provide a context basis for continued communication. This third culture C is an adaptive area, leading to accommodation strategies for intercultural effectiveness. It is important to discover the imprint of culture on communication.

The chapter documents a number of intercultural axioms concerning intercultural communication. These include the principle of difference, the content and relationship dimensions of intercultural communication, the role of personal communicator style in intercultural communication, reducing uncertainty about relationships and messages, the nature of perception in sensing differences, the centrality of communication to culture, and the importance of intercultural effectiveness as a goal.

You may not live in Pongo-Pongo, but you may live in Chicago, in a rural area of the United States, or in a region of the United States culturally different from the place where you grew up. Intercultural communication should, therefore, encompass a number of dimensions where culture and communication come together.

**Exercises**

1. How have recent trends in terrorism affected foreign travel? Perceptions toward other nations? How are people who are from different countries affected?

2. Interview an international student on changing patterns of communication style within his or her country. What are the differences in communication style between that person's home culture and the current culture in which he or she lives?

3. Your instructor will assign an intercultural communication book to each student. Scan and list all of the assumptions about communication that you can find in the book. Compare your list with the lists of other students, and compile a master list of assumptions. Evaluate the items on the master list and then redraft a final list of the communication assumptions that you think really say it best.

4. Conduct a newspaper scan for bias toward ethnic or social identification groups. How can you spot these reflections? How can you define them? What words or symbols would you use to alter perceptions of these groups if you were writing the newspaper story?

# Background to Intercultural Communication

After completing this chapter, you should be able to

**Objectives**

1. Identify the perceptual processes involved in interpreting intercultural messages

2. Distinguish between content and relationship dimensions of an intercultural communication situation

3. Describe the attribution process and specific negative perceptual processes indicated in the chapter

4. Discuss a brief and selected history accounting for the development of the field of intercultural communication

This chapter examines the background to intercultural communication, starting with assumptions about intercultural communication and concluding with a selected history of the development of intercultural communication. The undergirding variables of intercultural communication appear throughout the text. This chapter explores the fundamental beginning points, called *axioms*, that form the foundational principles concerning intercultural communication.

## Axioms behind Intercultural Communication

The axioms behind intercultural communication remind us how important it is to examine why we think about and act toward individuals and groups as we do.

### Intercultural Communication Assumes the Perception of Difference

Communication existing in a climate of cultural differences is a presupposition for the entire range of intercultural principles. The process begins with the perception that differences exist (Prosser 1978). Consequently, we focus on the message linkage between individuals or groups from two different cultural situations. There are a number of antecedents and consequences to that interaction, but it is the bridging of the intercultural gap that gives intercultural communication its fullest meaning.

The principle of difference implies that people often do not immediately share norms, thought patterns, structures, and systems. However, dealing with cultural differences alone and studying cross-cultural comparisons, while valuable, do not get to the point of contact and communication (Kim 1984).

Rather, it is precisely the perception of difference that explains communication tendencies. We may be motivated to avoid intercultural interactions when confrontation with difference becomes uncomfortable for us. On the other hand, an effective intercultural communicator recognizes difference as a positive opportunity to overcome misunderstanding and poor communication. The difference, once recognized, can motivate positive or negative "drives." To be successful in intercultural relationships, we must recognize differences as resources. An exact copy of ourselves can prove only to multiply our own flaws—the differences of others can provide a renewed resource of insight.

Seeing "difference" is a central facet to the intercultural communication model in chapter 1 involving perception—at the core is how individuals decide on similarity or dissimilarity. When they perceive "difference," the dissimilarity can be explained by three screening filters by which communicators size up each other. A form of distinguishing occurs. That is, social categorization leads to mental and emotional associations across three assessments: differences in culture or group, differences in personality, and differences in the way two people might view their particular interpersonal relationship. How does all this influence our practical communication?

This is where the axiom concerning the principle of difference helps us understand information and relationships. Evaluating the source of difference explains actions or thoughts of another person who appears different. We can explain the source of miscommunication, attributed to difference because of (1) culture ("This is the way my culture does things"), (2) personality ("You and I are from the same culture but we are individuals who think and act differently"), and (3) relationship history ("I thought I knew you, but I can't trust you anymore").

By its nature, intercultural communication assumes not only the message, but the social relationship associated with an interaction. We label this axiom as communication having content and relationship dimensions. Watzlawick, Beavin, and Jackson (1967) emphasize that communication does not exist in content isolation; ultimately meaning results from *what* is said and *who* says it. The relationship between two communicators affects how the message is interpreted. For example, if your best friend said, "Could we get started on this project?" you probably would interpret the statement as a simple request for starting a task. However, if the boss said, "Could we get started?" the meaning would likely be different. From the boss, the statement sounds more demanding and is much more likely to be treated with greater deference than your close friends's request.

**Intercultural Communication Has Both Content Relationship Dimensions**

While it is true that relationships alter meanings, the converse also works: messages alter relationships. For example, it is easier to feel positively toward a co-worker who compliments rather than criticizes. It is easier to like a boss who affirms constructively. In these cases, messages create a relationship, which in turn becomes the beginning for the axiom; the nature of the relationship then sets the stage for interpreting the next message.

When we say "message" or "information," those concepts are familiar and easy to understand. What is relationship, though? What is the gridwork through which we view another person? The principle of difference discussed previously, describes one fundamental relationship filter whereby we answer the question of how similar or dissimilar is this person. A second way people assess others involves believability, which communication experts call credibility. Together, perceptions of similarity/dissimilarity and credibility predict the nature of relationships. These judgments form the basis of information relationships. They even explain the friendship and network cultures of which we are a part. The influence of credibility as one parameter of relationships is illustrated by an international student from Thailand who expressed her negative evaluation of a certain American young man. However, once she reevaluated her attribution of various qualities about him, she perceived him as much more believable in ways that were credible for her home culture. Once that credibility was established, she began to view this same young man's messages as "very important." In the process, her alteration of the credibility relationship subsequently influenced messages between the two.

Intercultural communication involves skills that facilitate relationships, break down barriers, and create foundations for new visions.

## Personal Style Affects Our First Impressions, Which Influence Intercultural Communication

Intercultural communication can be described in terms of the communication styles used by people. Communication style means the personal qualities we infer from the messages and the manner of a communicator. For example, some people have a dominant communicator style; others have a submissive style. Some are warm and caring; others are cold and unfeeling. Some are authoritarian; others are open-minded. Some communicators are preoccupied; others are attentive. Other personal communication styles include being extremely friendly, being a mediator between people, being a counselor, being a critic, being a question asker, being an informed opinion giver, and being a victim.

Sometimes these "styles" or forms of social communication are conscious. In such cases, people communicate about the way they view themselves, and they intend to make a certain kind of impression. More often, people are not aware of their communication style. In this case, they act from habits formed in culture, family, and individuality. Very few of us remain unaffected by the various communication styles we encounter.

Intercultural communication depends upon reducing uncertainty levels about other people. In our interpersonal encounters, there is always some ambiguity about the relationship: "How does he feel about me?" "What are her attitudes?" "What can I expect to happen next in this relationship?" We experience discomfort with questions about relationships, and so to reduce our discomfort, we engage in behaviors that enhance our chances of maximum understanding with the fewest possible questions.

Intercultural Communication Involves Reducing Uncertainty

In the field of communication, predictability is something of the opposite of uncertainty and remains an important aspect of relationships. We seem to need a certain amount of redundancy to lessen the entropy (the "new" messages or the unfamiliar part of a message) in communication. In other words, the less guesswork about a message *and* a relationship, often the better we feel about the situation.

Communication with a person from a different culture poses *proportionately more* ambiguities and uncertainties. Some form of predictability is needed to combat the uncertainty. By employing some "standard" areas of predictability, we reduce the impact of what would otherwise be different, unusual, and uncertain. In greetings, for instance, there is a range of acceptable cultural practices. Throughout the conversation, various cultural rules guide the communication. If we share the same culture, the communication rules are implicitly understood, and the job of deciphering and interpreting the other person is significantly easier.

Interaction with someone from another culture, however, means that we do not necessarily share the same communication rules, and the ambiguity increases dramatically. There are significantly more possible behaviors during intercultural communication than during intracultural communication.

One answer to facing uncertainty is to offer predictability, using communication rules, customs, rituals, phrases, and features that match the other person's culture. A second way to face uncertainty is to understand and manage the interaction stages typical of people meeting: precontact, contact and impression, and closure.

*Precontact.* The first phase of reducing uncertainty involves precontact impression formation. In coming in contact with another person, we proceed from an unfocused scanning of the environment to a focused scanning (Barnlund 1968). We become aware that another person is a part of the immediate communication climate. At that point, we engage in *reciprocal scanning*. We gain information by interpreting the appearance and mannerisms of the other person, while the other person does the same with us. The strategies can be quite complicated, but we reduce uncertainty on a simple and efficient level during this first phase (Berger, Gardner, Parks, Shulman, and Miller 1976).

*Contact and impression.* The second phase of intercultural uncertainty reduction involves the initial impression within the first few minutes of verbal communication. Brooks and Emmert (1976) suggest that during the first four minutes, a decision is made to continue or discontinue the relationship. Even within the first two minutes, we form some rather important judgments: "Do I like him?" "Is she understanding me?" "Am I wasting my time?" "He sure doesn't look like much." This *four minute barrier* as it sometimes is labelled, may not take exactly four minutes, but the power of early impressions is certain.

*Closure.* The third phase of uncertainty reduction involves closure, or completion, of the intercultural relationship. This is not just a way of exiting or saying goodbye. It is the longer lasting attitudes based on the early impressions in stage two. There is a tendency to form a comfortable summary of another person, a mental picture or verbal phrase that profiles a final evaluation concerning the other person. These fundamental and powerful attitudes are the basis for the following intercultural communication axiom.

**Intercultural Communication Involves Fundamental Attitudes Toward Groups and Relationships**

When you read about racism, bigotry, and prejudice such words stir emotions. In the close of the twentieth century, how could anyone hold these attitudes, much less feel hatred or act violently toward "out-groups"? The daily news reports such tensions. What attitudes deny peace between coexisting cultures? What causes these attitudes, and what signifies their presence?

*Positive* intercultural attitudes lead to adaptive, functional outcomes, such as friendship, peace, increased understanding, and lasting bonds. The attitudes and accompanying communication behaviors emerge as openness, affirmation, questioning, supporting, listening, offering feedback, asserting, and suggesting.

*Negative* intercultural attitudes lead to nonadaptive, dysfunctional outcomes including prejudice, racism, ethnocentrism, discrimination, and negative stereotyping. These are related to communication behaviors such as withdrawing, blocking, closed-mindedness, authoritarian communication, slandering, condemning, and hating.

How do these and other attitudes originate? The perceptual processes are complicated, but in simple terms, there are four reasons.

1. *Attribution.* This theory refers to our understanding and summarizing others' behaviors by inferring their motivations. If someone does something we like, we attribute a positive motivation to that person because, after all, he or she practiced what we valued. Negative actions, however, cause us to infer a negative motivation—"He doesn't like me," "She's out to get me," "He's manipulative," "She really is working for a different position in the company."

2. *Impression consistency.* A related concept is called implicit personality theory. This theory implies that we seek consistency with our first "personality" assessment of another individual. If the first impression of a person's qualities is positive, then we ascribe additional positive qualities to that person. For instance, if Jim is energetic and assertive, then he will also be ____. What word did you think about inserting? Courageous? Intelligent? The theory predicts that some positive word will follow. In the same

way, if the first-known qualities are negative, we assess the unknown with more negative features. If Jim is described as dumb and clumsy, what additional personality adjectives might be included? Probably something negative, according to the theory. In other words, a positive or negative "halo effect" extends from described qualities to unknown qualities. What is unknown is consistent with the known.

3. *Incomplete information.* This also accounts for poor perception and can result in negative attitudes. Personal circumstances may lead to inadequate or poor sampling from which to draw accurate data about a person or a group. This leads to hasty or limited generalization.

4. *Following cultural attitudes.* By custom and adherence to cultural attitudes, one can slide into negative attitudes toward out-groups simply by following cultural caricatures, stereotypes, and attitudes. One university student once explained, "My hometown and school never had any Hispanics, so I never realized my prejudice and feelings of people 'not like me.' When Armando and I first met, my exclusive attitudes erupted into an ethnic dislike and blocked seeing what a caring, sensitive man he really is." Cultures, schools, and families teach us in silent, yet numerous ways, how to feel about others "not like me." It is all too easy to lift the stereotypes others have invented and unconsciously apply this "in-group" judgment without question.

Cultures inherently contain communication systems. Many years ago, Smith (1966) observed that "communication and culture are inseparable," a point echoed in more recent research (Hecht, Andersen, and Ribeau 1989). One implication of this insight is that cultures generate symbols, rituals, customs, and formats. To use a simple example, every culture has rules for achievement and attainment. In dominant U.S. culture, the symbols of these "rites of passage" include degrees, promotions, material objects, technology, and symbols of material wealth. A plaque of recognition, a certificate of merit, or a gold watch at retirement symbolize dominant U.S. culture's communication system. Nationals in Botswana use physical symbols also, but the symbols represent recognition in tribal terms and are symbolic of pride in the primary group and not just individual attainment. In this way, the communication systems we employ are rooted in the culture where they are used. Cultural misunderstanding occurs when we fail to match the appropriate symbols and general communication system to the culture. Just witness the awkwardness of an expatriate who attends a gathering in a host culture, but fails to wear the appropriate clothes.

A second implication of this axiom is not only should we employ the correct symbols with a culture's communication system, but also use the appropriate personal communication style. Communication styles refer to mannerisms, phrases, rituals, and communication customs appropriate for various situations in a culture. For instance, in Saudia Arabia interpersonal communication style upon meeting one's host is marked sometimes by flowery language, numerous compliments, and profuse thanks. Rarely does one publicly criticize fellow workers in a culture where such messages would appear disloyal and disrespectful (Harris and Moran 1991).

*Communication Is Central to Culture*

Some West Africans tend to exhibit an extremely friendly and warm interpersonal communication style. Some Asians are described as conscious of propriety, ceremony, and rules to a point of extreme display of respect and honor. Some dominant U.S. culture members appear informal, uninhibited, and preferring to come to the main point quickly in a linear manner. Some Britons seem to have a reserved subtlety, preferring understatement and control in interpersonal interaction. These examples remind us that it is crucial to understand the intercultural style of the people with whom we communicate. Of course, not everyone from a culture acts and thinks the same way, but the central tendencies you may come to discover about cultures can become a useful beginning for awareness and interaction.

## Intercultural Effectiveness Is a Goal of Intercultural Communication

Another axiom of intercultural communication involves communication effectiveness. The goal of this concept is positive intercultural outcomes. That success can take many forms: improved relationships, effective management, friendship, training (Brislin 1989), technology dissemination, and conflict reduction.

Overall, researchers are concerned about three intercultural communication outcomes: task, relationship, and personal adjustment. The *task* outcome is the result of intercultural communication on performance. Task means accomplishing a work-related purpose.

In the *relationship* outcome, we are concerned with what others think of us. Do they like us? Dislike us? Can we continue to work together? Understanding and friendship are two important subsets of relationship. Increased understanding makes mutual influence and accurate understanding possible (Ruhly 1976). One of the goals, of studying intercultural communication is to increase understanding and to decrease tensions.

A third possible outcome of intercultural communication is *personal adjustment*. A great deal has been learned in the last few years about the process of going through transitions and adapting to the cultural stresses that accompany communication in a culture different from our own. Learning to adjust and to acculturate are major outcomes of adaptation leading to effectiveness.

## The Origins of Intercultural Communication

While you may have some concrete ideas about speech or communication theory, it is possible you may have limited exposure to intercultural communication, a relatively new area of communication studies. The origins of this area of study are many and are complex, so the brief history below is selected from a dominant U.S. cultural perspective. At least the trends allow us to narrowly explore forces and conditions leading to the serious investigation of intercultural communication.

## Dealing with International Differences

Some observers claim that, prior to the Second World War, many people in the United States seemed to lack a world perspective. At one time in U.S. history, the Monroe Doctrine prompted leadership to embrace people in the world because it was "manifest destiny" to extend the doctrines of "democracy." We also learned from the experiences of travelers and missionaries. However, the events surrounding the Second World War seemed to jolt us, even more than the First World War, into a national consciousness that there was another world out there. U.S. isolationist views continued to erode under a move toward global awareness and interaction.

**Part 1    Introduction and Background to Intercultural Communication**

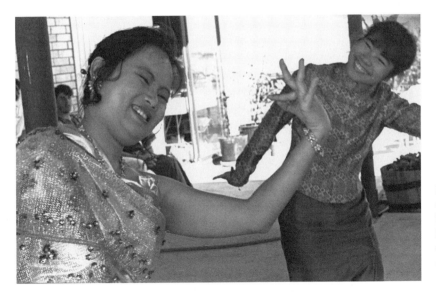

Encountering diversity is an axiom involved in intercultural communication. (Photo by Attitaya Indrakanhang.)

During the Second World War, leaders were faced with a practical strategic problem. How could nations such as the United States cooperate with residents of other cultures, when the U.S. leaders knew little about other languages or cultures? Anthropologists were then invited to study and discover culture of many of these new places. Through these investigations, the focus of cultural anthropology became more popular and took on new meaning. The study of culture became more widely known, setting the stage for the importance of culture and communication.

After the Second World War, a number of programs focusing on world situations and U.S. policy abroad influenced the development of intercultural communication studies. Of course, the establishment of the United Nations became a significant concern of foreign policy. With the United Nations occupying a prominent role in world events, the governments felt obliged to initiate new programs in interacting with leaders from nations throughout the world. This situation created a need to learn about the political, social, economic, and cultural life surrounding the representatives of these many nations. With the advent of the World Health Organization, the United Nation's assistance programs, the World Bank, and other agencies, the need to understand the culture of many developing nations and to interact meaningfully with citizens from these nations became a goal for some government agencies. Unfortunately, many of their attempts at communication across these cultural boundaries were superficial and sometimes dominated by economic theories of development that cast some doubt upon cross-cultural theories of social change. Often, some of the sincere attempts of United Nation's agencies and other organizations were overshadowed by the lack of cultural understanding of the peoples they were trying to serve.

Because the activity of the United Nations and other organizations inadvertently created a need to understand the interface of culture and communication, the U.S. Congress passed an act in 1953 that instituted the United States Information

Interaction between culturally different people creates a system that demands an understanding of each participant's need to reduce uncertainty.

Agency (USIA). The name was changed in 1977 to the International Communication Agency. This agency was charged with providing information about the United States through various communication media to nations of the world. The familiar broadcast "Voice of America" exemplified those efforts.

During the 1950s, early pioneers in this effort, such as Edward T. Hall, found that the USIA lacked cultural information, a point echoed in work by Leeds-Hurwitz (1990). The image of the "ugly American" seemed linked to poorly trained foreign service officers and travelers who lacked cultural awareness and intercultural communication insight. During this decade, Edward T. Hall drew upon his vast experience with the Hopi and Navaho Indians during the 1930s and 1940s and with foreign service officers in his capacity with the USIA and wrote the classic *Silent Language,* originally published in 1959. In some ways, this publication marked the birth of intercultural communication, since it synthesized what are now considered fundamental issues in understanding culture and communication.

In secondary education, foreign-language classes following the Second World War took on new enthusiasm, partly perhaps because language had become more "functional." The soldiers' return prompted a social, governmental, and educational awareness of a global society, and this enthusiasm quickly worked its way into school curriculum, though mostly as foreign language studies.

In the larger development of cultural studies, the geo-political aspects and needs presented awakened a segment of the academic culture to the ongoing work of the British and European social anthropologists, such as Malinowsky. Soon, the work of American cultural anthropologists such as Margaret Mead and Ruth Benedict become known, as well as the linguistic work of Edward Sapir and Dell Hymes.

As our national attitudes of the world began to change toward a more global view, the U.S. government's understanding about domestic cultures also began a gradual change that many experts conclude was long overdue. In 1909, for instance, the Bureau of Indian Affairs, working with other persons had arranged "The Last Great Indian Council," a meeting that was supposed to be a type of farewell to the "vanishing race" of Native Americans, despite the fact that Native Americans had been increasing in numbers, not decreasing (Faherty 1976). This lack of cultural awareness and denial was augmented by various national programs intended to assimilate the Native American into the dominant Anglo society. For instance, the handling of educational, welfare, and medical programs on reservations revealed little awareness of certain Native American cultures. Such examples involving governmental policy were said to typify the way in which a number of programs involving cultures were handled in the United States, including minority programs.

**Dealing with Domestic Diversity**

The 1960s in the United States also marked a cultural awakening. With the passage of the Civil Rights Act in 1964, the nation discovered its minorities. The same decade gave birth to many human rights issues in the United States. The questions, and sometimes the conflicts, made us painfully aware that communication between groups and cultures was no longer a matter of international expediency, but a problem of domestic urgency. Events in the 1990s will cause us to determine our future in part by our abilities to understand and to interact interculturally, a point well illustrated by riots in the Los Angeles area following the outcome of the first Rodney King beating trial, where police officers were on trial for beating a black motorist.

Another salient event with severe repercussions for intercultural communication was the Vietnam War. The interactions with Southeast Asians under the conditions imposed by the war overwhelmingly influenced the participants. The consequent overflow of refugees thrust a new generation of Americans into cultural contact never before known to them—overnight, elementary, high school, and college students were in classrooms with counterparts from Cambodia, Laos, and Vietnam. Educators faced a challenge with a cultural group with whom they had no experience, and communication challenges soared.

Of ongoing importance, too, are the continuing intercultural demands of growing multicultural societies throughout the world. In the United States regional demographic changes mean that groups once considered minorities will be the majority, a fact already having occurred in some areas and soon to occur in others. Economic and political oppression from regions of the globe, along with the growing human rights movement and continuing human rights unrest and political unrest in parts of the world, have heightened the concerns for intercultural awareness.

As treaties of economic significance in Europe, Asia, and North America continue to flourish, the intercultural needs accompanying these transactions correspondingly will rise. Furthermore, global ecology agreements require international and macrocultural analysis and finesse to communicate across these cultural boundaries.

## Developing an Academic Perspective

From these historical transitions, briefly reviewed, scholars continue to address investigations concerning the reciprocal impact of culture and communication. In the earliest days of intercultural communication, even the name for this area of communication investigation was inconsistent. Scholarly work was limited to pulling from a number of fields including rhetorical and communication theory, mathematics, social psychology, psychiatry, linguistics, anthropology, political science, philosophy, folklore and oral history, literature, rural sociology, and sociology. Today, numerous works are available from many researchers across the globe, each exploring new dimensions ranging in such areas as international concerns, interethnic and minority questions, dominance-nondominance issues, adaptation and competence, intracultural communication, diversity in the workplace, and intercultural communication training.

In his overview, Hammer (1989) concludes that intercultural communication shared a vision that has been cultivated and is still growing. To understand this field, he argues that first, we need to employ interdisciplinary and multicultural "maps." Second, the field is eminently practical, helping practitioners manage a number of interethnic as well as international needs. And third, intercultural communication addresses the concerns of people wherever groups are found.

## Developing Skills Dealing with Intercultural Communication Background

1. *Try to look beyond surface conditions, such as dress, custom, and environmental conditions (too cold, too hot, too humid, too dry, etc.).* Most of us tend to see and process new places on a tourist level.

2. *Develop a curiosity about the internals of culture, such as cultural structure, cultural thought patterns and logic, and cultural relationships.* A sense of internal culture can heighten intercultural experiences and foster better relationships.

3. *Look for ways in which various communication sources mold perceptions of groups.* Family, friends, media, and educational sources all leave us with information about cultural groups. Question your communication sources to develop a sharp focus on the accuracy of their stereotypes. A jaundiced view of all of our communication sources would likely be dysfunctional, but allowing ourselves a healthy critique of the perceptions invites growth.

4. *Discover ways that relationships affect content and content affects relationships.* How we feel about someone colors the message, and conversely, messages can heighten or flatten how we feel about a person. Unfortunately, not everyone means what he or she says, so working through the person-versus-the-message issue can be an important aspect of communicating.

5. *Broaden your views of culture from something "foreign" to the notion of collectives.* Where people relate and have tasks, communication bonds emerge. With these bonds develop a set of norms, structure, thought, procedure of relationship, and communication style. One measure of a person's intercultural growth is his or her ability to visualize those kinds of factors in a number of groups and to look for the ways in which a culture exists for that group.

6. *Where a set of negative attributes exists for you toward a group or a person within a certain group, work on balancing the negative attributes with positive attributes.* Unfortunately, many people selectively perceive negative features about others or what they define as negative features. The idea here is to develop the discipline to select and search for positive attributes to weigh alongside the negative.

---

**This Chapter in Perspective**

The chapter documents a number of intercultural axioms concerning intercultural communication. These include the principle of difference, the content and relationship dimensions of intercultural communication, the role of personal communicator style in intercultural communication, reducing uncertainty about relationships and messages, the nature of perception in sensing differences, the centrality of communication to culture, and the importance of intercultural effectiveness as a goal.

**Exercises**

1. In a small group, list as many microcultures as you can within the United States. Pick two or three of these cultures and identify the form, structure, and symbols of these groups. How do their forms and symbols foster or inhibit communication with other cultural groups?

2. Rent a video of the movie *The Witness,* a story involving the Amish culture. After viewing the movie, discuss the perceptual limitations people have of the Amish culture. What perceptual limitations do the Amish have of the larger macroculture? If you were in a position to resolve problem areas in intercultural communication between the Amish and others, what would you do?

3. Write at least three headlines from a newspaper that indicate culture or "groupness." How do they define culture?

# Part 2

# Perceiving Cultural and Social Diversity

# Chapter 3

# Elements of Cultural Systems

**Objectives**     After completing this chapter, you should be able to

1. Define culture

2. Identify elements of culture as a system

3. Describe institutional subsystems of culture

4. Describe the means by which cultures are changed

Perhaps the idea of cultural differences strikes some readers strangely, since, after all, we live in a world of mass media, where we can watch the evening news on television and see for ourselves the modernization among nations and peoples. The mesmerizing lights of television, however, may have dulled our sensibilities into thinking there are no differences across cultures. Realities continually remind us of groups of people, nations, continents, and a world divided not merely by political boundaries but by cultural barriers.

This chapter describes broad components of culture. A knowledge of these factors delineated in this chapter applies to global regions and national boundaries (called macrocultures) as well as microcultures around the world. Cultural differences are certainly broader than the following incidents, but even selected examples remind us that our world is composed of diversity. For example, Hindu ritual practices of cleansing differ from Islamic rituals. When we consider food and drink differences travelers encounter among different regions of the world, one can identify the meaning of at least a modest level of cultural difference. In 1979 and the early 1980s, during Iran's political transition, dissenters to the resurgence of a Moslem nation sometimes fell victim on a trail of executions and severe punishments. The Kurdish group in Iraq is victimized by an ethnocentric Iraqi power elite. Vandalism at a certain level in Singapore is punishable by "caning." Perhaps such an application of law and social control should be no more surprising than practices in portions of the United States not so many years ago when thieves were hanged for stealing a horse, but released or mildly punished for taking a life. The violation of minority rights and human ethics of fairness in the United States all too often sound like silent cries for the perpetrators but are actually loud cries of minority injustice. The mass suicide of nine hundred persons in Jonestown, Guyana, starvation in Ethiopia, crisis in the former Yugoslavia, war lords in Somalia, and a massacre in Beijing all remind us that ours is a world of different cultures.

A recognition of numerous cultural differences is not meant to create despair. Rather, as the central model in the text reminds us, effective intercultural communicators try to understand diversity in its many forms and to develop competent intercultural strategies in order to experience effective outcomes when we are faced with members of contrasting cultures. This chapter is designed to help readers visualize how cultures are systems of interrelated practices, beliefs, thoughts, hopes, and expectations of people who identify with each other as a group. These basic elements, found within most cultures, provide a framework to guide our observation of cultural diversity. It is also a framework directing our efforts to explain a number of cultural outcomes. By accounting for these features, we begin to adapt to the cultural differences we encounter.

## What Is Culture and Its Influence on Communication?

Culture can be defined in numerous ways: community, social class differences, minorities, social groups, nationalities, geo-political units, societies. All these have a place, for culture is multifaceted. In our examination of culture, however, we want to emphasize those features of culture that contribute to the perception of difference and hence influence intercultural communication. For that reason, culture is defined as follows:

> Culture is the holistic summation and interrelationship of an identifiable group's beliefs, norms, activities, institutions, and communication patterns.

This definition moves across a broad number of elements from values and beliefs to feelings and behaviors. The models of behavior for a culture's norms are expected or prescribed or both. The systemization of these norms and beliefs is evident in a culture's institutions. The use of verbal and nonverbal messages represents a feature of daily life, for culture is reflected in thought, speech, and action. Furthermore, cultural members are usually identifiable, often defining themselves. In sum, people develop and come to expect ways of *doing* and *thinking* that significantly organize their world.

## How Do We Learn Culture?

We do not yet fully understand how much of human behavior is instinctive and how much is learned, although most social scientists accept the notion that culture is mostly learned. In any case, culture is a powerful vehicle for learning and *socialization,* a term Brislin (1993) applied to cultural learning. That means we adapt to the group ways of doing and thinking. Usually, we learn in a group context, not in isolation. Schools, families, neighborhoods, churches, mosques, synagogues, and affiliative groups, represent instances of the social process associated with learning. Through the group factors such as language, habits, customs, expectations, and roles, individuals shape their world—and think, act, and communicate typically according to social group expectations. Of course, a person can reject or modify cultural influence, and one can exercise free will. Many cultural imprints are subtle and habit-based. Without scrutiny, culture's influence remains elusive, if not beyond conscious recognition.

## How Does Culture Primarily Influence People?

We are not suggesting that individuals are passive victims of a culture that mysteriously leads them. Culture is so basic to explaining human behavior, however, that we cannot ignore its pervasive influence, an influence that in recent years has been found to explain the previously unexplained, including communication activities. How does culture function?

First, culture *sets an agenda* of rules, rituals, and procedures. Attitudes toward time, how to dress, when and what to eat, when to come and go, and how to work, illustrate this first function of culture. Basic to socialization is developing a sense of proper and improper behavior and communicating within those cultural rules. For example, your family (an obvious significant cultural unit) may have warned you "not to point at people" with reprimands if you pointed anyway. The numerous cultural rules are assimilated over time.

Fundamental themes surrounding human development account for cultural rules, rituals, and procedures. We learn various ways to live ranging from survival (involving dependency), to group relations (involving interdependency), to

Culture is more than a place (such as Ghana shown here) or an institution. Culture encompasses the life patterns, customs, and beliefs of an identifiable group of people.

self-worth and autonomy (involving independence). These universal needs on a *dependent-interdependent-independent* continuum can be viewed as overlapping. Culture sets the rules on how these features of life and relationships are worked out. In this sense, the rules for exhibiting these themes or principles have cultural boundaries. A smile conveys sincerity and leads to interpersonal trust in one culture, but serves to hide emotions in another. This is a case of culture exerting boundary and agenda-setting influence on human actions and thought.

Second, culture *reinforces values* of good and evil and conveys belief. Consequently, we develop approaches to thoughts and beliefs about the world. Among the Kissi tribe of Kenya, for example, the grandmother assumes special responsibility for telling her grandchildren stories about the importance of family honesty, loyalty, and the nature of good and evil. In the sense culture influences these matters, culture teaches us what is beautiful or ugly, sexy or unappealing. As one overseas document for living abroad reminds us, culture teaches the value of hard work, thrift, privacy, competition, fair play, and directness (Overseas Diplomacy 1973).

Third, culture *teaches how to relate* to others, or how to communicate. *How* does culture relate to communication?

1. By encouraging communication style expected within each culture. In the science fiction "Star Trek" series the classic Klingons exhibit a demanding and harsh communication style. In many of the stories most of the Klingons interact ineffectively with other cultures, preferring confrontational if not a

warlike style of communication, a style that rarely produces positive outcomes (unless you are a Klingon who likes to blast people out of the universe).

Communication style is highly fashioned after the appropriateness of cultural communication expectations for each person. For example, loudness, pitch, rate, and certain stances and gestures characterize communication behaviors. The specific way a cultural communicator uses these may depend on that person's conception of the "ideal" cultural person. An American who speaks with a "normal" conversational volume contrasts with a "quiet" talking Thai national who interprets the American to be angry. In this case, the ideal cultural communication styles are in conflict, a conflict rooted in each culture's communication expectations.

2. By the power to shape perception. Ways of thinking, dominant symbols or images, and communication norms all are linked with culture. Some authors speak of the unique cultural interaction tendencies (Hecht, Andersen, and Ribeau 1989) and of verbal and nonverbal messages rooted and grown in culture (Matsumoto, Wallbott, and Scherer 1989). However you describe it, culture shapes perception by its categories. These act as a measuring device for judgment and interpretation. Depending on your culture's attitude toward people dissimilar to them, and how you were taught, you may have a good or a bad measuring device. The human tendency toward categorizing others is without question—and culture obliges by offering category systems to its members.

## Does Culture Imply Total Commonality Among a Group of People?

Culture is something like a glue that bonds people together. A person who refers to Mexican American culture probably is thinking of a large population with some commonalities of world views, attitudes, concept of self, and language. Obviously, one problem in identifying culture is overgeneralizing or stereotyping, since numerous differences among individuals exist in any one culture. To avoid this problem of stereotyping, we cannot then swing to an opposite extreme and argue for no commonalities. On the contrary, there is a middle ground where we can speak of *modalities* or commonly occurring tendencies among groups of people. By modality we do not suggest stereotypes as if to say a group always demonstrates certain qualities or never changes. Of course, numerous individual differences and a range of diversity characterize cultures. Too, the precise boundary where one culture ends and another culture begins is obscure. Nevertheless, we can approach the concept of culture perhaps as we approach the notion of group in small group communication, where we recognize the group's interdependence and its development of unique style, common features, and patterns as a whole, but realize individual differences.

## Elements of Culture

Culture is like luggage we always carry. From it we unconsciously lift daily needs: survival, information, prediction and maintenance of interpersonal relationships, and personal goals. From our culture, we apply what we consider the appropriate categories and communication tools as we interact. We do and think what our cultural learning taught us in each communication opportunity.

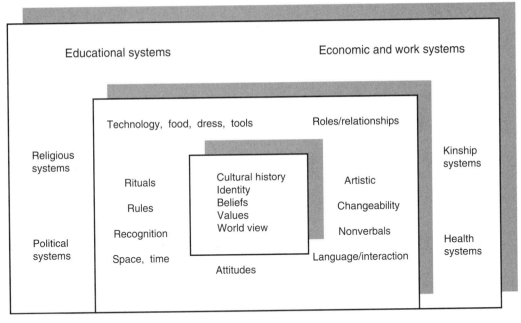

The figure contains the following labels:

Educational systems     Economic and work systems

Religious systems

Political systems

Technology, food, dress, tools     Roles/relationships

Rituals

Rules

Recognition

Space, time

Cultural history
Identity
Beliefs
Values
World view

Artistic

Changeability

Nonverbals

Language/interaction

Attitudes

Kinship systems

Health systems

**Figure 3.1**
This model demonstrates the many elements of culture composing a system. The inner core lies at the most significant level. The second and third set of elements are tied to the core, but remain an area for some degree of flexibility, fad, change, and crisis intervention.

Sometimes that means applying rules, while other times it involves operationalizing values. Or, we engage in a ritual all too familiar "back home" but misunderstood in a new culture. We begin in this chapter to open a cultural suitcase and unfold its contents. As we open each pocket, we explore an interrelated set of group beliefs, norms, activities, institutions, and communication patterns arising from these.

The model presented in figure 3.1 visually represents these cultural elements. As a system, culture contains these elements as major components, together comprising culture. True to what is called general systems theory, the elements outlined here function as an organized, holistic set to define a system. Applied to culture, a system and the elements in that system exhibit several qualities (Becvar and Becvar 1982):

1. mutually *interactive*;

2. each *part influences the whole;* each element has its own attributes or *properties,* but they contribute to the whole;

3. serve to define *boundaries,* or invisible lines differentiating one culture from another;

4. both *causes of and results of communication;* communication patterns are in a sense inseparable from the culture and the culture from communication;

5. typically has self-monitoring and feedback leading toward *balance and stability* when elements are out of balance or not functioning correctly;

6. systems can be open or closed; an *open* system exchanges energy or material with its environment, generally can alter its internal structure, and is open to change (unless too much openness violates the system's boundaries resulting in identity or integrity loss); *closed* systems lack outside stimulation, hold excessively rigid boundaries, and often cause diminished adaptation to growth and change.

Even though the elements mutually interact, a hierarchy begins in the inner parts of the model with cultural history, cultural identity, world view, and beliefs and values.

**Cultural History**

Historical development and tradition for people are a foundation for analysis—basic cues to understanding a culture. In the United States, for example, a family tree and family lineage afford identity and purpose, perhaps more in some regions than in others. Cultural history generates insight into norms of groups and individual behavior and explains many attitudes that seem to be shared by cultural members.*

For example, African tribes, such as the Ga and Ewe tribes of Ghana, highly respect the neighboring Ashanti because, as one non-Ashanti indicated, "The Ashanti are strong." Their respect has historical origins. In the slave-trading days, the Ashanti outnumbered and conquered neighboring tribes and sold them on the coast as slaves to European and American dealers. This historical origin permeates contemporary relationships of the Ashanti and their tribal neighbors. As another example, communication with various tribal Indians from Central and South America would be incomplete without a knowledge of their ancestral heritage, which includes being conquered by Spaniards and a 450-year history of submissiveness to social and economic domination.

Cultures have various ways of expressing their history, heritage, and traditions. Among some African cultures, a totem—often displaying elaborate artistry—is used to show tribal history. The totem's importance lies in its symbol as a record of the past, a reminder that for some cultures is a pervasive part of the present. The roots of history for almost every culture are so long that, from the past, comes norms and taboos for the present. A group's history provides a social continuity, an identity, as if to say, "This is who I am."

In some cultures, the past is recorded in books, or in some cases by local historians who specialize in memorization of a culture's history. For example, the noted American author Alex Haley's quest for his African heritage led to interviews with West African tribal members who specialize in memorizing generations of orally recorded history. In other cultures, temples, mosques, cathedrals, and other historic sites may symbolize significant cultural features.

No matter how a culture records its history, the point for the intercultural communicator is to appreciate a culture's past. For example, many European

*Ethnographic research can be found in the Human Relations Area File along with many other sources of published and unpublished material. Consult your periodicals and documents librarian for specific cultures.

Traditions and historical roots, illustrated by these Mayan ruins in Guatemala, are a part of culture that contribute to the current life of a group of people.

visitors to the United States wonder at the North American's fascination for the new and innovative. Enthusiasm for more efficient buildings, to replace old structures that could be remodeled, along with a quest for the latest gadgetry or technology contrast with cultures that believe in preservation and sufficiency of existing material objects. In many cultures, tradition is so important that anything new is viewed suspiciously. The effective intercultural communicator appreciates these emphases and sources of cultural pride and seeks to learn the history and geography of another person in order to understand possible attitudes and values, which are essential elements in intercultural communication.

Members of every culture have a sense of social identification: who they are and why. In other words, cultures can be likened to a group personality. The idea is akin to Cattell's (1951) syntality theory, in which he explained that groups are like individuals, since both have a "personality." Raymond Rodgers (1978) once explained that, through its folklore, a culture identifies itself with archetypal figures, such as heroes, and that these ideals become models to measure personal and group success.

Cultural Identity

One's cultural identity affects interpersonal relationships and expected models of individual personality behavior. From a sense of social identity (who *we* are), one receives a sense of personal identity (who *I* am). For example, in some cultures, decisions are collective rather than individual—even to the point of giving up individual rights in favor of decisions made by the leaders in that culture. To speak up against a village chieftain's decision would be inappropriate and inconsistent with African villagers' conceptions of behavior. Among the Ashanti tribe, individual decisions are made with the approval of the maternal uncle, maternal grandfather, and one's father.

## Cultural World View, Beliefs, Values, and Ways of Processing Information and Thought

Each culture has an interpretation of reality, or perceptual "window," through which people see self and others. Moreover, cultures hold assumed truths (beliefs), concepts deemed as holding ultimate significance and of long-term importance (values), and world view. World view is a specific belief system about the nature of the universe. More than just an outlook or philosophy of life, world view functions as a central construct related to how much control one believes is available (see chapter 6).

A culture's pattern of thought refers to the way a cultural group views such things as decision making, the kind of logical system and evidence usage practiced, and cognitive pathways of thought. For instance, many people in the Western Hemisphere accept cause-effect reasoning. Solutions to problems are simply a matter, they reason, of altering or controlling the causes to alter or control the desired effects. In contrast, some eastern cultures reason that no one can know the causes of life events and that the events are part of a natural plan that humans should not try to understand completely but to accept. Thus, the intercultural difference in this example is the divergent approach the interactants have toward the use of evidence, the way the universe operates, and consequently, the most useful communication styles for discussing solutions to problems.

Furthermore, members of some cultures think in terms of linear-sequential, time-ordered patterns (1, 2, 3, or A, B, C). In contrast, members of configurational cultures think in terms of pictures or configurations. The individual with a configurational pattern of thought follows a different order of attention to stimulus items than the linear thinker. Here, the stimulus items may follow an attention pattern unique to that culture; for example, 1, 16, 37, 2, or A, M, Z, B. The issue, which involves how a person collects and processes information, is being addressed by a number of learning theorists (Bandler 1985). Methods of information processing appear to be culturally dependent as well as individually derived, reminding us that perceiving culture requires an awareness of cognitive style and information processing differences. Foeman (1991) makes an excellent point that in diverse microcultures in the United States, we have categorized but failed to examine learning style differences sometimes associated with minority cultures, sometimes associated with individual differences.

## Cultural Technology

Probably the most salient features to most tourists abroad are the differences in a culture's technology; material culture—food, clothing, travel; and tools or machine technology. Unfortunately, some travelers offend host cultures by making light of their cultural methods of working out their basic material needs. Since technology is usually a matter of cultural invention and of intercultural contact with other technologies, it might be argued that no opportunities have arisen for acculturation of a technology, or perhaps the culture has rejected the technology.

Too often, we prematurely judge a culture by its material features. A person who values technological features may overlook a rich cultural heritage in such areas as art, language, and interpersonal relationships. Unfortunately, such myopia can damage intercultural communication.

Food preparation and eating habits are a significant area of difference for sojourners to new cultures, as for example in rural Ghana where "fufu" is a daily staple.

Sometimes a culture's technology and social functions intersect. For instance, an observer once described how women in a rural area of one East African country walked over a half mile to a river that supplied their families with water—two buckets at a time. One of this nation's governmental agencies decided that a water pump and a central water system would enormously benefit the villagers. However, the water-gathering routine was a means of social interaction and a very important method of making new relationships, enjoying friendship, and keeping up with village news. The government field staff also did not recognize the fact that routine excretory functions were performed off the beaten paths to and from the river. When the new water system failed because no one used it, the government was shocked to learn the reasons. The water system was abandoned, and life continued as before. This case illustrates that some methods and procedures are not always amenable to change without entire cultural imbalance and repercussions.

Material culture does not exist merely as a feature with functional value. *Overt* material culture may reflect a more subtle, *covert* peculiarity (much like the tip of an iceberg revealing only a small part of the total iceberg). For example, the Yir Yoront tribe of Australia had a central tool—the stone axe—for securing food, shelter, and warmth. Beyond its function of value as a material object, however, the stone axe symbolized masculinity and respect for elders.

In short, the stone axe represented authority, which was a controlling feature for these people, bonding together elements of their culture. Although the men owned the stone axes, women and children borrowed and used the tool according to customary rules of social relationships, and, in the process, reinforced the cultural glue of respect and authority. In fact, this artifact of material culture had such symbolic value that the subsequent introduction of the steel axe totally disrupted the social and economic bases of the culture (Sharp 1952). The culture literally disintegrated as thievery, drunkenness, and selling wives and daughters as prostitutes became commonplace once social order was removed.

Of course, customs surrounding material culture are complex and intricate. Effective intercultural communicators typically first try to understand existing customs, and second, seek to avoid a biased reaction from their own cultural standards. For example, the early dinner in some Northern European cultures strikingly contrasts with the late evening meals in Spain. You can well imagine the scene as hungry people in a new culture cannot understand why dinner is not served at the right time. Simple observation and adaptation are keys to interacting in any host culture. Like the stone axe, we should remember Rogers's (1983) description of technology. Technologies have *form* (what it is or how it looks), *function* (what it does, how it works), and *meaning* (what it represents).

## Cultural Roles

Cultural attitudes also revolve around categories of people and their expected pattern of performance or activity. These predetermined patterns, or at least prescribed and expected behaviors about categories people occupy, are called roles. Each culture has its expectations of us, according to various role areas.

*Age roles.* One obvious example of how culture determines role relationships centers on views toward the aged. Japanese students show respect for the elderly in various ways, including the use of greeting terms that show respect. The Ashanti of Ghana have a form of greeting any elderly man as, roughly translated, "my grandfather." The numerous examples demonstrating respect for the elderly and ancestral generations are well documented in many cultures. By contrast, global cultures in the western world are often said to lack respect for the elderly. Sometimes a senior person is perceived as nonproductive, an intruder in the lives of a busy, younger generation. This attitude is changing, but these role expectations have enormous emotive qualities, and contribute to acting out these societal conceptions. In a type of self-fulfilling prophecy, some elderly people actually perform less efficiently, develop more health problems, and feel alienated because of societal expectations.

*Occupational roles.* Occupational role behaviors are also culturally defined. The consequence is that a person in a certain occupation is expected to perform in a role-prescribed manner. Police officers, lawyers, doctors, and salespersons play certain roles congruent with social expectations. For instance, a police officer usually does not crack jokes while handing out a citation, not because of lacking a sense of humor but because of the social role.

*Friendship roles.* Even our relationships with friends, professors, family, and strangers are mediated by societal expectations. We usually communicate in full accordance with those unspoken but expected cultural rules for each role. For instance, bowing in certain Asian cultures correlates with the perceived social relationship: the higher the status of the person, the lower one should bow.

*Gender roles.* Role differences also involve the differing expectations of males and females. Not only are gender roles organizing factors for a culture, they also widely vary from culture to culture. Almost every culture, for example, has a division of labor decisively determined by the individual's gender. Among the Boran herdsmen of Kenya, women are expected to complete all household duties, gardening, and milking while the men tend to the herds. Traditional Vietnamese women are expected to eat smaller quantities of food than men at each meal, no matter how hungry they are (Hong 1976). In a research study of Hispanic males in North American dual cultural marriages, Baldwin's (1991) evidence suggests that the wife's overinvolvement counters an ideal role type and contributes to communication dissatisfaction. Family expectations and individual differences, of course, become additional sources for gender role expectations beyond one's culture.

The decision making and authority positions of men and women are constantly changing within cultures. Power, often associated with decision making, comes in variant forms. The Boran women of Kenya, again, decide who in the family gets the greatest allotment of milk. The role and the power attendant to that role hold survival significance in that culture. Power-status relationships, traditionally associated with gender, are decreasing at a rapid rate among world cultures. Nevertheless, norms and cultural roles still are highly defined and stylized in a number of regions. Effective communication adaptation requires understanding and cultural sensitivity to these norms.

Roles serve in three ways. First, roles help guide personal and social behavior. Second, they serve as standards in a stabilizing function, allowing members to predict certainty about what otherwise would amount to ambiguity in role relationships. Third, they give identification, as if to satisfy a need to know self and others. However, roles can be a source of stress, especially if (1) a person does not fit a cultural role, (2) there appears to be no adequate role model or if the guidance is too ambiguous, or (3) if a person is attempting to play multiple roles.

## Artistic Expression

Another element in cultural systems is the relevant artistic expressions of a particular culture. When we consider music, sculpture, painting, and weaving as reflections of underlying themes of a culture at a given time in its history, this element assumes deeper significance. The myriad of aesthetic differences and explanations of why one culture's view of "beautiful" is another culture's view of "ugly" go far beyond the scope of the artistic object or its manifestations. Artistic expression can reflect current, relevant *themes* of a culture, by which the

A culture's artistic expressions become one keyhole through which to view and understand a culture.

investigator gathers more and better insight. Or an investigator may discover a bit of artistic work to hold only *vestigial* significance, meaning the art once held unusual significance but no longer holds the original meaning. For instance, a particular design and color of cloth among Native Central Americans once identified tribalism but now means little more than pretty colors and design.

Play and recreation as art forms usually develop in two ways. Indigenous games either develop from within a culture, or they are borrowed from culture contact.

## Cultural Language and Interaction

The relation between language and culture is significant. Language and its categories filter, shape, and organize reality by the boundaries that linguistic systems draw, a point discussed in chapter 7. Every culture has a language, although of the thousands of language communities on earth, over one-fourth have yet to be written.

Every culture has a linguistic code and a sense of interactional rules (Dodd and Lewis 1991). In terms of the code, there is not only a language for every culture, but there are specific categories of that language that may not transfer to other cultures. For example, a Chinese man who spoke immaculate English was conversing with a North American who kept referring to words like "unique," "individual," and "self." Although the Chinese was excellent in English, he had a puzzled look on his face during most of the conversation. He finally asked, "What is this 'individuality' you keep referring to?" Although the grammar and vocabulary were similar, the concepts inherent in the North American's use of English were quite different from the Chinese concept of humility wherein individuality is rarely, if ever, brought forward. Even if two people share language, the thought processes lying behind the words may not be the same, separated by culture. Intercultural communication is more than knowing the right words. It involves using cultural competency also.

Many cultures use unusual codes, which may prevent others from understanding. For example, jargon, slang, or "in-house" codes allow rapid, shorthand-type communication. Cultures can speak telegraphically, where a single phrase has a wealth of meaning for people who have experienced the phrase. These codes can function for clarity, or they can function to hide meanings from others outside the subculture. With our own in-house communication system, people who do not share the jargon will sooner or later drop out.

This category of interaction and language also implies a set of linguistic usages expected in every interactional context. For example, there are certain words and phrases expected in greetings and leavings. In many African cultures you are expected to give signals of respect to other people who are older. For example, the word in one West African language that refers to older people is roughly translated "My grandfather" or "My grandmother," conveying the idea that a person who is not really your grandfather or grandmother deserves the same respect as your own family.

Leave-taking rules are also significant. You can abruptly stop a conversation, or you can proceed with culturally appropriate rituals. For instance, Americans end briskly with a minor apology, such as, "Well, I have an engagement, and it's time for me to go," or "I've got to leave right now." We typically thank people for the time together and offer summary statements, concluding the interaction with friendliness and smiles. However, for many cultures, leave-taking is a matter of the higher-status person breaking the conversation. Often there are more elaborate forms, and all of them take a great deal of time. Every culture has rules about forming relationships and using linguistic codes. The right form shows up not only in word choice, but in the tone of voice, pitch, volume, and number of expected words. For example, Middle Easterners are highly verbose, while Germans are more to the point. Furthermore, many cultures rely more on nonverbal cues than verbal codes. Great skill is necessary to read the situation and understand the use of silence, the flicker of an eyebrow, or the depth of a bow. However, in American culture, such features are not as important as the actual words spoken.

Another element of cultural systems assesses likelihood of a culture's change. What is the change potential in a culture? How stable or unstable is a particular culture? It is not immediately obvious why, but cultures can be analyzed on a continuum from *innovative* to *resistant*. For apparent historical and traditional reasons, some cultures have propensity for change; others do not. For example, Japan has demonstrated extraordinary adaptation into the world economy since World War II. Japanese values traditionally stress flexibility. By contrast, the ethnic wars of the mid-1990s in Europe and in Africa exposed traditional cultures, values, and communication propensities offering little in intercultural adaptation. Adaptive communication stresses adherence to cultural competencies and intercultural motivation. The exact currents of cultural

**Cultural Changeability**

streams predicting innovation or resistance are partly reflections of world view; researchers are still defining holistic qualities of innovative-resistance. Chapter 13 on social change offers methods of social influence.

## Ethnocentrism

Ethnocentrism is a unique element of cultural systems. More than simply an attitude, ethnocentrism refers to culturally shared notions of superiority in comparison with other cultures. Almost every culture exhibits some tendencies to judge others. The us-versus-them attitude is easily observed in interracial interaction when cultural categories remain stagnate or inflexible. In many nations, urbans look down upon rurals, elites scorn peasants, and white-collar employees devalue blue-collar employees. Some individuals within national cultures practice ethnocentrism. As an example, consider typical headline news stories: Iraqis Feel Superior to Iranians, Indians Belittle Pakistanis, Thais Devaluate Malaysians, Germans Isolate Turks, and Serbs Violate Croatians. On historical occasions, ethnocentrism has caused war, takeover, and a daily host of negative interactions between people.

This tendency to judge appears universal and is part of the attitude system sometimes lurking in intercultural communication climates. High ethnocentrism leads to negative stereotypes. What better way to prove one's superiority than to rely on negative caricatures to confirm the negative attributes of a disliked group?

## Nonverbal Behavior

Every culture has some system of nonverbal behaviors—gesture, touch, facial expression, and eye movement. The collective pattern of such behaviors, while usually in concert with spoken communication, is itself a symbol system. Nonverbal behavior, in this sense, becomes nonverbal communication and is loaded with cultural expectations. Researchers agree that a culture's nonverbal communication system is the most powerful communication system available, although not without its liabilities. The differences in nonverbal behavior among cultures can cause breakdowns in intercultural communication.

*Spatial relations.* One facet of nonverbal behaviors involves use of space. As a part of the dynamic interrelationship with other cultural elements, space is correlated with information and meaning inferences. Space is related to relationship development, perceptions of feelings and moods, inferences about intentions, and generalizations about personality. Inferences about spatial usage also leave wide ambiguities. For example, when a male from Iran stands close to a U.S. male from the midwest, the U.S. male may be conditioned to back away. The Iranian is confused by this cool and abrupt reception. How quickly intercultural communication fails!

*Time.* Time is also considered a facet of nonverbal behavior. Time's implications for intercultural communication begins with understanding how time is culturally rooted, and our use of time is wedded to our culture's cognitive perceptions surrounding time. Some cultures view time with great precision and expect you to be precise also. For example, Americans, Britons, Canadians, and Germans expect punctuality. A large share of these peoples' relationships are governed by the clock—and with some rigor: "Sorry I arrived a few minutes late," "Wow, look at the time! I've got to go." Furthermore, impressions in a time-conscious culture are based on one's ability to adhere to cultural rules about the time system.

By contrast, some cultures, such as African, Latin American, and Malaysian, are less time conscious. In these cultures, time does not dominate, except for situations where punctuality is the rule. Norms in the less time-conscious cultures seem to address the issue of people first, schedules second. Cultural rules in these cases are centered around internal relationships rather than external schedules.

Intercultural communication problems between time-conscious cultures and less time-conscious cultures involve task-conscious people, externally shaping their relationships with time and schedules, and interpersonal-relationship-conscious people, motivated by saving face and social lubrication. The task-conscious individual communicating with the people-conscious individual may experience unexplainable rebuffs. Such cool relationships are expected when our cultural time rules do not match those of the cultural system in which we are communicating. The powerful outcomes of nonverbal intercultural communication remain an area related to one part of adaptive communication competencies and skills.

Every culture has norms for understanding success and failure. Within the boundaries of cultural systems, relationships exist that express recognition and reward. Initiation rites, when successfully completed, represent a cultural method for advancement in tribes and clans. Proper behavior is usually rewarded in some way. Of course, what constitutes proper behavior is culturally variable. What constitutes rewarding is also culturally dependent. An American manager working in a Japanese cultural climate who insists on individually recognizing an outstanding employee may inadvertently create embarrassment. Traditional Japanese norms emphasize the individual in relation to his or her group, not usually individuals singled out.

**Recognition and Reward**

The kind of reward or recognition that is appropriate is a significant cultural difference. Money is appropriate in some cultures. Gifts, personal praise, written statements, future contracts, new titles, promotions in rank, acceptance into a group, initiation completion, and equality are but a few additional ways of showing recognition.

The most usual problem in intercultural communication concerning reward is that an intercultural participant simply does not know the cultural method for honor or praise. Consequently, a manager representing a multinational corporation hires, makes assignments, and offers promotions according to his or her corporate culture's methods: management by objectives, participatory decision making, and the like. However, the methods by which such techniques are administered, or even the techniques themselves, often fail because they simply lack cultural fit. The same goals can be achieved with culturally acceptable adjustments.

Cultural technology and customs, shown here in Guatemala, differ between global regions, as each culture meets its needs in a variety of ways.

## Cultural Rules and Procedures

Every culture has rules, meaning the regulations and expectations guiding the conduct about how things are to be accomplished. Procedures are related to rules and are the operational habits for enacting cultural rules. For example, a cultural rule is to manage your money. One procedure is to open a bank account. Doing so may be as simple as giving basic identification, signing a file copy, issuing checks, and depositing money. However, in many cultures of the world the procedures of establishing a checking account can be rigorous and exasperating. Many sources of documentation are required, perhaps a character reference is summoned, and long periods of waiting before writing checks or withdrawing money are standard. For months the account might be scrutinized. Banking is but one example of numerous differences in cultural activity rules or procedures or both.

Most people are aware of the way we are expected to perform in a culture. Unfortunately, the rules of a culture are rarely stated; nevertheless, we are expected to develop communication competence with those rules. In the American culture, for example, there are simple, but important expectations in the ritual of greeting. You are supposed to look someone in the eyes, touch them a certain way, and offer verbal recognition such as "Hello." However, such a simple procedure is totally different in another culture. No wonder visitors experience uncertainty and anxiety for those accustomed to the American style of greeting. In other cultures, such a procedure may be marked by lack of eye contact and lack of touch with few spoken words. In some parts of Japanese culture one bows, presents a business card, and waits for the person of higher status to initiate the conversation.

Many of us come from regions of the United States or from social systems with preconceived rules of interaction. Unfortunately, if the interactional rules are different, we get into communication trouble, since it is through interactional procedures that we are judged.

Rituals refer to activities customarily followed in a culture. Some rituals are formal, as in ceremonies, rites, formal occasions, initiations, solemn observances, or liturgies. Examples include weddings, births, funerals, baptisms, graduations, and a host of others. Other rituals are informal customary observances and lack the stiffness and solemnity of formal rituals. Examples include meeting friends after work, going to lunch at a certain place every week, crossing your fingers for good luck, or throwing bird seed at a wedding. In general, these are more casual. Rituals can be mixtures of formal and informal or be marked by a series of punctuations of formal/informal rituals (even routines) within a larger ritual.

Ways of acting concerning these systems elements discussed previously and other features become routine in formal ways within a culture. Patterns of expectation for an entire group's survival could be described as institutional subsystems of a culture.

Every culture has various mechanisms of dealing with economics and work, known as economic systems. These are defined as parts of the larger cultural system, so the term "subsystem" is used for a practical way of discussing the points. A practice among farmers in certain parts of the United States is to "swap out" work, whereby one farmer helps another harvest crops and the second reciprocates. Money is seldom exchanged in this process, although a system of informal, mental record keeping develops so that both parties are fully aware of who owes whom. While monetary economic systems play a dominant role in most cultures today, this example reminds us that other methods of exchange exist according to unique cultural situations. For instance, the highlanders of Papua New Guinea traditionally use the sweet potato as one unit of exchange. A missionary once described the mild surprise of foreign visitors to a church meeting where the indigenous church members contributed a large pile of sweet potatoes instead of money for a Sunday collection.

Like many cultural elements, concepts of family frequently are compared only with our own cultural experience. Our culture becomes a measuring rod with which to compare and contrast cultural views of social organization and marriage. The family is more important to many cultures around the world than to many North Americans. Successful intercultural communication involves, again, an understanding of the other person's total set of experiences. For a number of cultures, kinship is a highly integrated part of that set of experiences.

The forms and institutions surrounding the existence of the family differ from culture to culture. However, family needs are universal. Although models of family organization and system change constantly, theorists believe that the family functionally serves to meet the demands of a particular cultural group. Anthropologist Robin Fox (1971) summarized this position:

> I have tried to show how kinship systems are responses to various recognizable pressures within a framework of biological, psychological, ecological, and social limitations. Many anthropologists write as though kinship systems have dropped

**Cultural Rituals**

**Institutional Subsystems in Culture**

**Economic Subsystems**

**Family Subsystems**

from the sky onto societies—they're there because they're there because . . . . In truth, they are there because they answer certain needs—do certain jobs. When these change, the systems change—but only within certain limits. (p. 25)

Clearly, societies organize the family as they would any other aspect of a social group—to meet many needs in a practical way.

Because they face common problems and needs, family units adapt to meet those needs. For example, if an economic need exists for farm labor, a person from that cultural situation might deduce that having many children could supply that need. To foster that goal, the marriage practice of *polygyny* (polygamy is the generic word for more than one spouse, but technically one man with many wives is polygyny) may result as that culture's way of meeting its needs. Superstitions, magic, and various religious beliefs supporting such a marital norm may ultimately develop, thus making it, in a sense, an institution. Other basic modes of marital units, such as *polyandry* (one woman with more than one husband), *monogamy* (one husband and one wife), and *serial monogamy* (a series of monogamous marriages with different partners) develop in a similar way.

Researchers describe family units under two major classes. The first unit is the *nuclear family,* a unit referring to father, mother, and siblings. The second unit is the *extended family,* which includes the nuclear family and extends to incorporate the grandparents, uncles, aunts, cousins, and so on. Beyond these two classes, the trained cultural observer is concerned with the actual lineage, wherein group membership can be actually demonstrated from some common ancestor. *Descent groups* refer to groups where a common ancestor is assumed and where group members have ritual, property, or activity in common. A collection of lineages where common descent is not necessarily demonstrated is a *clan* (Fox 1971, 47–50). Collections of clans may become a *tribe.*

The fundamental family unit accrues only after *marriage procurement,* a process that also varies culturally. For example, some clans adhere to strict prohibitions, allowing marriage only within the clan (or even some other significant unit), a practice called *endogamy.* One reason for endogamy is the containment of property or perhaps sacred qualities connected with a lineage. For instance, the ideal marriage of a Yoruk of Turkey is between first cousins (Bates 1974). Another variation of marriage availability is the procurement of marriage partners from outside the clan (or other significant unit), a practice called *exogamy.* Sometimes exogamy occurs to strengthen ties with other clans or to ensure the exchange of economic resources through marriage. The Tzetal tribe of Mexico opposes intrafamily marriages, including marriage to even very distant kin (Stross 1974).

Kinship systems also involve the role of authority. Male-dominated authority patterns in the family are called *patriarchal,* while female-dominated authority patterns are called *matriarchal.* There is usually some question about the formal matriarchal society's existence, but British anthropologist Robin Fox (1971) summarized this position:

Early writers called any system that looked to them as though "kinship was through females only" either matriarchal or a system of mother-right (to contrast with the patrilineal, patriarchal, or father-right). This implied that power and authority were in the hands of women in such a system. This is, of course, just not true. . . . Such a sinister practice exists only in the imagination, although most people have at some time or another accused their neighbors of it, or at least of being in some way "matriarchal." Thus, Athens accused Sparta, France accused England, and now we are accusing the Americans. It probably arises from a deep-rooted fear on the part of men that they will lose their position, and the fear is projected onto disliked nations. Be this as it may, the true Amazonian solution is unknown. (p. 113)

If Fox's position is correct for formal levels within the cultural, we observe the many informal cultural circumstances of women's authority and decision-making, even if the power is not equally recognized or distributed in the culture.

Finally, qualities of inheritance or naming, or both, that come through the mother's side are found in *matrilineal* cultures. *Patrilineal* groups foster inheritance or naming, or both, emphasizing the father's side.

**Political Subsystems**

Universally, societies have some form of governing organization functioning on a formal level and an informal level. On the *formal* level, such governing organizations originate because of self-appointment, inherited rights, vote, consensus, or political takeover. A less obvious *informal* method of accruing perceived power, status, and leadership also exists. In various cultural groups, some leaders are assumed to have a certain degree of supernatural power. Many years ago, a group of South Sea islanders considered the power of *mana* (special power or magic) to dwell in certain individuals. This impersonal power was believed to cause its recipients to possess the equivalent of what we might term "power," since persons who were perceived to have high degrees of mana usually had greater financial prowess, inherent status, and attributed power. Individuals believed this power also resided because of some special charm or incantation formula. The term for this perceived power stuck—the word can still refer to a special leadership.

Aside from the concept of impersonal supernatural power residing in or near a person, traditional leadership in political organizations among traditional cultures seems closely linked with age and economic qualities. In Ghana, for example, village chieftainship and eldership appear to be related closely to father's role (inheritance factor), age, and economic ability. Reyburn's (1953) ethnographic report among the Sierra Quechua of Ecuador indicates that village leadership is a function of economic ability, marital status (only married men are considered for the post of *prioste,* responsible for fiestas), and priestly appointment.

**Subsystems of Social Control**

All cultures have methods of dealing with violations of norms (accepted modes of behavior) and laws. Societal punishment appears to be universal, although consequences vary from fines to banishment or death. For example, two visitors in an African country unknowingly walked through sacred African *ju-ju* ground, a religiously special place, and were fined the national equivalent of one month's wages. Physical punishment also exemplifies differing cultural solutions to the universal need for order as "caning" in Singapore illustrates.

Like every other element of culture, social control develops from specific cultural contexts. This chapter opened with several examples related to social control. A difficulty arises when we compare social control in one culture with its counterpart in another culture. Many international persons, for example, believe that the United States is far too lenient in its punishment for certain crimes; conversely, many U.S. citizens believe that some countries have enacted overly strict laws. Evaluation of cultural methods of social control depends on examining each culture from its own perspective.

## Health Management Subsystems

How a culture addresses the health of cultural members also poses a significant cultural system. As Harris and Moran (1991) observe, the very concept of meaningful health can differ among cultures. The methodologies by which people are medically treated can range from chemical medication by highly educated medical specialists to herbal application by village practiciners.

Hospitals and medical clinics are relatively new innovations in some cultures, and sometimes an interesting mixture of the traditional medicines with the modern medicines appears in hospital rooms. In Papua New Guinea, family medical tradition has sometimes combined with modern hospitalization as family members take turns in groups staying with a patient, cooking food, and practically camping out for days at a time in the patient's room. Health information is a topic currently significant for those working in developing countries. Not only is it important to understand the health system of a culture in order to manage it effectively from within, but the nature of health delivery is equally important in order to disseminate health information.

Cultural differences related to health care delivery unfortunately correspond to differential quality of life questions. Traditionally disadvantaged ethnic populations in the United States have higher than average infant mortality rates and overall fewer years life span on the average. While socioeconomic factors play some role in these differences, other cultural factors intervene. Brislin (1993) identifies a number of reasons for poor physical and mental health related to culture. Some of his reasons are adapted as follows:

1. with lack of insurance or personal resources people wait too long before calling a health professional;

2. traditional remedies may be used either because modern medicine is too expensive or because it is seen as ineffective;

3. little trust in health subsystems or in health professionals;

4. inadequate or inaccurate information provided for families;

5. cultural values toward the age at which mothers pay more attention to their infant's health needs;

6. accurate indicators of physical or psychological distress are not viewed as significant indicators of illness to report. In other words, symptoms a certain culture looks to as a sign of illness may be inaccurately linked to

the real illness, and conversely, symptoms that modern health professionals look for in examinations may seem irrelevant to an acculturated individual;

7. nonverbal signs typically associated with certain psychological disorders (like depression) are culture-bound, especially clinical diagnoses that involve interaction and rapport qualities and facial expressions. Mental health experts must conduct clinical evaluations using cultural base lines of normality.

To this list, we can add world view perspectives about the nature of the universe in a person's belief system:

8. world view intervenes in preventing modern medicine; for example, a person who believes in animism (witches and spirits) needs to be evaluated in light of the entire culture's beliefs. By western psychological standards, a person having a vision may seem mentally unstable, but by certain traditional African standards the person would be normal. We also can add fatalism, ancestor worship, the importance of silence, stoicism, language norms, and a host of other variables related to world view and values that intervene in accurate physical and mental health assessments.

**Educational Subsystems**

Cultural educational systems widely differ. In the British educational system, for instance, students are either university or vocational bound, influenced by testing by about age twelve or fourteen. Also, some European education is conducted bilingually. Many foreign universities are structured differently from those in the United States. At some universities, subjects are studied a year at a time, not by semester or quarter unit credits. The critical point for intercultural communication is recognizing diversity in educational subsystems and how those differences alter our perceptions and messages.

**Religious Subsystems**

Religious systems involve beliefs, ceremonies, places of worship, norms of respect, and linguistic concepts that can cause great embarrassment for those who do not understand them. Many visitors to mosques and temples, for instance, neglect basic etiquette by failing to remove their shoes or observe other norms of respect. Recognizing the external elements of religiosity in a particular culture not only prevents cultural mistakes but also can affect insights into macrocultural patterns, cultural beliefs, and cultural values. For example, during the holy month for Moslems, fasting occurs from dawn to dusk. As told by a Thai participant, several Thai workers (mostly Buddhist) who worked side by side with Islamic workers failed to appreciate the significance of the period of time and the rituals associated with the fasting. Consequently, the organizational climate during that month was tense and negatively altered communication patterns, work productivity, and morale.

**Theories of Culture Shift**

Elements and institutions around which cultures are organized have been identified. What phenomena account for a culture's changes? The topic of explaining culture shift is complex. Our discussion of cultural elements would be incomplete without briefly exploring social forces and theories leading to change.

**Cultural Borrowing**  External contact of one culture meeting another can produce change in one or the other or both. When the Pilgrims ventured to the United States, some of their habits changed; partially because of culture contact, they borrowed survival skills from Native Americans, such as planting and eating corn and other foods. Sometimes, cultural borrowing occurs deliberately. In the case of the Australian stone axe culture mentioned earlier in this chapter, acceptance of a culturally foreign object proved disastrous.

Many years ago, blackbirds were brought into the United States from England to control insects. However, today in some mid-southern states, these birds are creating an enormous health problem and millions of dollars of grain loss each year. Another example also illustrates this point. A hearty ground cover useful in Japan was imported to the United States for planting along roadsides. For some reason, the plant life grew so well that it became uncontrollable, covering fence lines, large trees, and waterways.

Similarly, cultural borrowing can significantly alter culture. Acceptance of imported products represents still another example of cultural borrowing and acculturation. The result often leads to cultural change and development. Culture contact that leads to change can be planned or unplanned. When planned, the culture contact typically is part of a strategic plan or special effort.

**Cultural Crisis**  Sometimes, cultural changes are the result of uncontrollable forces, such as floods, hurricanes, volcanic eruptions, and other spontaneous events that cause physical relocation or psychological alteration. Just as disasters create a need for cultural realignment, these cataclysmic changes in the life and history of a group of people can also forge a new culture from the old. For example, the severe Guatemalan earthquakes of 1977, which toppled entire barrios built on hillsides and engulfed mountain villages, caused relocation. The settled villagers of the mountains became the new settlers in plains regions. This shift has caused alteration of endogamy, authority structure, and language.

Contrived, human-made forces can be just as cataclysmic, and at least as forceful, as natural disasters in shaping cultural destinies. Wars, political coups, and installation of high dams along rivers seriously alter culture. For example, war-torn Vietnam, among other things, left a trail of refugees, many of whom settled in the United States. In some cases, highly skilled physicians, lawyers, or engineers worked at menial jobs as a result of their immigration. Family structures were also altered. Many of the younger Vietnamese showed greater acculturation capabilities than their elders. Despite family pressure to let the elders make decisions, pressure from the new culture sometimes pushed the younger generation toward family leadership and individualism.

As World War II encroached upon the South Pacific, New Guinea islanders were dramatically confronted with strange new ways. The war brought guns, machines of all sorts, vehicles, and hundreds of other things needed for life support and battle. The alien aircraft dropping their packaged cargoes from the sky surprised the islanders and yet enticed them toward these "miracles." When the hardware was removed at the war's end, an unusual cult developed. This new culture was termed the "cargo cult," and one of its tenets rested on the expectation of a return of the cargo. To this day, the quasi-religious culture still anticipates the return of the cargo.

Some economic changes induce social change. The Aswân High Dam on the Nile River has affected Egyptian rural life. Some observers believe that the many economic benefits of the dam may be partially balanced by its social effects. Many villagers have shifted occupations and live in newly-formed towns, a move that has eroded traditional lines of authority. The farmer, now a factory worker at a fertilizer plant, sometimes loses his personal pride as his superiors devalue his former life. Once prosperous river villages now lie under water, swept by the currents of a lake newly formed for a developing nation.

While cultural cataclysms have an immediate crisis-centered impact on a culture's development, cultural experts recognize that a culture's ecology also has a long-term, gradual impact. Certain environmental features may influence a culture's diet, dress, religion, and marriage partnerships.

## Cultural Ecological Theory

Ecological environment is important to culture for at least two reasons. One is that, as population increases, available land decreases. This population pressure pushes natural boundaries to their limit, and new frontiers are colonized. As a result of the new frontier environment, changes in agricultural practices, dress, diet, and word usages emerge. Also, hierarchical societies sometimes send lower-status members to colonize. New ranks then emerge in the newly changing culture.

A second reason that environment influences culture involves the distribution of products, services, and materials of neighboring cultures. For example, if the environment of culture C contains necessary items for cultures A and B, a symbiotic relationship develops. *Symbiosis* refers to fulfilling mutual needs between two or more cultures. Suppose that clans A, B, and C contain environmental productions of timber (A), construction stones (B), and fish (C) (figure 3.2). Inasmuch as all three of these subcultures desire these things, economic exchanges develop and symbiotic relationships crystallize.

As economic interplay heightens, significant cultural features may be borrowed or adapted, leading to divergence from tradition in cultural development. Members of a submissive culture may now become fierce bargainers or symbiosis may escalate, whereby exogamous clans (clans marrying outside their own clan) exchange those available for marriage.

Another theory for explaining culture examines major themes of culture. According to Benedict (1934), a dominant idea of a culture can reveal cultural members' fundamental values. Furthermore, these fundamental themes are more important than the functional relationship of cultural items to each other. Consequently, the cultural theme becomes the dominant force guiding action and thought.

## Dominant Theme Analysis

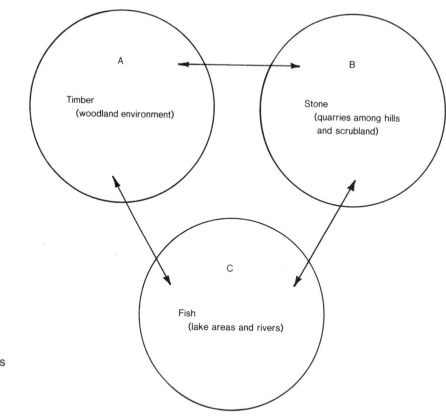

**Figure 3.2**
Economic symbiosis
based on
environmental
production.

Among the Zuni Indians, for instance, two cultural themes stand out. According to Zuni tradition, men submerge their activities into those of the entire group and claim no personal authority. A second theme is nonviolence. Even under attacks of insult and abuse, accepted behavioral systems provide nonviolent outlets. For example, if a man is unfaithful to his wife in Zuni culture, the wife may simply not wash his clothes, thus indicating to her husband and to the community that she knows of the affair. In some cases, this indirect, though passive-aggressive method, causes the husband to relinquish his extramarital affair.

National and regional macrocultures illustrate key themes that drive the nature of a culture. In Asian cultures, group harmony and subjecting self to the group is a predominant theme, a value strongly influencing culture. Some employees in Japan so identify with the company, for instance, that they introduce themselves with the company name first and then their own name. In one case, a Japanese engineer with an electronics firm so identified with the company that he called himself NJT Kanakamani, where NJT refers to the corporation and Kanakamani to his name.

Another theory of culture is called functionalism, developed by Bronislaw Malinowski (1944). From his work with the Trobriand islanders, he reasoned that cultural systems are an outgrowth of three underlying human needs: basic, derived, and integrative. Culture develops and organizes its values and practices around what the culture considers ways to deal with those needs. *Basic* needs refer to survival needs, such as food, water, and shelter. *Derived* needs refer to "social coordination," as Nanda (1980) describes it, including division of labor, distribution of food, and social control. The third need is *integrative,* or, as Nanda continues, the need for security and social harmony met by magic, knowledge, myth, and art. Malinowski's fundamental notion was that every aspect of culture can be summarized by one of these three needs and that cultures develop to satisfy these needs in ways functional for their situation and with their particular resources (Harris 1983).

**Functionalism**

You may find some of the following suggestions helpful. They are suggested with imperative verb forms for ease of understanding.

**Developing Intercultural Skills in Understanding Culture**

1. *Respect the dignity and personhood of others.* Even if you find yourself disagreeing with some values or other aspect of a culture, you may wish to avoid arguing. Respect the rights of others in their cultural situation, and seek to understand the culture rather than to criticize it. Try to enjoy people, looking at their personhood rather than their cultural background.

2. *Do not let others' criticism get you down.* In your attempts to learn a new culture, you will always find people who criticize your efforts to adapt and practice skills in intercultural communication. Be a bit thick-skinned. Do not let even your friends criticize your attempts if they are unwilling to try to understand a new culture themselves. Of course, if they are trying to tell you that you are reacting unduly, then be aware of their honest feedback. Keep in mind that you may be experiencing some forms of culture shock, and friends can help you with that experience.

3. *Do not feel as if you have to be liked everywhere by everyone.* The outgoing American may feel alienated in some cultures where members do not act as gregarious as the visitor may prefer. Everyone cannot be liked everywhere. Even if you feel that people do not like you, keep trying to communicate.

4. *Be careful in discussing monetary matters.* If you are visiting in another culture, you will soon discover that a number of cultures believe travelers are rich. Some southern Europeans perceive Americans to be loud, boastful, and ignorant of local customs. Do your best not to support that stereotype. Avoid talk of money and financial matters, except in clearly appropriate circumstances.

5. *Work on adaptability.* Studies show that being able to adapt quickly to new and different situations is essential to becoming a good intercultural communicator. In many circumstances, you may prefer to suspend judgment and listen to other people—and avoid merely reacting. Emotions quickly blind us, especially when frustration and emotional tensions are high anyway because of our arrival in a new culture.

6. *Work on initiative.* Be willing to take social risks. Try to open yourself to new cultural experiences. The principles in this chapter, including this suggestion, do not apply only to cultures outside the United States. Showing initiative and creativity can help you in everyday interpersonal communication and relationships. The words of Shakespeare seem particularly important as you ingratiate yourself with others: "Our doubts are traitors and cause us to lose the good we oft might win by fearing to attempt."

7. *Be observant.* Part of becoming proficient in intercultural communication involves watching and listening. You may find it helpful to write in a diary or notebook the things you observed each day. Write down things people say, stories you hear, or anything you think is important. Then, every couple of days, look over your diary or notes and reflect. You will be amazed at what you learn.

8. *Be ready for lack of privacy.* One of the things you probably value, sometimes without realizing it, is your personal privacy. In another culture, privacy as you may conceive it may be less than you prefer. Be ready for anything, and let things happen as they will without spending too much time preoccupying yourself with your "rights." Rude as it may seem, your personal privacy simply may not be a big factor in another culture's way of thinking.

9. *Do not superimpose your political values.* All too often a person in an intercultural contact converses about political systems to the exclusion of other topics of conversation. In fact, some people get into violent arguments about politics and misjudge a culture because of its political norms. Remember, a culture can be appreciated for topics and areas other than politics.

10. *Recognize perceived roles of women.* A number of cultures hold attitudes toward the role of women that may vary greatly from your attitudes. Though you may disagree with these attitudes, try to demonstrate respect for cultural traditions, whether you think they are right or wrong. Many intercultural relationships are lost trying to win ideological battles. You may win the argument but lose the relationship.

11. *Respect tradition.* Most of us who grew up in the United States have not learned the same respect for tradition that many members from other cultures hold. Many cultural members believe that traditional ways are tried and proven and that to disregard these matters is highly disrespectful.

12. *Get used to long lines.* Many cultures do not have systems that handle things as efficiently as you think they should be handled. Sometimes you will find yourself waiting in long lines. Thus, be prepared, and keep your frustration level down if you are impatient.

13. *Learn to give of yourself and to receive.* One reaction to facing differences in intercultural contact is to become reticent. This pattern of withdrawal, however, prevents interaction needed to learn a new culture.

## This Chapter in Perspective

The chapter discusses a number of different cultural practices and has treated cultural elements with a systems approach to some of these cultural practices. Beyond an appreciation for cultural elements, the goal has been to introduce the meaning of a culture's history, personality, material features, role relationships, economic methods, kinship and other social and political organizational patterns, social control, artistic expression, language, changeability and stability, belief system, and a number of cultural attitudes. The chapter also examines the numerous theories on how culture develops.

We do not become experts in intercultural communication because we now know how culture is a system composed of interrelated elements and institutions. This discussion, however, may help set the stage for understanding. Sensitization to another person's culture is a prerequisite for effective cultural communication.

## Exercises

1. Secure from some source person a simulation or game that emphasizes cultural differences, such as BA FA BA FA and Heelots and Hokias. After playing the game or simulation, try to spend some time debriefing. What made the exercise meaningful or not meaningful as far as learning about culture? What cultural variables came to light during the simulation?

2. Interview an international student on your campus. Then explain, to your class or a small group, a cultural element, a cultural theory, or a system of culture from the international student's home culture.

3. In almost every issue of *National Geographic* there are articles on other cultures. Pick an article that describes a culture of some interest to you, and give a brief synopsis. What theoretical point of view did the author of the article take concerning his or her description of the culture? Can you identify the major cultural variables uncovered in the article?

Chapter **4**

# Microcultures of Heritage and Group Attitudes

**Objectives**

After completing this chapter, you should be able to

1. Identify principles associated with in-group and out-group communication

2. List the rhetorical strategies used by in-groups and out-groups in their communication

3. Discuss a model and process through which individuals make judgments about in-groups and out-groups

4. Apply in-group/out-group communication with self-identity, worth, and confidence issues

5. List and actively discuss attitudes preventing competent intercultural communication between heritage culture members

6. Develop strengths and weaknesses of intercultural marriages

The term "heritage cultures" describes the perceived difference concerning ethnic and racial groups. The term represents a social matrix as a member of an ethnic or racial coculture and the pride and worth associated with one's cultural birth heritage. The term also opens a discussion of marriage or adoption into a heritage involving ethnic or racial group membership. To begin the discussion of communicating across what some have labeled as "minority" boundaries, let us recall two terms from chapter 1.

*Ethnic* groups are identifiable bodies of people noted for their common heritage and cultural tradition, usually national and/or religious. Examples include Polish American, Italian American, and Mexican American. These examples can be misused or occasionally misleading because the naming process to identify ethnic groups changes frequently, and some members of ethnic groups do not want to be identified in a unique way. Nevertheless, the idea is to indicate a person's origin, without any preconceived value to the naming intended.

*Racial* groups are defined by genetically transmitted and inherited traits of physical appearance. Examples include African American (although many members use the term "American blacks" or "blacks" to refer to Americans of African ancestry), Native Americans (American Indians), Asian Americans, and people of color. Since these examples focus from a U.S. cultural perspective, and could differ within countries outside the United States, we give only a few suggested examples to illustrate the concepts.

In the fundamental model in this text, it is argued that perceptual difference is triggered in ways that enhance or hinder accurate formation of attitudes or appropriate adjustment strategies or both. When ethnic and racial differences are encountered, given the negative attitudes from the past, these suggest primary areas of difference for some people to overcome. In writing on race relations, Anita Foeman (1991), commenting on an article from the *Harvard Business Review* about black managers states that, "After years of cross-cultural training activity many organizational members of color still report disappointment, dismay, frustration, and anger because they have not gained acceptance on par with white peers." She continues, noting that African American movement into upper ranks is unimpressive and that "while legal and political milestones may have been met, interpersonal acceptance has tended to lag behind" (p. 255).

Cultural differences in areas of race and ethnicity provide a significant and relevant arena in which to practice intercultural skills. Casmir (1991) reminds us that despite efforts to conceive of intercultural communication as individuals in interpersonal communication contexts, "it is the differences that create major challenges." While we think of ourselves as independent, Casmir argues that "human beings have always been *inter*dependent. . . . Along with the awareness of required interaction comes the recognition that we also have to deal

Dealing with multicultural pluralism is a major goal for every culture. (Photo by Angela Van Huss, Prague, Czechoslavakia.)

with ethnic and racial diversity or even confrontations, because interdependence means that we 'cannot leave each other alone'" (p. 231). Koester and Lustig (1991) indicate the importance of facing cultural pluralism in multicultural contexts in education. Brislin (1993) and Asante and Davis (1989) contend for the multiple communication encounters in the workplace involving cultural diversity.

These observations from intercultural researchers and educators match the many observations that stereotypes and intense prejudices condense into difficulty and ineffective intercultural relations. The assumption is made that most people are willing to communicate effectively with individuals representing cultural diversity in education, the workplace, in neighborhoods, in families, and in friendships. It is also recognized, however, that good motives need to be joined with good information about the nature and process of these dynamics of intercultural differences involving cultures of heritage.

## The Process of In-group/Out-group Communication

Group memberships play an important role in shaping a person's social behavior. Heritage cultures represent significant group identification. Considering a modality point of view, minority group membership sometimes predicts group patterns, although we must recognize many individual differences. From a person's identification with a heritage culture (and some people do not identify but have actively or passively rejected their heritage) how do cultural members draw upon their cultural roots in a way that influences intergroup communication? Recall in chapter 1 that the communication behaviors we see in others can reflect personality, culture, or perception of a particular relationship. We cannot lay every difference at the feet of culture.

### Social Categorization

The process of intergroup communication proceeds through several stages, as the model in figure 4.1 reveals. The first part of the process is actually a series of stages that occur called *social categorization* (Gudykunst and Gumbs 1989).

Social categorization can stimulate stereotypical attitudes, leading us to overlook the similarities between people.
(Photo by Attitaya Indrakanhang.)

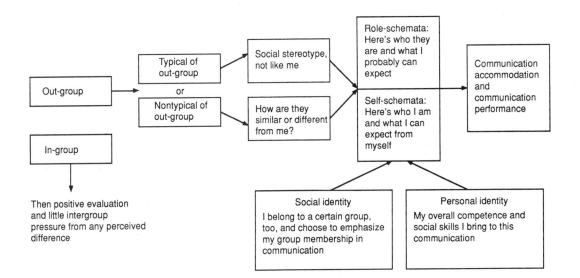

We perceive similarity or difference and assign typicality. Based on role and self expectations, the second rooted in social and personal identity, we then engage in communication accommodation and performance. The desire or ability to engage in positive communication and performance also depends on positive social and personal identifications. (See research by Gudykunst and Gumbs 1989, Gallois and others 1988, Ting-Toomey 1989.)

**Figure 4.1**
A model of social categorization.

It is like stereotyping. We put people in different boxes, and, unfortunately, build fences around the boxes. These boundaries lead to in-groups and out-groups, which are discussed later. For example, a person is either a Hispanic or an Anglo, an Asian or a black. Over time, we tend to build a set of expectations of how Hispanics, Anglos, Asians, and blacks are supposed to act. Some folks have more permeable boxes than others, but the point is the tendency to build these perimeters. Of course, we need to recognize, as many scholars have reminded us, that there are a number of personality factors that intervene or mediate in this social categorization practice. For example, people who are somewhat rigid and dogmatic tend to have narrower and less permeable categories than individuals who are more open and less rigid.

The model highlights stereotypes concerning out-groups. That is, people project various traits, emotions, roles, abilities, and interests of out-group members. Mental tapes are played that trigger our perceived certainties about this person's likes and dislikes: "She must like a certain kind of music, because she is from a certain particular ethnic group" or "He is probably a good athlete because he is of a particular racial heritage."

As it turns out, these social stereotypes operate mostly if we perceive a person as typical of a social group. If the person is not typical, another set of dynamics emerges, dynamics involving attribution concerning the other person. Social stereotyping, for the typical members, leads further into the process, a process affected by two kinds of internal perceptions: those about self and those about others.

## Self- and Role-Schemata

Perceptions about self in intercultural communication are called *self-schemata* (Gudykunst and Gumbs 1989). It is very similar to the idea of self-concept, but it refers to two specific identity issues. The first identification factor is called *social identity*—my perception of my identity in relation to belonging to a group. If a group, for instance, is very positive for me, and I choose to identify with that group, then I would have a very high social identification in my self-schemata. A second aspect of the self in interpersonal terms is my *personal identity*. This has to do with the question of personal capabilities or personal competence. These two identity issues of the self-schemata answer the questions, "Who am I in relation to my group in this communication situation?" and "What can I expect of myself in this communication situation?"

A second dimension, called *role-schemata,* however, overlaps at this point. Role-schemata answers the questions, "Who is the other group?" and "What can I probably expect from a person in this group?"

## Communication Accommodation

Based on the cumulative processing of this out-group member, (that is, stereotypes about the person, perceptions about specific attributes, what I can expect from him or her, what I can expect from myself), there is a motivation to engage in *communication accommodation* and communication performance, according to research by Gallois and others (1988). If social and personal identification are positive, we expect positive communication performance.

There are some factors that could easily prevent this model from being active. First, positive results will not occur if what is called *ethnolinguistic vitality* (the perceived prestige of a language group) were to result in arrogance on the part of one of the interactants. Second, if anxiety or uncertainty remains high following the stereotyping process, then that, too, would preclude effective communication. Third, certain personality factors could mediate the process and lead to ineffective outcomes. For example, a person who is highly rigid (high dogmatism, low category width), a person who adjusts poorly to communication needs in various communication settings (low self-monitoring skills), or a person who lacks judgment in discerning interpersonal relationships (low in cognitive complexity) can render communication ineffective. Fourth, the more we develop intimacy, knowledge about the other, friendship, and experience positive contact, the differences initially perceived become less important.

**Factors Altering the Social Categorization Model**

When we engage in intercultural listening, it is easy to see how intercultural groups with which we socially identify can help or hinder. Clearly, our perception of groups is hindered if we stereotype prematurely and draw upon negative attributions toward another person or group. If our own identities are insecure, lacking robust social or personal identification, it is less likely that we would listen very carefully (Ting-Toomey 1989). Also, our entire motivation to listen to others is undermined when there is no desire toward communication accommodation. Finally, if we lack empathy and sensitivity to the communication needs of others, we can fail.

As stated earlier, groups we identify with and whom we socially accept are called in-groups; those we do not identify with and are considered outcast in a person's category system are called out-groups. In many parts of the world, heritage cultures and origins frequently define in-group and out-group perceptions. For instance, the significant strife in the former Yugoslavia exemplifies, almost to the extreme, the in-group/out-group distinctions based almost exclusively on ethnic cleansing, as it has been called.

**In-group and Out-group Communication Applied to Heritage Culture Communication**

The characteristics common to interracial communication and interethnic communication may broadly apply to many intergroup interactions. While far more information exists about these specialized forms of communication,* the following areas (suspicion, stereotypes, solidarity, separation) reflect the rhetorical and communication phenomena often related to heritage cultural communication differences.

Some situations are frequently marked by mutual suspicions of group *A* toward group *B*. The erupting racial tension in schools, cities, and the workplace in the United States illustrates the intense feelings marking not just poor communication, but avoidance and hostility. The level of suspicion aroused is clearly irrational in most cases and is fueled by specific features, such as the "we-they" syndrome and mistrust.

**Suspicion**

*Works by Smith (1973), Rich (1974), Blubaugh and Pennington (1976), Gandy and Matabane (1989), Pennington (1989), and Asante and Davis (1989) exemplify these issues.

In-group and out-group communication is often characterized by alienation, a point experienced by this Apache Native American woman in the left of the photograph who, according to interviews, indicates her desire to intensify her friendships with Hispanics and Anglos.
(Photo by Attitaya Indrakanhang.)

*We-They dichotomy.* An accompanying characteristic of suspicion in the interracial and interethnic context is the distinction between "we" and "they." Such a distinction clearly heightens a sense of loyalty and group identity, both of which are necessary for social change. The words of Malcolm X (cited in Minnick 1979, p. 143) illustrate this principle:

> No, I'm not an American. I'm one of the 22 million black people who are victims of Americanism. One of the 22 million black people who are victims of democracy. . . . .

*Mistrust.* Suspicion is also aroused by attitudes of mistrust. Unfortunately, since contacts are often limited, people selectively perceive racial and ethnic groups that contrast with their own in such a way as to create mutual mistrust. The mistrust, however, is often predicated upon not only selective perception but also upon negative, erroneous stereotypes.

The principle behind the suspicious nature of in-group/out-group communication is well documented in Broome's (1990) case analysis of Greek cultural in-group/out-group communication where he describes the protection, trust, support, cooperation, sympathy, and admiration among in-group members. His analysis contrasts such positive factors to in-group relations with out-group members marked by suspicion, mistrust, rejection of out-group influence, avoidance, hostility, concealment, deception, and general lack of helpfulness.

## Stereotypes

Stereotypes develop as a way of organizing our world. Categorizing is a necessary part of daily functioning. However, stereotyping categories of people is often misleading, since all people within a category are not alike and since we may not always fully understand what we perceive.

Experimental studies confirm anecdotal notions of stereotypes and specify the ways in which those stereotypes operate. In a classic study of stereotypic attitudes toward Mexican Americans, England (1977) showed to one group, slides of a Mexican American male in various scenes—in a yard behind a frame house, carrying trash cans, raking leaves around a tree, and putting the leaves into a wagon. He was dressed in a work shirt, work pants, and an outdoor work hat. A second matched group was shown exactly the same scenes, except that the man in the slides was an Anglo male dressed exactly as the Mexican American stimulus figure. The respondents perceived the Mexican American stereotypically: having less education, working for others not self, and having a large family. More recent evidence continues to reveal a general population insensitivity. (See Jack Condon's *Good Neighbors,* or Deneve and Condon *Hispanic Cultures: A Kaleidoscope in Intercultural Communication.*) The problem is complex, but the following are helpful beginnings:

1. *Seek a common code.* Frequently, linguistic variations and dialectical differences cause people to close the door to further understanding and communication attempts. By seeking a common code, we can maximize our chances for a heightened overlap of experiences. Communication in establishing a common code should become two-way; asking questions and seeking to clarify are excellent ways to begin the process.

2. *Seek to build trust.* Trust comes from showing trust. An accompanying sense of empathy toward others can turn hostility into a meaningful relationship.

3. *Suspend judgments.* If interaction with a person from a different racial or ethnic background raises negative attitudes toward that group, then make a conscious effort to suspend those attitudes. Consider the uniqueness of each individual by carefully listening, expressing your view honestly, and then continuing to listen.

A third characteristic of heritage cocultures and their communication is the group's solidarity, often corresponding to a group's self-identity. This solidarity was well illustrated in the words of Martin Luther King when he declared:

Solidarity

> But one hundred years later, the Negro still is not free. One hundred years later, the life of the Negro is still sadly crippled by the manacles of segregation and the chains of discrimination.
>
> One hundred years later, the Negro lives on a lonely island of poverty in the midst of a vast ocean of material prosperity. One hundred years later, the Negro is still languished in the corners of American society and finds himself an exile in his own land. So we have come here today to dramatize a shameful condition.
>
> In a sense, we have come to our nation's capital to cash a check. When the architects of our republic wrote the magnificent words of the Constitution and the Declaration of Independence, they were signing a promissory note to which every American was to fall heir. (Minnick 1979, pp. 140–41)

The point of commonality, so eloquently stressed in this excerpt, was the mutual suffering and the future promise of mutual reward to a group showing solidarity (emphasized by the "we"). Again, not everyone chooses to identify with a heritage culture, or there may be loose-knit identification. To those whose identity is a major part of their racial or ethnic heritage, some important communication factors may coincide with solidarity: in-group code, in-group symbols, in-group expectations, and in cases of hostility encouraged by extreme solidarity, the in-group's enemy.

1. *In-group code.* By using a code system that only in-group members understand, a sense of belonging and uniqueness can result, facilitating solidarity.

2. *In-group symbols.* To the extent that the group encourages high levels of solidarity, use of symbols such as colors, musical lyrics, slogans, and significant objects, also foster solidarity.

3. *In-group expectations.* Solidarity also results from clear expectations. Whether one is a member of the group or not, norms and performance standards often are known.

4. *In-group enemies.* The racial tensions of our age starkly remind us of instances where in-groups portray out-groups in negative, hostile, enemy-like terms. For example, Broome (1990) explains the strong Greek cultural in-group/out-group system pointing to its intensity as well as its promises and liabilities in relationships. Outcroppings of racial and ethnic hostilities in schools, the workplace, neighborhoods, and large cities haunt our recent memories as phantoms that we thought were legislated out of existence. The daily news is filled with episodes involving in-groups of national origin, religious affiliation, and racial origin who conflict with out-groups.

**Separation**

A final theme of in-group/out-group communication is the separation theme. Evidence points to isolation, exclusion, and feelings of loss among heritage cultural members. This exclusion theme, noted as a value in chapter 3, is elevated when minority cultures find themselves not invited or at least disengaged within majority cultural relationships and systems. Gonzalez (1990) writes eloquently addressing this point from a Mexican American analysis. The separation theme is exacerbated all the more when one considers Gonzalez's point that the quality of Mexican "otherness" motivates this heritage culture to embrace an openness toward others, but the culture fears being rebuffed, even demolished. Out of the Mexican experience, notes Gonzalez, has come ambivalence, self-conscious resignation, withdrawal, and feelings of betrayal. These themes are rooted in the Spanish Conquest, but no doubt have streams of present reality as Mexican Americans interact in a dominant Anglo world.

The case presented applies to many oppressed cultures, where adjustment options become limited and dysfunctional: fight, get out, or deny. In each option, communication remains dwarfed, encased in a body of suspicious experience that prevents overlap of cultural experience and positive communication outcomes.

Dysfunctional attitudes arrest the development of effective intercultural communication. Investigators consistently identify attitudes that block open perception, and by their nature, limit intercultural relationships.

## Attitudes As Barriers to Effective Interethnic and Interracial Communication

### Ethnocentrism

As you may recall from chapter 3, ethnocentrism is an evaluation of one's culture as better than or superior to another culture. This attitude represents much more than technical or quantitative assessment, such as recognizing a culture has more technology or more resources than another culture. It is a cultural arrogance, loaded with emotions, and broadly applied to many out-groups. The resulting "my culture is better than your culture" belief weaves its way into thoughts and actions, such as arrogance, avoidance, withdrawal, faulty attribution, and faulty categorizing. Although the term normally appears in discussions comparing national and regional macrocultures, it is easy to recognize how ethnocentrism surrounds numerous cultures of diversity. The research on this topic also links authoritarianism and dogmatism to this attitude.

### Stereotypes

In chapter 2, one of the axioms concerning attributions or summary motives and impressions about groups and individuals was noted. Sometimes the information and consequent impressions are accurate. For example, to state that in general Japanese politely respect elders or that traditional Thais bow as a form of greeting to elder persons is an accurate statement about many members of those groups. You can always find an impolite Japanese or an inhospitable Thai person. The behaviors in those cultures, however, represent a modality of frequent actions.

Stereotypes also can be inaccurate. It is this area that causes many problems. How does inaccuracy occur?

First, the facts may be wrong, such as incorrect knowledge and information about a culture.

Second, negative qualities and intentions, attributed to a culture, may be unwarranted by the data. For example, to say "West Africans are late to meetings," may be an accurate statement in some rural settings. To then *interpret* a descriptive statement filling in attributions going beyond the observations is shaky at best. For instance, to add "Furthermore, they are late because of disregard or bad intentions" ignores the reasons for lack of clock watching among some rural Africans and has nothing to do with bad intentions.

Third, stereotypes that lead us toward a faulty extrapolation toward individual members, assuming that what is true of the group is also true of every member, violates a significant rule of logic. You cannot assume that everyone acts like the group, even if you accept the first premise about the group.

There are resulting *affective* or feeling components to all this that directly affects communicating between diverse cultures. Racial and ethnic tensions indicated by examples in the United States are represented for some urban blacks and Orientals, Hispanics and Anglos, Skinheads and Jews, Italians and Puerto Ricans. The in-group/out-group hostilities are explosive and leave little doubt of the deep-seated feelings lying underneath the diversity cultures' clash.

Racism and prejudice can be subtle, observed even in the way one stereotypes various groups.
(Photo by Mark Houston.)

Brislin (1993) writes excellent observations about the origins of the broader concept, prejudice, as a *socialization* process where pervasive negative stereotypes are passed on to children. If Brislin is right, the consequent intergenerational outlook is bleak. In this sense, emotion, not reason, captures our feelings of who is good and bad and how to feel about out-groups. Brislin's analysis forms a significant framework to understand the obvious and subtle ways of prejudice's forms, particularly as these evolve into hatred toward ethnic or racial groups, or racism (pp. 185–191).

*Intense racism.* People believe or act in a way indicating their belief that certain groups were born as outcasts. Consequently, they are viewed as being of low worth. Clusters of negative beliefs surround intense racism, beliefs that discriminate, devalue, ignore, withdraw from, and perpetuate negative or injurious myths toward the target of racism.

*Symbolic racism.* Brislin uses this term referring to out-groups as devalued not because of inherent inferiority, but because the group is seen as blocking basic cultural goals. In many cases, individuals are not disliked, but again, the out-group is perceived as causing trouble, disrupting habits and values, or moving too fast.

*Tokenism.* This subtle form of prejudice involves a person's small participation in activities appearing nonprejudicial as self-convincing proof of not being prejudiced. As an example, Brislin indicates giving small amounts of money or limited time and effort toward minority group activities in order to make participants feel good. Actually, the feeling is superficial, and hiding beneath the surface because of lack of involvement is a potential or latent prejudice or racism.

*Arms-length prejudice.* A final category chosen from Brislin's work is the behavior where nonprejudicial actions are clearly demonstrated in public, social settings, but warmth, friendliness, and intimacy are withheld in private settings. For instance, going to a party and being nice to out-group members, but later acting uncomfortably in a one-to-one visit over coffee or ignoring roommates, neighbors, in potential interracial/interethnic friendships in any private settings.

For many years, researchers and practitioners have explored the boundaries of how intergroup contact can work best. Intercultural authors such as Gudykunst (1977) and Brislin (1993), along with numerous authors from social psychology and sociology, have recommended strategies for enhancing intergroup contact, applied here to interracial and interethnic relationships:

1. *Make the contact personal.* Group meetings with little opportunity for sharing views and conversation beyond mere introductions does little more than allow for arms-length prejudice to continue. Contact alone does not work, but contact with intimacy has significant potential.

2. *Make the contact positive.* Sometimes structuring events that ensure positive contact and pleasant contact work best. A number of strategies exist to make the contact seem rewarding.

**Racism and Prejudice**

**Enhancing Interethnic and Interracial Relationships**

3. *Put people together with similar status.* In this case, role positions of similar rank or value are important. Pairing a lower positioned employee with an executive, for instance, works against the desired outcomes for the inter-group contact.

4. *Put people together with similar values.* As indicated in the last chapter, similarity of values fosters more rapid acceptance and assists credibility. For contact, the principle works to heighten positive evaluations toward an outgroup member.

5. *Reduce personal goals and agendas.* If the conversation pursues goals or agenda items that are relevant more to one than the other person in an inter-group contact session, this lack of empathy perspective (Broome 1991) and faulty listening make it less likely to experience positive communication adaptation outcomes.

6. *Show openness and respect.* These dual qualities work about as effectively in numerous intercultural contacts as almost any observation suggested. Openness implies response to differences that lead to inquisitiveness, willingness to learn, and tolerance of ambiguity. Respect carries an air of appreciation for differences and allows mistakes without judgment, expecting and creating mutual growth emerging from honest communication.

## Intercultural Marriages

In a chapter on heritage cultures, a discussion of intercultural marriages and family relationships is in order. Heritage cultures, as indicated early in this chapter, are not just accidents of birth but sometimes occasions of choice. To marry someone from another culture is a growing choice. Since those marriages are frequently between individuals of differing racial or ethnic background, it seems fitting to focus on the topic here. Intercultural marriages, sometimes called dual cultural marriages can come in various forms. Partners can be drawn from a variety of cultural combinations including rural, urban, interethnic, interracial, different macrocultures from a national culture perspective (Shuter 1990), mixed social classes, mixed religions, and mixed regions of the United States. Where there are significant group differences that mark the marriage, we choose to call it *intercultural marriage,* and refer to the partners as *intercultural couples.*

Studies examining intercultural couples reveal a similar theme: intercultural marriage partners experience unique issues related to culture, not just marital adjustment. Many times marital problems manifest themselves as rejection, discrimination, and even violence, according to Graham, Moeai and Shizuru (1985). However, cultural phenomena linked to intercultural marriage can pose problems in addition to "normal" marital problems.

## The Romeo and Juliet Effect

The Romeo and Juliet effect refers to intense feelings of attraction because couples are denied marriage. All of us are familiar with Shakespeare's story of Romeo and Juliet, where despite the Capulets' and Montagues' feud, Romeo and Juliet secretly married. Their passionate deaths ultimately brought peace between the families.

Certain forbidden relationships can intensify attraction, and as Markoff (1977) wrote, attraction in the early stages of intercultural communication can be stronger than that of intracultural couples. Unfortunately, this intense love can be short. Over time, the intercultural couple, once so intensely in love, now face increased and unexpected criticism, unwelcome and unusual interference by parents, low acceptance among the community, and decreased trust between the couple (Graham, Moeai, and Shizuru 1985).

Therefore, and unfortunately for all of us romantics who would like to believe love conquers anyway, cultural differences related to the Romeo and Juliet effect can be overwhelming. Successful marriages must engage in hard work and communication, conflict resolution, understanding, and working through prejudices and differences in life-style, values, attitudes, customs, roles, financial pressures, family relations, and a host of other factors. When cultural differences are thrown into the relationship milieu, some of these areas become compounded. Ironically, the Romeo and Juliet type attraction propelling the relationship can become the weakness that splits them apart. Evidence suggests that the occasional "forbidden fruit" or venturesome nature that partly plays a role in the romantic attraction can impair the judgments needed to forge the relationship. Rather than engaging in these long-fought, persistent battles over the elements mentioned, such as communication and conflict resolution, the couple is relying upon earlier feelings of attraction or intimacy, and assuming that such feelings will overcome the long-term demands needed in successful relationships.

Graham, Moeai, and Shizuru (1985) compared 170 intercultural and intracultural couples, including Caucasian, Samoan, Hawaiian, Tongan, New Zealander, Filipino, Chinese, and Japanese people. The results indicated a general satisfaction with the marriage, for both the intracultural couples and the intercultural couples. However, the intercultural couples reported 63 percent negative responses toward the marriage compared to 36 percent negative responses among the intracultural couples.

**Intercultural Marriage and Satisfaction**

This research study together with other data lead to a summarization of some major factors associated with intercultural marital satisfaction:

1. *Role expectations.* The wives in the study experienced greater difficulty in accepting their husbands' culture than the other way around. This is because wives experience more pressure to assimilate their husbands' culture and are expected to make greater adjustments.

    Baldwin (1991) found a similar result with Anglo-Hispanic couples; when the wife became "over-involved" or when other activities started taking her away from home more than the husband expected, ratings on communication satisfaction were reduced. On the other hand, when the husband became involved with child discipline, house cleaning, and decision making (in other words, areas of family involvement), the level of communication satisfaction increased. Finally, Baldwin found a positive correlation between communication satisfaction and marital satisfaction, indicating how intercultural communication impacts marriages.

2. *Extended family intrusion.* Problems surrounding intrusion or evaluation by the extended family also are indicated for some intercultural couples. For example, U.S. dominant cultural individuals may not recognize the significance of extended family influence in their intercultural marriage. In cultures that emphasize the extended family, literally dozens of family members may drop in unexpectedly and stay for long periods of time. For instance, in Papua New Guinea, I observed firsthand the *won-tok* system. The cultural rule is that if you "have" you are supposed to "give" to family members or friends from your home village. The feelings toward the habits and style of one's family by no means are limited to New Guinea, for different forms of extended family are seen almost everywhere.

3. *Collective-individualistic cultures.* Some cultures engage in a sharing/caring approach because of group commitments and group obligations, while others are more concerned with themselves and individualistic. For instance, the intercultural couples in the Graham, Moeai, and Shizuru study revealed a strong extended-family pattern for all the South Pacific (Polynesian) groups, which was described as a sharing culture. The interpersonal commitments of those from the sharing culture toward their extended family became an economic drain upon the family finances. Such a value system was a direct clash with their marriage partners who were from the "keeping" values of U.S. dominant nuclear families. Since a large percentage of the sample in this study involved American, Caucasian wives married to Samoans, it is easy to see why the sharing-keeping cultural clash predominated the findings in the study.

4. *Language and misunderstanding.* When two languages were spoken in an intercultural marriage, conflicts obviously resulted, particularly in instances of literal misunderstanding in language or wording, a psychological power struggle over who is going to control the household, and a question of which language will be used at home. According to Graham, Moeai, and Shizuru, when two languages are spoken in intercultural marriage, the children tend to learn the mother's tongue more fluently when the wife retains the dominant influence over the child or when she does not adjust as quickly to the husband's language or both. However, if the wife is bilingual, speaking her husband's language as well as her own, and the child is exposed to both languages, then the child is slower in language acquisition and comprehension. Furthermore, the authors reported that if the child is forced to decide his cultural identity, he will most likely follow the mother. In one case in which a Samoan mother was married to a Tongan father, the child was asked, "What are you?" The reply was, "I am a Samoan."

5. *Conflict styles.* Differences in styles of conflict resolution also mark a significant point of departure for intercultural couples. We can anticipate as chapter six illustrates that directness-indirectness, high context-low context cultures, monochronic-polychronic styles, and power distance are also factors related to conflict in intercultural marriage.

6. *Child rearing attitudes and practices.* Attitudes toward children and child-rearing methodologies represent another difference between the intercultural couples. Some cultures are much stricter with rules than other cultures, creating a value difference and a difference in the way values should be communicated and reinforced with children.

It seems that the major sources of conflict for many intercultural couples go beyond expected marital issues. Culture places still additional demands on the couple for optimal intercultural marital satisfaction.

In a study by Bizman (1987), 549 subjects were asked to evaluate a carefully devised description of three conditions of Jewish intercultural and intracultural marriages: a western Jew married to a western Jew, an eastern Jew married to an eastern Jew, a western Jew married to an eastern Jew. The conclusions indicated that for intercultural marriages (East-West) there was significantly less perception of compatibility and durability than for the intracultural couples. The respondents projected a 25 percent less chance of marital success for the heterogeneous couple than for the homogeneous couple.

**Intercultural Marriage and Attribution**

In her review of intercultural marriages, Beulah Rohrlich (1988) points to a number of sources and concludes that communication is the most prevalent issue. Also, in their book *Adjustment in Intercultural Marriage,* editors Tseng, McDermott, and Maretzki (1977) indicate that cultural factors clearly have many roots in how communication is dealt with in intercultural marriages.

**Intercultural Marriage and Communication**

If communication is a significant issue, then what are the particular intercultural adjustment options? Rohrlich describes a continuum from one extreme, in which a partner gives up his or her culture to adopt the ways of the other, to the other extreme, where both partners give up something of their old culture, producing still a new culture between the two of them. Consider the options for adjustment:

1. One-way adjustment: one partner adopts the cultural pattern of the other;

2. Alternative adjustment: at times one cultural pattern is consciously chosen and at other times the other is chosen;

3. Midpoint compromise: partners agree on a solution between their respective positions;

4. Mixing adjustment: a combination of both cultures is consciously adopted;

5. Creative adjustment: partners decide to give up their respective cultures in favor of a new behavior pattern.

Communication also relates to decision making and power in the relationship. For example, Ting-Toomey (1984) argues for different levels of satisfaction within the marriage based on the amount of power struggle. She says that intracultural couples are more likely to form intimate bonds than intercultural couples, simply because the former have a common basis for marital communication, decision making, and negotiation of everything from daily operations to important decisions in the family. Even in cultures that stress power distance, there is a continual defining of the boundaries of marital influence. Within Japanese culture, wives are supposed to be submissive to their husbands and compliant in fulfilling their wifely roles. Within those marriages, however, there is a subtle and sometimes nagging insistence in a search for power in a household domain, according to Ting-Toomey.

When it comes to decision making and power in the family, ambiguity, lack of role definition, and uncertainty produce much greater discomfort than a marriage where the roles are not under some kind of change or attack.

To marry an individual from another culture is to marry that culture. Lack of interest on the part of the spouse in the other's culture is damaging. To assume that the spouse is attached to the new culture is a serious mistake. The fundamental theme of the culture must be raised, discussed, and valued, if not shared, by both parties. As Gudykunst and Kim (1984) remind us, intercultural marriage involves adapting to a "stranger."

An awareness of cultural differences must proceed before sensitivity and appreciation can be developed. Cultural differences can actually be rich resources, providing, enabling, and complementing communication behavior. In that sense, cultural differences can be constructive. However, awareness of the differences is absolutely necessary before constructive and positive elements can develop.

**Developing Intercultural Skills Relating to Heritage Cultures**

1. *If you think you come from a dysfunctional family, be aware of the need to seek professional help.* Negative behavior can be passed on intergenerationally and needs to be addressed.

2. *Avoid the temptation to be overly passive or overly dominant.* Research shows that balanced assertiveness works well in working through family relations.

3. *Be aware of the need to explain yourself with elaborated code (see chapter 6).* It is too easy to lapse into a comfortable pattern of restricted communication code, which assumes an overlap of experiences. Unfortunately, a restricted code often lacks buffer, explanation, and reestablishment of the relationship, features badly needed, especially during conflict.

4. *Conflict-management skills (see chapter 11) are important for dealing with heritage culture differences.* Unresolved conflict only festers and makes things worse in the long run. It is all too easy to run from racial and ethnic differences, when these could be discussed.

5. *Identify potential prejudice.* Look for types of hidden prejudice in speech, thought, and actions. This type of self-analysis is difficult but critically important before improvement in communication skills can be attempted. These hidden attitudes leak out in unexpected ways, what I refer to in my consulting work as the "ooze factor." People can see hidden disrespect, negative stereotypes, and prejudice in our relationships.

**This Chapter in Perspective**

This chapter begins with the assumption that heritage cultures, usually ethnic and racial cultures, can be embraced or rejected, born into, adopted, or chosen. As in the case of reference groups, heritage cultures are also a source of identity, when one chooses to adhere to norms and expectations of the group. The chapter presents a model of the in-group/out-group process, a model that explains the adjustments people make regarding others and the perceptions they have about others and self. The chapter also deals with attitudes that prevent effective perception and thus lead to dysfunctional communication adaptation: ethnocentrism, stereotyping, prejudice (including many forms of prejudice, such as tokenism and arms-length prejudice). By identifying major rhetorical and communication themes between in-groups and out-groups, we stand in a better position to understand the interaction dynamics possible.

Finally, the chapter deals with the major concepts in intercultural marriages and their larger relation to the body of intercultural communication principles. The reader is alerted to the advantages and disadvantages of intercultural marriage. Several studies are presented to help us see this problem. Although most point to various categories of difficulty and stress placed on a couple by the various cultural differences, it is also clear that communication can play a vital role. The couple willing to significantly invest in their relationship will find that their differences do not have to be debilitating to their marriage.

**Exercises**

1. Interview intercultural marriages, or dual-culture couples as they are sometimes called, and ask for their evaluation of the ways they have worked out their differences and how their relationship has been affected.

2. Draw your own family tree showing as much extended family as you can. What influences came down through whom? What roles do you see yourself encompassing perhaps because of one or two major influences of family members?

3. Trace the influences of prejudice in your neighborhoods, schools, and workplace. Perhaps do library research about your community or conduct interviews to find out when attitudes have changed and why. People who have been around a company for many years are great sources for highlights and events over the years that resulted in heightening or reducing racial tensions. This assignment can be developed in a lot of ways, not limited to this brief description of target or resources.

# Chapter 5

# Microcultures of Social Identification and Group Relations

**Objectives**

After completing this chapter, you should be able to

1. Define how groups create and reinforce social identification

2. Identify features of reference group membership and the effect leading to individual conformity

3. List the effects of demographic factors, including how some people relate to demographic cultures and communication outcomes associated with these cultures

4. Identify attitudes of poverty cultures around the globe

5. Define organizational culture

6. Identify the influences of organizational culture and communication processing

7. Identify what constitutes a functional organizational culture

The model for the text again reminds us that we perceive others in terms of cultural difference. Those differences can be systemic orientations as indicated in chapter 3 or in-group/out-group factors as indicated in chapter 4. In this chapter we examine groups that comprise not only a part of a larger macroculture, but serve important *identity* and *information* functions for their members. Related to the concept of *significant others,* these microcultures of social identity exercise communication influence. Even in the most individualistic cultures, they act as reference points for individual filtering of thought and action. For example, a person deciding how to vote in a major election in the United States is often heavily influenced by family, friends, and associates. Group loyalties to associations with the people or the ideals of religious group, educational, or social class can involve a loyalty greater than other loyalties. They form the basis of reference group influence and represent another type of microcultural communication.

## Functions of Microcultures Involving Social Identity

Rodgers (1978) explained that these identity groups possess conscious membership in identifiable units, recognize their part in a larger culture, and recognize the importance of social identification as a powerful concept related to *interpersonal bonding.*

Self-image, Boulding (1972) argued, becomes a potent concept. How a group sees itself and how individuals within the group view themselves carry significant communication implications for self-worth. Attitude and opinion development also grow out of group images, to the extent that an individual bonds with the group and to the extent the group provides anchoring points.

## Reference Group Communication

Reference groups, sometimes called *primary association groups,* influence many of our decisions by (1) mediating information, (2) interpreting and reframing messages and issues, (3) symbolizing identification and self-worth, and (4) setting norms. Most reference groups center around family, play, or peer groups, committees, workers, and comembers in organizations (Smith, Bruner, and White 1956; Sherif and Sherif 1967; Berelson and Steiner 1964).

### Role and Function of Reference Groups

Most of us belong to multiple groups. By their nature, groups create drives toward conformity. In conforming to group norms, we receive two rewards: acceptance by the group and title to group beliefs, to which we can cling as a way of interpreting life's events (Abelson 1959).

Group membership offers an anchor for beliefs and evaluation of information. (Photo by ACU student media.)

There is security when the group acts as a source, reinforcement, and support, bolstering old attitudes and providing a context for future conversion to new positions (Sherif, Sherif, and Nebergall 1965). This communication web of influence is most meaningful, however, and works to *create conformity* under certain conditions. A list of those situations follows.

*Group size.* The smaller the reference group, the greater the pressure to conform. Within a large group, for example, less interpersonal interaction occurs, and thus the group looks to a leader to structure the communication (Bettinghaus 1980). The size of the group influences the amount and type of participation potentially available to members. Thus, small group members are more easily involved in discussion and accountability results.

*Frequency of contact.* Another group characteristic is the relationship between attitudes and frequency of contact. Researchers have observed that the more interaction within a group, the more likely that members will have positive feelings toward other group members. This process of in-group communication is obviously influential.

*Cohesiveness.* Cohesiveness, defined as the degree of group attraction for group members, is another factor in group influence. Cohesion implies a unity of group-centeredness and loyalty. In Back's (1958) classic study of cohesive and noncohesive groups cohesive members showed efforts toward uniformity and agreement; fewer individual differences emerged in the highly cohesive groups; and discussion was more effective, producing more influence and change than in noncohesive groups. In contrast, members of low-cohesive groups appeared to act independently, disregarding the needs and desires of other group members.

Group cohesiveness extends to several general principles that can be summarized as follows (Bettinghaus 1980). Members of cohesive groups tend to:

1. Have *fewer deviants* in their decisions;

2. Be *influenced by persuasive communication;*

3. *Communicate frequently and evenly* among group members;

4. Offer mutual *support* and *reject threatening messages;*

5. Experience greater *pressure for individual conformity.*

*Group salience.*    Salience refers to the importance an individual places toward a group. In a technical sense, salience also depends on personal awareness of the group norms and perceptions of their importance. Researchers tell us that resistance to change of group norms and attitudes is in direct proportion to the group's degree of salience. For example, Middle East terrorist groups would be expected to resist outside communication because of the salience the groups hold for their members. Conversely, the more salient and interesting the group is, the more a person conforms to its expectations. An example of this principle is the Jonestown, Guyana, religious cult and the David Koresh cult where group salience for both groups lead to an ultimate conformity of suicide and killing.

*Clarity of group norms.*    Studies concerning group norms have shown that the more ambiguous the group norms and standards of conduct, the less control the group has over its members. However, if the standards are clear and unambiguous, the pressure to conform is greater. Also, when ambiguity is prevalent within a group, interaction among group members reduces the ambiguity. For example, if the rules for a college fraternity are unclear, it is less likely that the fraternity will influence its members.

*Homogeneity.*    Homogeneity refers to similarity among many group members. Groups tend toward uniformity in actions and attitudes as homogeneity increases. Group homogeneity also contributes toward cohesiveness. When homogeneous attitudes prevail, an individual tends to hold personal attitudes more tenaciously. Homogeneity of opinion is most directly observable in reference groups, such as family, friends, and co-workers, a point still as true as when Katz (1963) first reported it.

*Issues.*    The issues confronting reference groups influence group members. The more relevant a particular issue is to a group, the greater the individual conformity to the group position. Also, when uncertainty about an issue exists, even when the issue is overly complex, individuals experience pressure to conform to group views.

*Inclusion needs.*    Reference group influence extends only as far as the boundaries of the personal needs allow. When group members depend significantly upon the group for satisfying high inclusion needs (that is, they fear rejection and have a

Friendships create a major part of our social identification in culture. (Photo by ACU student media.)

high need for acceptance), conformity to group expectations is more likely. This conformity may result from a need to resemble highly esteemed persons or to sustain social approval. Few people want exclusion, but some people fear its possibility more than others. In such situations, communication may become overly servile, since dependent members may offer frequent positive strokes to win the favor of high-status members and to receive positive strokes themselves.

Also, individuals who are strongly attached to the group are least influenced by later communication that attacks their group norms. A high need for acceptance and fear of rejection may explain why some people are compulsive joiners—they seek acceptance through group affiliation (Brady 1975).

*High task and goal direction.* In addition to reinforcing already held beliefs (for example, a person who already holds a position consistent with the goals of the organization joins a civic club), groups assist people in their personal quest. A group member might use a group to make sales contacts, for instance, and thus view the reference group as a stepping-stone for instrumental, individual purposes.

## Regional Cultures and Communication

People filter messages through what DeFleur and Ball-Rokeach (1976) called the "social categories" of communication. This idea proposes a similarity outlook that influences perception.

Regional differences are not merely geographical but examine social attitudes and communication differences. Regional diversity in attitude, speech patterns, and life-styles illustrate a few of the perceived differences raising uncertainty between potential intercultural communicators. To illustrate the diversity involved, consider attitudes and speech patterns.

Attitudes and values differ regionally within a national culture. Northern Germans differ in several social values from southern Bavarian Germans who in turn differ from East Germans. The regions within the national boundaries of Japan vary in several cultural and social values.

Evidence indicates that regional cultures within national cultures not only differ in attitude and values but in speech patterns and accents. Hundreds of examples exist. Spanish differs significantly from Castillan to Andalusian. Japanese language in Okinawa differs from Japanese in Tokyo; Spanish in Mexico City varies slightly from Torreon; Chileans in the mountains differ from the coastal areas. Bostonian English is different from midwestern and from Appalachian English accents in the United States.

Not only do attitudes and accents differ regionally, but regional cultures apply varying approaches to information management and communicator style. Observation concerning diversity of communicator style in the United States illustrates the point:

1. Perceived abruptness; speed of getting to the point versus delaying the main point.

2. Rate of speech delivery.

3. Amount of verbal buffering; that is, how many introductory phrases before getting to the point.

4. Amount of interpersonal buffering, level of informal rapport.

5. Amount of eye contact, touch, space, and verbal pausing.

6. Amount of verbal and nonverbal behavior surrounding phrases and messages before leaving a conversation.

7. Amount of perceived warmth and openness.

8. Amount of animation.

9. Amount of dominance.

10. Amount of contentiousness.

While these categories do not represent all possible regional differences, they highlight a number of common communication questions. (See Norton 1978 for original communication style inventory; numerous research studies use portions of this scale.) Regional differences can silently keep people apart. Some of the most sophisticated people seemingly let the subtle prejudices of regional differences affect their attitudes and relationships. This unfortunate waste of human resources is preventable.

**Rural Cultures and Communication**

In addition to regional differences, it is possible to identify characteristic norms of rurality. First, rural cultures emphasize personal know-how, practicality, and simplicity over complexity in approaching decisions. Skills at doing rather than being or knowing are often valued; perhaps such skills relate more to survival. Like all groups we attempt to describe, rural cultures are not all alike. Some favor innovation and change, while others embrace traditionalism. In some of my international field work and research, I spent time in a number of villages in West Africa and in southern, central India. Villages separated by only a few miles differed vastly on norms of innovation and change.

Second, norms toward interpersonal relationships persist within rural cultures. Indications are that bonds of friendship differ from urban cultures. It may not be surprising that norms of rurality in the United States hold traditional American values and themes of people helping people.

Third, rurality is a mindset. One can stay rural in the middle of urban life, or for that matter stay urban living in a rural region. For example, there are pockets of originally rural southerners in the greater Detroit area. According to personal interviews reported by Bill Goodpasture, many have retained some of the unique characteristics of their roots, despite a long passage of time.

Fourth, a study by Tichenor (1981) showed a higher degree of communication apprehension among persons from rural settings. She also found higher cognitive complexity for rural individuals, which indicates a higher ability to form accurate interpersonal impressions. This also means that rural individuals possess a more diverse set of categories by which to finely judge interpersonal relations. In fact, as Perrin (1980) writes, rural people can judge rather quickly according to some intuitive interpersonal rules.

Fifth, communication style differences of rural individuals involve cultural norms blended with regional practices. For instance, a General Motors plant in the United States relocated into a traditional southern rural area from an urban, midwestern region. The most evident problems were related to the communication style differences. Beyond accent and dialectical differences, some diverse approaches to managerial style of communication, many which match Perrin's (1980) observations, conflicted with a rural communicator style in the United States. Here are some examples:

1. Requests occur in a less demanding style.

2. Messages tend to be phrased in personal terms, rather than objective terms.

3. Respect is shown for the free will of the other person.

4. Story, image, and background scenarios play an important role in the communication style. Communication is filled with anecdotes and stories, often about family or friends, though in a number of cases about out-groups.

5. Messages are usually related to a unified whole. There is a kind of implicit theory about how this person or that event fits into the whole picture from a cultural point of view. For instance, "He acted kind of crazy. Probably because he's been working long hours."

6. Personal history behind events, people, and conditions serve organizing functions for messages, for instance, "He almost fell off the hay wagon. That's no surprise, considering his grandpa did the same thing twice when he was a boy."

## Urban Cultures and Communication

Obviously, urban life is complex, if nothing else given the massive numbers of people involved.

From a trend analysis among sources on *outlying areas* of urban regions, or the related areas known as suburbs, several observations meet communication needs. First, identification and joining behavior seem higher than inner city or rural communities. For example, from a census of Catholic Mass attenders in Montreal, Carlos (1970) discovered that the frequency of church attendance increased as people moved from the central areas of the city to the periphery. Although a certain amount of quality in religious practices diminished, Carlos explained higher church attendance as a need for community integration when people moved from the urban core to the suburbs.

Second, certain forms of neighborhood identification, such as when neighbors stand together on an issue, lead to cohesive neighborhoods.

Third, suburban or outlying residents overall tend to be joiners. Upward mobility and an emphasis on success symbols are associated with joining and group activity levels (McDonald 1985).

*Inner-city* cultures tend to be composed of isolated members with pockets or enclaves of group cohesion. Social participation outlets are limited, and isolation remains a significant theme. Housing problems and high crime rates affect social participation in urban areas and foster less dependence on interpersonal communication networks.

*Anomia,* a generalized isolation and loneliness, may result partly from crowded physical surroundings. Such conditions can easily lead to urban fears and suspicions predicated upon an urban dweller's experience with such things as increased crime and decreased personal territoriality.

## Class Cultures and Communication

Social systems usually stratify or result in class/status differences because of socioeconomic status variables, typically occupation, income, and education. That is, members of a society rank people into higher or lower social positions, producing a rank order of respect and prestige. Respect is conferred to individuals according to their conformity to a society's ideals. The result is a role-related position determined by the prestige, esteem, and value that other members of the social system place on the individual's social class and, therefore, on the individual. It is easy to see how intercultural communication perceptual differences result.

Overall, classes are inclined to depreciate the social differences between themselves and higher classes and to magnify differences with lower classes. Sometimes, this perceptual set is heightened so that a certain unity of outlook exists by allusions to "people like us" and to persons that are "not our kind." A feeling of "we-ness" especially occurs when expressing dissatisfaction with the upward mobility of the lower classes or resentment toward the higher classes. Unity is further intensified through common beliefs and patterns of overt behavior. The Indian caste system is an example of a highly ordered and rigidly determined class ranking, which in turn predicts attitudes and communication between different castes within the larger context of India's culture. Labor and management differences also reflect the attitudes that some classes hold toward other classes and of the importance of communication in resolving those differences.

Research also reveals unique tendencies concerning socioeconomic differences, friendship, prestige, and trust. First, compared with stationary members, those members climbing upward in the class system are not as likely to maintain close personal friendships. This phenomenon can partly be traced to their more frequent geographical movement, as Alvin Toffler's *Future Shock* and the data on high mobility in the United States remind us. Second, prestige and achievement become more valuable to middle-class members than to lower-class members and, especially, to upwardly mobile middle-class persons. Third, lower classes seem to be more distrustful of authority used by more powerful classes (Berelson and Steiner 1964; Daniel 1976).

## Poverty Cultures and Communication

Another coculture is poverty culture, which refers to a lack of financial and material resources. The economic condition of the poverty culture, however, is broadly associated with several beliefs and values. From the available research, the categories that follow appear consistent across many cultures. These are not racial, ethnic, or minority issues, but poverty issues and central tendencies characterized from available research. Rogers (1969) originally proposed some of the following categories, offering factors from a five nation study profiling attitudes among the poor. Research from Daniel (1976) adds to the list. Also, recent confirmation from qualitative analyses involving reviews of hundreds of welfare cases by a female, single-parent, African American manager (Parrish 1993) in a Texas social services agency gives us reason to consider a descriptive set of themes from poverty cultures.

### Perceived Limited Good

Some individuals in a poverty coculture believe the world's goods to be something like a pie with a limited number of slices. Consequently, if someone prospers, that prosperity is perceived to occur only at others' expense, since it is assumed that prosperity means one has taken an inordinate amount of the pie. It follows that neighbors may become suspicious of a community member who financially succeeds and thus violates the unspoken norms of this culture.

### Familism

Some members of poverty cocultures subordinate personal goals to the wishes and perceived good of the family. Called familism, family needs outweigh personal and individual needs or wishes.

Poverty cultures
worldwide
sometimes share
a similar outlook
(Photo by ACU
student media.)

Fatalism is a believed degree to which we cannot control the future. In many co-cultures, the future is often viewed as unknown and by nature certainly uncontrollable. Success and failure are seen as matters of luck. Unseen forces control destiny and people are victims of these forces.

**Fatalism**

Members of poverty cocultures typically are not able to purchase innovations. In some cases, resistance to innovation or change rests in values toward traditionalism and using tried and proven ways.

**Lack of Innovativeness**

Some individuals caught up in the poverty cycle have a low achievement motivation. Perhaps they have been burned. Or has a mindset developed that they do not deserve raising their economic status? While some poverty cultural members have given up trying to find a job or change jobs to one that is better, many poverty-level people try hard for economic opportunity, only to find those opportunities out of reach for a number of reasons.

**Limited Aspirations and Achievement Motivation**

There are two groups who spend now instead of saving for later. Some people who struggle within the poverty limits find it difficult if not impossible to save money for later purchases. One single mother reported that after rent and bills she had only $25 a month left to feed herself and her children. Deferring for the future is understandably elusive. There is also a here-and-now syndrome of reward for a second group within poverty culture, where immediate satisfaction overrides waiting for future rewards. As Daniel indicated, the future is difficult to envision, so live for here and now.

**Lack of Deferred Gratification: Spend Now or Later**

| | |
|---|---|
| Low Empathy | Members of poverty cocultures seem unable to project themselves into any situation or role other than their present one. This lack of projection may be why traditional poverty cultures around the world resist attempts at modernization. |
| Victimization | Some poverty cultures envision institutions or members of other groups as out to get them or as the cause of their poverty. The lines encircling legitimate cases where individuals have been victimized by prejudice or policy are real and frequent. Denial of fair treatment in many cases around the globe (consider South African blacks being denied fundamental human rights, prejudice in policy toward Hispanics in the United States, civil rights denied African Americans, abuse toward immigrant Irish Catholics, put-down of American Jews, and hostility toward immigrant Swedes in the United States) can create development of a victimization mindset. Examples also abound where reframing and reorientation leads to positive expectations, despite difficult circumstances. |

## Countercultural Communication

A counterculture is a group that stands in opposition or performs resistantly toward the larger culture. Features that serve to bind countercultural members include common code, common enemy, and common symbols.

| | |
|---|---|
| Common Code | Counterculture group members gravitate toward a common set of linguistic usages, such as jargon and slang, that are meaningfully interpreted usually only in light of the group members' assigned meanings to the code system. Street language, while constantly changing, is an example of specialized code usage in antisocial groups such as gangs. |
| Common Enemy | In a number of countercultures, there is a perceived common enemy, usually the dominant culture itself. When attention is focused on the common enemy, who allegedly is responsible for some ill affecting the countercultural group, the group then has a rallying point. In this way, group members are reinforced in their beliefs, and the reinforcement tends to bond the group into an even more cohesive unit. The numerous terrorist groups found throughout the world clearly employ such images of enemy hatred. |
| Common Symbols | Many countercultural members use symbolic objects, such as colors, highly prized objects, or drugs. These symbols emphasize commonality and unification. |

## Organizational Culture

Microcultures of social identification also include work cultures. In recent years, organizational culture has proven a rich metaphor to describe organizations. I am reminded of a middle manager, in a Fortune 500 company with whom a colleague and I were consulting, who presented us with extensive notes indicating conflict between his personal style and the corporate culture employing him. Like this manager, many people intuitively recognize the themes of organizational culture and how they are affected.

The potential for organizational culture to clash with the larger culture or with individual differences is illustrated in these examples:

A top manager from ARAMCO in Houston goes to work in Saudi Arabia for a branch office.

A high school principal is promoted to an assistant superintendent position and must adjust to central office norms.

David received his master's degree in his native Michigan and has been hired by Delco to work in their regional office in Oklahoma.

Deborah, a Canadian, works for the Canadian Development Office but has just been hired by Algoma Steel in Ontario, Canada to work in their computer division.

Samuel is joining a Japanese car sales force in his native Nigeria.

These examples illustrate adapting to macrocultures and to organizational climates. The differences these people encounter and the communication demands in these cultures represent an increasingly recognized focus of group influence (Sypher, Applegate, and Sypher 1985).

Organizational culture is an important metaphor to describe the norms, feelings, and shared interaction patterns of a group.

In this discussion, *organizational culture* refers to the communication climate rooted in a common set of norms and interpretive schemes (Carbaugh 1985) about phenomena that occur as people work toward a predetermined goal. In other words, we are dealing with organizational thoughts, actions, customs, and rules. Organizational culture for many people acts as a perceptual filter through which to create reality and use symbols. The idea is well summarized in Peters and Waterman's now classic work *In Search of Excellence* (1982), where they portray culture as the dominant idea behind the organization. They cite Delta's "family feeling," Maytag's Iowa work ethic, Levi Strauss's predominantly people-oriented philosophy, and Texas Instrument's innovative culture. One theme of the book underscores how productive, successful corporate cultures rely on fundamental image and metaphor. These images guide and influence employees and the larger cultural environment in ways of doing (norms) and thinking (values).

## Organizational Culture as a System

One way to describe organizational culture is to view it as a system. In most ways, systems theory really is an analogy, borrowed from the study of living organisms. For example, a pond can have input, output, and throughput. The input is the fresh water coming in, the output is the water spilling over the drainage part of the reservoir, and the throughput is the symbiotic relationship of the wildlife in the pond. A pond that has no fresh water intake or no outlet becomes a pond that is dead. Organizations can be dynamically open or closed, alive or dead like a pond. Further, organizations as systems can be described as having dynamic interchange, where there is interdependence among the organisms.

Such a metaphor leads to a creative approach to communication within the group. For example, if one has an organization that remains closed, then the strategy is to develop openness. If there is too much autonomy, where one unit is not aware of what another unit is doing, change is needed. A number of years ago, I discovered that one of three banks in a certain midwestern city had a very nonsystems view of employee management. Every department was so structurally distinct from every other department that executive management even denied access to promotions from outside each unit. For example, if you worked in the proofing department of the bank, you were allowed to be promoted only within that department. Of the three banks in town, this one was the oldest and best established, yet it had the highest turnover and absenteeism rates and the only known case of embezzlement in the immediate history of that town. Furthermore, their assets were lower and their reputation in the town had diminished significantly even before the embezzlement case.

What is the point? Simply stated, if we can look at an organization, borrowing the metaphor of system and layering on top of that the interpretive schema that the concept of culture provides for us, we have an even more fruitful way of examining organizations and their influence.

## Influence of Organizational Cultures

*The influence of filtering.* Organizational cultures have physical and psychological boundaries; that is, each organization has a way of defining itself. That process of definition, however, builds a perceptual filter that screens inputs into the organization (Harris and Moran 1991). While there are many advantages in a culture having a clear view of itself, images and symbols of an organizational culture can also insulate the culture from outside influences. Ultimately, this privacy can reinforce negative features of intercultural communication, such as stereotyping and ethnocentrism.

One solution for preventing what we might call an organizational cultural myopia is ongoing organizational development. In organizational development, there is continuous, planned change. The organization attempts to keep its members up-to-date. Where culture is involved, Harris and Moran (1991) point out that the most successful multinational corporations adapt themselves to the local culture while maintaining unique and distinctive features as corporations.

*The influence of adaptation to the larger culture.* Successful organizational cultures adapt to the local context. The kind of organizational adaptation envisioned here involves orienting typical management functions to cultural formats and methods of operation. Some typical management functions include coordinating, leading, communicating, decision making, planning, goal setting, motivating, controlling, negotiating, training, evaluating, and selection. Studies indicate where company policy calls for leadership style or practices completely out of step in a certain community or culture norms, that adjustment of the company policy to the culture is a successful strategy. For example, some cultures expect more directive leadership and control than others, as for instance some parts of traditional Greek culture. In cases, for instance, where standard procedure dictates a six-month period for job evaluation, a year may be more suitable. The need for flexibility is a significant intercultural issue. For example, when Nissan came to Tennessee, it brought its corporate culture. However, the company's success, as evidenced by low absenteeism and high performance, can be attributed to its cultural adaptation. Nissan melded its traditional corporate style of management into local culture in its attitudes toward friendliness, discipline, and listening.

*The influence of symbolism and message.* Organizational cultures have significant communication systems (Gudykunst, Stewart, and Ting-Toomey 1985; Frost, Moore, Louis, Lundberg, and Martin 1985; McPhee and Tompkins 1985; Putnam and Pacanowsky 1983; Williams 1992). Through the use of codes, values, heroes, storytelling, and other means of communication, an organizational culture develops a symbolic world. This communication and symbolism actually molds the organizational culture by shaping its norms. Through the stories that are told, workers sense how things are to be done.

Sypher, Applegate, and Sypher (1985) call this feature of an organizational culture its "implicit organizational communication." These stories are incredibly powerful and coupled with clear expectations, shape us more than we may realize. Some of the top performing companies, as Peters and Waterman (1982) explained, have "a rich network of legends and parables of all sort." A number of these stories surround the originators of the companies, such as J. C. Penney and his values toward business, honesty, and quality.

*The influence of explicit and implicit information.* A low-context culture makes meanings and information available and explains expectations. Information in these low-context cultures is explicit. Meanings are not in the context but in the verbal explanations provided. High-context cultures are the opposite. Expectations are inferred from the context. One is expected to know appropriate behaviors. Meanings are not explained but are implicit, (chapter 6).

In this way organizational cultures are no exception. Consider the case of the college graduate who was told by a major corporation, "You should know what to do within a couple of days. You have your accounting degree, and it should be no problem for you." While the manager in this case was intending to allow the new employee to be independent, the college graduate felt adrift. There was no orientation defining expectations or how the company typically engaged in certain procedures. Passing on corporate insights and defining the norms are functions of a low-context organizational culture. In this organization, however, the culture was high-context—the accountant was expected to automatically know what to do and how to accomplish the task.

*The influence of functional and dysfunctional organizational cultures in clarifying mission.* In their analysis of successful and less successful companies, Peters and Waterman (1982) concluded that good companies have clear norms and clear communication about those norms.

Without cultural norms as guides, a corporation becomes bogged down in decision making. The functional, excellent companies have a rich mythology and a set of norms, as Peters and Waterman indicated:

Everyone at Hewlett-Packard knows that he or she is supposed to be innovative.

Proctor and Gamble emphasizes quality over price, speaking of business integrity and fair treatment of employees without regard to cost.

Delta Airlines emphasizes a family feeling.

Texas Instruments is noted for a highly innovative attitude that permeates the organization.

Maytag claims its success in reliability is because of the strong Iowa work ethic where Maytags are made.

Levi-Strauss is highly people centered with a no-layoff philosophy that began after the San Francisco earthquake in 1906.

"IBM means service" is a company devotion to customer relations.

Dysfunctional organizations may have strong cultures, too, but they tend to focus on procedures. They also are highly concerned with costs and numbers. They tend not to realize that every person in the organization has meaning to the group, and most attention is concentrated on the top producers.

Consider some suggestions for intercultural skills. This list will stimulate your own response to your endeavors.

1. *Test your stereotypes.* As this chapter indicates, we may have negative impressions of others that are based on incorrect information. Ask yourself why you feel as you do, and try to correct false impressions.

2. *Treat cultural differences as a resource.* All too often, we treat cultural differences as something highly negative and thus approach intercultural communication with something of a jaundiced eye. We should look upon differences as an opportunity, a resource from which to learn exciting things about a new culture, a new person, and ourselves.

3. *Develop ways of handling uncertainty.* Intercultural communication by its nature poses various degrees of uncertainty—uncertainty about ourselves and about what to say and do. Thus, each of us needs to develop an ability to handle contradictions and uncertainty with grace and ease.

4. *Develop self-respect.* One of the best things that can help us in developing intercultural contacts is to take an extra dose of self-confidence. Be positive about others and that will help you become positive about yourself. Criticism and resentment only serve to hurt you, the intercultural communicator.

5. *Do not rely on past experiences to deal with every new situation.* The past comes from your own cultural background. The new culture represents a situation where your familiar cues are not present, and thus, to respond to features in the new culture as if you were in the old culture would be misleading.

6. *Outgoingness may not work.* If you handle new situations in your own culture with outgoingness, you may be surprised to find that being extra friendly does not necessarily work in the microculture where you are currently interacting.

7. *Competition may not work.* If you like competitiveness, do not be surprised if cultural differences preclude this value from being mutually appreciated.

8. *Progressivism may not work.* You may also hold strong attitudes toward goal orientation and progressivism. That is, you may expect a culture to be moving in a linear manner toward some goals that you have predetermined are good. Do not be surprised should such a direction not work for you.

9. *Stress areas of positive relations.* As we have already indicated throughout this chapter, look for ways to build bridges of understanding.

10. *Do not assume that your needs are like everyone else's needs.* Because you feel a certain way, do not assume that your feelings reflect anyone else's opinion. By listening and asking questions, you can quickly discover how your personal frame of reference does not match another person's viewpoint. That discovery is the beginning of effective intercultural communication between cultures.

11. *Learn the rules of the microculture.* You may think that cocultures do not have a systematized way of behaving, but like any culture, there are rules. Effective intercultural communication requires an understanding of the system.

## This Chapter in Perspective

This chapter highlights awareness of group membership and identification as essential components of a larger culture. To understand group differences is to increase insight into intercultural communication. Many intercultural communication problems emerge from reference group barriers.

Understanding the dynamics of reference groups is partially a matter of realizing their importance. Under a number of conditions, reference groups have an enormous influence on individuals. Also, individuals can affect reference groups.

This chapter also describes regional, rural, urban, and socioeconomic subcultures and their relation to communication. Members of various geographic locations, social classes, and age groupings can perceive messages in somewhat similar ways. The common elements among countercultural groups, another type of subculture, are common codes, a perceived common enemy, and perceived common symbols. The chapter also identifies attitudes sometimes associated with poverty cultures around the world: perceived limited good, familism, fatalism, lack of innovativeness, limited aspirations, lack of deferred gratification, low empathy, and victimization. Finally, an extensive section on organizational culture reminds readers of how organizational cultures function and how the culture influences its members' perceptions and communication.

## Exercises

1. Look at a cross sample of television programs, including reruns of older programs along with contemporary programs. What are the influences of group memberships in these instances? What are the group stereotypes? How are reference groups depicted, if at all?

2. In a public place, like your campus student center, observe people interacting with various groups. What patterns of behavior and interaction do you observe?

3. Interview someone from a poverty culture. Ask that person questions about his or her conditions. What conceptions do people have about the group? What conceptions does the poverty culture member have concerning people with financial resources? Are there different kinds of poverty cultures?

4. When you read newspapers, what kinds of articles about organizational or corporate cultures do you find? What model of organizational life is portrayed frequently in the popular media? Do you think these are accurate or inaccurate?

# Chapter 6

# Underlying Dimensions of Culture

After completing this chapter, you should be able to

**Objectives**

1. Discuss the importance of cognitive culture to communication

2. Understand cultural monochronic and polychronic orientations

3. Differentiate between high-context cultures and low-context cultures

4. Identify Hofstede's four factors of culture

5. Discuss concrete examples of how a culture's world view and values affect the attitude and behaviors of cultural members

6. List foundational cultural values

Culture is more than elements in a system. Culture also involves a shared perception about self and others. Culture includes how people think—their beliefs, values, world view, and information processing. These are all part of a less obvious yet highly significant nature of culture: *cognitive culture.* As we reviewed in chapter 3 culture has structure—it is a system with behaviors, rules, and institutional factors. However, culture involves vision, beliefs, truths, and outlooks that have an impact on its members. These are less tangible but undeniably powerful. What you believe or your assumptions about the nature of your place in the universe may sound a bit grandiose, but they qualify as considerable forces in guiding cultural behavior. Asians who value hard work and group responsibility take actions and process information in ways congruent with those values. Hispanic views of hospitality translate into marvelous care for family and others, as I have enjoyed and witnessed in visits in Texas, Mexico, and South America. A U.S. dominant cultural value toward time, reflected in phrases such as "Time is money" and "A stitch in time saves nine," influences communication patterns creating a shared perception about what is right and wrong, what it means to be late, and what happens if you fail to be careful.

## Cultural Differences in Information Processing

These illustrations of cognitive culture remind us that some fundamental ways of processing information are involved as we encounter cultural differences. Edward Hall has been creative in identifying some critical areas of culture that affect information processing, areas that are discussed in this chapter.

### Monochronic Time Orientation

Edward T. Hall's *Beyond Culture* (1976) expresses an important theory about the way cultures process time. Internal views of time have all kinds of implications about communication climates and consequent behaviors, including everything from irritation at being kept waiting to the very thought framework of time as cultural perception. According to Hall, the element of time structures our interaction. Indeed, there appears to be a continuum of time orientation, with monochronic time on one end and polychronic time on the other.

Monochronic time urges people to do one thing at a time. Time, for them, is like a long ribbon of highway that can be sliced into segments. Monochronics believe that accomplishments and tasks can and should be performed during each segment. Monochronics have a high need for closure—completing a task or coming to a conclusion in a relationship.

For example, one U.S. dating couple had diverse cultural outlooks in informational processing. The man was operating from a polychronic orientation, trying to process many of the couple's future relationship decisions all at once. The woman, on the other hand, was monochronic. She tended to focus on a single issue at a time and wanted closure, or completion, on each issue that the couple confronted in their dating relationship. Her need for closure was so high, in fact, that her demands for answers pressured the man into breaking up the relationship.

Monochronics are not all demanding, but they prefer seeing things finished. They are dissatisfied with dangling loose ends. Also, as a result, their tolerance for ambiguity is not high. As uncertainty rises, monochronics tend to articulate solutions and to work toward resolution, whether in conflicts or ordinary, everyday decisions. Monochronics usually think in a linear fashion. That is, they internally process information in a sequential, segmented, orderly fashion. For instance, monochronics schedule appointments linearly—arrival, meeting, conclusion, action—and they cycle through this same pattern all day long.

Being a monochronic is great if you are in a monochronic culture. However, when a monochronic is placed in a polychronic situation, or overall, in a polychronic culture, stress and poor communication usually result. For instance, a colleague and I were in India a few years back and on one occasion waited for a transportation ticket. We got there early (like good Americans) and secured our place in front of the ticket window. Nobody else was around, so we felt confident that our waiting would be minimal once the window opened. However, when the ticket window opened, about one hundred people came out of nowhere and crowded around us, squeezing us out of what we thought was our place in line. After a half hour of standing in the same place while everyone else crowded in front, we finally realized that in this culture there was no such thing as a line—it was everyone for themselves. Once we understood that, we soon had our tickets. We had structured our space just like our monochronic time orientation. The Telegu people of India, however, had a more polychronic view and apparently ordered their spatial relations accordingly.

If we examine situations in our lives that seem frustrating or nonproductive, we may find that part of the problem involves monochronic/polychronic conflicts. For example, many monochronic managers are faced with polychronic demands and must work with people who think polychronically.

Although monochronic individuals think in terms of linear-sequential, time-ordered patterns (1, 2, 3, or *A, B, C*), there are cognitive cultures whose members think in terms of pictures or configurations. The configurational pattern of thought that follows a nonlinear order of attention to stimulus is called polychronic time orientation. Here, the stimulus items may follow an attention pattern unique to that culture, as for instance, 1, 16, 37, 2, or *A, M, Z, B*. The issue involves how we collect and process information and is being addressed in the

**Polychronic Time Orientation**

learning style literature (Bandler 1985). The process of information processing, however, appears to be culturally dependent as well as individually derived. Thus, a significant part of understanding cultural differences involves examining methods of thought.

Polychronic individuals tend to think about and attempt to do a number of things simultaneously. In Latin America, for example, a businessperson may conduct business interviews by inviting a number of unrelated clients into his or her office at once, entertaining them for hours, and jumping from one to another and back again. Sound unusual? Well, the one-at-a-time method seems unusual to polychronic cultures.

Actually, it appears more correct to talk about *individuals* who are monochronic or polychronic. While American, British, Canadian, and German cultures are largely monochronic (as evidenced by the school systems and the organizational patterns of most businesses and the military) and Latin American, African, Middle Eastern, and southern European cultures tend toward polychronism. Clearly individuals tend one way or another.

Research indicates some fascinating results of university students and microcultures. Through critical incident surveys I conducted at Abilene Christian University, and with a sample of over six hundred upper division college students, approximately 50 percent of the Anglo respondents report extreme or moderate levels of polychronic processing. Phipps (1987) conducted a study of 212 Mexican and Anglos and found that about half of the U.S. Anglo adults were slightly monochronic and statistically were not significantly different from both a Mexico sample and a Mexican American sample. However, he found that 62 percent of the Anglo students in his study were polychronic. Within the Mexico sample, he discovered the Eastern Mexico sample from Merida were slightly polychronic (53 percent) while the Monterrey sample was monochronic (76 percent). Furthermore, comparing monolingual Anglos with bilingual Anglos indicated a fascinating discovery: monolingual Anglos are about half monochronic and polychronic (51 percent M, 49 percent P) while two-thirds of bilingual Anglos are polychronic (34 percent M, 66 percent P).

Most people describe a basic style or an overriding tendency to function within either a monochronic or polychronic cognitive style; it would be something like a preferred approach all things being equal. In actuality, we have discovered that we are monochronic or polychronic depending on certain situations. Phipps adds that college students, particularly, function polychronically because of role demands and having numerous study demands bombarding simultaneously.

Monochronic tendencies can become dysfunctional in situations that demand polychronic performance. Some organizational cultures, groups, systems, and families think, schedule, and operate in a monochronic fashion. Thus, a polychronic person can feel rather stressful, even depressed, in such a group.

Polychronics may experience high degrees of information overload. That is, they are trying to process so many things at once that they feel frustrated. They may also experience procrastination. They seem to struggle harder to articulate abstractions without visualization. In fact, they seem to be very visually oriented people. These observations may in further research be found to correlate with the theories of left- and right-brain orientations, where it is asserted that right-brain-dominant people think creatively, visually, and artistically, while left-brain-dominant people think mathematically and linearly.

In any case, how we process time seems both cultural and personal, and this monochronic-polychronic continuum has an important influence on communication behavior. You might choose to measure your information processing style at this point with the M-P scale in the appendix.

Another way that cultures process information revolves around how much its members are expected to know about procedures and rules without being told. Some cultures expect you to know what to do in certain situations. Other cultures do not make these assumptions. To put the idea another way, some cultures are not high in providing members with information about routines or rituals or about how to behave in common, everyday situations. Other cultures, however, provide information to equip members with procedures and practices in a number of situations.

**High- and Low-Context Cultures**

A culture in which information about procedure is not overly communicated is called a high-context culture or HCC (Hall 1976). Members are expected to know how to perform, so information and cultural rules remain *implicit*. The context is supposed to be the cue for behavior. For example, a supervisor says, "Here's the task—you have a college degree, so get started on this project." In situations like this, procedures are incompletely stated.

In a low-context culture, or LCC, information is *explicit*; procedures are explained, and expectations are discussed. For instance, a supervisor says, "Here is the task, and here is our procedure for accomplishing this task." Information levels are adequate for performance.

The most frequent intercultural communication difficulty, considering high-context and low-context systems, occurs when one person assumes a high-context mind-set, while the other person expects explanation, looking for a low-context condition. These assumptions are rarely understood, much less discussed between intercultural participants.

This high/low context phenomenon is evident in macrocultures around the globe. While the Japanese have HCC tendencies, American culture is considered to be on the low-context side. By comparison with other cultures, a relatively large amount of information provides cues for how to respond. For instance, some Americans use signs, instruction lists, and standard operating procedures. In contrast, some Japanese expect one to sense the context and act

High-context cultures use implicit meanings without necessarily overt communication of rules and explanations. Each person in an HCC knows what to expect from another. (Photo by Mark Houston.)

in an expected manner, whether the situation calls for proper bowing, silence, nonverbal expression, or observance of conversational rules. Although there are numerous exceptions, in general, northern Europeans, western Europeans, and North Americans tend toward the low-context condition; Middle Easterners, Africans, and Latin Americans tend toward a blend of low and high context culture; and Asians tend toward a high-context condition.

Stella Ting-Toomey (1985, 1988) provides several additional communication principles concerning low- and high-context cultures. First, low-context cultures encourage communicators to separate the issue from the person, sometimes however, at the expense of personal relationships. Often, the rhetorical ideal of avoiding attacking the person is clearly the ideal: "Just get the facts." By contrast, high-context cultures tend not to separate the person from the issue. If you attack the issue, you are assumed to be attacking the person and would create embarrassment or ill will. Such perceived attacks, from a high-context-culture viewpoint, need smoothing. Thus, the motive to *save face* is usually very strong in high-context cultures.

Second, members of low-context cultures typically do not like things they do not understand. That is, they typically avoid uncertainty, which explains the small talk in conversations. Comfort results from answers to cultural questions: Who is this person? What makes that person the way he is? How can I be accepted and succeed with this person? What is the product and its workings? In contrast, high-context cultures live with more ambiguity. They want information, of course, but they can process information amid uncertainty. Often silence is used as a major part of the strategy in high-context cultures.

Third, low-context culture members use a very direct style of communication. They seek and absorb quantities of information and direct the communication process. A good example is a conflict style that centers around an informational and somewhat confrontational approach. In contrast, high-context cultural members use more indirect styles of communication. For instance, among Japanese cultures, extreme politeness and extreme tact are standard. They are concerned about group harmony, and a nondirective social style may be the best way to engage in communication accommodation. Given that cultural motivation, one can understand strategies of cooperation and participation.

Fourth, negotiation differs. People in low-context cultures tend toward linear logic. Analysis is essential for such cultures—in short, a cognitive, using-the-head approach marks the bargaining style. In contrast, high-context cultures use a soft bargaining approach, preferring communication involving feelings and intuition; it is a communication style of the heart (intuitive) rather than the head. On one occasion in Hong Kong I was interested in buying an opal necklace for my wife. I went from one store to the next, scanning necklaces and gleaning all the facts I could, only to be frustrated when it seemed my opponents in bargaining—namely the store owners—did not negotiate American style. Looking back, I can see that they were engaging in an intuitive style of bargaining, while I was much more interested in a logical, analytical style. I finally managed to strike a good bargain and came home with a beautiful opal necklace. (See, my dominant U.S. culture tells me I need to assert that I was competitively successful.)

Fifth, low-context cultures seek interpersonal data emphasizing personal, individual aspects, not social or group aspects (Ehrenhaus 1983). In contrast, high-context cultures emphasize social factors in their interaction. In other words, each culture searches for different categories. Because they are scanning for totally different categories, what is heard may not be what was said. An LCC person wants prediction about this individual (who he is, what he does, his worth, his competency). An HCC person is listening for group loyalties (organization, family, national loyalty, value) in order to answer questions of trust and respect. No wonder communication opportunities fail. One person's communication expression surrounds the presentation of self and others, while the other person is clearly looking for harmony, social participation, and issues surrounding trust. These low-context culture members tend to be verbose and open and to center on personal data, while high-context culture members seem more cautious. After all, mistakes could be made and errors cause shame or loss of face. In low-context cultures errors are part of the risk one takes in getting good, solid information. After all, an LCC might think such errors can be corrected by adequate explanation.

As we can see, a high-context culture's concern over ease of relationships is really intense. In fact, communication within high-context cultures is so finely tuned on these matters of relationship ease and communication comfort that complex, intricate systems exist. Ting-Toomey (1985) reminds us of several preventive strategies typical of Japanese interpersonal and organizational communication conflict (see chapter 12).

## Hofstede's Cultural Dimensions

During the 1980s, a great deal of research uncovered factors related to cultural themes. One of the major works during this decade was by Hofstede (abridged edition 1984) in which he analyzed questionnaire data from multinational corporate employees in over forty countries. He asked a number of extensive survey questions and applied these to a statistical process by which four central factors indicated significant communication qualities about members from those cultures. These four factors include individualism-collectivism, masculine-feminine, power-distance, and uncertainty avoidance.

### Individualism-Collectivism

The concepts of individualism and collectivism have encouraged the most amount of research of Hofstede's factors. Triandis (1987) surveyed anthropologists and psychologists from many parts of the world and concluded individualism-collectivism is a powerful relationship indictor.

Individualism concerns personal achievement. In contrast, collectivist cultures are those that emphasize community, groupness, harmony, and maintaining face. We would expect the accompanying communicator style to be correlated with each of these cultural dimensions. For instance, one could expect a great deal more assertive behavior, self-disclosure, and other personal-advancement issues to arise in an individualistic culture. On the other hand, we could expect far more strategies of people pleasing, solidarity, relational issues and face saving to occur in a collective culture.

Empirical research by Kim, Sharkey, and Singelis (1992) confirms the interactive or communication qualities associated with each facet of this cultural dimension in their study of Koreans (collectivists) and Americans (individualists). They indicate significant communication expectations across a number of studies, which have been adapted and summarized here.

*Individualists* emphasize:
- —concern for clarity, directness
- —truth telling, straight talk
- —meeting personal needs and goals rather than group
- —self-referent messages, more "I" than "we"
- —more independent
- —linear pattern of conversation

*Collectivists* emphasize:
- —indirect communication
- —concern for others' feelings, avoiding hurting others, saving face (not causing embarrassing situations)
- —avoiding negative evaluation from a hearer
- —less goal direction
- —more interdependent, group concerned
- —fewer linear patterns of conversation

Hofstede statistically identified the cultures that fit into these categories. Among the top individualistic cultures are the United States, Australia, Great Britain, Canada, the Netherlands, New Zealand, Italy, Belgium, and Denmark. The top collectivist cultures are Columbia, Korea, Pakistan, Peru, Taiwan, Thailand, Singapore, Chile, and Hong Kong. Notice that the collectivist cultures tend to be Asian and Latin-American, while the individualistic cultures tend to be North American and European.

Although Hofstede is frequently credited for this factor, individualism-collectivism, Harry Triandis also has numerous pioneering works applied to this area. Triandis (1990) observes that people can act collective-like (he calls them *allocentric*) or individual-like (he calls them *idiocentric*) across any culture. (See also Triandis 1987.) Also, Sudweeks (1991) underscores the importance of the individualism-collectivism dimension in developing more effective intercultural communication and sensitivity. For instance, she reminds us to be familiar with in-group norms, be aware of the collectivist's discomfort with competitive situations, and generally avoid saying "no" or criticizing in environments such as U.S. classrooms.

Hofstede's work borrowed the masculine-feminine metaphor to describe a gender role differentiation in cultures. By suggesting characteristics traditionally associated with masculinity or femininity, Hofstede's masculine cultures are those that exhibit work as more central to their lives, strength, material success, assertiveness, and competitiveness. Masculine cultures also differentiate gender roles more than feminine cultures. Feminine cultures are those that tend to accept fluid gender roles, embrace traits of affection, compassion, nurturing, and interpersonal relationships (Sudweeks 1991).

**Masculine-Feminine Cultures**

There are also communication-style differences that seem to emanate from these cultures. The masculine cultures tend to use more aggressive styles of communication. Their problem-solving methods and conflict-management techniques would center around bottom-line issues, strict coping and debriefing information techniques. In contrast, the feminine cultures are probably much more capable of reading nonverbal messages and are better prepared to deal with ambiguity. Perhaps not so surprising is that masculine cultures display higher levels of stress and also have lower percentages of women in technical and professional jobs when compared to feminine cultures.

The highest masculinity-index scores come from Japan, Australia, Venezuela, Switzerland, Mexico, Ireland, Great Britain, and Germany. The countries with the highest feminine scores are Sweden, Norway, the Netherlands, Denmark, Finland, Chile, Portugal, and Thailand. Hofstede observed that machismo is present in the Caribbean, but not particularly evident in the remainder of South America. This point could be debated at some length, based on evidence from other sources.

This sacrificial altar in Central America was believed to represent a place where spirits could be appeased. The belief in impersonal power and its influence is prevalent in many parts of the world.

## Power-Distance

Still another dimension of Hofstede's research involved what he called the power-distance index. Cultures with a high power index are said to accept inequality as the cultural norm. In other words, these cultures are vertical—that is, they are hierarchical cultures. People expect hierarchy, and authoritarian style communication is more common. We could expect much more oppressive behavior in high power-distance cultures, as well as more formalized rituals signaling respect, attentiveness, and agreement. Countries highest in the power-distance dimension are the Philippines, Mexico, Venezuela, India, Singapore, Brazil, Hong Kong, France, and Columbia. In general, many of the African and Latin American countries exhibit a high power-distance index as well.

Those cultures that are low in power-distance are more horizontal. That is, they are not fundamentally organized around hierarchical relationships. The countries with the lowest power-distance scores are Australia, Israel, Denmark, New Zealand, Ireland, Sweden, Norway, Finland, and Switzerland—mostly European-style countries.

Several theories have been used to explain the power-distance phenomenon, including ecological, technological, and climate issues (Hecht, Andersen, and Ribeau 1989). However, such arguments tend to ignore migration patterns, original tribalism, religion, and a host of other factors that enter an explanation. These cultures represent a fascinating profile.

## Uncertainty Avoidance

Our central model in chapter 1 and an axiom in chapter 2 referred to uncertainty and ambiguity. Hofstede questioned the extent to which a culture would avoid or tolerate uncertainty. Obviously, some cultures cannot stand the unknown. For them, avoiding uncertainty would be very difficult without increasing the number of rules of behavior to compensate for the uncertainty. These cultures include Greece, Portugal, Belgium, Japan, Peru, France, Chile, Spain, and Argentina.

Other cultures, however, seem more comfortable dealing with diversity and ambiguity. These include Singapore, Denmark, Sweden, Hong Kong, Ireland, Great Britain, India, the Philippines, and the United States.

Hofstede's work concerning this factor reminds us that cultures that place a premium on avoiding uncertainty will probably exhibit communication that tries to get a straight answer. In fact, members of such cultures may even be a little more emotional in the process of gathering that information. Identifying with a cultural communicator in a way that allows him or her to feel the most comfort and commonality with the communication interactant is a good strategy. It is not necessary to become something that you are not, for clearly that would be superficial and inadequate. However, to the extent that a match is created between communicators and another person anxiety is reduced.

## Cultural World View

A Nigerian student attending a major university spoke to his faculty advisor about a scene he had witnessed in his home country. Many onlookers, including the Nigerian student, observed a demonstration where one person allegedly brought a razor-sharp sword down upon the arm of another person wearing a special charm, but the person wearing the charm suffered no harm. The student then described the amulet and the secrets connected with this cultural phenomenon.

This student was reflecting one of the most fundamental concepts about the nature of culture, called cultural world view. World view is a belief system about the nature of the universe, its perceived effect on human behavior, and one's place in the universe. World view is a fundamental core set of assumptions explaining cultural forces, the nature of humankind, the nature of good and evil, luck, fate, spirits, the power of significant others, the role of time, and the nature of our physical and natural resources. Because it is so fundamental, world view affects communication.

Discovering a culture's world view involves finding out a culture's belief regarding various forces explaining events. For instance, many tribal Kenyans believe that disease is the result of evil spirits. Some Latin Americans believe wealth comes from a pact with the devil or possibly luck in finding buried treasure. The Nigerian discussed previously believed in what is called "ju-ju" in West Africa. Voodoo and the evil eye are well-known belief systems in Caribbean cultures. In another example, a middle-school teacher working among a group of economically disadvantaged students faces examples of fatalism in communication with such language as "Why try?" and "No one else will let me." Our interactions may be less than perfect for a number of reasons, but differences in world view intervene as one cause of misunderstanding in intercultural communication.

| Elements of<br>Cultural World<br>View | By examining some of the typical concepts by which cultures order their worlds, we have assembled a category system with which to assess some fundamental belief structures of a group of people. A knowledge of those belief structures can improve intercultural communication, a point reviewed by Cecile Garmon (1984) and adapted for our discussion. |
|---|---|

*Shame and guilt cultures.* Some cultures can be characterized by their perceived sense of personal guilt (usually found in individualistic cultures) and shame (usually found in collectivist cultures). This organizing feature of shame suggests that cultures feel a sense of obligation when things go wrong. In Asian cultures, for instance, shame is not good, almost as bad as losing one's group identity. In traditional Japanese culture, disgrace potential is an important element in decision making. If a policy or a person has the potential for bringing about shame or loss of face, then such risks are not likely to be sought. According to Marsella, Murray, and Golden (1976), Chinese and Japanese Americans both show tendencies to be more negatively sensitive to shame than Caucasian Americans. In fact, Japanese chief executive officers have been known to commit suicide if the organization experiences financial failure.

Shame cultures have a way of looking inwardly for obligation and responsibility. If duty is overlooked, it could cause shame to someone else, which in turn would cause you to be shamed. In Thai culture, for instance, it is especially important not to engage in any behavior that would show disrespect for parents or elders. To do so would bring shame.

In contrast, guilt cultures (often individualistic) experience remorse for personal actions but not for group mistakes. These cultures feel a need to reduce guilt and lean more toward personal blame than for group blame.

Both guilt and shame cultures develop systems for atonement and purification and often rituals to expiate those needs. Jimenez (1987) noticed this sense of guilt in his therapy practice with upwardly mobile Mexican Americans. His analysis revealed that economic mobility set in motion a number of guilt-provoking messages for certain individuals: "I don't deserve this; why am I so lucky and others so poor?" He based his analysis, in part, on his recognition that the culture in which his clients lived emphasized qualities that provoked guilt, but the culture simultaneously inculcated a sense of group loyalty. Thus, clients experienced a combination of guilt and shame.

The general theme of saving face, which is identified earlier in this chapter, is also related to the guilt-shame continuum. Several Middle Eastern, African, and particularly Asian cultures engage in communication styles that enhance relationships and avoid embarrassing another person. To publicly communicate personal attacks, relentless negative statements, or to display inadequate listening would likely not only be personally ineffective, but such behavior could trigger shame emotions among nonwestern friends.

*Task and people cultures.* Some cultures emphasize task accomplishment over relationships, while other cultures emphasize relationships over task. There is reason to believe that a fundamental belief system is part of the task-people

Values ranging from individuality to social responsibility are culturally rooted. (Photo by ACU student media.)

dichotomy. Task cultures may well have an underlying cognitive world view structure of what makes a person good. Task world views stress how self-worth comes from accomplishment and success. Therefore, working hard and successful task completion are methods to prove oneself. Task cultures certainly have many friendships, and obviously, people are not totally pushed out of the way. Such organizing themes as "Get ahead," "No gain without pain," and "Move upward" are the surface structures of a deeper, underlying cognitive dimension of how people are viewed in comparison with tasks. Americans, for instance, are considered highly task conscious.

Relationship cultures, of course, also accomplish tasks. The driving force, though, is thinking of others and finishing the relationship needs ahead of personal goals and schedules.

*Spirit and secular cultures.* Another important continuum by which a culture can be evaluated for its cognitive cultural world view involves whether or not the culture accepts the notion of a cosmos filled with spiritual beings and forces or whether a spiritual dimension plays a lesser role or any role at all. Anthropologists traditionally have labeled this factor as sacred-secular, meaning that some cultures accept a spiritual vitality or the presence of culturally defined spirits and beings, while other cultures reject or devalue a spiritual dimension in their world view. Marshall Singer (1987) describes a Guatemalan village whose water source ran dry. The government arranged to pipe water from a nearby village who had ample water. The government levied a water tax on the village, but the villagers refused to pay. A friend of the villagers, Mr. Green, visited the village and discovered the reason for the refusal: Everyone knows God gave water free. When Mr. Green explained that while God gave free water, humans made metal pipes, and would the villagers mind paying back the government for the pipes and installation. The villagers then had no problem and gladly paid the tax.

The story illustrates how cognitive beliefs impact relationships and how a secular view (the government framed the problem as purely economic) can counter a sacred view (the villagers framed the issue initially from a sacred perspective).

This continuum explains an area of difference not always appreciated as a part of a culture's perceptions and explained as a matter of an open or closed system. Francis Schaeffer (1968), a noted European philosopher, concludes that a secular culture has an implicit faith in the presupposition of the uniformity of natural causes in a closed system. A spirit culture accepts the presupposition of an open system, implying the alternative of categories for God and spiritual dimensions. Essentially, a spirit (or sacred) culture places faith in the spiritual realm, which a secular culture does not accept.

Communication differences arising from this cognitive continuum can be sizable. With this cognitive position, members of a secular culture may label alternative cultures as untrustworthy, unintelligent, uninformed, and biased. Likewise, members of a sacred culture may view secular cultures in the same negative ways. A number of social philosophers, such as Schaeffer, believe that the presuppositions of the nature of the universe as open or closed to any force is the fundamental difference involved. Intercultural communication proceeds on the assumption that dialogue and friendship can transcend the spiritual-sacred continuum. There are clearly significant differences involved in these two cognitive schemas, but the differences need not be barriers for interpersonal relationships, task productivity, intercultural friendship, or group effectiveness.

*The role of dead to living.* Some cultures are characterized by their view of the relationship between living and dead. The well-known ancestor rituals in certain Asian and African cultures remind us that some people see death as an event that can be bridged with ceremony and ritual. The world view of the Ashanti of Ghana, for instance, is diagrammed in figure 6.1 and shows how ancestors are considered as a part of an Ashanti's daily life. Thus, at weddings and funerals, palm wine is poured on the ground to satisfy the thirst of ancestors.

The assumption indicates a layered universe. Some of the powers available to a person are believed to come through ancestors, at a certain layer in that universe, who can be called upon to perform certain things on behalf of the person asking. This same layered world view, however, may also involve impersonal spirits, magic, formulas, and rituals that perform services for the living.

Among the Yaruro of southern Venezuela, their gods and the dead are understood as being in a relationship with the living. The Yaruro visualize existence as having age levels divided into steps, something like a continuum, of which the dead and the gods are the two highest levels (Bock 1969).

Among the Navaho, the ghosts of the dead are greatly feared, and anything connected with death is carefully avoided. Not only do the Navaho have no desire to contact the dead, but they practice rituals to drive away the dead spirits and ghosts; certain illnesses are believed to be caused by contact with death. Navaho patients have even been known to flee a hospital upon learning that a death has occurred there (Bock 1969).

Some cultures hold assiduous beliefs about ancestors, though in a somewhat different way than beliefs about the afterlife in general. True *ancestor cults* remain in Oriental and African societies in which each major lineage honors its

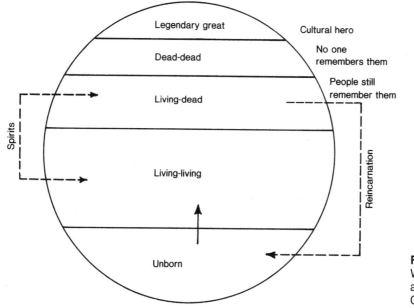

**Figure 6.1**
World-view structure among Ashanti of Ghana, West Africa.

own set of founding ancestors. The Kai of New Guinea customarily swindle their ancestral ghosts, just as they try to swindle each other. In some cultures, the members try to outsmart the ancestral spirits by lying to them. Cajolery, bribery, and false pretense are common means of influencing the supernatural. In other cultures, ancestors are appeased in hopes that offerings and special ritual treatment will please the ancestors, who in turn will offer some benefit to the worshipper.

Another example deals with ancestor propitiation among the Mapuche or Araucanian Indians of Chile (Faron 1961). Ancestor worship or the belief in the spirits of the dead most clearly emerged in funeral activities of the Mapuche. The ceremony begins with the attempt to exorcise the dead person's spirit and other lingering evil spirits. During the ceremony, the dead person's life history and ancestry are recounted in a loud voice, not for the benefit of the living, but to invoke the ancestors to accept, help, and protect the dead person's spirit from attack by the lurking evil spirits. Spirits are supposed to go to the spirit world and live tranquilly. However, if a spirit were to stay longer on earth, it may be captured and put to a bad use by a sorcerer. Therefore, an unpropitiated spirit returns to earth to haunt relatives, not to do them harm, but to remind them of their obligation to him or her.

*Nature of humankind.* According to Kluckhohn and Strodtbeck (1961), cultures perceive humans in one of three ways. The first is that human nature is considered good. The implications of this view are that people can handle responsibility, do the right thing, and make their own decisions. Suppose you were working for a group and your primary organizational role is to coordinate information. With this world view position, would you assume they are telling the

This photo of Lake Atitlan in Guatemala reminds us of a perceived mystical link of humans to earth, a link traditionally valued by Native Americans.

truth or lying? You would assume that people are inherently good and will tell the truth. You may have read of McGregor's Theory Y in management, which also assumes the goodness of humankind, a point that may help illustrate the pervasive nature of world view in daily communication experiences.

A second positive of the nature of humankind assumes a mixture of human goodness and evil, while a third position assumes that humans are basically evil. With this presupposition, communication strategies gravitate toward such variables as control, regulation, protection of information, and a communication climate stressing upward and centralized communication. This cognitive world view position would lead to a Theory X approach in managing, according to McGregor. In this case, the hypothetical information coordination role noted previously would demand checks and balances to insure accurate information.

*Humans and nature.* Another element of world view is the amount of control over nature one believes. There are three possible positions here, too. One cultural position is that humans are subject to nature (Kluckhohn and Strodtbeck 1961). As Sarbaugh (1979) explains, a person believes nature was not meant to be controlled. A second position is that humankind should be in harmony with nature, preserving and working in coordination with natural conditions. A third position is that humans should control nature especially in ways that benefit humankind, such as placing dams in rivers or cutting forests.

Interestingly enough, these cognitive cultural positions define some of the controversies in global environmental issues. One faction argues for total preservation of natural resources, while another faction argues for productivity and usage of many of the world's natural resources.

*Doing and being cultures.* The doing-being duality is another world view difference between cultures. One cultural pattern is to prefer activity and productivity and measurable accomplishment. In fact, a doing culture often develops strategies to invoke guilt on its members for inactivity and loss of productivity. Such cultures emphasize goals, functional information, and less interpersonal dimensions. Many of the world's technology cultures typify this type of culture.

Being cultures emphasize a meditative value, stressing personal thought, discussion, interpersonal relationships, spontaneity, and harmony. Consider, for example, a couple where one person is a very meditative person, preferring quiet time, but the other person enjoys going places and being constantly on the move. Their communication difficulties may relate partially to their cultural differences on the doing-being continuum.

*Life cycle.* Several examples noted in this text imply that life can be viewed in two ways. One view suggests that life is linear—that birth, life, and death mark each person's existence. According to this view, there is no rebirth, only this life in which to accomplish. Therefore, use of time is considered important. Individuals who maintain this linear view may or may not believe in an eternal existence after death.

A second view suggests that life is cyclical—that birth, life, death, and rebirth mark each person's existence. This view also affects use of time. Since another earthly life follows, cyclical cultures may believe that time pressures are not as important. Some analysts have argued, for example, that the United States was at an immediate disadvantage during the Vietnam War because of differences in these two time views. The North Vietnamese were prepared to fight for scores of years; the United States was accustomed to war's quick end and grew weary when such an ending seemed illusive. These expectations justifiably may have resulted from each culture's view of time and life cycle.

*Fatalism.* Rogers with Svenning (1969) defined fatalism as "the degree to which an individual recognizes a lack of ability to control his future." A fatalistic outlook on life

> results in a failure to see a relationship between work and one's economic condition. Having enough is thought to be almost entirely due to luck and is never believed to be brought about or furthered by personal initiative. (pp. 32–33)

Fatalism is said to produce two totally different results. It can produce what has been characterized as failure qualities, such as passivity, pessimism, acceptance, endurance, pliancy, and evasion. However, it can also be credited for success. Fate is credited for bringing good luck, wealth, ability to go on, new opportunities, and new relationships.

Fatalism results from a perception that something beyond our control causes our immediate circumstances. That cause may be random luck or manipulation of spiritual forces directed by someone else. The important point is that high fatalism suggests a low degree of control over one's actions and one's environment.

In addition to the elements of cultural world view, we also can identify the mechanisms by which world view beliefs are said to operate. These mechanisms are said to represent the methods by which members engage their world view.

**Mechanisms of Cultural World View**

*Mana.* Mana is the belief that material objects have special powers. Originally a South Sea Island belief, this force is believed to be inherited, acquired, or conferred. An amulet worn about parts of the body serves in a special way to ward off evil in some Melanesian cultures. To some Americans, luck is a form of mana in material objects like a rabbit's foot or magical charm.

*Animism.*   Animism refers more broadly to the belief that impersonal spirits dwell in material forms of nature, such as rocks, rivers, plants, weather, certain places, and special places. These spirits are believed to be capable of a benevolent or a malevolent influence. Among some Ghanians, it is believed that proper respect for animism can bring about certain benefits by the power of ju-ju. Voodoo and the evil eye in Caribbean cultures invoke similar forces. Sometimes a special ambassador, called a shaman, is believed necessary to manipulate the spirit world.

In a study of the Mapuche Indians of Chili, Faron (1962) noted a dualistic world view most often categorizing good or bad as left or right. Cultural aspects classified as left are evil, death, night, sickness, evil spirits, sorcerer, underworld, poverty, and hunger. In corresponding cultural classifications on the right are good, life, day, health, ancestral spirits, shaman, after-world, abundance, and fullness. In this culture, for example, if anyone is startled by a bird's song near at hand, and the bird is on the right, it signifies good fortune. If the bird is on the left, it presages evil. As another example, when, in this culture, there is a dream of reaching a fork in the road and the person takes the left fork, he or she will have only bad fortune. If the person turns to the right, he or she will enjoy riches, huge quantities of food, and general good fortune.

Even natural elements and directions coincide with this dichotomous world view. On the left are west, north, winter, cold, moon, water, speech, ocean, below, blue, black, layman, and sin, while on the right in corresponding categories are east, south, summer, warm, sun, blood, ritual language, land, above, yellow, white, priest, and expiation. These, along with many more examples, led Faron to the conclusion that the Mapuche live in a dualistic or dichotomous society, where animism is associated with this position.

*Shamanism.*   A shaman is an individual who acts as a diviner, curer, spirit medium, or magician. The belief in a shaman's power is called shamanism. A long training period may be demanded before a novice can attain the rights and privileges of some shaman positions. Shamans are recognized by others as being different from the ordinary and usually take the lead in religious ceremonies, magical arts, or curing especially in traditional cultures. It is believed that a shaman's power makes it possible to enter into contact with spirit beings and to exercise some degree of control over supernatural forces. Sometimes, spirit possession and entering a trance are believed to be a part of a shaman's activities. While in this condition, the shaman in some societies acts as a medium, transmitting messages from the living to the dead and vice versa, predicting the future, finding lost objects, identifying the cause of illness, prescribing cures, or giving advice.

**Personal Communication and World View**

Scholars are interested in how world view influences communication. The term applied to this question is personal communication world view (PCWV), defined as how much control characterizes one's communication climate. Research developing this construct identifies how individuals cope with everyday communication situations (Dodd and Garmon 1987). What assumptions does a person make concerning managing one's communication climate?

The fundamental theory of PCWV posits that individuals have a communication construct concerning the operation and management of communication control. We organize information about ourselves and develop a communication style that reflects fundamental beliefs about the amount of control believed available within communication contexts. In this sense, one end of the continuum measured by PCWV relates to metaphors such as helplessness, powerlessness, external locus of control, and fatalism, while the opposite is true for the other end of the continuum.

The research connecting personal world view to intercultural communication holds far-reaching implications (Auletta 1989). First, this construct appears to influence values (Dodd and Garmon 1987; Driskill and Norton 1989). Second, PCWV explains specific communication qualities known to be important to intercultural skills and culture sensitivity. For instance, a person with high communication control finds choices and decision making easier. That person typically exhibits a communication style consistent with numerous communication qualities including: openness, low communication apprehension, innovativeness, high self-esteem, organizational cooperation, cognitive complexity, and opinion leadership. The opposite characterizes those individuals who feel little control over their communication climate.

This concept appears very useful in describing barriers or facilitators to intercultural communication. For you to check your own tendencies in communication control, see the PCWV scale in table 6.1 (Dodd and Garmon 1991). According to norms based on testing over 2,400 people, individuals below 60, may exhibit less communication control, 60–80 moderate control, and 80 or above high control. As you might expect, your score depends on immediate life's circumstances: broken relationships, failures, difficulties. Finally, the instrument predictably differentiates individualistic cultures from collectivist cultures and high power-distance cultures from low power-distance cultures.

A growing body of research compares cultures and world view differences. For example, Long, Javidi, and Pryately (1993) found that communication control (one of the top indicators of what is called communication motives, based on a communication motives instrument by Rubin, Perse, and Barbato 1988) resulted in highlighting cultural differences and communication style comparing Japanese, Ukranians, and Americans according to the study. Ukranians were the highest on communication control, followed by Americans, and then Japanese. They also found communication control motives anticipated certain communication style outcomes for each culture: Ukranians with high communication control are higher on impression leaving and contentiousness; Americans with high communication control use more contentious, dramatic, and dominant communication, but a less friendly style; Japanese with high communication control exhibit dominance and friendliness, but less relaxation. The study concludes: "Consistent with other studies, this investigation assumed that American, Japanese, and Ukranian groups would possess different world views and, ultimately, different moves [communicator style] for satisfying communication motives [one of which is communication control]" (p. 24).

**Table 6.1**   Personal Communication World View

Read each item carefully to be sure you know what that item is stating. Then circle your response to the item. The responses range from strongly disagree (SD), to a less intense disagreement (D), to a position of being right in between agreeing and disagreeing (N), to a position of agreement with the item (A), to strongly agree (SA). You are being asked to indicate your attitude/belief about each item, honestly expressing your personal opinion.

| | | 5 | 4 | 3 | 2 | 1 |
|---|---|---|---|---|---|---|
| 1. | No matter how much effort I make to communicate clearly, it really seems my level of happiness is not changed by what I say or do. | SD | D | N | A | SA |
| 2. | Both the bad things and the good things that happen to me are beyond my control. | SD | D | N | A | SA |
| 3. | In my view of the world, the future is already set in motion, so my choices are limited; even if I communicate convincingly, or use helpful decision processes, it will not do much to change the way my future looks now. | SD | D | N | A | SA |
| 4. | Frequently, other people have more effect than I on whether or not I attain my goals. | SD | D | N | A | SA |
| 5. | Luck and circumstances play a major role in my life, regardless of my communication efforts for influencing my situation. | SD | D | N | A | SA |
| 6. | Many times I could be described as a victim of people or circumstances beyond my control. | SD | D | N | A | SA |
| 7. | There is not much use in trying too hard to please people; if they like you, they like you, and if they don't like you, you can't do much to change the situation. | SD | D | N | A | SA |
| 8. | My destiny depends mostly on the plans of others, who alter many of my decisions. | SD | D | N | A | SA |
| 9. | Getting a job or being promoted in a job depends on my being in the right place at the right time, not on my personal ability or personal communication skills. | SD | D | N | A | SA |
| 10. | Many times I could describe myself as having little influence over the things that seem to happen to me or over the people in my life right now. | SD | D | N | A | SA |
| 11. | The future lies before most people like a long ribbon that cannot be altered or shaped very easily but mostly just followed. | SD | D | N | A | SA |

**Table 6.1** *Continued*

|  | 5 | 4 | 3 | 2 | 1 |
|---|---|---|---|---|---|
| 12. With people who just don't respond well to me, even if I try to pay more attention, listen better, and interact the best I can, my efforts don't work; the relationship seems already set and I can't seem to do much about it. | SD | D | N | A | SA |
| 13. I've found that when I make choices to help or influence people, my decisions really do not change them—usually it's the circumstances and not what I say or do. | SD | D | N | A | SA |
| 14. I wish I could take more control over the direction of my life, but people, groups, and circumstances regulate me too much. | SD | D | N | A | SA |
| 15. It is not always wise to plan too far ahead because many things turn out to be a matter of good or bad fortune anyhow. | SD | D | N | A | SA |
| 16. The way I see it, I can try to communicate and interact, but I'm finding that changing my circumstances is not very likely. | SD | D | N | A | SA |
| 17. In reality, I tend to think and do things the way my family does things. | SD | D | N | A | SA |
| 18. I often think that few of us have a control or predetermined purpose that we understand clearly. | SD | D | N | A | SA |
| 19. My culture, friends, and circumstances usually direct and influence me more than anything else. | SD | D | N | A | SA |
| 20. What is going to happen will happen, regardless of what I say or do. | SD | D | N | A | SA |

Scoring:

All SD = 5; D = 4; N = 3; A = 2; SA = 1. Add the rating for each item, and total across all twenty items.

20–59 = low communication control; personal choices and communication management not as strong as relationship, luck, circumstances.

60–79 = moderate communication control; personal choices and communication management equally as strong as relationships, luck, circumstances.

80–100 = high communication control; personal choices and communication management stronger than relationships, luck, circumstances.

(reliability = .86, Cronbach's alpha)

Carley Dodd and Cecile Garmon, 1991 introduced in this text.

The Dodd and Garmon research over a ten-year period reveals an average 20 percent of U.S. Americans and 30 percent of Latin Americans and Asians who experience low communication control. Garmon (1984) and Cardot (1990) found significantly higher communication control among faculty than administrators in American colleges and universities. Garmon (1980) in an early investigation discovered that American college students exhibit more communication control than high school students. Roper (1986) found that high communication control college students were less likely to drop out of college their first semester. Driskill and Dodd (1989) reported that high communication control college students in a dorm environment were more likely to be opinion leaders and express an open communication style.

## Values and Intercultural Communication

Values refer to long-enduring judgments appraising the worth of an idea, object, person, place, or practice. Sometimes, our opinions and attitudes reflect deep-seated and fundamental values. While attitudes tend to change, values are long lasting. For example, an incumbent political candidate supporting humanitarian aid to an impoverished nation may have won your vote because that person holds values similar to your values. Your attitude (evaluation of goodness or badness of something) may be positive toward the candidate because of a link with a value you cherish, altruism. This value even might relate to some of your other values. Fundamentally, values relate to questions of whether something ought or ought not to be—when we discover the why of those questions, we discover the values. A number of influential sources may prove useful to you as they were to me in framing the next few pages of this discussion, and these are gratefully acknowledged for further reading on this topic.*

Value differences affect intercultural communication. For example, a person may elevate the importance of extra effort and hard work, believing it produces success. Imagine the potential difficulty if this person were teamed with an individual who devalues hard work, believing that just getting by is enough, so that there will be more time for enjoying life. Their communication may be strained under this system. An understanding of values, therefore, can pinpoint the differences between two individuals from separate cultures—-intercultural communication can proceed from an understanding of those differences.

### Relationship with Family

A number of values center around evaluations concerning family and kin, especially values toward elders, parents, and ancestors.

*Respect for elders.* Almost every culture shows some degree of respect for its elders. In North America, for many years the young used last names in a formal manner when addressing older or respected persons. In some rural areas

---

*Values are discussed by numerous sources, but several authors influential on this point are indicated here: Arensberg and Niehoff (1964); Kluckhohn and Strodtbeck (1961); Rokeach (1968); Condon and Yousef (1975); Asante (1990); Brislin (1993); Gonzalez (1990); Kalbfleisch and Davies (1991); Seelye (1993); Lewis, Dodd and Tippens (1992); and Klopf (1991).

of the United States, the practice existed not too many years ago of addressing an older person as "Aunt" or "Uncle," even though no actual kinship was evident. Among North American family members, there is a degree of respect for age—up to a point. Some seem to lose respect for their senior family members and senior citizens in general, from retirement age on. Norton's (1991) research identifies an elderly microculture and implies feeling's of rejection and oppression from the larger culture.

The respect North Americans have for their elderly is indeed pale compared with the high value placed upon the elderly in other cultures. For many Asian and African cultures, age and its accompanying wisdom stand as a salient element—in some cases, a focal point—of culture. Many African men under twenty-five years of age will not make decisions without consulting older family members. Someone recently observed to me that North American parents value their children and their needs more than the parents' parents or grandparents. Just the opposite is true in Asian cultures where the elders are honored ahead of the children. This concept plays out in many circumstances from eating habits to resource management in the family.

*Respect for parents.* Value of parental authority also varies culturally. North Americans typically stress individuality and making one's own decisions by the midteens. Accompanying this emphasis seems to be a disregard for parental authority and much less communication with parents—at least in a large number of cases. Such actions would be regarded as dishonoring parents in African and Middle Eastern cultures. In these cultures, to honor one's parents throughout life is considered one of the highest virtues.

*Respect for ancestors.* Although most North Americans typically do little more than occasionally remember a deceased relative, many people in other cultures pay deep homage to their ancestors. This value partially stems from some world view beliefs that ancestors can influence one's life and provide special benefits, as indicated earlier in this chapter. In some parts of Africa and among some subcultures in the United States, family members take out large newspaper ads featuring a picture of a deceased family member and a personal letter addressing the deceased, as if that person were fully aware of the message. This form of communication with immediate ancestors or other deceased family members reflects not only an interesting communication form but also the importance of values. Respect for ancestors sometimes coincides with life cycles, illustrated in the ancestor-reincarnation view of the Ashanti (figure 6.1).

*Source of identification and self worth.* Family serves as an organizing social unit from which to develop personal identification. "I am a Martinez," or "a Schleyermacher," or "I am from the family of Lin Chan," or "My family is Abramson," represent examples relating to identity and ultimately a source of self-worth in many cultures. The cultural vitality of the family as a source of personal worth depends on respect and dignity factors offered in two-way processes of affirmation and confirmation between parents, grandparents, and children.

*Obligation.*    Another family value varying across cultures is obligation to family. In many cultures families must take precedence over self. Obligation in many cultures, however, is broader than just family. A PBS special on African culture entitled "Legacy of Lifestyles" emphasized how successful, urban Africans take their obligations to their rural tribes seriously. An African with good income often makes frequent visits to the village and helps with things like fertilizer, school fees, conflict resolution, and pays respect to older villagers. This example is but one of many cultures where the migration from rural to urban life does not exclude obligation to family and friends. When I was in Papua New Guinea, I observed the won-tok system, whereby material wealth brought with it the culturally accepted obligations to family. In fact, won-tok is so pervasive, that any villager or good friend is allowed to enjoy the material advantages of their friends.

*Shame.*    The collectivist concept of shame in contrast to individualistic cultures that experience guilt was discussed earlier in this chapter. We recognize how family members in certain cultures cause group embarrassment, or shame, for all family members. Anytime a child violates norms or law, the shame potential exists. In some Asian and Latin American cultures, a daughter who dates a young man without the parents' approval brings dishonor to the entire family. In certain cases, the dishonor forces the father to disenfranchise the daughter. Shame, embarrassment, and loss of face are broader issues than just family, often affecting entire communities (Brislin 1993).

## Relationship with Others

Another set of values focuses on interpersonal relationships. One's personal dealings with others is considered a sacred trust in some cultures but is treated casually in other cultures.

*Equality of people.*    In the United States, people generally accept the norm of equality among people, at least philosophically. Among many other cultures, however, norms prevail concerning the rules of inequality. Members of these cultures accept status and role differences and in some cases espouse those differences as natural for orderly existence. As the discussion on power-distance earlier in this chapter indicated, there is a value placed on hierarchy in some cultures. In a number of those cases, the vertical differences between people are justified on the basis of harmony and good for all in the culture.

Equality not only functions to provide a sense of order, the concept has philosophical roots as a key theme in some cultures. In the United States, the thematic importance of equality is well known and works in institutional life, law, and norms. In reality, there is inequality in status and roles but the philosophical commitment to equality and consequent personal freedoms are deeply embedded. What appears to a North American as submission and loss of personal freedom in other cultures can be reframed in terms of value differences.

*Humanitarianism.*    Cultures vary on their obligations to people outside their family, tribes, and friends. In some cases, it is assumed that each significant social unit, like a family or tribe, can help its own members. Thus, obligations are not extended beyond those units to outsiders. Other cultures operate on the assumption that altruism operates broadly and is expected to persist for strangers as well as associates. Most cultures have a sense of altruism, compassion, sympathy, as these values affect helping others, but the cultural rules for operationalizing these values differ.

Also, mitigating situations circumscribe acting on humanitarian values. For example, conditions in some urban environments may prevent a person from interpersonal helping activities even despite positive personal values toward altruism. In the long term, it is possible that anomia and fear will replace altruism, eventually prompting a reordering of cultural community values.

*Honesty.*   Most cultures have some taboo against dishonesty—under certain conditions. A Middle Easterner who values slyness and cleverness, for example, may be fully acceptable as long as he is considered sly in bargaining and not perceived as dishonest. Of course, one person's definition of honesty becomes another person's definition of cleverness—the United States businessperson who can cheat and not get caught is sometimes considered shrewd. That person's foreign counterpart is considered dishonest. In some cultures, a bribe is perceived as dishonest; other cultures view the same activity as a courtesy, as payment for a favor, or as an extended tip.

These points highlight the ongoing discussion among experts concerning the relativity of cultural values and personal/social ethics. The intent of this discussion does not give license for corporations operating overseas to violate ethical standards or for a country to violate human dignity and rights, any more than an individual visiting another or living in a host culture should alter personal codes. However, the problem of universal absolutes and of values seemingly held without question in one's home culture versus alternative and diverse values in a host culture raises ongoing and acute dilemmas.

*Harmony.*   Earlier discussions already have alluded to the importance of harmony with others. East-west relationship building often stresses this consideration and requires communication activity accompanying this important value. Asante's (1990) analysis concerning traditional African court and trial procedures reminds readers of trust as essential to producing harmony. Overall, a number of important communication strategies relate to interacting with cultures emphasizing harmony.

—face-saving at all costs; regardless of who is right or wrong, saving face contributes to overall harmony

—developing consensus; individual comments or long speeches are acceptable in harmony cultures so long as the speaker ultimately accepts the group's choice and facilitates rather than takes away from the group; as the Japanese proverb goes, "the nail that sticks up gets hit"

—cooperation as an expectation

—truth as an organizing principle

—appropriate ambiguity or silence used in a timely manner

—avoid directness and confrontation

—respect for tradition as a pattern to keep in mind, but not always a primary concern, as Brislin reminds us (1993).

*Mentoring relationship.* In recent years, research has highlighted interpersonal values toward role models or mentors. Investigating the value that black professionals place on interpersonal helping roles, research by Kalbfleisch and Davies (1991) indicate the race of the mentor is the best predictor of professional development, according to their survey of black professionals. It appears that a system that values role modeling and mentoring is vital and healthy for relationships.

*In-groups and out-groups.* The distinction between in-groups (those valued usually because the source describing the perspective is a member) and out-groups (those devalued because the source describing the perspective is not a member) is a source of interpersonal value difference. For example, Broome (1990) reminds us that Greek in-group/out-group distinctions are significant, even historically meaningful organizing principles to a larger extent than in western societies. In this example, the entire culture's predominant interpersonal orientation revolves around this classification schema. In the broadest sense, then, cultural values toward others depend on group memberships and group loyalties surrounding those memberships. Successful interpersonal relationships are culturally bounded by a matrix of associations and one's personal reference group's acceptance or rejection of those associations.

*Inclusion and exclusion.* Cultural values also differ on the role of how much interpersonal psychological distance to keep from others. How much emotional closeness or distance (in communication literature, this concept is called immediacy) is appropriate and has enormous communication consequences arising from the value assigned by each culture. For instance, Al Gonzalez (1990) defines Mexican otherness and points out how the Mexican Americans appear to push others away. In reality, the separation is a mask hiding the pain of oppression and exclusion from larger social processes. Just as important to some Mexican Americans is the drive toward inclusion and the embracing of value toward a host culture and others that is positive and highly motivated. Inclusion, in fact, is probably the dominant force. What Anglos perceive as ambivalence toward others is in reality a struggle beneath the psychological surface of dealing with identity and acculturation in a new culture, while facing the pain and grief over a conquered past, according to Gonzalez.

## Relationship with Society

Another set of values predisposes cultural members toward salient societal behavior. Some of these values relate to personal behaviors, and some relate to group behaviors. In either case, it is very clear in many cultures that personal action and thought affect the group. In those cases, individuals or families are monitored for implications affecting the entire group. In Singapore for instance, the national culture enjoys wealth and success, but these come at the expense of subjection of personal liberties. This dynamic relationship between society and self is understood by members in light of their culture, although foreign visitors remain puzzled if not occasionally angered by the perceived personal losses. Such a rank ordering of society over self, or for North Americans, self over society, reflects this question of society values—their elements and diversity.

*Morality and ethics.*    Morality and ethics seem highly personal to North Americans. But for many people around the world, morality is a group matter. Inappropriate premarital activity can cause a family to lose a certain bride price otherwise gained for a daughter. Incorrect use of property can become a grave societal offense among some African cultures. Not using appropriate silence or disclosing too much can be offensive among some Native American tribes.

*Personal freedom.*    Personal freedom is not only defined differently, but also not valued the same across cultures. In some cultures it is inappropriate to discuss personal choice in a way other than the individual's relationship to the group at large. One of the contrasting features that seems to surprise visitors from the United States to a host country is the sense of groupness. For instance, the Japanese sense of group relationship, loyalty, and hierarchy contrasts with the North Americans' sense of individuality (Doi 1976). Conformity to social norms exists practically universally. Within the boundaries of social norms, some cultures stress groupness while others stress individualism. Of course, readers will recognize that harmony and its communication applications noted previously connect with the diversity of personal freedom indicated in this section.

*Emotions.*    Some cultures value emotional expression, but other cultures prefer reservation. While there are exceptions, Asian cultures generally practice reserve and emotional restraint. The idea of extreme emotion, such as loud sobs during a funeral or boisterous laughter on festive occasions, would be considered too emotional. To a lesser extent, some Scandinavian cultures appear publicly reserved. Britons and Germans appear more reserved than Italians, Greeks, and Czechs.

The use of emotion in communication, therefore, varies according to the relevant culture. For example, the speech one makes in Lagos, Nigeria, should differ from a speech in Denmark in terms of emotional elements of communication style. Similarly, we should not be surprised to find our intercultural communication colored by a high emotional pitch in some cultures or affected by little enthusiasm in other cultures. To certain Europeans, North Americans appear pushy and too emotional; to Latin Americans, the same North American mannerisms appear cold and unfeeling.

*Work and play.*    Many cultures separate work and play. In these cases, work demands diligence, concentration, even tedium. Since play is considered frivolous, combining work and play is unreasonable. Work and play do not mix! That view dominates some North American thought. In contrast, other cultures blend work and play. For the North American to insist on the divorce of work from frivolity and to judge others negatively is to invite estrangement (Arensberg and Niehoff 1964).

*Time.*   Time is valued more by some cultures than by others. To the U.S. businessperson, "Time is money." To the Ecuadorian storekeeper, time is relatively less important to one's friendships and other social obligations. The values that cultures place upon time, however, cause numerous misunderstandings, as you can imagine.

*Tradition.*   If Tevia in the *Fiddler on the Roof* was right, then adhering to the past supersedes the present. Although as Tevia discovered, traditional values change. Cultures can be thought of as if on a continuum from relying on tradition at one end to embracing innovation on the other end. Individuals within a culture find themselves in consonance or dissonance with the mainstream values, as Tevia found about his children and their rejection of traditional ways.

## Relationship with Self

Another set of value variables deals with personal values toward success and material well-being. These values also relate to personal qualities of individualism.

*Success.*   The idea behind getting ahead, winning, and generally being above average has deep roots as a North American value. Competition also is valued, since it purportedly stimulates success. However, this notion of success and failure lacks correspondence in many other cultures. In many cultures, cooperation is fundamental.

*Individualism.*   Success in North American values is linked with personal achievement and rugged individualism. Individualism pervades concepts of personal freedom in which each person has the right to pursue choices (Seelye 1993). In contrast, many other cultures do not highly esteem individualism. Again, some Asian cultures emphasize group cohesion and loyalty. Many African cultural members thwart personal goals for the sake of the family, village, tribe, or larger cultural unit. Some international critics have likened the North American's view of freedom to an adolescent who lacks self-restraint. The point of view, of course, depends upon the values one holds toward individualism, freedom, and other related concepts.

*Material well-being.*   Many cultures value material accumulation of goods and wealth. Cattle herdsmen of East Africa, for example, prize their animals partially as a measure of status and wealth. In a similar way, North Americans accumulate goods as a measure of wealth and success. However, material well-being and accumulation of wealth can become ends valued in and of themselves—sometimes as the single most important value. The symbols of material well-being and wealth, obviously vary among cultures. Perhaps even more importantly, the rank order of these symbols differs considerably among cultures.

## Relationship with Natural Resources

In her pursuit of intercultural communication, Diane Schwalm's literature findings alerted me to the significance of values centered around land and animals. The larger issues, however, are actually how cultures come to view the totality of their natural resources. Cultural rules for the working out of natural resources become intricate and could appear quite foreign to a culture that does not place importance on natural resource values.

*Relationship with land.* First, consider the importance of *land as a cultural value.* For instance, farmland in China is related to a sense of security. It can be passed through generations; money may be used up, but not the land. Land values often center around kinship ties. This tie is reinforced by ancestor worship and creates a bond between a man and his land. It is not impossible for a man to sell his land but to sell breaks the bonds of filial piety. Because these bonds are so rarely broken, from childhood onward, a man develops a sense of personal identity with his land; it becomes a part of his very personality.

Like the Chinese, the Maoris of New Zealand feel quite strongly about the inheritance of the land to develop an ancestral continuity. These feelings have more immediate consequence for the Maoris than for the Chinese, according to Metge (1976).

> It is a tangible link with the heroes and happenings of a storied past. Even more important, inherited rights in Maori land are bound up with rights of precedence in Maori community life and on the open space used as a gathering place. The older generation, in particular, recognize an almost mystical connection between land and personal standing. (p. 107)

Metge also defined aspects of social standing based on land.

> In each local district, Maoris give a special status to those they call *tangata whenua* (literally, people of the land). To qualify for this title and the privileges attached to it, a Maori must first of all be descended from a line of forebearers who lived and owned Maori land in the district continuously over many generations. (p. 107)

With no ancestral connection to the Maori land, a person is considered an immigrant, frequently barred from public office and rarely listened to in public discussions.

Among the Navaho, a matrilineal kinship rule gives a woman her own plot of land, and the returns she reaps from it are strictly hers. The man does the same with his property. Even the children may be given designated pieces of land or a few animals and be expected to take care of these things as soon as the children are old enough (Leighton and Leighton 1944).

However, the land and its productivity are not a status symbol to the Navaho, even when they bring in a considerable amount of money. They have a high regard for possessions but feel that anyone who becomes extremely wealthy must have come by the wealth dishonorably. Therefore, they advocate that the wealth must be distributed among the wealthy's less fortunate friends and relatives.

Though the ownership of hunting grounds among the Kwakiutl Indians was specified, nature itself was believed to be controlled by a supernatural power.

Animals, rocks, waterfalls, islands were all approached by prayer, and a person could seek their help or offer thanks for their contribution. Some pieces of land had particular supernatural powers. For example, the soil from a land otter slide was believed to influence the weather.

The Plains Indians of North America were also hunters and gatherers, but their philosophy did not allow for a man's ownership of the land. To the Plains Indians, "All things are contained within the Medicine Wheel, and all things are equal within it. The Medicine Wheel is the Total Universe." A Blackfoot Chief explained the relation between the Indian and his earth as follows:

> Our land is more valuable than your money. It will last forever. It will not even perish by the flames of fire. As long as the sun shines and the waters flow, this land will be here to give life to men and animals. We cannot sell the lives of men and animals; therefore we cannot sell this land. You can count your money and burn it without the nod of a buffalo's head, but the Great Spirit can count the grains of sand and the blades of grass of these plains. As a present to you, we will give you anything we have that you can take with you; but the land, never. (Storm 1972, p. 5)

This concept of the land was not only related to the equality of all nature, but to the view of the earth as a mother. In most Indian literature, the earth is referred to as the Earth Mother. Her daily power and influence on the lives of the Indians is reflected in the following passage by Chief Luther Standing Bear, chief of the Lakota, a western band of the Sioux Indian tribe:

> The Lakota was a true naturist—a lover of nature. He loved the earth and all things of the earth, the attachment growing with age. The old people came literally to love the soil, and they sat or reclined on the ground with a feeling of being close to a mothering power. It was good for the skin to touch the earth, and the old people liked to remove their moccasins and walk with bare feet on the sacred earth. Their tepees were built upon the earth, and their altars were made of earth. The birds that flew in the air came to rest upon the earth, and it was the final abiding place of all things that lived and grew. The soil was soothing, strengthening, cleansing, and healing.
>
> That is why the old Indian still sits upon the earth instead of propping himself up and away from its life-giving forces. For him, to sit or lie upon the ground is to be able to think more deeply and to feel more keenly; he can see more clearly into the mysteries of life and come closer in kinship to other lives about him. . . .
>
> The old Lakota was wise. He knew that man's heart away from nature becomes hard; he knew that lack of respect for growing things soon led to lack of respect for humans, too. So he kept his youth close to its softening influence. (McLuhan 1972, p. 6)

This love and respect for the earth is in opposition to the agrarian societies, who would often clear and plow the ground for agricultural purposes. One Wintu Indian woman expressed these beliefs:

> The White people plow up the ground, pull down the tree, kill everything. The tree says, "Don't. I am sore. Don't hurt me." But they chop it down and cut it up. The spirit of the land hates them. They blast out trees and stir it up to its depths. (McLuhan 1972, p. 15)

*Relationship with animals.*    Another set of values considers the *importance and roles of animals* in a culture. The sacredness of all life to the Hindu is well known (Harris 1974). The cow, for instance, is highly symbolic of reincarnation. Also, the elephant represents nobility, patience, grace, wisdom, and beneficence (Naravane 1965).

Jewish and Islamic peoples condemn pigs and pork. Other societies revere the pig. The Maring, a remote tribe living in the Bismarck Mountains of New Guinea, hold a pig festival approximately every twelve years. During the festival, a massive number of pigs are sacrificed, and a battle is waged on enemy clans. Following the battle, a prayer is offered to assure the ancestors that the fighting is over and that the coming years will be spent replenishing the pig supply. The total concept of pig love is explained by Harris (1974):

> Pig love includes raising pigs to be a member of the family, sleeping next to them, talking to them, stroking and fondling them, calling them by name, leading them on a leash to the fields, weeping when they fall sick or are injured, and feeding them with choice morsels from the family table. But unlike the Hindu love of cow, pig love also includes obligatory sacrificing and eating of pigs on special occasions. Because of ritual slaughter and sacred feasting, pig love provides a broader prospect for communion between man and beast than is true of the Hindu farmer and his cow. The climax of pig love is the incorporation of the pig as flesh into the flesh of the human host and of the pig as spirit into the spirit of the ancestors. (p. 46)

Some cultures, such as the Balinese, do not regard animals as being on the same level as humans and carry a revulsion of animal-like behavior within the culture:

> Babies are not allowed to crawl for that reason. Incest, though hardly approved, is a much less horrifying crime than bestiality. (The appropriate punishment for the second is death by drowning, for the first being forced to live like an animal). Most demons are represented—in sculpture, dance, ritual, myth—in some real or fantastic animal form. The main puberty rite consists in filing the child's teeth so they will not look like animal fangs. Not only defecation, but eating is regarded as a disgusting, almost obscene activity, to be conducted hurriedly and privately because of its association with animality. Even falling down or any form of clumsiness is considered to be bad for these reasons. Aside from cocks and a few domestic animals—oxen, ducks—of no emotional significance, the Balinese are aversive to animals and treat their large number of dogs not merely callously but with a phobic cruelty. (Geertz 1973, pp. 419–20)
>
> A blood sacrifice is offered to pacify the demons among the Balinese people. No temple festival can be permitted until such a sacrifice has been performed, despite their hatred for many kinds of animals.

The traditional Kwakiutl on Vancouver Island, on the other hand, claim animals as their ancestors, as Boas (1966) described:

> According to Indian theory, the ancestor of a *numaya* appeared at a specific locality by coming down from the sky, out of the sea, or from underground, generally in the

form of an animal, took off his animal mask, and became a person. The Thunderbird or his brother the gull, the Killer Whale, a sea monster, a grizzly bear, and a ghost chief appear in this role. (p. 42)

When the Kwakiutl hunted, an equality was established between the hunter and the actual and spiritual qualities of the animal they hunted. A certain ritual etiquette was observed by the hunters. The chiefs were the only real hunters of the tribe, because they embodied the spirits of the ancestors.

The Plains Indians of North America, because of their belief in the total harmony of the universe, also had a distinct respect for the animal. Any buffalo killed would have its heart left on the prairie as a sacrifice and as a symbol of the Indians' desire for the buffalo to prosper. Each person would receive a medicine animal at birth, a symbolic name of an animal that represented his or her character (Storm 1972).

## Developing Skills in Dealing with Cognitive Cultures and Intercultural Communication

The following list of suggestions is intended to stimulate your continued thinking about world views and values and thus, in a way, to extend some of the principles that were discussed into some further areas of application.

1. *Do as others do.* Whenever you are visiting another culture, try to observe the methods of respect toward symbols within the new culture. For example, if you are visiting a special shrine or some holy place, try to practice respect for the feelings of culture members toward their symbols.

2. *Develop self-awareness.* The ability to know yourself is truly helpful. Puzzling, demanding situations are the norm in intercultural communication. Understanding world view can provide tremendous insight into your own cultural background and the background of the host culture.

3. *Try to understand missing social cues.* When we go to another culture, familiar social cues are missing. In their absence, we can become confused, a disorientation especially augmented by extreme differences in world view. Realizing this principle and striving to keep ourselves learning new cues can be helpful.

4. *Do not assume that you know a world view.* This chapter may leave you with the impression that, because you know some of the categories of world view, you now know all there is to know about a particular culture. Cultural belief systems are very complex, so do not assume that you have a handle on a new culture's belief system. Instead, keep asking questions, observing, and listening.

5. *Discover when to use formal and informal modes.* Almost every culture has cues that relate to those times when, according to the belief systems, you are supposed to behave formally. Other times, it seems everyone is a lot different, somehow more relaxed. The difference may be one of formality and informality. After a while, you will find yourself easily conforming to the role-switching situations.

Cognitive culture, or underlying dimensions by which people perceive self and others and by which they process information, is a pioneering metaphor to explain intercultural phenomena. Monochronic-polychronic dimensions of culture involve singular or simultaneous time processing. High- and low-context cultures refer to expected information and meanings inherent in the situation or how much is expected to be articulated. Hofstede's work identifying four factors underlying culture explains a great deal of communication behavior. World view is a significant element of culture and represents the means by which cultures organize their world and their place in the universe. Cultural world view compels practices, rituals, attitudes, and communication behaviors.

The chapter contains data on elements of cultural world view. Those elements include shame and guilt, task and people, sacred and secular cultures, role of dead to living, nature of humankind, humans and nature, doing and being cultures, life cycle, and fatalism. The chapter also describes systems of cultural world view and the concept of personal communication world view.

Cultural values were discussed. Many values revolve around relationships with family, friends, and associates. Attitudes and values with respect to the elderly, parents, ancestors, others, self, society, the land, and animals were examined.

Each dimension said to underlie culture has consequences for explaining intercultural communication. Sometimes these dimensions are useful for explaining the perception of difference in the first contact with a person or group. How the other person thinks or processes information becomes an assessment of similarity or difference, as our model indicates. A second consequence for intercultural communication is how underlying cultural dimensions explain communicator style differences. As the third culture adjustment takes place and individuals seek to enact communication accommodation strategies, style differences appear at this level, too, and thus explain why people relate to each other differently.

**Exercises**

1. Interview several people to assess more about world view. For instance, ask five people about their feelings about luck or owning personal property or about their views of the past. There is certainly much more to world view than these items imply, but the responses you receive may help you to understand more of how people view themselves in relation to forces in the universe as we perceive them.

2. If you have seen *Star Wars* or any of its sequels, then do an analysis of the world view of the main characters. (Also, you can read the book if you have not seen the movie.) For instance, what is Darth Vader's world view? Luke Skywalker? Han Solo? C3PO? What are their respective values?

3. Try to secure a copy of precinct voting records in your area. Are the patterns of voting different or similar among various precincts? Are any patterns of voting related to residence? How? Do these suggest values?

4. In what way do you and your friends use M-P styles differently? Do you think you are a high- or low-context individual? What about your family? Discuss with friends or family these differences. Ask your professor in a class discussion or in private consultation how these cognitive factors influence your communication, relationships, and approach toward tasks.

# Understanding Intercultural Information

# Chapter 7

# Cultures of Linguistic Diversity

**Objectives**    After completing this chapter, you should be able to

1. Give examples of the significance of language for understanding culture

2. Describe the reciprocal influence of language on culture and culture on language

3. Demonstrate the workings of the Whorf and Bernstein hypotheses

4. Describe perceptual differences and attitudes people hold toward minorities and foreign speakers

5. Identify theories of why certain dialects suggest prestige

6. Identify the relationship between speech and employability

7. Identify ethnolinguistic theories of identification

8. Describe why ethnolinguistic categories are important for communication between cultures

Still another way to perceive cultural differences, according to our central model for the text, is our assessment of a person's culture or personal identity because of language or accented speech patterns. The importance of language as an indicator of culture is well illustrated in the numerous occurrences of our creating unintended meanings through our usage of language. For instance, an insurance company discovered that fires inadvertently occurred because warehouse employees acted carelessly around "empty" barrels of gasoline, although they previously had exercised great caution around "full" drums of gasoline. The terms *full* and *empty* seem to mask the real danger in working with gasoline drums—empty drums are extremely combustible, while full drums pose far less threat. Yet, empty drums seemed harmless, from the linguistic perception of that word to the workers. A story is told of a Christian Scientist who refused to take vitamins, since the recommender described them as "medicine." However, the same person gladly took the vitamins when he was told they were "food." Several years ago, Swedish citizens were embroiled in a controversy over the pronoun *ni*. This word was a term reserved for speaking to those of a lower social status. Apparently, some persons who were equal or superior in social status brought suit in court against those individuals who used *ni* toward them; the connotation of the word had evoked such strong images that it was almost literally a "fighting word" (Kluckhohn 1972).

Examples of linguistic misunderstanding could be dramatized by countless failures across cultural boundaries. During the 1976 presidential campaign, Jimmy Carter used the term *ethnic purity,* which evoked a round of strong criticism from the African American community in the United States. The actual meaning of words and phrases, as this example indicates, stems from our cultural experiences—in addition to the nuances of language. Blacks perceived the phrase as racist, an interpretation framed by that culture's experiences. Carter apologized and interpreted the phrase to mean the need to uphold ethnic heritage and customs and to prevent their being swallowed up by a dominant culture. Cultural experience with and connotations of the word *purity* overshadowed the meaning Carter apparently intended.

## The Interface of Language and Culture

Not only is language a part of culture, language shapes perceptions. Also, language usage is a function of the cultural context. The Whorf and Bernstein hypotheses suggest the active roles that language and social context play in determining our perceptions and also our behaviors.

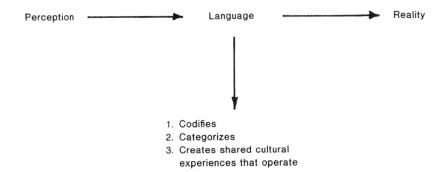

Figure 7.1 Model of
Whorf hypothesis.

1. Codifies
2. Categorizes
3. Creates shared cultural
   experiences that operate

Whorf Hypothesis

Many years ago, Benjamin Whorf wrote that language functions not only to report information but actually to shape our perceptions of reality, a point illustrated in figure 7.1. This idea revolutionized linguistic science—and intercultural communication specialists recognize today the continuing importance of language and culture on perceptions. One observer wrote that

> language plays a large and significant role in the totality of culture. Far from being a
> technique of communication, it is itself a way of directing the perceptions of its
> speakers and it provides for them habitual modes of analyzing experience into
> significant categories. And to the extent that languages differ markedly from each
> other, so should we expect to find significant and formidable barriers to cross-
> cultural communication and understanding. (Hoijer 1976, p. 116)

The term *linguistic relativity* applies to language as the shaper of reality (Whorf 1956). Since languages differ, linguistic communities differ in their perceptual experiences of the world around them. Language acts like a filter, molding perception. A slightly different idea, *linguistic determinism,* refers to Whorf's assumption that language determines thought, which is to say that higher levels of thought hinge on language (Dale 1972). Let us focus on linguistic relativity for the moment.

Clearly, language categorizes our world. Just as the biologist uses a scientific taxonomy to classify organisms, so the normal speaker uses language to classify reality. For example, one word may stand for an entire cluster of things, like the word *animal,* which refers to an entire class. You may already realize that colors are categorized differently in different languages. What you may not realize is that the native speaker's actual perception of the colors is influenced by this categorization process. For example, English contains seven basic colors on a type of color spectrum ranging from red on one end of the spectrum to violet at the other end. When this spectrum is laid end to end and compared linguistically with two tribal languages, the Shona and the Basa, the result is that the Shona language has four words and the Basa language has only two words for the spectrum, as illustrated in figure 7.2 (Gleason 1961). Undoubtedly, few people would argue that the Basa tribe sees nothing but "hui" (the bluish end) and

English

| Violet | Indigo | Blue | Green | Yellow | Orange | Red |
|---|---|---|---|---|---|---|

Shona

| Cips$^w$uka | Citema | Cicena | Cirs$^w$ka |
|---|---|---|---|

Basa

| Hui | Ziza |
|---|---|

**Figure 7.2**
Color spectra for English, Shona, and Basa.

Language, like music, is said to be inherently pleasant or unpleasant. The test of pleasant sound may be found in cultural norms, too.
(Photo by ACU student media.)

"ziza" (the reddish end). Of course, they can see the physical color (language does not change the retina), but Whorf's theory suggests that the language classification forces a category system that alters our perceptions where shades of difference become relatively unimportant.

Various anecdotal sources also underscore this point between language and cultural thought and activity. In English, the word *snow* is a category for all types of snow, although we can use phrases to describe variations, such as "fluffy snow," "wet snow," and so on. In Eskimo languages, however, no one word is sufficient, and some claim that there are some twenty-five different words for snow. In Brazil, scores of words exist for coffee. Kluckhohn (1972) reported that Arabic contains numerous words for a camel and its parts. The languages of certain Native Americans, such as the Sioux, do not have grammatical structure for past and future tenses.

These examples, and for that matter the entire Whorfian theory, do not imply unequivocally that people of one culture cannot think of objects for which another culture has plentiful vocabulary, like the camel parts. The fact is not that we cannot, but that we do not. That we do not think of such specificity may mean that such matters are unimportant or irrelevant to our life-styles. As figure 7.2 illustrates, language categorizes our experiences, almost without our full awareness. If we were to describe our experiences in linguistic terms, the very act of description would then reinforce the initial mental implant of the experience. For instance, how would you describe this text when you go to the library? Do you call it a book? A pamphlet? A text? A volume? Your perception of this "thing" is a perception partly influenced by your culture—whether you are a college student or a professional person—by your experience with books and by your language, which tells you what it is. You perceive the book partly by what you call it (a book is usually "better" than a pamphlet, for instance), and you name it based on how you perceive it. Every time you describe the book, you reinforce the very linguistic concept of book. Since other people in your culture also reinforce the use of the term book, then language and its perceived meanings become culturally shared. That is one reason why many cultural members share similar perceptions.

## Bernstein Hypothesis

It is obvious that humans usually adapt their speech to the social context. For instance, as you pass a friend in a corridor, the constraints of the social situation act selectively on your speech with the friend. This momentary social structure may cause you to speak to your friend in a code familiar to both of you: quips, phrases, single words, and interrupted sentences are understood because you know the other person and his/her meanings. An outsider listening to your conversation may not share your mutual experience and consequently may not understand this jargon. This common experience, though, has important scientific underpinnings, a relationship Basil Bernstein (1966) once described:

> Speech . . . is constrained by the circumstances of the moment, by the dictate of a local social relation, and so symbolizes not what can be done, but what *is* done with different degrees of frequency. Speech indicates which options at the structural and vocabulary level are taken up. Between language in the sense defined and speech is social structure. (p. 428)

Bernstein's conceptual explanation of dyadic social relations expands to include a broader social structure. Once we think of social structure as not only momentary social context but as a culture, microculture, or social system, then speech, communication behavior, or linguistic code result from the cultural contact. A graphic representation of Bernstein's hypothesis emphasizes

Whorf indicated that our linguistic categories influence our perception of reality.

the mediating nature of social structure. We actually convert a potential reservoir of language into speech behavior, or what is actually said, and the model that follows illustrates that principle:

| *Language* | *Social Structure* | *Communication Behavior* |
|---|---|---|
| 1. Lexicon (vocabulary) | 1. Social context | 1. Restricted code |
| 2. Syntax (word relations) | 2. Culture, subculture, social system | 2. Elaborated code |

In other words, what we say and how we say it comes directly from our perception of the cultural climate in which we find ourselves.

Given a closed group or a larger cultural context, speech, or what is said, emerges in one of two codes: restricted or elaborated. The *restricted code* involves message transmission understood by the people in a networking culture, highly predictable, and approaching redundancy. Both the vocabulary and the structure are drawn from a narrow range. As Bernstein (1966) explained:

> The speech is played out against a backdrop of assumptions common to the speakers, against a set of closely shared interests and identifications, against a system of shared expectations; in short, it presupposes a local cultural identity, which reduces the need for the speakers to elaborate their intent verbally and to make it explicit. (pp. 433–34)

Restricted codes, then, are like jargon (argot) or "shorthand speech" in which the speaker is almost telegraphic. The earlier example indicated close friends often make brief references to something, and yet each is reminded of a wealth of experiences or concepts. An outsider would have difficulty understanding you because of your shared experiences; you know what your friend means sometimes even before he or she finishes speaking. Even special communication found among professional groups represents a type of restricted code, such as medical or engineering terminology. Bernstein observed that lower-working-class children in Britain tended to use only a restricted code, while

A restricted code is often used within a culture that shares common meanings and experiences. This bell choir, who has performed throughout the United States, is a group of linguistically disadvantaged students in a special school program.

middle-class children used both elaborated and restricted codes. In his field research of a communal cult, Dodd (1975) found that a highly formalized restricted code played a major role in strengthening a counterculture's norms and self-image. Restricted code communication also provided common ground for members from divergent backgrounds so that they could talk about the same things in meaningful ways. Restricted codes also arise in such closed communities as prisons, military units, gangs, clubs, and families.

*Elaborated codes* involve messages that are low in prediction. Hence, the speaker must employ verbal elaboration to communicate effectively. Since we cannot anticipate what is actually said, the verbal channel dominates. This dominance contrasts with restricted codes, where new information and uniqueness emerge primarily through nonverbal and paralinguistic channels.

## Ethnolinguistic Variation

Several years ago, a U.S. Commission on Foreign Languages and International Studies noted that, in some foreign markets, cars with the interiors labeled "Body by Fisher" were advertised as having "Corpses by Fisher." When Pepsi was first introduced to Taiwan, the slogan "Come Alive" was translated into Chinese as a rather sacrilegious message: "Pepsi brings your ancestors back from the grave."

Such nuances of language remind us how language becomes a keyhole through which to view culture. However, that relationship extends beyond the confines of language and culture to include ethnolinguistic variations. This term refers to language used by a group of persons, called a linguistic community, and has unique features of pronunciation, vocabulary, or style usage. It includes dialect and accented speech. Many investigations have examined the existence and effect of dialectical differences.

> Empirical research has clearly established that listeners form differential attitudes toward speakers on the basis of dialectical characteristics of speakers' linguistic presentations. (Mulac and Rudd 1977)

> A large number of studies have now accrued suggesting that, in many cultures, there is a type of speech, peculiar to a given language community, that has more prestige than other varieties of that language. (Giles, Bourhis, Trudgill, and Lewis 1974)

> Considerable data have been accumulated in recent years on the way in which a person's dialect affects others' attitudes and perceptions of him. (Whitehead, Williams, Civikly, and Algino 1974)

Clearly, then, speech behavior is related to social groups and attitudes that others hold toward those groups. Additionally, speech patterns serve as a cue, causing listeners to assign certain characteristics to a speaker with one dialect or another.

One way people have explained attitudinal differences concerning ethnolinguistic variability has been to assess linguistic features of a particular dialect (such as its rate, melodic qualities, and other pronunciation characteristics) and attribute prestige or desirability because of its inherent pleasantness. For example, in Britain, speakers of the accented form of English known as Received Pronunciation are perceived as more competent and receive better attitudinal ratings than speakers with regional accented speech (Giles, Bourhis, Trudgill, and Lewis 1974). Listeners evaluate styles other than the Received Pronunciation style as less standard and more unpleasant. Does this sort of rating imply that some dialects are inherently pleasant and others inherently unpleasant?

**Inherent Value of Linguistic Features Theory**

Empirical evidence for the inherent value hypothesis is intriguing. In one study, French Canadians rated speakers of European-style French as more intelligent, ambitious, and likable than speakers of Canadian-style French; they also regarded their own French dialect as less aesthetically pleasing than European French. However, when a sample of Welsh respondents, totally unfamiliar with the language, listened to the two French dialects, they did not attribute more prestige or favorability to the European-style French speakers (Giles, Bourhis, Trudgill, and Lewis 1974). These neutral observers did not perceive inherently pleasing sounds between the dialects. Apparently, the linguistic cues provided in the two French dialects simply triggered perceptions of *status* differences based on cultural norms, not innate qualities of the dialects.

It seems that voice quality, as such, is not a universal gauge by which people judge dialects as pleasant or unpleasant, superior or inferior. For example, a nasal voice quality is associated with highly unpleasant Australian accents, although the same feature is considered pleasant to what is regarded as nice, normal British English. In the same way, guttural voice is a quality the working-class Norwich people consider unpleasant, although this same feature marks high-status German and Arabic accents (Giles, Bourhis, Trudgill, and Lewis 1974).

One other study illustrates the point again as we put the question of inherent qualities to the test. Giles, Bourhis, Trudgill, and Lewis (1974) selected forty-six British undergraduates, with no knowledge of Greek, to listen to two Greek dialects. The Athenian dialect is the prestigious form of Greek and is considered by native speakers to possess inherent pleasantness. The Cretan dialect of Greek produces stereotypic reactions among Greek respondents in that the Cretan speakers are perceived as less intelligent and sophisticated, but more amusing and tougher than Athenian speakers. Unknown to the respondents, the two audiotape versions of the two dialects were prose readings delivered by the same person, who simply performed bidialectically throughout the thirty-second recording. The results indicated that no significant differences between the two dialects occurred in terms of prestige, aesthetic quality, intelligence, toughness, amusement, and sophistication.

These linguistic studies cast doubt upon the inherent value hypothesis to explain prestige of one dialect over another. Apparently, dialectical differences produce stereotypic reactions—listeners judge speakers more by the associations of dialect with preconceived notions of what all dialectical speakers are like.

## Linguistic Norms Theory

Sociolinguists have proposed another explanation for the judgments people make about dialectical differences or accented speech. The linguistic norms hypothesis argues that pleasantness and prestige are best accounted for by *cultural norms* toward accented speech. The cultural norms advocating favorability toward a particular accented speech pattern, furthermore, are often products of historical development. Thus, prestige is linked to the social group status from which the dialect originated. For example, "had the English Court in the Middle Ages been established in another region of the country rather than the southeast, then it could be suggested that the national news would now be broadcast and televised in what is considered today a nonstandard, regional accent" (Giles, Bourhis, Trudgill, and Lewis 1974, p. 406).

Proponents of the linguistic norms hypothesis argue that linguistic communities simply have notions of what they like and dislike—and the outcome is clearly linked to cultural norms forged through history and circumstance.

A related issue to the linguistic norms hypothesis concerns the norms of a given linguistic community where speakers of that linguistic community prefer one dialect over another. In fact, we can create a "we-they" subcultural attitude through the use of language. For example, Miller (1975) found that English Canadian subjects responded more positively to a source described as English Canadian than to a source described as French Canadian. The attribution of these sources provided a cue strong enough to produce a feeling that English

Accented speech creates ethnic stereotyping. Intercultural communicators must guard against negative attributions from speech patterns alone. (Photo by Attitaya Indrakanhang.)

Canadians preferred one of their own dialect. In a field survey, Korinek (1976) asked southern listeners during the 1976 presidential campaign to evaluate such speakers as Jimmy Carter, Gerald Ford, Ronald Reagan, and Walter Cronkite. The results revealed a significant difference between Carter, who was evaluated as similar in speech and linguistically close to the listeners, and the other three (Ford, Regan, and Cronkite) who were described as sounding very different in speech characteristics and were rated as less interesting. These examples provide some data to suggest that sometimes groups evaluate speakers based upon their linguistic similarity or difference. One exception to this generalization, however, occurs when there is mobility away from one's regional association or some other reason to disassociate oneself from a region.

## Attributions toward Ethnolinguistic Variation

Most of us occasionally use unique speech markers to identify and judge people. Fast, slow, slurred, drawled—they all tell us something about the speaker. Those variations of linguistic patterns capture our attention and bind us to stereotypes associated with those speech forms. Social attitudes stem from ethnolinguistic input or at least the interpretation our perceptions provide. The process is complex, but the impact is unmistakable.

An individual from the South was overheard to say, "I don't know what everyone else thinks, I like Bill Clinton. I like how he sounds, and I trust him." This example illustrates the influence of speech upon listeners' attitudes. Speech behavior, in the form of accented speech, establishes a cue (steeped in recall and experience with speakers of the dialect in question), which in turn triggers an attitude based on a listener's perception of the accented speech. Those perceptions encompass many varied aspects of listener perceptions of speakers, the first of which is language and social status.

## Ethnolinguistics and Social Class

Several major efforts have studied the relationship between language and social stratification. The classic language research by William Labov (1966) in New York City and Roger Shuy and his colleagues (1967) in Detroit represented a working combination of sociological and linguistic research methods.

William Labov examined the relationship between language and social stratification in New York City, focusing on frequently occurring linguistic patterns. After categorizing subjects from "lower class" to "upper middle class," the researcher then varied their speaking situations to elicit different styles of speech for each situation, including casual, formal, interview, reading, and overall word lists. The results indicated a relationship among the social class of speakers, the variations in the speech situation, and the performance difference on several linguistic variables. Among other things, higher social-status respondents used fewer /d/-like sounds for the voiced "th" consonant as in "that," used more high vowels (generally /æ/) as in the words "bad," "bag," and "cash," and used fewer /t/-like sounds for the unvoiced "th" consonant as in "think" (see figure 7.3). Labov could detect social class from these specific linguistic variations (Williams 1972).

In another study, Roger Shuy used a random sample of approximately seven hundred residents in Detroit. Researchers attempted to evoke varying styles of speech, ranging from "careful" to "casual." The study provided a wide range of potential types of response data for the identification of linguistic variables. Results showed a correlation between social status of informants (index of occupation, education, and residence) and particular linguistic usages, particularly multiple negation ("He can't hit nobody"). Multiple negations increased

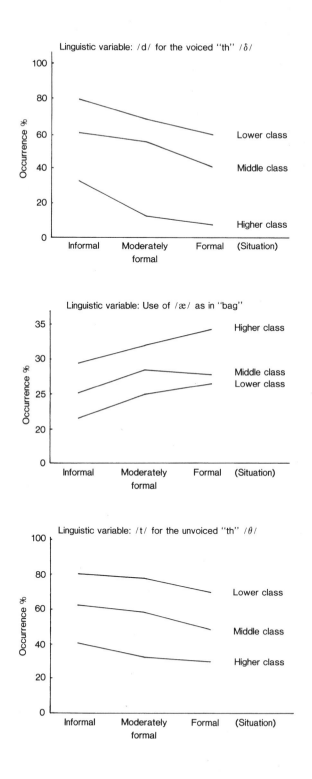

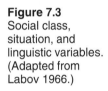

**Figure 7.3**
Social class, situation, and linguistic variables. (Adapted from Labov 1966.)

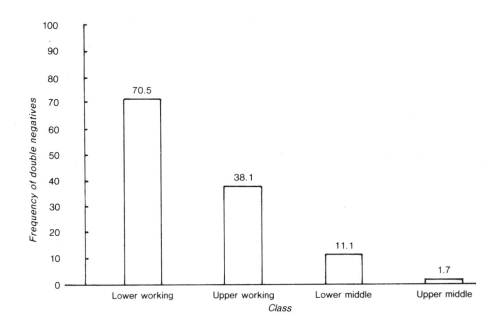

**Figure 7.4**
Social class
differences and
frequency of multiple
negations. (Adapted
from Shuy 1970.)

dramatically from 1.7 for upper-middle social status to 70.5 among the lower-class respondents, thus indicating that the percentage of multiple negations is significantly higher in lower-working-class than in upper-middle-class respondents (figure 7.4). Once again, social class was linked with linguistic usage.

Often, students are asked to alter their pronunciation and conform to the practice of the educated members of the community. They are expected to change from substandard speech to socially acceptable speech. Is linguistic change a useful goal? Or as Harms once asked, "Is it possible to tell who a person is from the way he or she talks?" An experiment involved nine speakers of low status, middle status, and high status (on the basis of education) taping a forty- to sixty-second recording of "content-free" speech. Listeners rated the speakers on status and credibility. The study revealed that speech is related to perceived status and credibility. This suggests that there are speech cues present that enable a listener to recognize the status of the speaker and to attribute credibility to the higher status speakers (Harms 1961).

## Ethnolinguistics and Impression Formation

In a study of stereotypes, Delia (1972) invited student volunteers at the University of Illinois to listen to a taped speech delivered in three different American dialects: general American, southern, and New England. After hearing the tapes, the students wrote their impressions of the speaker. Among other things, the results showed that when these general American listeners heard the southern or New England dialects (dialects usually different from their own), they not only correctly identified each region by its dialect but ascribed certain traits to the speaker, including their perception of the speaker's social role and status. Among other things, we apparently use language as a cue to form impressions.

Another study examined listeners' expectations concerning two dialects speaking for and against George Wallace (Delia 1975). People who had general American accents (University of Illinois students) listened to tapes of a general American and a southern speaker (actually one person varying his dialect), each giving a pro- and an anti-Wallace speech. When they heard the pro-Wallace speech by a speaker with a general American dialect, the respondents did not agree with the topic position, but they rated the speaker as having character. Similarly, they rated the southern anti-Wallace speaker to have high character. In other words, when speakers, perceived only by dialect, went against the norms stereotypically expected from speakers in that region, they were considered more credible. Again, dialect provides a cue for attitude formation.

Still other studies focused on the effect of dialect differences in other cultures. Miller (1975) compared the effect of dialect and ethnicity on communicator effectiveness, using English Canadians and French Canadians as the focal ethnic groups. Each group was exposed to English speakers using French Canadian and English Canadian dialects, speaking on two topics, one relevant to each group. After listening to the tapes, subjects completed questionnaires concerning their perceptions of the communication and the author of the communication. On both messages, people agreed more with the English Canadian dialect speaker. On the French topic, the English Canadian also was considered more competent, even though he was English. English Canadians tended to rate French Canadians in stereotypic fashion as poor, quiet, ignorant persons.

In another culture, Howard Giles (1973) was concerned with the question of prestigious accented speech in Britain. He used the four basic accented speeches of (1) Received Pronunciation (considered the nicest and thus most acceptable), (2) South Welsh, (3) Somerset, and (4) Birmingham in messages on capital punishment. Subjects heard four persuasive speeches, each using a different accented speech. The subjects had been pretested to determine their opinion on capital punishment. After the speeches, posttests determined any shifts. In rating the quality of the argument, subjects preferred the Received Pronunciation (the standard), but they were persuaded more by the nonstandard speech. Perhaps because the nonstandard speaker was associated with the lower class and was perceived as being more informed on crime, he was considered a more credible source. On another topic, Giles noted, the nonstandard speaker might not be as persuasive.

These studies suggest two major principles. First, a speaker's accented speech and dialect influence our attitudes toward the speaker. Second, speech forms outside the linguistic norms of the listener usually are evaluated negatively, except where the accented speech conveys the impression of experience with the topic or task at hand.

Several studies have assessed how teachers evaluate the speech of pupils, particularly in terms of the students' "sounding disadvantaged." In one study, tapes of 40 speech samples from fourth- and fifth-grade, African American and white children, males and females, sampled from low- and middle-income

**Ethnolinguistics and Perception of Children**

homes were evaluated. After listening to the children's responses to questions, teachers rated the children's speech along two dimensions: confidence-eagerness and ethnicity-nonstandardness. The children who hesitated a lot were perceived as less confident-eager. The children who used some nonstandardizations in English were perceived as ethnic and nonstandard. Also, teachers associated "sounding disadvantaged" or "low class" with perceiving a child as reticent, even more so when the child sounded ethnic or nonstandard in his or her language usage (Williams 1970).

Williams, Whitehead, and Miller (1971) carried this research further to assess the effects of ethnic stereotyping. Four videotapes of fifth- and sixth-grade male children, one each of an African American and a Mexican American child and two of Anglo children, showed a side view of the child assembling a plastic car. As the child worked, he described what he was doing, but observers saw only slight lip movement. Groups of undergraduate education majors viewed (1) an African American or Mexican American child whose nonstandard speech, unknown to the respondents, had been replaced by dubbing in the speech of a standard English-speaking child; (2) an African American or Mexican American child speaking nonstandard English; and (3) an Anglo child speaking standard English. Findings indicated that the videotape image, showing the child's ethnicity, affected ratings of the child's language in the direction of racial stereotyping. African American children were expected to sound more nonstandard and ethnic. The same was true for Mexican American children, and they were expected to be more reticent and nonconfident. It seems likely that this relationship also would affect teacher judgment of certain academic ability. These extended examples represent numerous research efforts that point to similar themes: ethnic children often are rated by ethnic labels, skin color, and teachers' academic expectations.

One exception to these negative evaluations comes from the work of Piche and his colleagues (1977). These researchers had preservice elementary teachers form a composite impression of individual children based on videotaped samples, selected social class information, and samples of children's written compositions. African American and white fourth-grade children, interviewed on videotape, used casual speech. These teachers viewed nonstandard English and white standard English and good and bad compositions allegedly written by the African Americans and whites. Neither the dialect and ethnicity nor the quality of the written compositions caused major perceptual differences. Aside from other conditions, the authors concluded that dialect does not always exert a straight-forward effect—it depends on the teacher's expectations.

Overall, however, research indicates that stereotypic impressions result primarily from perceived dialect, although in most studies even the same speaker merely switched accented speech in what is called bidialectical speech or using a matched guise technique. The effects toward the accented speaker may extend beyond an attitude toward the speaker to what is called the *Pygmalion effect.*

Pygmalion, a Greek mythological character, sculptured a woman so beautiful that he fell in love with his creation. His wishes and expectations concerning the sculpture came true when Venus made the woman real. Similarly, the expectation of an event can actually create a self-fulfilling prophecy and cause the event to become reality. A teacher's stereotypes, based solely on linguistic dialect cues, may create negative impressions that become self-fulfilling prophecies; that is, the teacher expects the child to perform poorly, and the child obliges.

Hopper and Williams (1973) extended the previous studies on the effects of accented speech on person-perception into the world of business. They were interested in how people tend to evaluate prospective employees on the basis of their speech. They used four ninety-second tapes, each consisting of four different speech types, including (1) standard English, (2) African American English, (3) Spanish-accented English, and (4) southern English. Employers evaluated the tapes and then indicated which speakers they would hire and their attitudes toward them. Results showed that the following characteristics were potentially of primary concern to the employers: (1) intelligence and competence, (2) cooperative spirit and dependability, (3) self-assurance, and (4) Anglo or non-Anglo. Remember, these factors were assessed from the voices of four speaker types. Specific elements relating to specific jobs were (1) competence and intelligence (these people were chosen as executives and supervisors) and (2) being relaxed and self-assured (chosen for clerical work). While cooperation and dependability did not appear as a major reason for hiring, ethnicity (perceived through the voice) had a slightly negative influence on hiring choices.

**Ethnolinguistics and Employability**

Stereotyping is a process by which we make sense of stimuli around us. By stereotyping, we categorize others, particularly out-groups. Stereotypes create expectancies about others and how they conform to our expectations. We create self-fulfilling prophecies. Ethnolinguistic variations activate stereotypes. For example, Susan, a twenty-two year old student, met an international student from England. Her first reaction was that this person must be incredibly intelligent because of the way he talked. In other words, all of her biases concerning the elitism of British pronunciation flooded her thinking. Later she discovered that he was like any of her other friends in many respects. She had simply acted on her stereotypes.

**Ethnolinguistic Variation and Intergroup Communication**

Many of us let language lead us into avoidance or sensitivity, indifference or sincere caring. A number of judgments, from social class to social attitudes, are rooted in ethnolinguistic variation.

The ethnolinguistic features promise bold implications for understanding, attribution, and intercultural listening. For example, Giles and Franklyn-Stokes (1989) provide prolific evidence concerning groups where we really remain at risk as far as cultural misunderstanding. Such groups include cancer patients, the bereaved, physically handicapped individuals (Emry and Wiseman 1987), the elderly, Native Americans, Hispanics, and African Americans. Their evidence, citing various scholars, shows how Anglo teachers question with nondirective methods designed to elicit specific responses. The Anglo students understand and respond accordingly. However, children from African American cultures are used to a more direct form of questioning to elicit the correct information. When teachers do not understand this phenomenon, ethnic-minority children can be seen as unresponsive, lacking understanding, and underachieving (Rubin 1986).

## Ethnolinguistic Identity

A great wealth of evidence indicates that people use ethnolinguistic speech for identification. Scholars conclude that language is a vital aspect of any ethnic group's identity. As a result, one's self-concept derives from how one sees himself/herself as a member of a particular group. Indeed, there is emotional value attached to that particular membership (Gudykunst, Ting-Toomey, Hall, Schmidt, 1989). Researchers label this property of the identity secured by emotional attachment to one's ethnic language *ethnolinguistic identity,* a label first applied by Beebe and Giles (1984).

Expanding this notion, Ting-Toomey (1989) indicates how the amount of confidence people have about their ethnolinguistic identity predicts their confidence toward out-group members. If they are secure about their ethnolinguistic identity, intergroup confidence prevails. However, insecurity about this ethnolinguistic connection leaves them less confident in dealing with out-group members.

Studies also indicate that members who feel good about self-identity, which is tied to ethnolinguistic identification, also indicate more self-awareness, self-knowledge, and self-acceptance. As a result, these individuals engage in active information seeking and thus are more likely to be information rich in a number of social situations. It seems that members who feel secure in their identities are not afraid of losing the personal self. Rather, out of a sense of "Who I am" and "Where I fit in my group," there is strength and confidence that lead to positive motivation. This is particularly evident in one's personal enabling and risk taking while reaching out to members of groups not from one's own ethnolinguistic identity.

Finally, Ting-Toomey goes on to indicate a number of other dynamics of intercultural capabilities concerning people who have this very high sense of ethnolinguistic identity. Those behaviors include the ability to take different roles, to be rhetorically sensitive, and to be highly self-monitoring. In short, these people are able to deal with relationships in the most positive of ways—including areas of relational, taboo topics. Their vulnerability comes about because of their confidence rooted in the self, and the self, in this case, is rooted in ethnolinguistic identity.

## Ethnolinguistic Vitality

Ethnolinguistic identity also hinges on an assumption that one's linguistic community is acceptable in a number of ways. The degree of prestige, acceptability, and importance attached to a group's language is known as *ethnolinguistic vitality.*

This term might sound unusual at first, but it makes sense. When I am faced with an ethnic or cultural group obviously different from my own, this encounter could be somewhat brief if I have the feeling that my ethnic or cultural group is being put down. Since my language is one of the most clear-cut surface ways that I am identified, it is quite easy to see how my confidence could suffer if my language is indeed somehow also disparaged.

I remember very well the story of Bill, who came from a rural coculture. On entering a rather large university, Bill was informed by his mass media professors that his rural accent was insufficient for radio and TV. No linguistic vitality here, Bill was told, so like any intercultural communicator, Bill adapted to a new set of expectations and thus met the norms of the more prestigious general American patterns of speech. When Bill went home for Thanksgiving, his somewhat uneducated mother literally would not let Bill in the house because when he knocked and called out, she did not recognize his voice. Her response? "If that's you, Bill, you better start talkin' right, boy, or you're not gettin' in this house." Even more tragic for Bill, is that he never finished college. The role expectations based on the two linguistic communities were too much for him to handle. If he could somehow have learned to be bicultural, perhaps the problem would have been solved, but the roles were too much for Bill to take.

People who attempt to identify with out-groups by using what is called in intercultural terminology *communication accommodation* (the term linguistic convergence is used by some researchers) generally find themselves appreciated by the group for whom the accommodation is intended. However, in-groups do not like out-groups to accommodate communication, or linguistically converge, when the in-group tries to maintain distinctiveness or perceives some malicious intent on the part of the out-group in communicating this way. If you find yourself accommodating in your communicating style, and it is perceived that convergence toward the other group has some hidden attempt or some hidden dimension, then you could be in trouble.

**Communication Accommodation**

Some fascinating studies have indicated the influence that occurs when communication accommodation takes place. Gudykunst, Ting-Toomey, Hall, and Schmidt (1989), for instance, cite evidence that when salespeople accommodate to the language of their customers they are more successful. Customers in banks accommodate to the clerk's language usage and seem to be more comfortable in that situation. A number of other studies indicate the same principle. When an individual perceives the situational norms—or the favorite way of talking for the in-group—interpersonal accommodation is more likely to take place. In the case of bilingual speakers, that accommodation takes place by speaking the more prestigious language for that situation. In the case of dialectical differences, speakers use the favored code for that particular situation. Incidentally, this process of using the code most appropriate for the situation is also called *code switching,* a frequent and usually successful process. Remember, people use communication accommodation for a number of reasons: personal agendas (such as social approval), maximizing information sharing, and heightening persuasion.

Ultimately, we need to use strategies by which we can be more effective in relating to out-groups and in-groups. One strategy, mentioned previously, is to use communication accommodation and thus to converge toward normative usage for any one situation. A second strategy comes from our review in chapter 6 of how intercultural communication misunderstanding occurs because of stereotypical thinking and poor attributions.

A third strategy is to explore the advantages of a second-language competence. A number of scholars make a fascinating case for expressing thoughts and feelings from a second-language perspective. For one thing, it seems obvious that we need to communicate in the "heart language" of the culture (heart language refers to the emotional attachments to one's native language). One Mexican American informant told me an important principle a few years ago on the topic of achievement phenomena among Mexican Americans:

> You must understand that Hispanics in Texas and throughout the Southwest fall into two groups. Those who want to adapt to the larger Anglo cultures, and their counterparts who choose not to have such motivation, have one major barrier. That barrier is that English does not convey the emotion and feeling level that we can feel in Spanish. The phrases in our language are too rich to be ignored. And so, if acculturation means we must lose our heart language, I choose not to acculturate.

These words were spoken by a person who was completing a master's degree, had an excellent executive job, and was a leader in the Hispanic community. She articulated a very important point: if we are to penetrate another culture and be effective, second-linguistic competence with that other culture is obviously important; otherwise, feelings, experiences, and subjective messages all are missed. Obviously, a person is disadvantaged without a second-language ability. In some ways it is tempting to think we can get by, especially since English is such a world language. However, people deeply appreciate the efforts we take to relate to their world—a world for them identified by their language.

A fourth way to relate to ethnolinguistic differences is to remember Ting-Toomey's (1985) findings that when people from collectivist cultures intend to engage effectively with people from individualistic cultures, the individualistic cultures place a higher premium on fluid, articulate, and information-laden messages because tolerance is low in those situations. Evidence indicates that for the Japanese—a clear example of a collectivist culture—second-language competence leads to a more personal set of relationships and a greater sense of perceived harmony with U.S. persons.

A fifth observation is the pressure exerted on ethnolinguistic members to abandon their minority-language use. The point is well made by a number of scholars that when ethnic groups have low political, social, and economic status and low demographic representation, at least compared to other groups in a community, and when support for their ethnic language is low, the pressure to lose their ethnicity and assimilate the out-group language is intense (Giles and Franklyn-Stokes 1989). The pressure is so great that ballots have been cast in some states requiring homogenous adherence to English as the official language of those states. No one can deny any lawmaker's desire to maintain unity, harmony, and singularity of purpose, and there is evidence to suggest that adherence to a single language can promise solidarity over time. However, what such political observers and policymakers may overlook is that language is so closely identified with personhood that minorities feel the policies are a slap in the face. Probably such policies were never intended that way, but ethnic language is the string that pulls the heart. In fact, we may have only begun to understand the deep-seated sociolinguistic creativity embedded in this issue.

Sixth and finally, evidence indicates fundamental differences among cultures and their beliefs about talk and silence. Empirical studies show that cultural groups can be placed on a kind of continuum, ranging from assertiveness and control of situations on one end, all the way to tolerance of silence on the other end. In one study, Caucasian Americans saw talk as important and enjoyable and saw themselves as initiating conversation. Furthermore, they were much more likely to take advantage of opportunities for talk than were the Chinese foreign students who were in the study. In short, Americans saw talk as a way of controlling a situation, but the Chinese seemed to use silence and were more tolerant of silence than were the Americans. If we can but learn to look for the dynamic ways that users incorporate amounts of information or silence, perhaps it would give us greater insight into the true feelings of communicators, thus enabling more effective communication.

## Developing Skills in Language and Culture

1. *Listen for unintentional meanings.* In intercultural contacts, users of a second language in this interaction may read unintended meanings into the word usages.

2. *Listen for emotional meanings.* A word understood denotatively by both parties nevertheless may carry strong emotional feelings that are culturally conditioned for one person but not for the other person. For example, the word *government* conjures images of political systems and institutions, power, and elections for North Americans. Yugoslavians view the same word as representing high position but, to a lesser extent, power, and few, if any, view the word with regard to elections, political systems, or institutions (Szalay 1974). Thus, a word that appears unequivocal may produce different images for the intercultural users of that word. We cannot assume that the word means the same thing to each person; we can only assume that words and phrases are culturally conditioned.

3. *Ask for clarification.* When someone speaks to you in a restricted code, ask for clarification. Invite the person to restate and amplify. The alternative, sometimes, is pretending you understood when, in fact, you did not.

4. *Offer clarification.* Our own cultural experiences make it unnecessary to elaborate in intracultural communication. Thus, we may unintentionally use a restricted code in intercultural contacts and produce confusion with conversational style and words that any of our intracultural friends might understand perfectly well. In intercultural communication, we should avoid slang, jargon, and personal references that exclude another person's experiences. Also, it may be helpful to avoid lavish words; try to be direct.

5. *Give others the benefit of a perceptual doubt.* Remember that not only our cultural experiences but our language can shape how we see things. The foreign national in our country or the host country national when we travel may categorize his or her world differently. Try to understand that world, and communicate as best you can within that person's framework.

6. *Meet people on their cognitive territory.* As the person who has studied intercultural communication, you must take the initiative in meeting people where they are cognitively. As you step into their cognitive territory, you will be more effective and broaden your self-insight.

7. *Learn greetings.* If you find yourself in a culture where the language difference suggests your learning a new language, then at least learn appropriate greetings. Of course, learn the entire language, but knowing how to greet others is imperative immediately.

8. *Realize that meanings are in people, not in words.* The dictionary does not really tell us everything about the meaning of words and phrases. The same word *bad* can mean something that is good or something that is awful, depending upon your cultural outlook and your use of language.

9. *Speak slowly.* If you are conversing with a person from another country, perhaps a visitor to this country, speak distinctly. Do not fall into the trap of compensating for the other person's broken English by speaking loudly. That only embarrasses you both.

10. *Do not give up.* When your attempts fail at language or at the larger considerations of intercultural communication, stay with the attempt.

11. *Learn when to be direct and indirect.* In Italy, you are expected to tell things to people in a straightforward manner; tell things as they seem to you. However, in Japan, people are concerned with saving face; you would rarely tell people something directly, especially if you know more than they about a particular matter. Rather, you would speak indirectly. In England or Scotland, one needs to be indirect also. One suggests but does not order or dictate (*Overseas Diplomacy* 1973).

---

**This Chapter in Perspective**    The Whorf hypothesis suggests the mediating effect of language on reality. Implications of an adapted Bernstein hypothesis indicate that salient cultural features of a culture and social structure predict communication behavior. Communication behavior, or speech, is of two types: (1) restricted codes involve narrow, jargon-like messages understood by other members of the subculture; (2) elaborated codes include messages that necessitate verbal elaboration of meaning. Implications for intercultural communicators include feedback, clarification, renewed understanding, and initiative in encoding messages with the other person's cognitive framework in mind.

In view of the literature, we can conclude that: (1) people judge others by their speech, (2) upward mobility and social aspirations influence whether people change their speech to the accepted norms, (3) general American speech is most accepted by the majority of the American culture, and (4) people should be aware of these prejudices and attempt to look beyond the surface.

In formal and informal speaking situations, we should not only realize our prejudices and try to understand more thoroughly various dialects, but also realize how our own dialect can affect others. This self-perception will help us to become better intercultural communicators. Also, through this knowledge of the effects of speech behavior, as teachers, researchers, or practitioners, our evaluations of others should become less narrow, and we should begin to see a total picture of others' communication behaviors. Finally, the chapter reviews ethnolinguistic theories affecting social attitudes and, more importantly, intergroup and interethnic communication.

**Exercises**

1. Can you think of other examples of language differences between you and English speakers from other countries? Scan the newspaper for examples of how language seems to affect culture and how culture affects language.

2. Interview someone from another English-speaking country (Canada, Nigeria, India). Make a list of familiar concepts, and find the corresponding word in that person's use of English. Are different English words used for the same concept? Why?

3. Make a list of as many American English words for money as you can (for example, bread, greenbacks, change, skin, bucks). Do you think other cultures have as many words for money? Do Americans have many words for kinship, friendship, or other interpersonal relationships?

4. By talking to some of your professors and by looking at some relevant books in the library, try to ascertain which dialect or accent of English your region speaks. Try to find out what attitudes prevail toward that accented speech pattern. Why do such attitudes exist? How are those attitudes changed? Should those attitudes be changed?

5. Talk to several area employers—both in business and in universities. Are there any discernible attitudes toward employment that stem from linguistic usage? What about a person who uses bad grammar?

6. The chapter noted that sometimes teachers inadvertently rate their pupils on linguistic grounds rather than on competence. Discuss how this occurs and how this can be prevented.

# Intercultural Communication and Nonverbal Messages

**Objectives**

After completing this chapter, you should be able to

1. Describe categories of kinesics

2. Identify oculesic movement and facial movement as indicators of emotion

3. Discuss greeting behaviors most often associated with nonverbal communication and their relation to cultures

4. Identify kinesic, proxemic, chronemic, and sensoric differences among cultures

5. Describe particular touching behaviors and their implication for intercultural communication

6. Identify the role of paralanguage in structuring meaning and interpersonal understanding

At a health clinic in downtown Los Angeles, a thin, stoop-shouldered, expectant mother made her way through the crowded waiting room to find the one remaining chair. Her obvious nervousness made the sound of her dropping a paper cup of coffee resound more like a cannon than a whoosh—at least to her overanxious ears—as the coffee blackened the tile floor. One of the other patients merely sighed and rolled her eyes, another mumbled something gruff under her breath, while a nurse standing by the counter released a rather loud "umph." Still others showed looks of disgust, amidst a mass of skewed mouths and arched eyebrows. Such scenes illustrate how actions can produce silent messages of approval or disapproval. The meanings we interpret from nonverbal behaviors are culturally conditioned—and significant. Our behavior often speaks louder than our words.

Adapting to cultures is not merely using the right verbal language and following procedures from the cultural system. Intercultural communication modifies nonverbal behavior in order to manage the perceptions interpreted by another person. Since interpretive schemas for nonverbal behaviors vary culturally, this area provides a rich and fertile topic for refining intercultural communication skills.

Nonverbal behavior is a significant area of communication study for at least three reasons, which are explained by Garner's (1989) analysis. First, nonverbal behavior *accounts for much of the meaning* we derive from conversations. One level of meaning is the actual stated message. Label this the *cognitive content.* It is the part we consciously process. We also have a feeling about another person and the conversation we just had. This feeling is called the *affective content.* For instance, your roommate is lying in bed as you enter the room. Your roommate says something about his day and mentions he is feeling fine. Later you may find that he was really depressed because of an earlier test and because of dating problems. The cognitive content of this encounter consists of what was said openly. The affective content is the conveyance of feeling. Mehrabian (1981) indicates that 93 percent of meaning in a conversation is conveyed nonverbally—38 percent through the voice and 55 percent through the face. Even conservative figures suggest 70 percent of meaning stems from nonverbal components. Nonverbal behavior is significant because it accounts for most of the feeling expressed in conversations.

## Overview to Nonverbal Intercultural Communication

## Significance of Nonverbal Communication

Second, nonverbal behavior is significant because it spontaneously *reflects the subconscious.* We normally attempt control over the words we say. Occasionally we may slip up, lose control over our words, and have to apologize, but usually some degree of control is there. However, with nonverbal behavior, we may leak our true feelings in other, more subtle, behaviors. In fact, even accomplished liars can be detected by subtle nonverbal cues they unknowingly emit. Hence, because we assume that nonverbal behavior is spontaneous and not easily manipulated, we tend to believe it, even if it contradicts the verbal (Garner 1989; Malandro and Barker 1983; Hickson and Stacks 1985).

A third reason that nonverbal communication is significant is that we *cannot not communicate.* Even if we choose silence, the nonverbal dimension of our communication is always present. Even if we remove ourselves *bodily* from the scene of interaction, our absence may speak loudly.

## Definition and Functions of Nonverbal Communication

Unfortunately, the phrase nonverbal communication is open to many interpretations. Do we mean the behavior or signal produced, or do we mean the interpretation of actions? Nonverbal signals are not isolated from verbal. As Mark Knapp (1980) states, "Generally, when people refer to nonverbal behavior they are talking about the signal(s) to which meaning will be attributed—not the process of attributing meaning. . . . The term nonverbal is commonly used to describe all human communication events that transcend spoken or written words. At the same time we should realize that these nonverbal events and behaviors can be interpreted through verbal symbols." (p. 3, 21)

Nonverbal communication serves several functions. First, nonverbal communication may *complement* a verbal message. If you smile and say, "Hi, how are you?," these behaviors complement each other.

Second, nonverbal behavior may *contradict* other messages. Breaking eye contact while saying, "Nice talking to you," contradicts a speaker's positive verbal message. Shrinking back and frowning while saying, "I love you" is another example of a nonverbal message contradicting a verbal message.

Third, a nonverbal message can *repeat* a verbal one. For example, a librarian says, "Let's be quiet" as he places the index finger to his lips. In our culture, the index finger to the lips is a nonverbal symbol of the need to be quiet. It will send a clear message without verbal utterance.

Fourth, nonverbal communication serves to *regulate* communication. It is the major means of controlling the flow of conversation between interactants. By head nods, eye contact, vocal inflection, and body leans, we can tell if it is our turn to enter a conversation.

A fifth function of nonverbal communication is to *substitute.* Nonverbal messages may substitute for verbal ones in certain settings. The small child may point to a toy instead of saying, "I want that." In your classroom, you may wave to a friend and point to a meeting place instead of yelling across a crowded room.

Nonverbal intercultural communication is rooted in cultural and social rules. (Photo by ACU student media.)

## Nonverbal Behavior as Cultural Rules

Nonverbal behavior is very much a culturally rule-governed communication system. Rules dictate all of our communication behaviors, but rules are especially evident in our nonverbal communication. The examples are countless but include greeting, leaving, politeness, entering a room, friendship expectation, and classroom behavior. Furthermore, the rules are governed by culture, and the rules and nonverbal behavior differ among cultures.

By looking at categories of nonverbal behavior we come to a better understanding of the many ways intercultural meanings are inferred.

## Kinesics: Our Body Language

The term *kinesics* refers to gestures, facial expressions, eye contact, body positions, body movement, and forms of greeting and their relation to communication. Certain kinds of body movements are physiological, such as yawning, stretching, and relaxing. Other kinesic patterns—staring, walking slumped over, raising a clenched fist, showing a victory sign—are personally and culturally conditioned. For instance, when you say, "Hello," you may use a greeting gesture such as the palm of your hand extended outward with the fingers pointed upward, in the manner of waving, moving the palm from side to side. As they say goodbye, North Americans place the palm of the right hand down, extend the fingers, and move the fingers up and down. In India, West Africa, and Central America, such a gesture would imply beckoning, as if we were calling a cab or asking someone to move toward us. The way we fold our arms, the direction of our body orientation (toward or away from the other person), the direction and manner of our eye contact, and our manner of walking and sitting in the presence of others are significant kinesic behaviors that differ culturally. Other people can quickly decide if we are angry or pleased with them, if they are members of our culture and share our nonverbal code.

In the intercultural setting, kinesic behaviors can trigger totally unintended responses. In Indonesia, for instance, it is common to enjoy conversation with a person in his or her house while sitting on the floor. As you sit, however, great care must be taken not to point the soles of your shoes or feet toward the other person. Such a behavior is offensive, for the gesture, no matter how innocently intended, indicates that you consider that person beneath you. In certain parts of India, one does not point the toes or the soles of the shoes in the direction of hanging wall pictures of certain deities. This behavior is taboo in that culture. One of the first objectives in intercultural communication is to understand and observe the other culture's kinesics.

Misuse or misunderstanding of kinesic communication behavior has enormous consequences. In a well-known example, during the cold war between the United States and the former Soviet Union, Nikita Khrushchev visited the United States, and as he emerged from the airplane, officials, news reporters, and other visitors greeted him cordially. In response, Khrushchev clasped his hands together and raised them above his shoulder. To television viewers and U.S. observers, the gesture appeared like a boxer raising clasped hands signaling victory. However, Khrushchev intended the gesture to represent a clasping of hands in friendship.

Consider the sometimes deleterious effects of unguarded kinesic behavior illustrated in the following example:

Several years ago, a popular American politician took a trip to Latin America. Upon his arrival at the airport, he emerged from the airplane, stood at the top of the loading ramp, and waved to the people awaiting his arrival. Someone shouted out, asking him how his trip was. He responded by flashing the common "OK" gesture. Shortly thereafter, he left the airplane and engaged in a short visit with a local political leader. Following that visit, he went to the major university in the area and delivered an address on behalf of the American people. During his talk, he emphasized that the United States was most interested in helping this neighboring country through economic aid that would help develop the economy and relieve the difficult economic surroundings of the poor. His speech, in fact his entire visit, was a disaster.

Why? Everything this gentleman did verbally was quite acceptable. But nearly everything he did nonverbally was wrong. To begin with, a photographer took a picture of our visitor just as he flashed the "OK" sign to the person who asked how his trip went. That picture appeared on the front page of the local newspaper. You may wonder, "What is so bad about that?" The gesture, which we use in the United States to signal "OK," is a most obscene gesture in this particular Latin American country.

After this "excellent start," our representative went to the university to give his speech, apparently unaware of the fact that this university had recently been a scene of violent protest against that government's policies. His choice of that place to speak was interpreted by the government as showing sympathy for the rioting students, but perceived by the students as an invasion of their territory by a friend of the government. Further, while our representative was presenting an excellent speech in English, concerning our interest in helping the poor people of that country, the speech was being translated for the audience by an interpreter in full military uniform. The interpreter was a clear symbol of the military dictatorship that was in control of the country at that time.

It is certainly not surprising that the intended goodwill visit of our representative had a contrary effect. This is an excellent example of what can happen when people are unaware of, or unconcerned with, their nonverbal behavior. (McCroskey 1972)

Some researchers classify kinesic research into three categories: prekinesics, microkinesics, and social kinesics. *Prekinesics* is concerned with the physiological aspects of bodily movements. Prekinesic research focuses on describing all bodily movements, regardless of their cultural meaning. This process of classification uses an elaborate taxonomy to accomplish this goal. (The fundamental unit of pure kinesic behavior, without any implication of attached meaning, is the kine.) In a sense, the value of prekinesic research is the same as any "pure" scientific investigation where the scientist examines something without specific regard to its application. Of course, some scientific discoveries were built on the foundations from pure research. Similarly, the immediate application of prekinesic findings may be reserved until later discoveries.

*Microkinesics* is concerned with the attribution of meaning to bodily motions, both intraculturally and interculturally. For instance, although prekinesic research indicates eleven discernible positions of the eyelid, microkinesic findings reveal that only a very few of these positions actually communicate distinct meanings. The study of prekinesics sorts and classifies individual kines, while microkinesics sorts and classifies individual kinemes—bodily motions that represent different meanings.

A third area of kinesic research is that of *social kinesics,* which concerns the social role and meaning that different bodily movements convey. Consequently, this area usually includes comparing kinesics between two cultures. For example, LaBarre (1976) noted that spitting in most Western cultures is a sign of disgust and displeasure, but for the Masai people of Africa spitting is a sign of affection. Among some traditional Native Americans, spitting can represent an act of kindness, as for example the medicine man spitting on a sick person to cure him.

Most often, intercultural communication interests center on microkinesics and social kinesics. In those areas, codes and meanings for communication take on their greatest significance.

**Gestures**

Gestures, or hand and arm movements, fall into several categories. As we discuss these various aspects of gestures, determine which ones you frequently use and how you use them. In the process, you may learn a lot about how gestures interact in intercultural communication.

*Adaptors.* Some of our gesturing behavior occurs primarily out of a physical bodily activity we must perform at the moment. For example, holding our hand over our mouth as we cough or sneeze is a North American cultural response to that bodily need. Shading our eyes with our hand in bright sunlight also represents an adapting type of gesture. Our hand and arm movements in opening a door also represent gestures that of necessity involve a set of arm and hand movements. In some ways, even these movements, which are physiological responses or skill oriented, are traced to cultural influence: some African cultures do not cover the mouth when coughing. Nervous habits go into the adaptor category, as well.

*Emblems.* Nonverbal emblems are gestures that have a relatively precise, clear referent and thus are culturally assigned some meaning. For instance, holding your index and middle fingers upward in a "V" represented the victory emblem during World War II. During the peace movement in the United States during the 1960s, the "V" sign became culturally accepted as a peace symbol. During the 1976 Olympics, the black civil rights movement used the raised fist as an emblematic symbol of black power and thereby increased self-awareness of African American culture.

*Illustrators.* Illustrative gestures serve to complement spoken words (Ekman and Friesen 1972). In pointing when we give directions to someone, we are illustrating the verbal message with a gesture, using perhaps the index finger to emphasize the direction. Sometimes a person's hand slashes through the air to accent some word or phrase. A speaker who uses the hands to "draw" a picture in the air also applies an illustrator. Other categories include

1. *Batons.* Illustrators that emphasize or accent a word or phrase (Example: bringing hand down on a key word)

2. *Directors.* Illustrators that point (Example: pointing with a finger)

3. *Ideographs.* Illustrators that sketch a direction of thought (Example: a speaker says, "I want to pursue this line of thought" and offers a sweeping arm gesture or raises a finger for a first point, second point, and so on)

4. *Kinetographs.* Illustrators that depict bodily action (Example: moving both arms as if you were jogging, thus depicting the idea of running as you converse)

5. *Pictograph.* Illustrators that "draw" a literal picture in the air (Example: using your fingers, hands, and arms to illustrate the shape of a football)

6. *Regulators.* Illustrators that depict pacing. Also, regulators such as eye contact and silence can indicate turn-taking (Example: snapping your fingers to coincide with a musical beat or the gesture "stop," thus regulating)

7. *Spatial.* Illustrators that depict spatial relationships (Example: a speaker says, "Imagine three groups of people," and then gestures to the left for group one, the middle for group two, and the right for group three, as if to help the listener to spatially define three distinct groups)

Gestures become especially revealing in ongoing conversation (Wolff and Gustein 1972). For instance, illustrators tend to increase with a speaker's increasing enthusiasm, and they also increase if it seems the listener does not understand. How many times have you observed people talking with a foreign national resort to using illustrators when language barriers appear?

Also, some studies show that, among North Americans, gestures reveal discrepancies in a speaker's words. When someone is lying, the hands and feet sometimes leak a message that tells us that something may be concealed. That mismatch between words and action also is evident in eye movement and facial expression (Ekman and Friesen 1972).

**Posture**

Like gestures, posture is a significant aspect of kinesic behavior. Although many people can describe posture when asked, it is not by any means universal, since posture differs with culture, personality, religion, occupation, social class, gender, age, health, and status (Sheflen 1964). Despite these differences, there are three basic behaviors in posture: (1) inclusive postures, (2) interpersonal postures, and (3) reflective postures.

Inclusive postures involve using the body to block off or separate groups or individuals. One type is the "bookend" gesture, in which group members form a circle, or extend their legs or arms, to close off their group from outsiders. For example, while someone may extend his or her legs "simply to stretch," that person often will extend the legs in such a way that they form a barrier to any people outside the group. Another type of inclusiveness is intervention, in which someone intervenes between individuals who are disputing or being distractive.

Interpersonal postures involve seating arrangements where two people sit face to face. If two people sit side by side to view a common object, their interpersonal posture is parallel and focused away from the other person. Sometimes, a person can be both interpersonal and parallel by splitting the body in half (the upper torso turned parallel, the lower torso turned interpersonal) and in this way include more members in a group.

Reflective postures involve repetition of one's posture by another. For example, often when two people sit across from each other in a group, one person will begin to reflect the posture of the person opposite. Also, when one person in a group shifts postures, others often follow this shift.

## Body Movement for Beginning and Ending Conversation

Body movement can also be used to detect the beginning and end of discussions or statements. According to Knapp, Hart, Friedrich, and Shulmen (1973), group members give the following clues when they want to change topics or want to speak:

1. Leaning forward 40 degrees

2. Breaking eye contact

3. Smiling

4. Major nodding movements

5. Change of posture (trunk or legs or both)

6. Foot contact with the floor

These cues can effectively and subtly alter communication. Consider the person who stands with arms crossed, looks constantly at a clock, taps the foot repeatedly, and breaks eye contact frequently. These signals usually mean it is time to go.

## Oculesics

Another aspect of kinesics that affects intercultural communication is oculesics, or eye behavior, which may account for a good deal of our meanings in communication. According to Ellsworth and Ludwig (1972), eye contact varies with personality and sex but can greatly influence credibility. They reported that dominant and socially poised individuals seem to have more eye contact than do submissive, socially anxious persons. They also noted that, when people feel included in a social situation, they tend to have more eye contact. The study also indicated that females use more eye contact overall than do males. Finally, Ellsworth and Ludwig revealed that a speaker who uses more eye contact seems more informal, more relaxed, and yet more authoritative. In other words, credibility increases with the use of eye contact, at least in the United States (Beebe 1974).

Cultural differences in oculesics indicate why intercultural communication is sometimes ineffective (Asante and Davis 1989). If a white teacher reprimands a young black male, for instance, and the student responds by maintaining a downward glance, rather than looking directly at the teacher, this behavior may anger the teacher (Yousef 1976). Members of certain segments of black culture reportedly cast their eyes downward as a sign of respect; in white culture, however, members expect direct eye contact as a sign of listening and showing respect for authority. Navaho Indians ascribe personal eye contact as a harsh way of indicating disapproval; thus, one does not meet the eyes.

Johnson (1976) observed that, among blacks, eye rolling expresses impudence and disapproval of a person in authority. Usually, the process begins by staring at the other person (though not an eye-to-eye stare) and moving the eyes quickly away from the other person. The eyelids are slightly lowered as the eyes move in a low arc. Furthermore, eye rolling occurs more frequently among black females than males. Perhaps this oculesic behavior may explain the common black phrase, "Don't look at me in that tone of voice."

Other eye movements also hold culturally distinct meanings. For example, eye winking among North Americans means, "I'm teasing about this," or under some conditions connotes flirting, especially with the opposite sex. When Nigerians wink at their children, this eye behavior signals the child to leave the room. A "friendly" wink may be perceived as an insult in India (Smutkupt and Barna 1976).

Like other kinesic signals, oculesic behaviors are culturally dependent for their meaning. To illustrate, consider the various meanings of a widening of the eyes (Condon 1976):

| Significance | Intention | Culture |
|---|---|---|
| Really! | Surprise, wonder | Dominant Anglo |
| I resent this | Anger | Chinese |
| I don't believe you | Challenge | French |
| I don't understand | Call for help | Hispanic |
| I'm innocent | Persuasion | Black American |

We can easily mistake a Hispanic child's plea for assistance, for example, as some other emotion, unless we understand cultural kinesics.

**Greetings**

Cultures have unique greeting kinemes that are rich in diversity. The American handshake, or the hug and a pat for more intimate acquaintances, finds parallels in various other cultural systems.* Several examples from LaBarre (1976) illustrate the diversity of greeting kinemes. For instance, Polynesian men greet by rubbing one another's back while embracing. An Ainu man, greeting his sister, "grasped her hands in his for a few seconds, suddenly released his hold, grasped her by both ears and gave the peculiar Ainu greeting cry; then they stroked one another down the face and shoulders." In Matavai, a formal greeting after a long separation involves abrasively scratching the head and temples of the other person with a shark's tooth, to the point of bleeding.

Handshaking represents a common greeting in North America, although shaking hands is inappropriate as a greeting in some cultures. Many Asians bow the head slightly and put the hands in front of the chest to show respect. Vietnamese men, for instance, do not shake hands with women or with older people, unless the old people or women offer their hands first. Also, two Vietnamese women do not shake hands.

---

*Among peoples of the United States, intricate patterns of greeting and leaving have developed, some of which are described in the late Eric Berne's works *Games People Play* and *What Do You Say After Hello.* Similar rhetorical modes are developed by Knapp, Hart, Friedrich, and Shulmen (1973).

The practice of waving to someone as a greeting is insulting as is slapping someone on the back to signify friendship, at least to the Vietnamese. In the first place, waving motions are used by adults to call little children, but little children do not call adults in this fashion. Similarly, backslapping is considered rude and especially insulting to women.

One must also consider the relationship of the person one greets. In many parts of Asia, for example, bowing occurs at more precipitous levels, depending on the relationship and the status of the other person—in general, the more status, the lower the bow. The same type of principle holds true for the order of greeting. In North America, one greets persons in a group by convenience and proximity to each person. However, in many parts of Africa and Asia, one must greet the head of a family or older persons first, then the younger ones (Hong 1976).

Clearly, greeting kinemes involve intricate behaviors, for misusing them creates a negative intercultural first impression that may be difficult to erase. Perhaps these examples will remind you to observe, ask, and even experiment to learn this important element of kinesics—the nonverbal greeting.

## Facial Expression

The human face comes in many shapes and sizes. Sometimes, we make judgments about other people based on facial features. However, we also infer what people "really" mean by their facial expressions Mehrabian (1981) claimed that 55 percent of our meanings are inferred from facial expression. Studies have indicated that we can detect emotions from facial expression.

In fact, several research studies have documented six universal emotions: sadness, happiness, disgust, anger, surprise, and fear. A seventh, contempt, appears headed for further research (Matsumoto, Wallbott, and Scherer 1989). Researchers typically examine facial expression captured by hidden cameras of people from different cultures who are watching stress-inducing films. Since the film watchers are unaware of being watched, their nonverbal reactions are spontaneous and uncensored. The mask is off. Most experts agree that different cultures exhibit the same basic facial responses.

However, when scientists are present as respondents watch these stress-inducing films a second time, some cultures more than others mask their true emotions. Ekman and Friesen (1972) first described this phenomenon as *display rules* when they observed Japanese hiding their negative expressions with a smile during the emotion-packed films.

Some emotions are more universally conveyed by facial expressions than others, according to St. Martin (1976): sadness, happiness, and disgust (contempt is also identified as disgust [Matsumoto, Wallbott, and Scherer 1989]). The following emotions have more diversity in their interpretation: anger, surprise, and fear (Knapp 1980).

All cultures do not reveal or perceive emotions exactly alike. For instance, Leathers (1986) describes how Germans are far more sensitive than Americans to facial disgust (distaste, disdain, and repugnance), but insensitive to sadness and specialized anger (rage, hate, annoyance). Many emotions

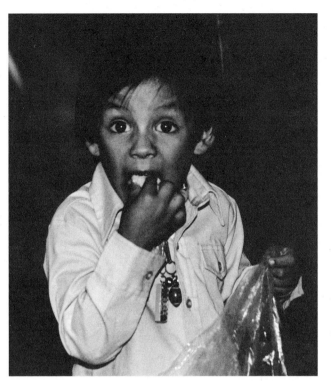

Through facial expressions, we convey our emotions, such as happiness and surprise.

are neurophysiological—for example, fear—and thus are universally and biologically shared. However, people learn display rules and learn how to manage emotions in culturally appropriate ways (Boucher 1974; Matsumoto, Wallbott, and Scherer 1989).

## Proxemics

Proxemics refers to the study of spatial relations. The study of proxemics includes not only fixed features of space (such as architecture and spacing of buildings), but semifixed features (such as seating arrangements and furniture arrangements) and dynamic space (use of personal space).

## Fixed Features of Space

Visitors from parts of the southwestern United States, who are used to wide open spaces, seem amazed at the closeness of residences in the northeast. In the southwestern and western United States, for instance, a person can drive on a highway for miles and never see a sign of people or dwellings, a rare occurrence in more populated sections of the United States. North Americans from the United States visiting a foreign country sometimes express surprise about the proximity of individual dwellings and the narrow roads. There is probably some truth to the observation that Americans use more space than nationals of many other countries. Intercultural communicators need to realize that cultures have alternative approaches to space and ways of using it.

The shapes of our buildings affect individuals. An elaborately structured building may, in a sense, communicate modernity because of its architectural uniqueness. Other buildings may give a perception of power and strength. Obviously, values, economic factors, and even religion play roles in determining architecture, but a culture's values (or the architect's values) determine the use of space.

The size of rooms is also a subject of psychological impact. A large office in the United States communicates status and perhaps power. The smaller the office, the less status appears connected with the office occupant. In an office complex, office staff who share space are perceived to have less status, higher status employees have their own corner or partitioned area, and the highest employees enjoy the most private, largest, plushest offices. This arrangement of status by space is expected in North America, but different cultures use and perceive room size differently. In some countries, high government officials may share an office with six or eight lesser employees in a fifteen-by-twenty-foot room. Within the United States, however, status differences among employees is often communicated by the structuring and use of the space provided for offices. This unspoken language of space is so strong that employment problems may arise when one person gets a larger office than someone else. For instance, in one large manufacturing firm in the United States, two corporate officers, on an equal level in the organization, received new offices. However, one office was six inches wider than the other, a fact that created a perception among office workers that management had sent a signal—the fellow with the larger office was being promoted. Although this message was inadvertently conveyed, this person actually was being chosen for a promotion; the space assignment told it all, even before any formal announcement (Hall 1973).

The origin of fixed, semifixed, and personal features of space began with cultural needs over territoriality. That concern sometimes translates into geographical and political boundary questions between cultures and also converts to the ways cultures use buildings and fixed features of space in screening behavior. Screening refers to our permanent and semipermanent use of our territory. For example, a fence marks a territory in much the same way we use hedges or survey posts. The message in these cases is clear, revealing private ownership and covertly saying, "Respect this boundary—this is mine."

Screening behavior is evident among Germans, who value privacy. In that culture, a closed door in an office represents expected behavior. In North America, a closed door can indicate that the person behind the door is hiding something. A manager often attempts to maintain an aura of openness by leaving the door open. When an employee enters the office and closes the door, other employees receive a message that something is secretive, depending upon how long the conference lasts and the facial expressions after the conference.

Semifixed features of space refer to spatial arrangements of movable objects within a room, such as furniture, accessories, screens and file cabinets. In the United States, a small, cluttered desk implies low status; a larger desk usually indicates higher status. However, the position of the desk and the arrangement of the chairs in a business office are of communicative importance as well. If the chairs in an office are directly in front of the occupant's desk and if the occupant does not come from behind the desk, a nonverbal tone of impersonal behavior may be perceived. As we might expect, again, the use of space and material objects is culture bound.

Semifixed features of space can be arranged to encourage face-to-face participation, called *sociopetal* arrangement according to E. T. Hall. Living areas in personal dwellings in North America and meeting rooms of various sorts normally encourage interpersonal communication because of the furniture arrangement. *Sociofugal* arrangements tend to diffuse communication since the arrangements lead conversation away from interpersonal relations to impersonal relations.* Many lecture arrangements, waiting rooms, and libraries are sociofugal.

Semifixed features of space differ interculturally. For example, in the evenings, Syrian men converse sitting across a room from each other, with the furniture arranged to facilitate this pattern. Certain cultural groups, like the Chinese, seem to prefer furniture located in side-by-side seating arrangements for personal communication, rather than sitting with direct eye contact. The following example vividly illustrates the semifixed features of proxemics and the importance of this feature of nonverbal communication:

In 1968, the majority of the American people were very concerned with getting peace talks started in Paris to seek a solution to the Vietnam war, but it seemed that it would take forever before the talks could begin. The problem centered around the seating of the various delegations for the peace conference and the shape of the table. The United States and South Vietnam each wanted two sides at the table; North Vietnam and the Viet Cong each wanted four sides. Four sides would put the Viet Cong on an equal status with the other three parties in the talks, something the North Vietnamese and Viet Cong insisted on, but that the United States and the South Vietnamese were unwilling to accept. After eight months and literally thousands of deaths and injuries on both sides, a compromise was reached whereby the North Vietnamese and the Viet Cong could interpret the table settled upon as four-sided while the United States and South Vietnam could interpret it as two-sided. Almost anyone not directly involved in those negotiations would agree that the behavior of these parties was absurd. Nevertheless, this extreme sensitivity to the nonverbal communication of the shape of the table resulted in months of delay and thousands of deaths. The importance of nonverbal communication in this setting could hardly be overestimated. (Note: The table selected was round.) (McCroskey 1972)

*E. T. Hall (1973) highlighted the terms *sociopetal* and *sociofugal*.

**Chapter 8 Intercultural Communication and Nonverbal Messages**

At its root, spatial usage stems from a deep-seated concern over territoriality. For many years, scientists have explored how people feel about not only their cultural or national territory but also their personal territory, including personal space.

**Personal Space**

Use of space often focuses on variable space. Personal space refers to an individual's unconsciously structuring the microspace immediately surrounding the physical body. This space is not only culturally determined but results from varying relationships. That is, among North Americans, friends usually stand closer than strangers. Furthermore, Hall (1973) observed that space communicates and thus affects our intercultural relationships:

> The flow and shift of distance between people as they interact with each other is part and parcel of the communication process. The normal conversational distance between strangers illustrates how important are the dynamics of space interaction. If a person gets too close, the reaction is instantaneous and automatic—the other person backs up. And if he gets too close again, back we go again. I have observed an American backing up the entire length of a long corridor while a foreigner whom he considers pushy tries to catch up with him. This scene has been enacted thousands and thousands of times—one person trying to increase the distance in order to be at ease, while the other tries to decrease it for the same reason; neither one being aware of what was going on. (p. 180)

In Middle Eastern countries, being close enough to breathe on another person is proper. In fact, the breath is like one's spirit and life itself, so sharing your breath in close conversation is like sharing your spirit (Yousef and Briggs 1975). That many cultures stand closely in conversation explains why some U.S. government officials, field workers, and visitors return from the Middle East, southern Europe, or Latin America and say things like, "It's all right if you don't mind garlic breath in your face," or "It's fine once you get used to having your eyeglasses fogged up in conversation." Their complaints center around the close interpersonal distances normally maintained in these cultures.

Research on personal space reveals several patterns of interpersonal distance. For example, Rosegrant and McCroskey (1975) analyzed American black and white contacts and found that (1) males established greater interpersonal distance from males than they did from females, than females did from males, or than females did from females; (2) whites established greater interpersonal distance from blacks than they did from whites or than blacks did from whites; and (3) female blacks established closer distances than female whites or either black or white males. Whitsett (1974) also examined spatial distances between blacks and whites under controlled conditions. The subjects in his experiment were asked to interact first with a stimulus person of their own race and then with a stimulus person of the opposite race. The stimulus person (one black and then, for the other condition, one white) were instructed by the experimenter to maintain a constant position. A one-way mirror enabled

Personal space varies interculturally. Misunderstanding of personal zones creates a source of intercultural conflict. (Photo by Serene Goh.)

the experimenter to observe and record measures of dynamic space. His results showed that whites stood closest to the white stimulus person and blacks stood closest to the black stimulus person. Also, the blacks felt more comfortable in moving around, even changing their body orientation dramatically in conversing with other blacks, but not with whites. The subjects later explained that they "did not trust the whites" and thus felt uncomfortable in any personal space but head-on, face-to-face.

The reason for these phenomena relates to a smaller sense of territoriality—something like our personal body space, a kind of body bubble. Although the idea of personal space has no particularly startling value, for it may seem commonplace knowledge, it has enormous consequences. Applbaum (1973) reminds us that, when others enter our personal bubble, we react with nervousness, discomfort, defensiveness, and uncooperativeness. At the same time, we use body space to convey personal attitudes toward those whom we address. In general, we establish shorter distances with people with whom we seek approval (Rosenfeld 1965) and maintain greater communication distances from those about whom we feel negatively (Mehrabian 1969).

Personal space is culturally related. For example, North Americans tend to prefer greater distances between themselves and others than do Latin Americans, Arabs, and Greeks (Hall 1973). When these proxemic expectations are violated, embarrassment or even hostility can result. Comparing intraethnic proxemic stability with interethnic stability, Erickson (1975) concluded that, at least among the blacks and Polish Americans whom he studied, the intracultural communication produced far more proxemic stability (black with black, Polish American with Polish American) than in interethnic communication (black with

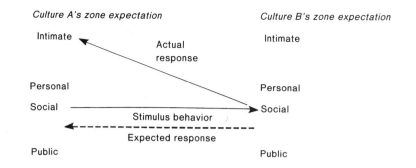

Culture A's zone expectation

Culture B's zone expectation

Intimate

Intimate

Actual
response

Personal

Personal

Social

Social

Stimulus behavior

Expected response

Public

Public

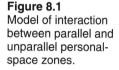

**Figure 8.1**
Model of interaction
between parallel and
unparallel personal-
space zones.

Polish American). In their videotaped analysis of dyads from seven countries, Remland, Jones, and Brinkman (1992) reported that the English use more space than the French or Italians. French and Italians in turn use significantly more space than the Irish and Scottish. It seems, therefore, that a comfort level exists intraculturally that lends itself to stability. When two persons with different ethnicity interact, they experience discomfort because they do not know the proxemic rules of the other person's subculture. Shuter (1990) calls for an increased understanding of intracultural patterns, a point made clear in the many examples of nonverbal differences.

Perhaps we can better understand why intercultural proxemic differences produce discomfort by discussing four zones of personal space. The *intimate* zone encompasses touching and a distance of up to eighteen inches and, for North Americans, is a zone reserved only for very close, intimate relationships and touching. The *personal* zone ranges from one and a half to three and a half feet and is used for confidentiality. The *social* zone is the normal conversational space for North Americans and includes space from about four to twelve feet. The *public* zone is used for talking across a room and for public speaking and includes distances of twelve feet and larger.

Our difficulty in intercultural communication comes from conversing in unexpected and different zones. For instance, North Americans usually converse in the personal and social zones. Many Middle Eastern and Latin American individuals, however, converse in North American intimate but Latin American personal zones. As a result, North Americans are perceived as distant and cold, and these other cultures are perceived as pushy.

These unexpected spatial violations are expressed in a model of interaction between personal space zones, as indicated in figure 8.1. When a culture A person expects to communicate within the social zone, then appropriate distance and action is initiated. In response, that person expects social distance to be reciprocated. However, if a culture B person expects to communicate within, say, an intimate zone, then this second person in actual response moves closer to establish what he or she now considers the proper distance for communication. Now, the culture B person expects A to reciprocate an action that does not occur.

Instead A moves back, B moves forward, and so on. In terms of this model, the principle is simple: Interaction between parallel personal space zones is comfortable, but interaction between unparallel personal space zones is uncomfortable.

Our understanding of time falls under a class of nonverbal communication called chronemics and is influenced by culture. Time is a potent force, communicating as powerfully as verbal language. In North America, for instance, lateness for a business appointment communicates lack of interest. A recent news report indicated that certain U.S. workers can be docked half a day's wages for being as little as one minute late, according to one labor contract.

**Chronemics: Our Use of Time**

In intercultural communication encounters, ours and the other person's concepts of time may influence our communication behavior. It is not unusual for village meetings in Africa to begin when everyone is ready. A forty-five minute wait may not be unusual for a business appointment in Latin America, even though such a period seems insulting to a North American. The ensuing conversation between the Latin American and the United States businessperson is likely to be evaluated negatively because of misunderstanding between the two cultural clocks.

In other research focusing on analysis of differential time conceptions, Horton (1976) noted that street time among blacks is mediated by culture, emotion, feeling, and situation. In some cases, researchers point to language as the cause of contrasting time conceptions, as in the case of the Sioux Indians, whose language lacks words dealing with time, such as *late* or *waiting* (Porter 1972). In other cases, differences may be a function of world view, economic motivation, outside contact with other cultures, need for achievement, or other factors.

North Americans tend to think of time as a road or long ribbon stretched out in a progressive linear path, having a beginning and an end. They also believe that this road has compartments, or segments, that should be kept discrete from one another. This compartmentalization of time is so distinct that the term *monochronic time* applies to many North Americans, a concept meaning that cultural members prefer doing one thing at a time. In contrast, many other cultures prefer operating with several people, ideas, or projects simultaneously, illustrating the concept of *polychronic time*. Observers sometimes condition us to mark Latin American differences with North Americans in terms of these categories, with the Latin Americans falling into the polychronic time category. Other observations lead us to believe that monochronic or polychronic time is not only cultural, but based on training, occupation, personality, and right- or left-brain orientation (see chapter 6).

Time can also be viewed in terms of cultural *synchrony* (Hall 1966). Cultural synchrony means the rhythms, movement, and timing of a culture. For instance, when walking on the streets of New York, we have to move in a faster-paced manner than we would in a rural town in Montana. East Africans move with a methodology quite apart from Germans. The rhythms themselves have a time dimension to them. Part of effective intercultural communication involves being in sync with those timed rhythms.

In general, North Americans feel that time is a commodity, something to be used, bought, wasted, saved, spent, and in other ways manipulated. By contrast, many cultures, including African, Latin American, and Southeast Asian, view time more flexibly. A number of Southeast Asian cultures view time cyclically rather than linearly, a contrast that may explain the North Vietnamese attitude during the United States conflict in Vietnam of, "We will wear you down." The Americans were used to a quick end to war because of their history and their attitudes toward time, but the enemy was accustomed to waiting scores of years, even centuries, for desired results.

One reason for these differing views of time is the difference that cultures maintain concerning *types* of times (Hall 1973). *Informal* time refers to loose calculations of time, such as "after a while," "later," and "some time ago." *Formal* time refers to exact points in time, such as "by 2:00 today," and "yesterday at 5:00"; in other words, more of a clock time. *Scientific* time refers to ultra-precise designations of time, such as laboratory timing of experiments. One of the most frequent intercultural communication breakdowns occurs when one cultural member operates on formal time and a member of a different culture operates from an informal time orientation. The one person shows up for a meeting at 2:00 P.M., and the other person arrives sometime in the afternoon, whenever circumstances allow, if at all. Our understanding of these different perceptual expectations can enormously reduce our stress level in intercultural communication.

**Sensorics: Sensory Perception in Intercultural Communication**

Sensorics indicate the communicative and perceptual functions of the human senses. Our senses can be considered instruments of functional nonverbal communication. For example, some people are often turned off to another culture because of the *smell* of foreign situations; one cultural group thinks the other has a somewhat obnoxious odor. Highlanders of New Guinea saturate their bodies with mud and pig grease and hardly ever bathe. Compare that situation with a Ghanaian, who typically bathes once or twice a day, and imagine the intercultural barriers between these two engendered by the one variable, smell. Scholars such as E. T. Hall increasingly consider the olfactory sense a highly significant feature of cultural transactions.

The sense of *taste* differs culturally, as any international traveler knows. *Color* and *texture* preferences are likewise visual features that are culturally appreciated. (Perhaps some of the initial conflicts during the 1960s' generation gap arose because of the color schemes in the clothing of a subculture.) *Auditory* preferences are also culturally influenced. Consider, for instance, widely divergent musical preferences among and within various countries. The notion of *thermal* sensory communication, in which we perceive others' body heat, may also be considered sensory perception. Some people actually seem to radiate more heat than others, and Hall (1966) has suggested that this factor may account for our descriptions of others as warm or cold personalities.

Our sensoric perceptions work together, interacting with the cultural context, to shape a total view of a culture and our intercultural contacts. One way to describe our intercultural reactions comes from the following formula:

$$\text{Degree of sensory difference} = \frac{\text{Importance} \times \text{Number of disliked sensory experiences}}{\text{Importance} \times \text{Number of liked sensory experiences}}$$

This formula illustrates that, if our disliked sensory experiences outweigh the liked ones, then the ratio of our feelings, weighted and added according to their importance, is high. The resulting ratio is the sense ratio difference. The higher the number, the greater the degree of sense ratio differences.

All of these contrasting differences bombard the senses simultaneously and account for some of the reasons that people experience culture shock. Overcoming sensoric nonverbal differences is an important part of intercultural adjustment.

Intercultural communication also involves cultural touching and its effects. The nature and importance of our use of touch is called haptics.

## Haptics: Our Use of Touch

### Factors Related to Haptics

A number of factors have been linked with haptic behavior. The most obvious area is gender differences where a number of studies conclude that female and mixed-gender dyads touch more than male dyads, except that males initiate touch more in mixed dyads.

Observations of touching during North American communication show that males avoid touching other males, but females express themselves in touching other females during conversation. If there is a link between haptic behavior and gender of the communicators, its roots lie in cultural roles. Males are inhibited from touching other males because of cultural taboos against homosexuality, though females are allowed flexibility in touching other females. However, cultural roles restrict females touching males, though males are often permitted greater flexibility in male-female communication. However, those general findings are mediated by age, situation, and culture.

### Intercultural Differences in Haptics

A body of observations suggests that some cultures are highly touch oriented, while others are nontouching cultures. For example, Arab, Jewish, eastern European, and Mediterranean cultures have been characterized as touching cultures, while Germans, English, and other white Anglo-Saxons are characterized as infrequent touchers (Mehrabian 1981; Sheflen 1972; Montagu 1971). However, these observations should be coupled with other findings. For instance, one empirical study compared German, Italian, and North American tactile displays in

Touch is a fundamental, universal need by which we communicate many of our interpersonal feelings and attitudes, as this village scene in Ghana illustrates.

an extensive field survey using trained observations in natural settings (Shuter 1977). Shuter's findings partially deny national stereotypes in that generalizations about contact and noncontact cultures partly depend on several factors, such as the gender of the interactants. For instance, males interacted farther apart and touched less in both Germany and the United States than in Italy. Italian males, however, stood closer and touched significantly more than Italian females. It also appears that Italian males interact nonverbally in ways considered appropriate only for German and American women. However, Shuter found that German females were more tactile than Italian women and that U.S. women showed as much tactility as Italian women.

When we find ourselves in a contrasting culture, we should initially observe, ask, and probe—and avoid operating on stereotypical information only. It is imperative that we become observers of nonverbal behaviors in a host country to avoid the barriers that only nonverbal behaviors can erect. Obviously, a toucher in a nontouching culture can be just as uncomfortable as a nontoucher in a touching culture.

First among several very important principles concerning haptics is that touch differs dramatically among cultures. For example, Latin American contact differs dramatically from British contact. Most of us have discovered what Hecht, Andersen, and Ribeau (1989) renamed from Hall as *contact* cultures and *distance* cultures. The contact cultures using more touch and less space include Latin America, Middle East, southern and eastern Europe. They prefer sensory involvement. In contrast, North Americans, Asians, and northern Europeans are considered low-contact cultures and express more of a distancing style, although Asians typically use a little more of this style than the other two.

**Paralinguistics: How We Say Things**

Paralanguage is that set of audible sounds that accompany oral language to augment its meaning. In other words, speech carries symbolic cues, not only through verbal and nonverbal cues, but also through vocal qualities to which various linguistic systems ascribe meaning. Again, Mehrabian (1981) reported that, under a situation of induced disagreement, where Americans communicated feelings, words accounted for 7 percent of the messages, paralanguage for 38 percent, and facial expressions for 55 percent of the total feelings communicated.

The following examples may clarify the importance of paralinguistic cues in intercultural communication (Taylor 1976, p. 36):

1. I'll see you tomorrow. (declarative statement of fact)

2. I'll see you tomorrow? (question)

3. I'll see you tomorrow! (excitement)

4. *I'll* see you tomorrow; I'll *see* you tomorrow; I'll see *you* tomorrow; I'll see you *tomorrow*. (contrast)

In this statement, the words alone do not carry the meaning. Rather, we interpret the feelings and emotions of the speaker by perceiving the variations of vocal quality. Furthermore, a number of variations in vocal quality, intensity, tone, and pitch height can alter the simple declarative statement of fact as illustrated in the examples that follow:

5. (matter-of-factly) I'll see you tomorrow.

6. (demandingly) I'll see you tomorrow.

7. (resignedly) I'll see you tomorrow.

8. (conspiratorially) I'll see you tomorrow.

9. (invitingly) I'll see you tomorrow.

For good or ill, it is precisely the paralinguistic features of language of which many learners of English remain unaware. Also, mistakes in paralinguistic features cue native speakers to develop negative attitudes toward a speaking style used by many learners of English as illustrated in the following example:

10. (evenly segmented, flat intonation, incomplete terminal contour) I will see you tomorrow.

Native speakers react defensively to this last utterance "since the foreign speaker sounds insistent and demanding" (Taylor 1976, p. 36).

In another way, perceptions we create about ourselves to listeners clearly develop from paralanguage. Dynamism in credibility largely stems from vocal expressiveness. Many people understand our emotional involvement and sensitivity from vocal and facial cues. In this way, our vocalics may reveal our feelings to others. For example, Thai people use silence to show respect, agreement, or even disagreement, depending upon how the silence is used (Smutkupt and Barna 1976). Also, speaking softly shows good manners and education. Consequently, many Thai feel that the people in the United States are angry because Americans speak more loudly than Thais.

## Meaning of Nonverbal Communication

Nonverbal messages may complement, contradict, repeat or accentuate, regulate, or substitute, the verbal message. How does an interpretation of nonverbal behaviors (kinesics, proxemics, chronemics, sensorics, haptics, and paralinguistics) work? How do we organize codes into behaviors with meanings? Each culture perceives nonverbal behaviors, converting them for communication value, along several dimensions—clusters of how we usually organize nonverbal messages.

Messages of *immediacy* refer to those nonverbal aspects of approach, accessibility, and openness at one end of a continuum and avoidance and distance at the other end. For example, high-immediacy behaviors in the United States include smiling, touching, eye contact, open body position, closer distances, and vocal animation. Along with these behaviors, immediacy also includes how we regulate privacy (Hecht, Andersen, and Ribeau 1989). As you might expect, high-contact cultures, by their very definition, also evaluate people as similar and more credible if they engage in immediacy behaviors.

Evidence also points to *status* and *power* as part of an interpretive cluster. That is, we use and interpret nonverbal messages to indicate status or power. A primary example is furniture arrangement and size in a large office—or even the large office itself. Consider the way we attempt to control others by leaning over people, touching in dominant ways, or taking up more space. Furthermore, we often interpret nonverbal messages around the dimension of *responsiveness.* Scholars such as Mehrabian use this term to indicate the way we react to people, things, and events. For instance, if we speed up our own speech rate, others interpret us as more responsive to a special need or even to the people around us. If we were to increase gestures or use more eye contact, these too would make us appear more responsive to our environment. Up to a point, this change in activity level makes a person appear more attractive and in some ways more credible.

A final interpretative aspect of nonverbal behavior is *metacommunication,* meaning a message about a message. Nonverbally, we communicate a message about a message, like the perceived message of empathy as we lean forward and touch while verbally giving bad news. During negative performance appraisals, for example, our tone of voice and use of eye contact may say, "You're OK; you'll make it." More than just a function of reinforcement, people look for the hidden messages, or the metacommunication, which serves as an important category for interpreting nonverbal meaning.

You may find some of the following skill suggestions helpful in improving non-verbal communication:

1. *Observe and discover specific kinesic behaviors for any one culture.* When people do things that puzzle you, ask them why they are acting in that manner.

2. *Avoid letting your emotions get the best of you.* In many cultures, people will touch you and bump you, and you may feel emotionally insecure or angry. Remember, some cultures simply do not think of private, personal body space. Sometimes, fifty Africans can crowd into the same amount of space that holds only twenty North Americans. The reason is that the Africans' personal space suffers no intrusion from crowding and touching.

3. *Notice spatial positions.* To figure out the appropriate interpersonal distance in an intercultural contact, plant yourself and avoid backing away. The other person will then stop at the culturally relevant distance.

4. *In practicing eye contact, observe what is appropriate within different contexts.* In some cultures, you may observe males maintaining eye contact, but a male and a female avoiding eye contact. Thus, you can learn how to respond.

5. *If you think you acted incorrectly, ask people, if it seems appropriate, what you did wrong.* Only by asking will you learn, because a host national normally will not volunteer information.

6. *Certain sensoric differences can be frustrating because our old social cues are removed.* To counteract this tendency, remind yourself that differences do not have a wrongness about them. By enthusiastically trying new foods and enjoying new sounds, for instance, you can create a pleasant feeling for yourself. In two words, be positive!

---

**This Chapter in Perspective**

Clearly, a significant element of intercultural communication is the silent language of nonverbal communication. Kinesics refers to gestures, posture, body movement, eye contact, facial expression, and greeting behaviors and their effects on communication.

Dimensions of space emit silent messages, especially as cultural members structure their interpersonal body space according to cultural norms. The study of proxemic behavior, particularly because of its obviousness and frequency, may be one of the most significant aspects of nonverbal communication.

Another element of nonverbal communication involves chronemics—our understanding of and use of time. Perceptual misunderstandings with regard to time create frequent intercultural communication breakdowns.

Understanding the relationship of familiar senses to unfamiliar sights, sounds, tastes, smells, and touches of a host culture leads the intercultural communicator to try to avoid overreaction and to probe deeper meanings of a new culture. The most evident way that the effects of a large sense ratio can be overcome is by further understanding of predictable stages of psychological intercultural distress in the process of culture shock.

This chapter also discusses cultural touching behaviors and their effects. Finally, the chapter briefly describes the nature of paralanguage.

In reality, nonverbal communication operates under incredibly complex rules. It is hoped that the basic concepts introduced in this chapter will be enough to prepare you for the meanings of nonverbal communication.

**Exercises**

1. Spend some time in the student center or some public place and make a list of the nonverbal communication behaviors you observe. What do these behaviors mean? When are they used?

2. With your list of nonverbal behaviors from exercise 1, go back another time and look at nonverbal communication in terms of interpersonal relationships. What type of oculesic patterns do you observe? What kind of relationships produce what types of proxemic behavior? What is the role of sex on nonverbal behaviors that you observe?

3. Interview some international students about haptics in their culture. What cultural practices differ from your own cultural practices? Ask the international students to describe their feelings when they first came to the United States and attempted to interact meaningfully in nonverbal ways. What did they do to adapt to the new culture? What principles does this suggest for you in adapting to intercultural acculturation?

**Chapter 9**

# Cultures of Networking and Information Flow

After completing this chapter, you should be able to

**Objectives**

1. Determine the effects of similarity/homophily on intercultural contact

2. Delineate basic dimensions of homophily

3. Give examples of how homophily enhances information flow

4. Use a measure of interpersonal homophily

5. Develop an explanation for interpersonal attraction

6. Identify elements of intercultural credibility

7. Apply strategies to manage credibility images in intercultural interactions

8. Define opinion leadership

9. Assess opinion leadership influence in network cultures

10. Identify information roles in social networks and their influence in intergroup interaction

One way to understand intercultural information is to consider the networks through which messages flow. There is a networking culture, which is a group by virtue of the information flow and relationship formed between people. Three important qualities of perception lead to these information groups: similarity, credibility, and opinion leadership.

## Communicator Similarity: Homophily

Many interpersonal relationships begin because we discover similarities that draw us toward another person; sometimes they end because we find differences that repel us. This propensity greatly affects our intercultural relationships, for we hang mental labels on others of "similar" or "different" and often act in a manner consistent with our evaluation.

Imagine for a moment an ambassador from Saudi Arabia talking with an ambassador from Sweden; a British agricultural extension representative attempting to persuade a Boran herdsman from Kenya; a middle-class Anglo selling furniture to urban ethnic group members; or an Anglo school teacher persuading a Mexican American community to adopt youth recreation programs. Each of these situations involves potential circumstances where understanding how information flows through personal networks is important.

A fundamental focus of our model in this text is how perceived differences can prevent clarity and foster mutual suspicion, distrust, and ambivalence. This perception of difference is a primary assumption about intercultural communication: the need to recognize differences and to adapt through communication. The term referring to difference between two people is *heterophily*. The degree of similarity is called *homophily*. The tendency to communicate with those similar to us is called the *homophily principle*. Furthermore, clusters of individuals in information sharing networks form around similarity as one dimension of communication relationship development.

## Appearance Homophily

In general, persons who have similar physical characteristics judge one another as similar. This feeling applies not only to generalized appearance, but also to looks, size, and even clothing. The problem of cultural stereotyping is partly related to this perceived factor. For instance, a North American student and an Iranian student see each other approaching in the hallway. Based solely on appearance, they may come to the mutual, though silent, conclusion, "This person

According to the homophily principle, we tend to interact with other individuals similar in social characteristics.

is different from me." In turn, that heterophily perception may precipitate little more than a greeting—or worse, hostility. Many people close their thinking at the point of appearance only.

We also judge others on our perceptions of age, education, residence, and other demographic features, ratings of similarity that we call background homophily. For instance, McCroskey, Richmond, and Daly (1975) found that perception of social class, economic situation, and social status highly influenced most of their respondents' judgments toward others. In many diversity culture studies, the gap between the higher and lower social classes is well known. In these cases information typically passes within a social class. In other words, homophily was so predominant that information did not "spill over" to outside groups differing in background homophily.

**Background Homophily**

Attitude homophily includes commonality of personal attitudes and opinions. These similarities are attractive to forming and maintaining friendships as Shuter (1990) implies.

**Attitude Homophily**

Another element of homophily is a perception of similarity in morality, sexual norms, ways of treating people, and other general values. Value homophily, sometimes referred to as morality homophily, requires an assessment of long-enduring judgments of good and bad conceptions. As an illustration, consider cultural values in Sweden's antispanking law, which prohibits parents from spanking their children. The reasons advanced for this law included norms of

**Value Homophily**

Our circle of friendships is highly conditioned by homophilous individuals, usually interpersonally attracted by task and social skills.

**Personality Homophily**

antiviolence and arguments that spanking would lead to child beating and abuse. Various microcultures disagreed, claiming that it stripped parents of their natural rights to correct their children by what they consider tried and proven methods. At its root, this clash focuses on values of protection on one hand and values of physical punishment as a means to a greater end on the other hand.

In addition to these other dimensions of homophily, people also perceive similarity or dissimilarity of personality. Research studies indicate that we attribute greater feelings of friendship and attraction to people we perceive as similar to us (Byrne 1961). Also, friends are more similar in personality than nonfriends (Berscheid and Walster 1978). Furthermore, there is a tendency to project onto our friends the very characteristics we lack (Beier, Rossi, and Garfield 1961).

These projected characteristics are often characteristics of a culturally ideal person. For example, males typically attribute more masculine interests to their friends than to themselves, but not to nonfriends. If a person is introverted and perceives a culturally ideal person to be extroverted, then he or she will typically project extroversion qualities on a friend. Therefore, if we are not similar to our friends, we mentally make them over in an image more compatible to our ideals.

Baldwin's (1991) research on Mexican American/Anglo dual cultural marriages supports the same point. Spouses engaged in idealized expectations; communication satisfaction was lowered when these ideals were shattered by reality.

Many times we obtain information from interpersonal networking cultures with daily reference group relationships—friends, family, work associates. The homophily principle explains the theory behind the influence and why we develop the networks we do. As a result of similarity, information is received more readily and persuasion occurs more frequently (Rogers 1983).

The Homophily Principle and Intercultural Communication

*Homophily information sharing.* The consequence of homophily is best described in the homophily principle, which is to say that we share information with similar persons. Consequently, communication is generally more effective than heterophilous communication (Rogers and Bhowmik 1971).

A number of examples reflect the homophily principle: political voting choices are usually discussed among people of similar age and education; farmers talk with other farmers perceived to have attitude and value homophily; Chicago inner-city dwellers talk about family planning with other inner-city dwellers of similar social status, age, marital status, and family size; Indian villagers discuss social questions with other villagers of similar caste, education, and farm size. Information rarely crosses social strata as the following research indicates:

> For example, in the Colombian villages, there was the tendency for informal interaction to occur between farmers of generally similar social status. Seldom did a small farmer initiate a discussion about an innovation with a very large landowner (*hacendado*); perhaps the small farmer thought the *hacendado* would be an inappropriate role model for his adoption behavior, or maybe the *hacendado* was socially inaccessible to the small peasant. The lines of communication in a peasant village seem to flow horizontally within social classes, rather than vertically between those of different social classes. (Rogers with Svenning 1969, p. 235) This principle is illustrated in figure 9.1.

The homophily principle is further illustrated by a study in Ghana (Dodd 1973), in which respondents were asked their sociometric choices for opinion leadership. African villagers in that study preferred opinion leaders who were homophilous in terms of their filial relationship, village residence, and religious membership. They preferred friends or relatives, someone in their home village, and someone of the same religious membership across widely variant topics.

*Homophily and persuasion.* Research indicates that homophily can facilitate persuasion. For instance, Berscheid (1966) found that communicators who were homophilous with their audience members in a laboratory setting responded by changing their attitudes toward a topic more often than under conditions of heterophily. The classic study by Marsh and Coleman (1954) found that farmers who adopt a large number of new farming practices typically had a high number of kinship relations (first cousins or closer), close friendships, and

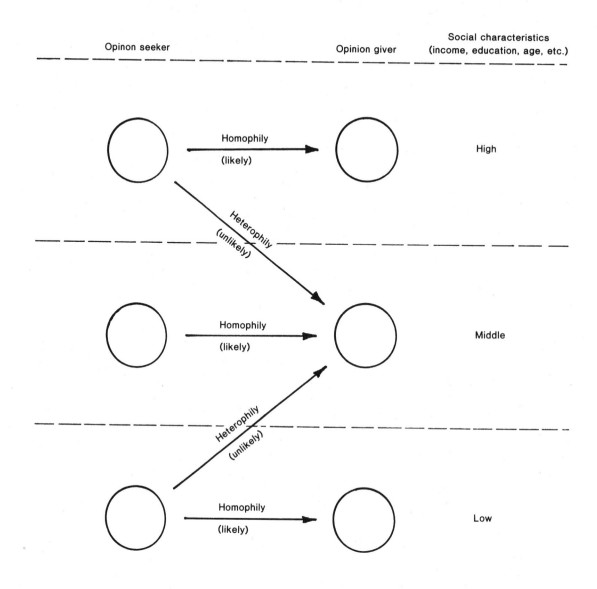

**Figure 9.1**
Homophily principle: people communicate and share information with individuals similar in social characteristics.

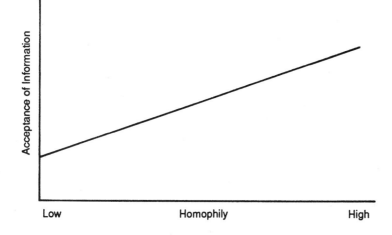

**Figure 9.2**
Acceptance of information increases corresponding to increases in homophilous relationships.

work ties with other families and individuals who likewise had adopted a high number of new farming practices. As homophily increases, there is a corresponding increase in information acceptance, thus depicting one part of networking cultures (figure 9.2).

This principle is further illustrated in a well-known scientific research effort in which researchers followed the prescribing of a new drug in a New England community among physicians practicing in the community. Not only did they discover the predominance of clique groups (figure 9.3), or what we are calling networking cultures, but also the extreme similarity among group members in age, ethnicity, religion, father's occupation, and specialty. Furthermore, adoption of the new drug followed lines of clique-group membership, so that clique groups, marked by their homophily, tended to adopt around the same time (Menzel and Katz 1955). These classic studies have been followed by network research built on these findings but focusing more on theory development. Network theory research confirms how information and influence are outcomes of networking cultures (Rogers 1983; Weimann 1989).

*Optimal heterophily.* There is a range of tolerable difference in information relationships called *optimal heterophily.* This concept clearly recognizes a simple fact: if two people are perfectly homophilous, then one would know little more information than the other. That makes good friendship, but neither knows more than the other. Problem! Solution? Seek a person heterophilous in knowledge, but homophilous enough in social characteristics to feel socially comfortable. For instance, suppose an Ethiopian villager was deciding upon a new type of seed for seasonal planting on the farm. Depending upon motivation, the farmer would need information from someone more knowledgeable than he and yet someone with whom he could identify. A scientist might be too

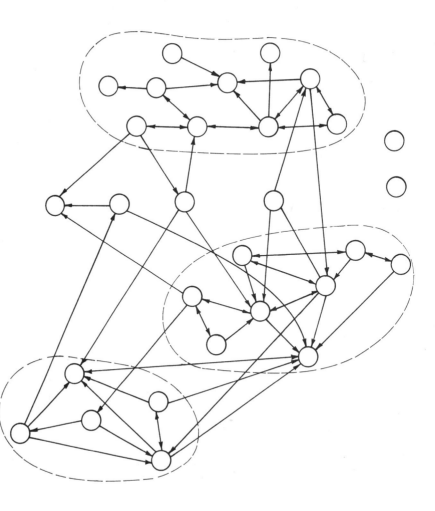

**Figure 9.3**
Illustration of new drug diffusion among New England physicians. The study showed who talked with whom on social occasions. Clique groups tended to adopt simultaneously.

heterophilous and a close relative too homophilous. Ideally, the farmer could discover someone with homophily in some characteristics but heterophily in knowledge. This situation calls for optimal heterophily.

So how do similarity and networking cultures affect me? I don't live in a village—or in another country. These principles are described for two reasons. First, social networks in many parts of the world are major social forces. It is difficult to fully comprehend the dynamics of many cultures without understanding this closeness and interpersonal bonding. The sense of bonding is particularly strong in collectivist cultures (Ting-Toomey 1989). In fact, perceptions of similarity form a major axis upon which social identity is built. Being identified with a significant group has enormous implications for self-worth. Even in individualistic cultures, many find strength in the homogeneity among the group membership. For this reason, we can better understand the network dynamics of unity among peer groups and friendship groups.

In traditional towns and villages, information tends to flow horizontally and informally among people with homophilous social characteristics, illustrated by this Guatemalan village.

Second, similarity theory explains our tendency to cluster around in-groups and to avoid out-groups. In-groups hold attraction and the promise of self-worth. The comfort-zone reflected here is common within cultures. As long as we remain in a cocoon of network similarity, we lose the power inherent in difference. We learn, grow, and develop when interaction includes some differences. The opposite breeds ethnocentrism, negative stereotypes, and bias. That is not to mention the possibility of incomplete or inaccurate data. The studies of *groupthink* remind us of the political, social, and economic disasters resulting from intolerance of difference.

**Measuring Homophily**

The easiest method for measuring homophily is the use of a scale, primarily focusing on interpersonal dimensions of perceived homophily (McCroskey, Richmond, and Daly 1975). This scale, shown in table 9.1, has high reliability and validity and continues to be useful for perceived homophily. Its use has been demonstrated across samples of high school, college, and adult populations, though only in the United States. By asking respondents for their attitudes toward a target individual, the higher the number (after appropriate reversal from 1 to 7 and 7 to 1 for opposite worded items) the greater the perceived homophily.

**Intercultural Credibility and Networking Cultures**

In addition to similarity-dissimilarity (homophily-heterophily), intercultural information is influenced by the perceived credibility of another person. To be effective, as A and B develop a successful third culture C between them, they must each feel believability or else motivation to use competence and communication adjustment may be missing.

A few years ago, Helen Sohns, a German nurse, worked among the Mataco Indians at the northernmost part of Argentina's border and described her attempts to introduce better birth delivery techniques. At first, the Indian women eyed her suspiciously, but gradually, after a series of special lessons for birth

**Table 9.1**   Scale for Perceived Homophily

With a person in mind, evaluate the similarity or difference between you and the person you have selected using the following evaluation items.

**Attitude Dimension**

| | | |
|---|---|---|
| Doesn't think like me: | 1 2 3 4 5 6 7 | :Thinks like me |
| *Behaves like me: | 1 2 3 4 5 6 7 | :Doesn't behave like me |
| *Similar to me: | 1 2 3 4 5 6 7 | :Different from me |
| Unlike me: | 1 2 3 4 5 6 7 | :Like me |

**Background Dimension**

| | | |
|---|---|---|
| *From social class similar to mine: | 1 2 3 4 5 6 7 | From social class :different from mine |
| Economic situation different from mine: | 1 2 3 4 5 6 7 | Economic situation :like mine |
| *Status like mine: | 1 2 3 4 5 6 7 | :Status different from mine |
| Background different from mine: | 1 2 3 4 5 6 7 | Background similar :to mine |

**Value Dimension**

| | | |
|---|---|---|
| Morals unlike mine: | 1 2 3 4 5 6 7 | :Morals like mine |
| Sexual attitudes unlike mine: | 1 2 3 4 5 6 7 | Sexual attitudes like :mine |
| *Shares my values | 1 2 3 4 5 6 7 | :Doesn't share my values |
| *Treats people as I do: | 1 2 3 4 5 6 7 | :Doesn't treat people as I do |

**Appearance Dimension**

| | | |
|---|---|---|
| *Looks similar to me: | 1 2 3 4 5 6 7 | :Looks different from me |
| Different size than I am: | 1 2 3 4 5 6 7 | :Same size I am |
| *Appearance like mine: | 1 2 3 4 5 6 7 | :Appearance unlike mine |
| Doesn't resemble me: | 1 2 3 4 5 6 7 | :Resembles me |

Source: McCroskey, Richmond, and Daly 1975.
*Scale for these items should be scored in reverse direction, 7 to 1.

attendants, her credibility as a trusted source increased. She particularly credited the following message, presented during her lessons, for some of her increased credibility:

> When you make bread, you need flour; when your husband makes a chair, he needs wood (most men here are carpenters). In the same way, woman in whose body a baby is growing needs enough food to form the baby's body. If she does not have enough food, the baby will be weak, and her own body will suffer and get weak. Have you noticed how the women's teeth go bad after having a baby? That is because the baby takes what it needs to form its bones, and the mother's body suffers. Now, your custom is that a woman who is expecting a baby must eat very little during the last three months so that the baby will be small. It is true that we do not want an enormously big baby that will cause difficulty in delivery, but we do want a strong baby. There are some foods that make a person fat, such as bread, noodles, sugar, semolina, rice, etc. It is right that an expectant mother should not eat too much of

these. But there are other foods which give a lot of strength and do not make a person fat, such as meat, fish, eggs, milk, fruit, and vegetables. A pregnant woman should eat plenty of these, so that the baby will be strong without being fat. (Sohns 1975, p. 314)

As a result of several efforts similar to this presentation, Sohns reported a greater sense of trust from the birth attendants in this traditional setting and found them calling upon her much more frequently and readily. What happened as a result of this speech that produced that heightened trust in this highly personal, intercultural communication situation? The villagers perceived trust, expertness, and a certain oneness with this nurse, or, as she went on to state, "They do not regard me as a rival now, but as a colleague."

This case identifies a common question when people are speaking or listening. How can I reduce my uncertainty or anxiety about this person? There is a dynamic perception on the part of listeners causing them to interpersonally believe or disbelieve, trust or mistrust, praise or blame. What are those qualities perceived between people? Credibility alters our relationships and impacts the information roles among networking cultures.

Credibility, or believability is a multidimensional concept (McCroskey 1966; Berlo, Lemert, and Mertz 1966; Applbaum and Anatol 1972; Tuppen 1974). The importance of these elements is in the underlying dimension of how people perceive one another—an obvious ingredient for cultures. As Dorothy Pennington (1989) states ". . . the phenomenon of interpersonal power and influence operates across cultural lines" (p. 261). Her analysis supports the multidimensional nature of power and influence on intercultural contexts. The first dimension of intercultural credibility is authority.

## Authority

Perceived authoritativeness does not indicate that the influential people in a network culture are authoritarian. Rather, the concept refers to knowledge and insight. Other key words are competence, qualified, informed, and expert. Authority itself is multidimensional, particularly encompassing two basic features: competence and power.

*Authority by competence.*   People in networks are attracted to or seek information from others partly because the people with whom they interact have perceived competency in relevant topic areas. Across cultures, the role of expert advice is well known. Skills involving reliability, relevancy, and high levels of information are but a few actions that can increase perceived competency.

*Authority by power.*   Power is associated with the qualities of influencing others. Like many social scientific constructs, it too is multidimensional, as classic work by French and Raven demonstrated (1959). The following factors comprise elements of power, which is the perceived ability of one person to *influence or control* another person.

*1. Positional power.*   This kind of power accrues when a person is selected to play a certain role. The cultural means of selection are varied ranging from voting to mana and magic. Those given power to rule are sometimes called *elites*. They are believed to be influential less because of information and more because of the positional role they play.

In a study of immigrants in Israel, Eisenstadt (1966) reported on the role of various power elites and their influence. His interviews with immigrants streaming into Israel reveal that the most effective communication comes from leadership sources.

| | |
|---|---|
| Formal, impersonal | 10 percent |
| Personal appeal from official to immigrant | 25 percent |
| Through leaders (elites) | 65 percent |

The 65 percent who found the leaders' communication to be most effective stressed the perceived authority and yet personableness of these informally powerful persons, illustrated by these statements:

> "We do not want only to hear orders from far away people, even if they are very wise and know everything. Our rabbis know that the best way is to gather all of us in the synagogue and to tell us about it and to explain it to us. Otherwise, we do not listen. . . ."
>
> "In our place, they (old leaders) were really very important and honored as they knew everything about our tradition, how to arrange things, the right ways to behave. But here it changes, it is otherwise. . . . They do not always understand this, and they cannot help us in getting our way here. That is why I became interested in the new (political) organizations and frequent these meetings. The organizers here are really important people and know how to advise you, and so some of us are going there." (Eisenstadt 1966, pp. 581, 584)

2. *Referent power.* Referent power refers to a person's ability to influence because of hero status or attractive features. Famous people or well-known entertainers illustrate this type of power.

3. *Reward and punishment power.* Reward and punishment power refers to the ability to mete out reward or punishment in ways that go beyond choice and free will. Individuals in relationships or roles who have such influence can be said to hold coercive power. The famous cult examples of David Koresh in Waco, Texas and Jim Jones in Jonestown, Guyana represent unfortunate negative examples of this power.

4. *Expert power.* By nature of a person's competency, power is available. Credentials are often said to be significant in this type of power. The idea involves possessing special talents or knowledge.

5. *Informational power.* Those who hold relevant or significant information also hold influence and persuasive ability over others. Fortunately, most of us can find information even if one's credentials are not expert. What is relevant and significant, of course, is culturally dependent.

## Trust

Trust, honesty, unselfishness, virtuousness, and character—these also create feelings of high credibility. During the cold war years of the 1950s, for example, the credibility gap between the United States and the former Soviet Union was a

Trust and coorientation are ingredients in credibility, leading to a wide range of interpersonal choices, from friends to national choices such as our political leaders.
(Photo by AP service.)

trust gap. Neither side could be certain that the other would not trigger a nuclear war. The tensions became so great that steps were taken to ease the tension that threatened a world holocaust. According to Windt (1973), for the Russians to be successful in gaining their concessions, Khrushchev needed to alter American's perception of his being a "communist devil" to one of his being a trustworthy source. During his visit to the United States in September of 1959, Khrushchev attempted to create credibility by creating a perception of trustworthiness. For instance, in the Camp David talks with President Eisenhower, he modified his position and thus gave Americans "one piece of evidence that Khrushchev was not as unreasonable as he had been portrayed" for he "contributed to a modification of our perceptions of him. He conveyed the shadow, if not the substance, of a reasonable politician, a man prepared to negotiate" (Windt 1973, p. 204). In contrast to a demagogue like Hitler, bent on world destruction,

> Khrushchev was entirely different. A preacher of peace and understanding, he looked more like a businessman than a politician. One reporter likened him to "any prosperous, hard-working, penny-pinching farmer who has reached the chairmanship of the local school board by sheer weight of his own toilsome success with the field." Furthermore, he had a sense of humor he displayed publicly and often turned on himself. His wife, Nina Petrovna, added to his image. No Mata Hari she, but rather a kind and gentle-looking matron who moved another American reporter to write: "There was the feeling that anyone who had the good sense to marry her, stay married to her, and bring her over here couldn't be all villain, no matter what he was doing during Stalin's regime." (Windt 1973, p. 208)

> In this way, Khrushchev skillfully replaced the devil image with that of a trusted politician, or as Windt continued, "His agile and human responses to situations conveyed to the American people a leader who broke the mold of their stereotyped dictator" (p. 208).

In other examples, President Jimmy Carter's successful peace negotiation during the Camp David talks in 1978 between Prime Minister Begin of Israel and President Sadat of Egypt stressed trust and sincerity. Carter's respect for both leaders, his high expectations, and his encouraging an atmosphere of ultimate trust lead to the historic settlement. It is unlikely that such success would have occurred had President Carter held ethnocentric attitudes, mistrust, or lack of respect toward either of the other men. In sharp contrast, the Beijing massacre of June 1989 revealed little or no trust, only coercive power. The deathly aroma of powder-burned, lifeless bodies testifies to the ill effects of credibility gone sour.

The first Rodney King trial of 1992 in which four Los Angeles police officers were tried and acquitted for beating black motorist Rodney King, lead to extraordinary riots in Los Angeles. The lack of trust in particular and low credibility overall in the judicial system was a major factor in this situation.

## Coorientation

According to Tuppen (1974), another factor of communicator credibility is *coorientation,* a perception of oneness or commonality. People judge other people by their value systems, group memberships, likability, and personal goals and quickly form attitudes based solely on those characteristics. One of the goals in intercultural communication is to give your cocommunicator the perception of wanting the same things, or in other words, to establish coorientation. The German nurse's communication, as noted earlier, clearly sought to establish identification with the villagers, as if to say, "We truly want the same things—we have a common goal."

Consider, for instance, Indonesian President Achmed Sukarno's speech to the United Nations in 1970, in which he clearly allied himself with a prevailing theme at that time of rule by the will of the people in the third world.

> Today, it is President Sukarno who addresses you. But more than that, though, it is a man. Sukarno, an Indonesian, a husband, a father, a member of the human family. I speak to you on behalf of my people, those ninety-two million people of a distant and wide archipelago, those ninety-two million who have lived a life of struggle and sacrifice, those ninety-two million people who have built a State upon the ruins of an empire. (Prosser 1973, p. 165)

One of the crucial mistakes of third world leaders of a decade or two ago may well have been their failure to establish a perceived similarity between themselves and their people. In not coorienting themselves with their people, leaders of nations can suffer dire consequences, as Prosser (1973) wrote:

> Among the four charismatic leaders whom Lacouture treats, Bourguiba, Nasser, Nkrumah, and Sihanouk, all were masters of propaganda and public relations. Still only Bourguiba remained in power in mid-1972. Sihanouk's "government by

laughter" fell because he was so insensitive to his inability to communicate effectively with his followers that he, like Nkrumah, dared to leave his country, opening himself to a bloodless coup. (p. 166)

Few of us are in a position in which a government would topple so we fail to use coorientation concerns. However, these illustrations should heighten our awareness of the importance of commonality and empathy in our various intercultural relationships.

In a perceptive research article dealing with political communicator credibility, Winn (1978) called attention to a fact of political ethos that applies to intercultural credibility. Blending historical forces, Gallup Poll findings, and a factor analysis of the Carter-Ford presidential debates of 1976, Winn concluded that credibility depends upon rhythms of history. Apparently, for a given people, political communicator credibility depends on cycles of history, which in turn dictates their demand for certain dimensions of political ethos. For instance, Winn's factor analysis revealed four major factors in the Carter-Ford debates: leadership, consubstantiality, trustworthiness, and dynamism. Ford scored higher on leadership, but Carter scored higher on the consubstantiality dimension, which was defined broadly but similarly to coorientation. Winn anticipated the ultimate victory by Carter, since American history was ripe for a sense of plain-folks commonality in a post-Watergate era. At another time in history, the coorientation of Jimmy Carter may have yielded to a perception of authority and leadership of some other political candidate, which may explain the 1980, 1984, and 1988 Reagan-Bush victories. In 1992 the Clinton victory indicated the curve has turned again toward the coorientation dimension.

The point of Winn's study for our discussion is that history repeats norms significant to communicator credibility. During one period of a culture's history, coorientation may indeed be the most important factor in establishing credibility. Another era may demand high leadership or power, depending on historical rhythms. This insight suggests that we sensitize ourselves to culturally preferred and culturally diverse avenues of credibility.

**Charisma**

Another element of intercultural communicator credibility is *charisma*. Charisma is a type of leadership based on (1) a leader's extraordinary claim to remedy a distressful situation, and (2) an acceptance of this leadership. To put it another way, when people believe that a person has special gifts or powers to lead them out of a crisis, charismatic leadership can take root, depending on the strength of the leader's claim. For instance, many British citizens believed Winston Churchill to be extraordinarily talented and accepted his charismatic authority to lead England out of World War II. In another direction, Jim Jones led converts to accept his messianic role as cult leader and to believe that he was the only one able to deliver them from various world crises, including nuclear fallout and worldly concerns.

While an in-depth exploration of charismatic leadership is the subject of an extensive work by Max Weber and later writers interpreting Weber, the following are five characteristics of charisma as a part of credibility.

*Charisma is perceptual on the part of followers.* Each of the factors of credibility is perceptual in some ways, but charisma is especially dependent upon the followers' faith that the charismatic figure can lead them into a promising future. Dow (1973) convincingly underscored this point when he wrote of charismatic leaders

> who reveal a transcendent mission or course of action which may be in itself appealing to the potential followers, but which is acted upon because the followers believe their leader is extraordinarily gifted. By accepting or believing in the leaders' extraordinary qualities, the followers legitimize his claim to their obedience. (p. 188)

During the early Cuban Castro regime, he was perceived as a charismatic leader illustrated by statements from some of his followers:

> "Fidel has the same ideas as Jesus Christ, our protector and guide."
> "I would kiss the beard of Fidel Castro."
> "My greatest fear is that some mean person might kill Fidel. If this happens, I think I would die."

The point of charismatic leadership depending upon a foundation of perceived power is particularly heightened by the bravery perceived in Fidel Castro, as Fagen (1973) continued:

> The theme of historical blessedness and protection received popular reinforcement from the circumstances surrounding Castro's return to Cuba from Mexico in 1956 with eighty-two men and the avowed purpose of overthrowing Batista. Only Castro and eleven others escaped to the Sierra Maestra, where they launched the guerrilla action which culminated in the downfall of Batista two years later. All the elements of high drama and miraculous escape were attached to the story of the guerrilla band during these two years. At one time, Castro was reported dead, and subsequently, a price of $100,000 was set on his head. (p. 223)

*Charisma is contextual.* Charismatic leaders arise during times of extraordinary stress. In this way, charisma is contextual, so that a charismatic leader in one situation may be ineffective in another, or as Fagen (1973) emphasized, "there are no universal charismatics" (p. 215). There is no "right time" for a charismatic leader to emerge; such leaders arise not because of facilitating conditions but often because of adversity (Dow 1973). For example, a man like Churchill could inspire his listeners to visualize victory, despite Germany's devastating air strikes on England during World War II. Each crisis context seems to produce charismatic leaders who believe in their control over the destiny of a particular crisis, much like Hitler, Churchill, DeGaulle, and Roosevelt during an intense saga of world history.

In her analysis of the well-known Jesse Jackson visit to Syria in December 1983 to seek the release of hostage Robert Goodman, Pennington (1989) concludes that Jackson's success in influencing the ultimate release in 1984 was partly trust, but largely a context-specific multidimensional charismatic leadership. Pennington associated Jackson's communication style with sincerity, religiosity, morality, and personal trust toward the Syrians, a feature perhaps difficult to duplicate at another historical time. His charismatic style is evident in Pennington's article:

> I didn't come here on a mission seeking justice. I didn't come here because America is morally correct. I came on a mission of mercy. I don't argue the rightness or wrongness of Goodman. I am seeking mercy and the lowering of the temperature of war so that peace may come.

His ability to raise the context above politicality to morality and spirituality may well have matched a middle eastern cultural view of credibility as personalized and passionate, features more resonant with nonwestern cultures than logical-reductionist arguments or deductions of right and wrong.

*Charisma is missionary.*   The charismatic leader is highly motivated toward a mission, which Max Weber described as "new, outside the realm of everyday routine, extraordinary and revolutionary." The leader believes in shaping the destiny and history of his or her people. There is a type of bond, an identification between leader and led, that makes the leader's appeal one of a "secular savior" (Dow 1973).

Beyond mass perception, the charismatic leader's self-concept is one of master of history, transcending the moral order of things and inspiring the people to maintain their confidence in the leader. A good example of this principle again springs from the Cuban revolution under Fidel Castro. He viewed himself as one who was appointed and protected as part of a larger, blessed historical movement, or as Fagen (1973) wrote:

> First, Castro perceives the Revolution as part of a greater historical movement against tyranny and oppression. . . . Second, the Cuban leadership and Castro in particular are seen as blessed and protected by the larger historical movement of which the Revolution is a part. Castro's famous speech ending, "Condemn me, it doesn't matter. History will absolve me," is a classic, early articulation of this idea. Finally, because the leader is seen as acting in concert with larger historical forces not always visible to more ordinary men, he alone retains the right to determine the "correct" behavior in the service of the Revolution. (p. 219)

Under stressful conditions, such as poverty, war, and despair, it is possible that leaders like Hitler can convince nations of their mission. Charismatic leaders like Ghandi, Churchill, Roosevelt, and Martin Luther King believed in their task and perhaps viewed themselves as extraordinary people able to lead their nations from stress into victory.

*Charisma is unstable over time.*   A key element in Max Weber's classic work on charisma is that charisma is effervescent—but over time, the charismatic leader usually suffers demise. Fagen (1973) cited several reasons why charisma is short lived. One reason is that the leader's image of infallibility is naturally tarnished because of inevitable failures, leading writers to note a "natural entropy of the hero's charisma" (p. 215). A second reason, according to Weber, is that the charismatic leader, over time, naturally must attend to the affairs of state, a concern that causes the leader to be perceived as bureaucratic. This new image stands contradictory to the charismatic leader's earlier denunciation of the previous regime and thus produces a popularity loss. This circumstance, caused by the need to attend to daily administration, is called the *routinization of charisma.*

*Charisma is passed on by social ritual.* Almost every culture has ways of passing on official charisma or charisma of the office. Power is passed on by ceremonies, charms, incantations, and the like. In the Serbian culture, for instance, the mother spits over the head of her baby in a religious initiation ceremony as a method of passing on blessings and a good spirit. Many cultures practice "laying on" hands as a way of passing on special powers. Coronations of kings and inauguration ceremonies of heads of states illustrate formalized ways that cultures imbue recipients with *impersonal charisma* (Dow 1973).

## Dynamism

A final element in intercultural credibility is dynamism, which refers to enthusiasm and personal involvement. Dynamism is often described in terms appraising a communicator's aggressiveness, empathic nature, boldness, activity, and energy.

Dynamism certainly intersects with charisma, since a charismatic leader is often dynamic. The key ingredients for dynamism involve verbal and nonverbal elements. The inflammatory rhetoric of terrorism, for instance, is marked by dynamic qualities both in rhetoric and in terrorist action. Campus protests are often remembered for their dynamic qualities. African rhetoric and preaching is highly dynamic and stylized in its performance (Asante 1990).

Research in communicator credibility across a variety of situations in North America, at least, reveals that the importance of dynamism depends upon specific situations. For instance, Applbaum and Anatol (1972) found that authority and trust considerably outranked the importance of dynamism in a classroom lecture or a speech to a social organization. However, when subjects in their experiment rated credibility for a sermon in a church, dynamism jumped from the least important factor to the second most important factor. Only trustworthiness was rated as more important than dynamism in the church context. These results suggest that dynamism is more important in some contexts than in others. It depends upon the cultural expectations of time, situation, and norms. Many intercultural situations demand a strong dynamic quality, for many cultures do not share European and North American emphasis upon scientific proof and logic. In fact, persuasion in parts of Africa and Latin America occurs in significant measure through emotional appeal and dynamic delivery, not syllogisms and cold logic.

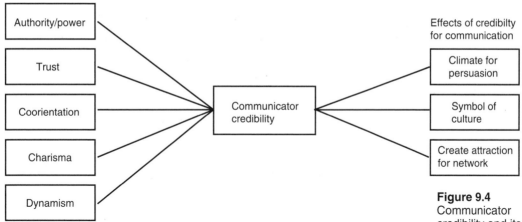

**Factors of source credibility**

- Authority/power
- Trust
- Coorientation
- Charisma
- Dynamism

→ Communicator credibility ←

**Effects of credibilty for communication**

- Climate for persuasion
- Symbol of culture
- Create attraction for network

**Figure 9.4**
Communicator credibility and its effects.

Certainly these factors of communicator credibility influence communication outcomes.

**Effects of Credibility on Culture**

The first effect of credibility in the intercultural situation is its effect on persuasion. Writers as far back as Aristotle confirm that communicators perceived as highly credible are more persuasive than communicators with low credibility.

Climate for Persuasion

Communicator credibility symbolizes a culture and identity. This quality makes credibility an important ingredient in networking cultures.

Symbol of a Culture

A final effect of credibility is the ability of credible persons to attract and influence others. The very fact that people are in a group network testifies to friendship and the mutual believability of peers.

Create Attraction toward a Networking Culture

Several years ago, while conducting fieldwork in Africa, I learned an important lesson about opinion leadership. One purpose of this trip was to speak with large numbers of villagers and to collect data for my dissertation. Upon entering a village where few foreign outsiders had traversed for a while, I went directly to the chief's hut—though not without the fanfare of a couple of dozen children and about half a dozen dogs. Although the chief was meeting with the other elders of that village, my arrival seemed no bother, and they welcomed me. After a visit of some forty-five minutes, in which I explained the purpose of my visit and engaged in conversation of several current topics, the chief suddenly asked me, to my surprise, if I wanted them to ring the gong gong. Being too embarrassed to question what the gong gong was, I simply said yes. With such affirmation, the chief and other leaders went to the front of the chief's hut and rang a large bell, after which all the village family heads gathered within a matter of minutes. Unfortunately, I was speechless by the process, so that the few words I spoke were

**Opinion Leadership and Networking Cultures**

Opinion leadership lends interpersonal influence in a context of information seeking.

probably not worth the trouble it had taken the villagers to gather. However, the remainder of my stay in that village was filled with warm receptions from many households.

This incident solidifies a number of elements of a larger concern—and a principle of intercultural communication often discussed in the literature as opinion leadership. My going to the chief and village leaders tapped an interpersonal network that legitimized my work in that village. Within any cultural system, individuals develop informational and social networks.

## Opinion Leadership as Information Role

In one sense, every person we meet has some influence on our decisions, but all people do not exert equal amounts of influence. Those individuals, however, who have a greater influence on the opinions of others are called *opinion leaders.*

By definition, opinion leadership is not necessarily community leadership. Rather, people influence people informally where respect and communication exists. There is a web of interpersonal relationships from villages to modern cities.

The discovery of opinion leadership in the interpersonal network sense emerged from an unlikely set of studies. For almost the first half of this century, people assumed that the mass media were all powerful, able to sway passive audiences, shaping them into malleable culture moved by the whims of those who controlled the mass media. Second World War propaganda in Nazi Germany, Orson Welles's "War of the Worlds" broadcast in 1938, and the influence of

Madison Avenue advertising in electronic and print media created a perception of mass media power. This theory of mass media was called the *hypodermic needle theory* and conveyed an image of a message being injected into the minds of passive audience members.

However, researchers using this model overlooked the important information roles interpersonal networks play. When Lazarsfeld, Berelson, and Gaudet (1968) investigated the influence of communication on voters' choices during the 1940 presidential election, they were convinced their study would demonstrate mass media influence contributing to voters' decisions in elections. To their surprise, they discovered that fewer voter choices were influenced directly by the media than by interpersonal sources. When these interpersonal sources appeared to influence three or more people, they were called opinion leaders.

In another study, Steinfatt, Gantz, Seibold, and Miller (1973) highlighted the importance of interpersonal sources of communication in serious news events, such as assassinations. They compared several cities for news sources and reported the predominance of interpersonal communication sources for the following events:

| Event | Percent Hearing from Interpersonal Sources |
|---|---|
| 1. John F. Kennedy assassination | |
|    a. San Jose, California, sample | 50 percent |
|    b. Iowa City, Iowa, sample | 55 percent |
|    c. Dallas, Texas, sample | 57 percent |
| 2. George Wallace assassination attempt | 70 percent |

Not only do these figures accentuate the importance of interpersonal communication sources in news events, but they illustrate the prominent role of interpersonal communication networks.

Starosta (1974) underscored the highly interpersonal nature of information sources within Ceylon:

> These disquieting conclusions are replicated in my own field study of three villages in central Ceylon, where many villagers relied almost exclusively on the words of neighbors, shopkeepers, and "others in the market" for their information. . . . The radio set or the newspaper is always to some degree an intruder. The villager who would have a prescribed ritualistic response for his dealings with the village headman might be overwhelmed by the tremendous volume of ideas that would flow from the media to the degree where he would set up defenses against the influx of impersonal and alien stimuli. (pp. 307–308)

This relative value of interpersonal networking has been documented in numerous studies across dozens of other cultures.

Opinion leadership is a major part of social networks and information flow, as illustrated in a rural area of Ghana.

Not all interpersonal communication is with opinion leaders, but all relationships with opinion leaders are interpersonal. Because this bond is unique, subtle, and influential, it represents a significant intercultural communication role relationship.

## Communication Qualities of Opinion Leaders

By noting the communication qualities associated with opinion leadership in networks, we do not mean to suggest that the concept is static or one-way from leader-to-follower. The relationship is subtle and dynamic. Influence goes two ways. When we isolate, for purposes of analysis, the apparent leadership qualities of individuals within networking cultures, some evident communication features emerge.

*Information competency.* Opinion leaders have interest, accuracy, and familiarity with the issues. They are *information rich* and are exposed to relevant mass media and interpersonal sources to gain information access (Sherif and Sherif 1967; Rogers 1983).

*Interpersonal communication competency.* In addition to their information sufficiency, opinion leaders also practice interpersonal communication competency. One way is their ability to pass on good advice. Decisions concerning grazing domains among herdsmen in Kenya, for instance, are made through respected leaders who pass on advice, decisions, and information through dialogue.

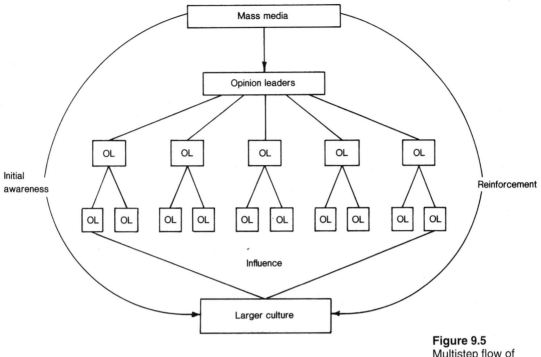

**Figure 9.5**
Multistep flow of
information.

A second communication competency is their ability to network with other information sources. Opinion leaders are often part of a complex chain of opinion leaders, actively tapping other outside networks and opinion leaders. This intricate process is called the *multistep flow,* shown in figure 9.5.

A third quality of communication competence is their openness. Driskill and Dodd (1988) found opinion leaders scored higher on a communication openness index and concluded that communication competency is a vital part of understanding the opinion leadership relationship.

Fourth, opinion leaders tend to be interpersonally accessible not only in openness but also accessible geographically. Typically, they live near, where people can find them (Rogers 1983).

*Socioeconomic levels.* Opinion leaders usually emerge from the upper levels of each occupational division. Educationally, within each socioeconomic status level, opinion leaders tend to come from the more educated members of the group. They also tend to be slightly higher in income than those they influence.

*Interpersonal contact.* As a source of personal influence, opinion leaders' personal contact is frequent and effective. Friendships are important to them, and they are highly active in social networks (Rogers 1983).

**Table 9.2** Comparison of Opinion Leadership Assessment Techniques

| Technique | Concept | Example |
|---|---|---|
| 1. Sociometric choice | Ask respondents to whom they go for information and advice about a particular topic. | A respondent says: "I go to person A for information about a new type of seed." |
| 2. Self-report | Ask respondent if anyone has sought his or her advice over a certain period of time. | Person A responds: "Yes, three people have asked me about this new type of seed." |
| 3. Key informant report | Ask a person of the culture in question to tell you who is influential on specific questions. | The informant indicates: "Well, most people would probably go to Person A, since he really understands new things about farming." |

*Range of opinion leadership: monomorphic and polymorphic.* In some cultures, opinion leadership is *monomorphic,* meaning that a person is an opinion leader in a specialized topic. Monomorphic opinion leaders are influential in a limited field, while *polymorphic* leadership works with more than one topic (Rogers with Svenning 1969).

Polymorphic opinion leadership was indicated by 76 percent of people in an African sample (Dodd 1973) where respondents preferred the same person for advice/information on such divergent topics as farming, disputes, and religious questions. However, a culture's monomorphic or polymorphic style mostly depends on its specialized information needs. In general, monomorphic styles appear more in technical information cultures, while polymorphic styles are associated with less technically information-concerned cultures (Ho 1969; Korzenny and Farace 1977).

Richmond's (1980) college life study showed opinion leaders more likely to try more new things (called innovativeness) and less apprehensive in their communication. Driskill and Dodd (1988) also examined university relationships and reported that polymorphic opinion leaders are more likely to be "super OL's" who influence a larger network of people than monomorphic opinion leaders who typically work within very small networks.

Overall, opinion leaders function as sources of information and evaluation. Persuasive efforts are likely to be more effective when the message is focused toward opinion leaders, who in turn influence, or at least pass on information, among those homogeneous groupings of people with whom they typically interact (figure 9.6).

## Measuring Opinion Leadership

Over a period of years, three techniques have proved useful for assessing opinion leadership: the sociometric choice technique, the self-report technique, and the key informant report. From all indications, while these three techniques generally produce similar results, they are presented in rank order in Table 9.2 which summarizes the methods.

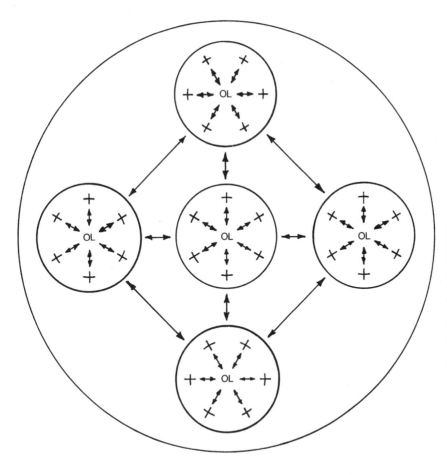

**Figure 9.6**
Opinion-leadership communication as part of a social network. Opinion leaders pass information on to those they influence, and opinion leaders influence one another within a cultural communication network.

*Sociometric choice technique.* With the sociometric choice technique, the researcher asks the respondent to whom that person would go for information or advice or both about a particular topic. The exact nature of the specific questions depends upon the culture, the topic under consideration, and so on. Typically, however, the sociometric choice technique asks respondents for their choice of a person in specific categories, some of which are noted in the following:

1. *Value relationship:* Asking the respondents which people they value for the way they do their work. *Example:* "Which two farmers do you consider good farmers?"

2. *Communication-task relationship:* Asking the respondents to whom they would most likely go for advice regarding a decision. *Example:* "To whom would you likely go for advice on adopting a new farm program?"

3. *Communication-social relationship:* Asking the respondents with whom they like to socialize. *Example:* "With which two farmers do you most frequently visit?"

4. *Liking relationship:* Asking the respondents which people they like the most. *Example:* "Which farmers do you like the most?" (Van den Ban 1973).

*Self-report technique.* The self-report technique is largely a matter of asking respondents if anyone has asked information of them over a certain period of time. For instance, a typical question might ask if anyone has specifically asked for advice on certain topics within the last month. If a respondent reports that he or she has had as many as three or more requests for information, then there is a likelihood that the respondent is an opinion leader.

*Key informant report.* A third method of locating opinion leaders is to ask a key informant of the culture for that person's analysis of people to whom others go for information and advice concerning topics under consideration. This method extends ethnomethodology by working closely with informants who typify the culture in question. These informants are more than "guides," for they should be able to discuss a number of factors about the culture and serve as translators (when necessary); many times they provide excellent case studies.

## Networking Cultures

Homophily, credibility, and opinion leadership are major reasons why informal networking cultures evolve. Homophily heightens attraction and information sharing; credibility opens believability and influence; opinion leaders facilitate information flow and influence while also networking with still other opinion leaders. The term *networking culture* in this text refers to a *communication network* formed by the flow of information between individuals in a system. As Weimann (1989) defines it, a communication network is stable over time, predictive of behavior, and is a major part of a culture's social structure. The basic concept is to ask "Who talks with whom?" When these associations are determined the result is an interconnected group of individuals exhibiting a patterned flow of information between them (Rogers and Kincaid 1981; Rogers 1983).

*Structure of networks.* First, when an entire organization or system is the unit of analysis, communication flow between members of the system results in a *sociogram.* A sociogram shows who talks with whom. The smaller groups of friends or associates are cliques. A *clique* is a subgroup within the larger system whose members interact more often with each other than with other members of the network.

Second, the individuals within a communication network are *nodes* who may or may not hold role and communication functions, such as opinion leadership. A *link* is the communication tie between nodes (on the individual level of analysis) or between cliques, organizations, and cultures (on a group level of analysis). Examples of links are illustrated in figures 9.7, and 9.8 by the lines between people inside and outside the cliques.

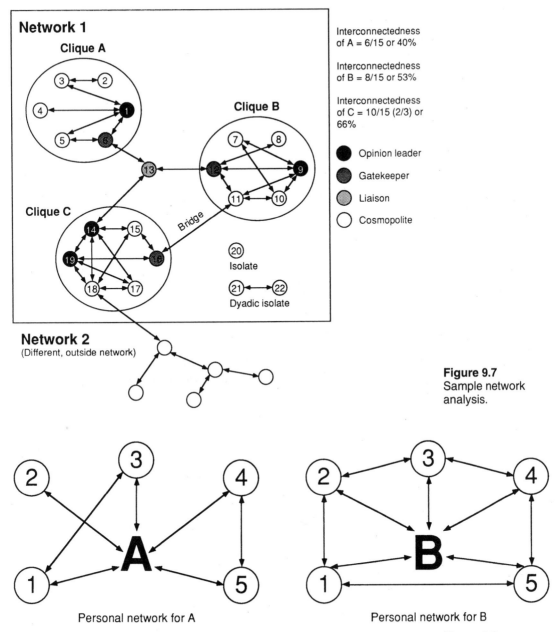

**Network 1**

**Clique A**

Interconnectedness of A = 6/15 or 40%

Interconnectedness of B = 8/15 or 53%

Interconnectedness of C = 10/15 (2/3) or 66%

● Opinion leader

◓ Gatekeeper

▨ Liaison

○ Cosmopolite

**Clique B**

**Clique C**

Bridge

20 Isolate

21 ↔ 22
Dyadic isolate

**Network 2**
(Different, outside network)

**Figure 9.7**
Sample network analysis.

Personal network for A

Personal network for B

**Figure 9.8**
Personal network interconnectedness or integration.

Third, members play certain information roles. *Gatekeepers* let information pass into a clique. *Opinion leaders* evaluate information and are sought out for their advice. *Liaisons* link two or more cliques but themselves are not members of any one clique. *Bridges* are members of one clique who link information to another clique. *Cosmopolites* link the entire network or system to other outside networks. *Isolates* have no links. *Dyadic isolates* link with each other but have no other contact (Weimann 1989; Rogers 1983). Weimann's research describes how the *intragroup* flow of information is orchestrated by the centrally positioned people, such as gatekeepers and opinion leaders. The *intergroup* flow of information is carried out by people outside the cliques, such as liaisons or cosmopolites.

Fourth, we can examine the overall nature of these cliques and networks. For instance, if members of a clique interact frequently, the clique is highly interconnected. The *index of interconnectedness* refers to the amount of member interaction within a unit, such as a clique (Rogers 1983). The formula is the *actual* links in a group divided by the potential links. Potential links are derived from the formula $\left(\frac{n(n-1)}{2}\right)$, where N is the number of people in the group being evaluated and that number is multiplied by that number minus one and the entire result is divided by 2. In figure 9.7 the first clique in the network has a lower interconnectedness index than the second or the third. The actual links (6) divided by potential links $\left(\frac{6(5)}{2}\right)$ or $6 \div 15 = 40\%$. Cliques B and C have 53 percent and 66 percent respectively.

Finally, we can focus more exclusively on any one individual within a clique and analyze that person's ties to the group. In the material presented previously, the clique group was the unit of analysis for interconnectedness and identifying the roles within the network culture. Now, we examine communication not looking in on the group, but by looking out from any one group member's view as to how many people are connected with that one individual. Thus, a *personal network* analyzes the communication among individuals linked to a focal person. In figure 9.8, person A and B are each linked with the same number of people: each is linked to persons 1 through 5. However, there is a difference in the two personal networks. A's personal network of 5 are not connected with each other to the extent that B's personal network of 5 are connected with each other. When a personal network has overlapping, interrelated, interconnected people with each other as well as with the target individual, it is also said to be an *interconnected personal network*. (This term is used to avoid confusion, but some researchers use the terms interlocking versus radial and high versus low communication proximity to describe this phenomenon.) Links serving multiple purposes with one tie are called multiple ties, as when 1 and 2 are simultaneously friends or fellow workers. (Weimann 1989).

Overall, high interconnectedness usually results in a faster flow of information within the group. This is because information is heard more rapidly and accurately within the group. Also, acceptance of innovations is expected to occur more frequently (Rogers 1983).

1. *De-emphasize backgrounds in cases of wide economic disparity in background.* Too often, a person may unconsciously view wealth and power as a solution to many problems, rather than specializing in developing healthy intercultural relationships. It may be better to value attitude relationships, where you can build friendships in the absence of appearance and background homophily.

2. *Seek a common ground.* If one person values material possessions, for example, a second person who finds these values extreme may feel little commonality. Build common ground by emphasizing areas of similarity.

3. *Tolerate differing values.* Inevitably, values between persons of different cultures clash. Despite these differences, you can build a "homophily" of respect and of tolerance for difference. Encourage communication about those differences and strive to build bridges of affection and empathy.

4. *Try to understand different views of knowledge.* Some people view knowledge as personal only, while other people perceive knowledge and attitudes as valid for everyone (Ruben 1977). Differences in knowledge and attitudes between two people should not be viewed as I am right and you are wrong, but as differences to be shared. Rather than assume knowledge and attitude heterophily, suspend judgment and invite dialogue.

5. *Develop sensitivity to values.* By remaining alert to others' needs and values, you can turn heterophily into productive interaction. Heterophily gaps can serve to fill areas where you find yourself not very knowledgeable, but you must initiate the discussion.

6. *Find cultural models.* Understanding culturally preferred models can help us grasp a role standard. For example, observing highly credible communicators within a culture can help us discover if the culture relies more on emotion or logic, wisdom or science.

7. *Do not misuse authority.* Many visitors to a host country, for example, feel compelled to share knowledge. Unfortunately, some cultures take this behavior to mean that the visitor is acting without humility. In Japan, a U.S. naval officer stopped to assist a Japanese man whose motorcycle needed emergency repair. The officer acted judiciously, offering indirect advice, asking for permission to try an "experiment" on the motor. The reason for this indirect advice to the distressed motorcycle owner stemmed from the culture's value of not embarrassing people by causing them to feel that they do not know how to do something. A quiet humility was appropriate—the cycle was repaired, and a friendship was established.

8. *Discover how to be trustworthy.* Studies among North Americans show that self-disclosure, friendship, and trust interact. The more trust we reveal, the more likely the chances of establishing and maintaining friendship, as long as we do not come across too strong early in a friendship. Similarly, intercultural relationships rely on trust—and in some cases, the trust extends far beyond our own cultural expectations. For instance, trust in some cultures

results from offering hospitality or showing wisdom and insight. Other cultures withhold trust unless there is some proof of loyalty, or in some cases, courage. Developing credibility in the context of intercultural relationships begins by probing ways to be trusted.

9. *Show personal concern for others.* Coorientation is important and translates into a genuine concern for others. Build common ground interculturally; focus on similarities, not differences. Practice empathy.

10. *Be natural but flexible.* Sometimes, being natural can be offensive to other cultures. Then again, a person cannot be radically opposite of his or her basic nature. Be yourself, but talk and act as consistently as you can with the culture. Patience, humility, empathy, and willingness to try are characteristics that may help you maintain naturalness with yourself but flexibility in meeting people from other cultures. Couple with that a willingness to learn and a respect for others, and you will have overcome many beginning pitfalls.

11. *Facilitate a heightened sense of respect for yourself and foster interpersonal relationships by personally adopting some opinion leader qualities, such as gregariousness, amiability, and empathy, as well as knowledge about the topic of concern.* When you interact with other people, for instance, if you "cut them off" or in some way show disrespect, it is unlikely that such people will continue a long-enduring friendship with you. Look for rapport-building efforts that often begin with a keen interest and a lot of listening.

12. *Know when and how to involve opinion leaders in message facilitation.* Opinion leaders can add credibility to a message in a way that often reduces the "emotional blinders" and suspicions that sometimes prevent adequate attention to a topic of potential interest. When someone you respect asks you to listen to something, you are more likely to do so than if an impersonal source invites your attention.

13. *Be aware of links, cliques, and networks.* Information travels fast, especially among people who are closely connected. Realizing that people represent their information networks helps us to understand why our interpersonal communication is not the only voice they hear.

The concept of homophily implies similarities in social characteristics. Heterophily implies differences, while optimal heterophily indicates a tolerable range of heterophily, where two people are socially homophilous but heterophilous on competence and information. Appearance homophily refers to similarity of dress, looks, and so on. Background homophily refers to similarity of residence, education, social status, race, and so on. Attitude homophily refers to perceived similarities on topics, while value homophily involves outlook and long-enduring judgments of good and bad. The chapter includes the influence of homophily in communication, such as in persuasion. A scale to measure homophily is presented, also.

This chapter indicates the nature of intercultural communicator credibility and its effects in intercultural situations. Authority and power, trust, coorientation, charisma, and dynamism are foundational concepts. Their effects are found in their contribution to perceived communicator credibility, which in turn produces a climate for persuasion, a symbol of a culture, and source for cultural identity. Obviously, these factors and their effects do not work independently—they work in concert. However, any one factor may be dominant, depending upon cultural expectations and specific crises facing a culture or a nation.

Opinion leaders are information-rich people in role relationships with others similar to them in a communication network. They have high interest and competence in the subject, are accessible, have access to relevant information, and are similar to the people they influence. An opinion leader in one particular group probably will not be an opinion leader in another group, unless the needs and conditions of the groups are similar. Functionally, opinion leaders open channels of information. They also reinforce group norms and individual opinions and provide a source of social support.

Some opinion leaders serve a communication information role for only one topic area (monomorphic opinion leadership). Other opinion leaders function as information sources across a variety of topics and are called polymorphic leaders.

Social opinion leaders are vital parts of social networks. And social networks, with their accompanying communication roles, influence our interpersonal communication; for in part, we interact not with individuals but with their social networks.

**This Chapter in Perspective**

**Exercises**

1. Ask some of your friends to complete the interpersonal homophily scale with regard to a person mutually known and somewhat respected. Now have them complete the same scale for someone in the news from a foreign country. What differences do you observe between the two?

2. Ask an international student to discuss with you the nature of interpersonal relationships in his or her country. In what ways does the homophily principle operate the same as in the United States? In what ways is it different?

3. Observe interethnic, intercultural, and intracultural communication in a public place. Do you see some ways in which homophily operates in these situations? How? In what ways does heterophily operate? Why?

4. Ask your friends what they admire most about specific national leaders. Then ask them what they like least about the same national leaders. How does this list compare with the factors mentioned in this chapter?

5. Examine newspaper articles about various cultural leaders both in the United States and abroad. What features are emphasized in these articles? How do these emphases match the five credibility factors found in this chapter?

6. When a highly credible leader takes an unpopular stand on some major issue, list what people around you say about this leader. Does the leader's credibility seem to rise or fall? What kinds of messages change credibility?

7. List examples of charismatic leaders whose routinization of administrative details leads to their unpopularity. What could such leaders do to retard this demise? Ask people in your class to whom they go for information concerning some topic of significance. Who are the opinion leaders? What characteristics do they seem to have? Do they offer opinion leadership on a number of topics? Why or why not?

8. Spend some time in an organization, asking who talks with whom about various topics. Why do patterns of informal communication emerge? What are the interpersonal networks and relationships in the organization?

# Cultural Adaptation and Communication Accommodation: Applying Intercultural Competencies

**Chapter**

# Adapting to Culture

**Objectives**

After completing this chapter, you should be able to

1. Cope with anxiety upon entering a culture

2. Adjust in a new culture more effectively understanding adjustment models and strategies presented in the chapter

3. Train others, informing them of the acculturation and adaptation processes

4. Identify the negative effects of poor intercultural adaptation

5. Describe reverse culture shock

6. Develop skills for cultural reentry

We begin a new unit in the text by examining our communication and adaptation to culture. As the central text model reveals, in the heat of uncertainty or anxiety when confronted with perceived difference we strive to find a dissonance reducing solution. We develop a third culture C. Out of the third culture context, we develop competent communication accommodation, largely involving adaptation. However, we might adapt well or poorly, depending on how functional our intercultural competencies and accommodating strategies leading to effective intercultural outcomes, or how dysfunctional we might be leaning on past stereotypes, engaging in ethnocentrism, withdrawing, ignoring, and a host of other behaviors. This chapter synthesizes the processes of how people reduce their uncertainty and anxiety upon entering a new culture. There are many transitional experiences and shocks we face: job shock with a new position, role shock when changing relationships, life transition shock when going through a family or personal epoch. In this material, we deal with culture shock and identify the larger concerns of communication adaptation.

When one enters a different culture, a natural anxiety emerges. This normal tendency to feel somewhat worried about the new culture and your response to it, however, can become an overwhelming fear, turn to inordinate mistrust, and lead to an eventual return from the culture earlier than we expected. We do not have to leave the United States to enter a second culture—sometimes another culture is only a few miles away. This chapter focuses on the process of adapting to the new culture and the related process of learning its ways.

The problem of cultural adaptation is well illustrated by the following statements from people who entered a new culture:

"At first, I felt as if this country was the best place in the world. But after a while, I began to feel as if they were all crooks."

"I don't know what happened to me. I hadn't been in this place for more than three months when I had a compelling urge to return home. It wasn't just homesickness, which I expected to feel, but it was a kind of compulsion."

"My anxiety about the country did not really have to do with the food. I developed what I now guess was a phobia about the place and my interaction with people. Back home, I was always outgoing, but in the new country, I hardly felt like leaving the compound. I was almost scared to death."

These statements typify people's feelings, which fall rather predictably into a pattern we call *culture shock*. Culture shock refers to the transition period and the accompanying feelings of stress and anxiety a person experiences during the early period upon entering a new culture.

Culture shock can leave the person entering the host country with a feeling of alienation and can result in decreased intercultural contact.

There is no right or wrong to experiencing culture shock—it happens to almost everyone, although it occurs in varying degrees. After all, your nervous system is working overtime, and your surroundings are very new. It is normal to experience some level of culture shock. However, just like anxiety in your own culture, culture shock can become overwhelming. Knowing what to expect and knowing how to cope with culture shock should assist you in handling these feelings. When you experience this phenomenon, you may even feel temporary physical symptoms, such as a slight headache, an upset stomach, and sleeplessness. The following general symptoms also can surface (Oberg 1960; Adler 1975; Bennett 1977):

1. Excessive concern over cleanliness and health

2. Feelings of helplessness and withdrawal

3. Irritability

4. Fear of being cheated, robbed, or injured

5. A glazed stare

6. Desire for home and friends

7. Physiological stress reactions

8. Anxiety, frustrations, and paranoia

9. Loneliness and disorientation

10. Defensive communication

Because of its disorienting qualities, adapting to a new culture presents some unusual blocks to effective intercultural communication. To put it in perspective, again, adapting to a culture has analogies to many transitions, such as entering college, moving to a new house, taking a new job, moving to another city, or losing a loved one. For those reasons, we can experience transition shock, job shock, role shock, and, according to Alvin Toffler (1970), shock related to rapid cultural and technological change, called future shock.

The good news is that we can understand and develop skills in adapting to new cultures that reduce the negative qualities.

## The Early Adaptation Experience

A number of writers have explored the causes and symptoms of culture shock and have outlined the phases that people enter and leave throughout the transition process (Oberg 1960; Adler 1975; Bennett 1977; Stewart 1977). In addition to these works, the United States Navy manual *Overseas Diplomacy* (1973) outlines a number of phases and subphases that commonly occur. These include eager expectation, everything is beautiful, everything is awful, and everything is OK.

### Eager Expectation Stage

In this stage, you plan to enter the host culture. The planning and development of the trip and the purposes of the entry make you simultaneously excited and wary. You may be looking forward to new food and yet remain apprehensive. You may be enjoying the new language and yet remain concerned about using it properly. You anticipate how new people will respond to you and yet worry that they might reject you. However, you face the future with optimism, and the planning continues.

### Everything Is Beautiful Stage

When you arrive in the new culture, you feel a sense of excitement, pleasure, and self-satisfaction for making the decision to come to this beautiful place. During this phase, nearly everything appears wonderful. The food is exciting; the people seem friendly. Although you may experience some of the symptoms mentioned earlier, such as sleeplessness and mild anxiety, your enthusiasm and curiosity quickly overcome these minor discomforts. The sense of euphoria is so great that some writers call this stage the honeymoon stage. You should have come long ago—you think to yourself—to this piece of heaven. The people are polite and gracious, unlike some people you know back home, and so you may come to feel that you have discovered utopia.

Studies indicate that this stage varies significantly from a short time to months. However, this stage of ecstasy is lost to a period of anger, depression, or denial.

| Everything Is Awful Stage | The honeymoon is over! Now, things have gone sour. After a while, you begin to feel more anxious, restless, impatient, and disappointed. It seems you have a more difficult time saying what you mean. You are meeting more people who do not speak English, and yet your foreign-language knowledge has not improved dramatically. Perhaps you begin to realize that the eager expectations were just a fantasy, colored by the honeymoon stage, reinforced by your euphoria when you first arrived. Now you feel that you were wrong. |

There is increasing difficulty with transportation. Shopping seems to come too often, and you are getting a little tired of having to bargain for almost everything you purchase. Even with these surrounding problems, no one seems to care. The host country seems indifferent. Today, you learn that devaluation of the dollar has shrunk your purchasing power in the new culture. Besides that, your wallet or purse was stolen.

This period of adaptation is marked by a loss of social cues and a time of inconvenience that you had not experienced earlier. The confusion heightens with the unfamiliar smells, sounds, food, and cultural customs. Not only do some of the physical symptoms set in at this stage, but depression, loneliness, and fear pervade your attitudes and feelings. The reaction is predictable.

The "everything is awful" stage can last from a few weeks up to several months. Some people never experience this stage at all, though others experience it more seriously. The goal, of course, is to work toward a balanced view of the people, the customs, and self.

Most people in the "everything is awful" stage cope with the frustration in one of the four ways that follow (*Overseas Diplomacy* 1973).

*Fight.* Some people in the "everything is awful" stage of culture shock scoff at the host country. They may also reject the nationals of that country, thinking that the people in that culture have inferior ways—in short, they look down on the culture of the host country and act ethnocentrically. Other people in this situation actually destroy property, which only fuels the guilt and makes the situation worse. For example, one teenage boy, whose father served as a change agent in a foreign country, reacted not only with insolence to his classmates at the international school but also destroyed personal property of some of his father's friends in the new culture. To say the least, the fight reaction during the "everything is awful" stage can lead to legal difficulty in the host culture. Symptoms include excessive irritation, angry outbursts, defensiveness, and frustration over minor things.

*Flight.* Other people in the "everything is awful" stage of culture shock remove themselves from the culture. The most obvious examples are the people who leave for home shortly after arriving in the host culture. Even if these people do not leave, other symptoms accompany this coping behavior. For example, they may withdraw from all contact with the new culture. Not only do they avoid speaking or trying to learn the new language, but they avoid contact with the host nationals. During this episode, they may develop nervousness, depression, alcoholism, mental debilitation, excessive homesickness, loneliness, disorientation, and general withdrawal.

*Filter.* Some people in the "everything is awful" stage of culture shock can experience three kinds of filtering behavior. The filtering behavior refers to a denial of reality, and it occurs in several ways.

First, people can *deny differences* between themselves and people in the host culture or between their hometown and a city in the new culture. Some people in this condition go to great lengths to argue the harmony and similarity between home and host cultures. One international student in a North American university, for example, spent a great deal of time in his conversations with North Americans trying to convince them of how few differences he had noticed and "how wonderful America is." He, like all of us at times, was denying differences.

A second way people filter is by *glorifying their home* culture. For example, a North American from the United States may forget all about the problems back home and remember only the good things. This process is something like the old statement about looking at things through rose-colored glasses. Only in this case, the tinted glasses are framed by a need for security. This distortion of perceptions extends into views toward the host culture. One underlying reason for glorifying home is a disgust, contempt, or ethnocentric attitude toward people in the new host culture.

Still a third reaction within this filtering behavior is to *go native.* Sometimes, people totally reject their old culture and enthusiastically adopt the host culture. Of course, the problem is that these people are never accepted in the new culture for anything but what they actually are, so this behavior really does not work.

*Flex.* A final behavior within the "everything is awful" stage is flexing. In this more positive phase, the visitors or new residents observe, try new things, and reflect on events, trying to sort out the frustrations and understand them. During this situation, they begin to look at life in the new culture, to reflect on why the people act in a certain way. Then, they go out and try some new food, habits, and customs. Eventually, this process leads into the final stage of culture shock—the "everything is OK" stage.

**Everything Is OK Stage**

After several months in the new culture, you may find that you view both the negative and the positive in a balanced manner. You finally have learned a lot more about the culture, and while you still do not like some things, you now like more things than a few months ago. Not everyone is a crook, you think to yourself, and, in fact, there are some good folks along with some bad. By now, you have become more accustomed to the foods, sights, sounds, smells, and nonverbal behaviors of the new culture. Also, you have fewer headaches and upset

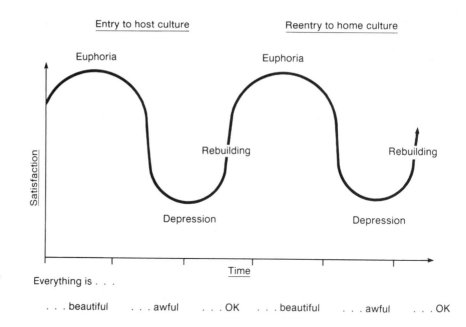

**Figure 10.1**
Entry and reentry
stress curve:
W-curve.

Entry to host culture   Reentry to home culture

Euphoria   Euphoria

Rebuilding   Rebuilding

Depression   Depression

Satisfaction

Time

Everything is . . .

. . . beautiful   . . . awful   . . . OK   . . . beautiful   . . . awful   . . . OK

stomach problems and less confusion, uncertainty, and loneliness. Your physical health and mental health have improved. Normal contacts with host nationals are increasing, and you do not feel that you must defend yourself. You can accept yourself and others around you. Congratulations! You have just made it through the worst of culture shock.

As previously mentioned, some people experience culture shock in varying degrees. Also, because culture shock occurs over a period of time, you may not always realize that its stages are temporary. The best thing to do is to admit that you are experiencing culture shock, try to identify your stage of culture shock, and work toward becoming more familiar with the new culture. Feeling good about yourself before you go into the new culture is important (Stewart 1977; Bennett 1977). A positive self-concept alleviates self-doubt and allows you to experience new things with less stress.

Furthermore, these features apply to any diverse context, domestic or international. People can experience just as much adaptation difficulty moving to a new city as moving to a new country.

The process just described has been referred to as the U-curve for entry and the W-curve referring to the entry-reentry cycle. The model in figure 10.1 refers to the stages in the W-curve.

**Long-Term Adaptation**

How would you feel if you moved to a new town, changed schools, or undertook a new job? As you can guess from the previous discussion, there would probably be some degree of culture shock. What if you were an immigrant coming to a

The process of acculturation involves adaption to the host culture.

new country, an international student entering the United States or a Native American moving from a reservation to Chicago? The process would be more difficult. Beyond culture shock lies the process of acculturation. *Acculturation* refers to the long-term process of adapting to new cultural behaviors that are different from one's primary learned culture. Although a number of observers are interested especially in how acculturation works with relatively new immigrants, such as the influx of Cubans, Vietnamese, and Koreans into the United States, the principles of acculturation apply broadly to moving to a new location, changing jobs, and adapting to ethnic diversity in education and in the workplace. To understand acculturation is to discover interpersonal relations, the effects of prolonged culture contact, and how a person changes to adapt to a new culture. All this involves a learning, socialization process—it is not easy and takes time.

People living in a new culture for a short time, or sojourners, do not necessarily have to rely on the host culture as much as long-term adapters. Many investigations, such as Young Yun Kim's (1988) research in this area, illuminate the variables involved.

What happens when a person lives a short or long-term in another culture? Beyond the culture shock stages are important assumptions of what happens in the adaptation process.

**Assumptions behind Cultural Adaptation**

*Adaptation involves survival skills.* Part of the process of acculturation is learning survival skills—how to cook, eat, work, rest, do banking, seek transportation, and the scores of other things that bombard the new person who plans to live permanently in the new culture. The daily press of living becomes the dominant concern (Stewart 1977). From an understanding of

Maslow's hierarchy of needs we can learn that once these physiological needs are met, a person seeks more psychological assurances, such as security, self-esteem, and acceptance. If the survival skills are not adequately dealt with, a person may suffer lessened adaptation.

*Adaptation and growth.* Culture adaptation assumes attitudes and behaviors will ultimately change. Without an understanding of positive conditions bringing about the changes, ethnic people can remain trapped, victims of negative experiences that prevent acculturation. In the long run, growth results from stretching and experiencing the inevitable stresses.

Kim explained the growth process in her stress-adaptation-growth model. Kim's (1988) research proposes that adaptation is an accumulation but progressive series of positive and negative experiences. There may be two steps forward and one step back as we move toward adaptation only to be pulled into stress. We do not always adapt in a smooth, continuous process. Pictured as a coiled spring, which stretches and grows but is pulled back by its own tension, the stress-adaptation-growth dynamic ultimately depicts adaptation in the new culture (figure 10.2).

## Communication Factors Influencing Long-Term Adaptation

A number of variables have been examined in an attempt to identify the communication and participation activities arriving to live permanently in a new culture. Although many studies are very specific, dealing with particular ethnic groups, the following principles emerging from these studies apply to our discussion of adaptation.

*Ethnic identification.* Whenever a minority culture is faced with learning the new ways of a contrast culture and surviving in that culture, there is a strong ethnic identification. By that we mean that the minority person or immigrant seeks identification with familiar people, customs, and language. Thus, the barrios of New York mark almost precise boundaries of numerous immigrant and minority groups. In recent years within the United States, these groups have been encouraged to maintain their ethnic ties in what is termed *cultural pluralism.* Such a view conflicts with an earlier notion in the United States that this country was a melting pot, where all become one culture, so to speak. The reality of minorities testifies to the fact that cultural pluralism exists historically and probably will continue in most macrocultures. Young Kim's (1977) study of Korean immigrants in Chicago indicates that ethnic identification is high, especially in the early years of acculturation. Interpersonal and organizational involvement among this group remains stronger than ties with the host nation, although the number of intercultural contacts increases over a period of time. However, too strong a network of ethnic relationships can reduce adaptation (Jin Kim 1980).

*Intercultural friendships.* Although ethnic identification remains higher than intercultural identification, studies of successful adaptation indicate that, as time passes, intercultural friendships develop. For example, Kim (1977) reported that, among her Korean respondents, the number of casual friends who are

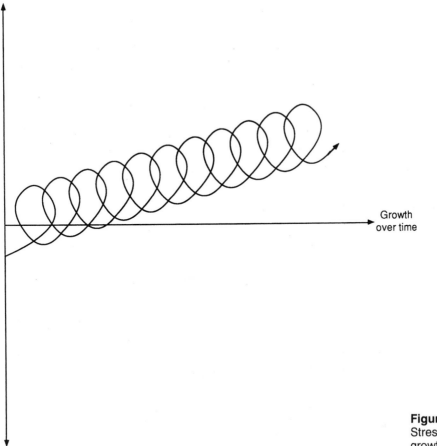

**Figure 10.2**
Stress-adaptation-
growth dynamic
(Kim 1988).

Americans increases significantly after the Korean immigrant has been in the United States about five years. After a few more years, the number of Korean casual friends decreases but always remains greater than the number of American friends. The same principle works for intimate friends: the number of American friends rises dramatically, and the number of Korean friends decreases somewhat. In other words, as the immigrants begin in the new country, they attach themselves to friends within their ethnic group. Although they maintain these ties, the new immigrants branch out and develop interethnic friends after a number of years. Jin Kim's (1980) analysis of Korean immigrants reported that communication with nonethnic sources (this is, intercultural communication) significantly facilitates the acculturation process.

*Cultural involvement.*    The longer a person lives in a new culture, the more that person tends to become more culturally involved, at least under the following conditions (see Kim 1977, 1988):

1. *Acculturation motivation.* If a person is highly motivated to be acculturated, he or she usually becomes more culturally involved with group memberships in the host culture than a person who is not motivated to acculturate.

2. *Linguistic competence.* English competence is important for explaining why some Koreans acculturate faster and better than others in the United States.

3. *Education.* Education also affects acculturation and cultural involvement, since more highly educated persons entering the host culture seem to develop more friendships and join more groups than less educated people.

4. *Dual membership.* People involved in the ethnic culture, through group memberships and friendships, also tend to be involved in the host culture. Exposure to one medium is highly related to exposure to another medium. This dual cultural involvement effect can be called the *centripetal acculturation effect.* Only in this case, acculturation and involvement in one's own culture predict involvement in a host culture—involvement breeds involvement, up to a point.

5. *Occupational status.* Kim's data also pointed out that occupational status facilitates the acculturation process (Kim 1979; Inglis and Gudykunst 1982; Baldassini and Flaherty 1982). The more one is expected to interact and the higher the status of the occupation, the greater the adaptation.

6. *Uncertainty reduction.* Gudykunst and Hammer (1988) indicate that uncertainty-reduction skills facilitate increased adaptation. They also theorize that reduced anxiety heightens the adaptation process (see also Kim 1989). If Pearce and Kang (1987) are correct, too wide a variety of interacting with individual differences and significant diversity of communication experiences of immigrants with the host culture confuses the ethnic sojourner. In this case, uncertainty not only remains unresolved, it could go up or increase anxiety.

7. *Mass media usage.* As Kim's model indicates, mass media involvement stimulates processing and adaptation to some extent. The media become a source of language trial-and-error as well as a source of humor and general cultural features.

8. *Communication skills.* Without the right communication skills in place, research shows that various communication difficulties act as major detractors from cultural adaptation. For instance, Lakey (1988) demonstrated significant findings in his survey of communication difficulty among Thai students.

Working through cultural adaptation involves stress, but accompanying growth by making new friends, developing positive attitudes, and trying new things.
(Photo by Attijaya Indrakanhang.)

He selected and developed a highly reliable scale, refining items from an earlier scale by Furnham and Bochner (1982) and found the following skills to be most important:

a.  Managing and regulation
b.  Interpersonal relationships
c.  Learning rules of social behavior
d.  Mismatch between home-culture skills and host-culture skills
e.  Inadequate stereotype and picture of host culture because of incomplete information
f.  Differences in interpretive functions—thinking and interpretation about American thought and logic that are inaccurate, leading to less adaptation
g.  Too low a level of enmeshment; that is, low internalization and contact

Overall, Lakey describes his findings as communication and social-skill deficits. He laments, along with Furnham and Bochner (1986), a lack of social-skills orientation applied to cultural adaptation, particularly in everyday situations.

Overall, the adaptation process can be viewed, as Kim (1988) indicates, as a model predicting adaptation (figure 10.3). She links a person's adaptation predisposition (acculturation motivation, change orientation, personal resistance) and the host culture's receptivity. These two influence the immigrant's communication competence and social participation in interpersonal and mass communication. These communication factors, in turn, activate adaptation outcomes (including stress, intercultural identity, and functional abilities). In sum, the idea is that one's personal motivation and the host culture's facilitation opens up windows of

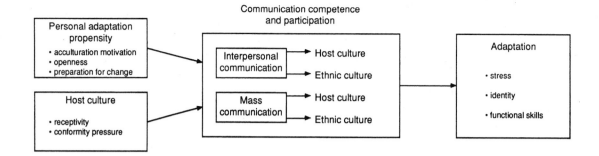

**Figure 10.3**
Adaptation of Kim's
(1988) multi-
dimensional model
of intercultural
adaptation.

possibility for immigrants to communicate interpersonally and be exposed to mass communication. Communication with the host culture and, to a lesser extent, with members of the ethnic culture, leads to adaptation.

Acculturation does not occur in everyone's life in the same way. Some people are motivated to acculturate, while others are not. At least for first-generation immigrants and for immediate culture contact, total integration is gradual and depends upon several factors. Even then, however, perhaps we are recognizing the reality that cultural pluralism is a fact for the future. The challenge for intercultural communicators is to recognize the dynamics of the cultural adaptation and acculturation factors and apply these principles, along with personal competencies and communication accommodation, to meaningful relationships.

## Intercultural Reentry

A body of literature has been evolving that documents the process of reentry into one's home culture after a stay in another culture. The research in this area reveals staggering information about what Austin (1987a) cited as a "conspiracy of silence." No one wants to admit that he or she is having difficulty readjusting to the home culture, so the reentry process has often involved people suffering a quiet stress. Austin, a leading researcher in reentry, having surveyed and counseled in his psychological practice hundreds of returned government, missionary, and business personnel, noted that a slight majority of people returning face stress in reentry and that in some cases the need for counseling is severe (Austin 1987b). Among children, 10 percent are reported to need psychological counseling. Data also suggest that returning children may experience a delayed adolescence by as much as ten years (Davis 1990).

The cycle of reentry stress is similar to the cycle of entry stress experienced upon first arrival in a new culture. Thus, a W-curve best represents a model for understanding the entry/reentry cycle (see figure 10.1). Upon first returning home, there is a sense of relief and excitement about being in familiar surroundings, seeing old friends, and so on. However, to the surprise of everyone, especially the returning expatriate, a sense of depression and negative outlook follows the initial reentry honeymoon. Symptoms described earlier in the chapter may result. Research in reentry has revealed some special factors that contribute to a downturned part of the reentry cycle. First, *self-concept decreases*. There is a feeling of nonacceptance of the self and a general search for identity (Austin 1987a). In fact, evidence suggests that returning Vietnam veterans especially experienced this loss of self because they came home to a U.S. culture that rejected their role. A second factor that can lead to reentry depression is a *homesickness and nostalgia* for the country the person just left (Moore 1981). The home culture looks so negative at times that the reentering person longs for the "good old days" in the country where he or she lived for the past several years. A third reason for reentry depression, according to Austin (1987b), is that persons facing reentry may experience a *value change*. One of the most obvious areas of value change is a kind of disgust with American materialism and feeling an embarrassment of riches. Fourth, a change that contributes to a depression stage following reentry includes the returned person's dissatisfaction with the *fast-paced way of life* and a desire for a simpler life. Fifth, a desire for *deeper friendships* and relationships accompanies reentry. In the host culture, great effort was expended to make friends and all that has to happen again, but it does not seem as automatic as the returnee expected. Sixth, a heightened *concern over ecology and politics* is a change of many repatriates way of thinking. The overseas experience often leads one to see waste and conservation in new ways. Seventh, many repatriates return with a heightened *awareness over minority issues and racial prejudice*.

Practically speaking, reverse culture shock, or cultural reentry, is a cultural vertigo because of the dizzy feeling persons experience when returning from overseas to find that the home culture is no longer the same. The mental snapshot they took when leaving is now blurred. Reactions to cultural vertigo have been documented by Schmidt's (1986) interview research and include the following observations:

1. You're not the same person upon returning, and you have a new outlook on the country.

2. It's difficult to use your experience from overseas, and people can't deal with you—it's hard to fit in.

3. You find that you're two years behind the times in clothing, slang, and other things.

4. You don't have a network to help you, as you had overseas, which makes it difficult to break in and hard to make friends.

5. Preparing for reentry is a little like preparing for old age. It doesn't begin at age seventy.

6. Find a friend or mentor before going overseas who can keep you abreast of things at home and see that your name is brought into conversations.

7. Keep in communication with people back home, and keep them up-to-date with you but also ask what changes they're going through. Don't flaunt your foreign experience. Some suggest writing two letters a week—one to work associates and another to family/friends.

8. Indicate new skills being developed and how they might be used back home.

9. Make preparations (information gathering) before returning and be prepared for changes—home will be new.

10. Distill the essence of your overseas experience because people won't want to sit for hours listening to you and seeing slides. Don't assume that you are the person who has had the exciting time—listen to others.

**Developing Skills in Intercultural Communication and Cultural Adaptation**

Overall, adapting to new cultures involves first working through culture shock. The following suggestions should assist you not only in culture shock but also in longer-range adaptation.

1. *Do not become over-reactionary.* This advice stems from the tendency to become overly frustrated during various stages of culture shock. Patience goes a long way; if you control your emotions, you can more easily see yourself and others.

2. *Meet new people.* Force yourself to go out of your way to meet others. By engaging in these new friendships, you gradually gain personal confidence and ultimately learn a lot more about the culture than by your sheer determination. A new friend can tell you things that you may spend months learning otherwise.

3. *Try new things.* Being creative and trying new foods, clothes, and so on can assist you in meeting the stress of the new culture. Trying new things is not easy, but if you can try them gradually yet persistently, you will enjoy the new culture quickly.

4. *Give yourself periods of rest and thought.* Adapting to a new culture is like being in school for several hours a day—it is hard, mental work. Like any other serious learning endeavor, you need time to rest properly. Also, you need time to reflect and put your thoughts together. Do not be a recluse, but a little time to yourself can prove beneficial.

5. *Work on your self-concept.* The mind can be directed toward positive or negative thoughts. While this idea may seem oversimplified at first, try feeding yourself a diet of positive thoughts. Of course, you can go

overboard and distort reality, but positive thinking can help you. Tell yourself that you are really not so bad and that most other people go through the same experiences that you face during culture shock.

6. *Write.* Sometimes writing in a diary or some other medium can release tension and frustration. Also, reflecting at a later time on what you have written can prove insightful to personal growth.

7. *Observe body language.* As stated in chapter 9, body language and nonverbal communication in general are subtle but persuasive. Part of the frustration of culture shock is not knowing the culture's system of body language. People bump into you without apology, and people may not smile at you the way they do back home, and so you miss the cues once so familiar. By learning the nonverbal rules, you may discover that the behavior of the people of the new culture does not indicate anger or any other dissatisfaction with you personally.

8. *Learn the verbal language.* Take time to learn as much of the host culture's language as possible. Not only does using the native language compliment people in the host culture, but it obviously aids your survival skills.

---

## This Chapter in Perspective

This chapter describes physical and psychological symptoms of transition into a new culture, called cultural adaptation. Some of those symptoms include upset stomach, slight headache, obsession with health and with material things, irritability, homesickness, and defensiveness.

The chapter also outlines four stages of culture shock: (1) the eager expectation stage refers to the planning stage and the accompanying excitement; (2) the "everything is beautiful" stage involves a sense of euphoria and pleasure with the new culture; (3) the "everything is awful" stage is typified by a flurry of negativism in which one fights, flees, filters, or flexes; and (4) the "everything is OK" stage characterized by a balanced view of the new culture.

During and after culture shock, however, people who plan to be permanent residents of a host culture face the long-term stress of adapting to new people and customs. An obvious part of acculturation is first learning survival skills. We typically change our attitudes toward host nationals following culture contact, but only under a number of conditions. Long-term acculturation includes the stress-growth-adaptation dynamic. The chapter discussion of adaptation also highlights the importance of communication factors in facilitating adaptation.

This chapter also documents processes and suggestions for meeting the demands of cultural reentry. The psychological stress underlying reentry can be understood and dealt with. A number of useful suggestions are provided.

**Exercises**

1. Interview a business or professional person who has been working overseas for a while. Ask for impressions of his or her psychological states during the earlier and then during the later period of this person's stay in the host country. What patterns emerge? Why?

2. Discuss with some ethnic leaders in your community the problems of acculturation of minorities in your locale. Ask them for their advice as to how ethnic groups or other minorities can acculturate in ways mutually beneficial to ethnic group members and the dominant culture.

3. Do some research in the library or in some of your other university or college courses about the theory of cognitive dissonance. What parallels do you see between that theory and the patterns of culture shock discussed in this chapter? How can dissonance theory reduction techniques be used in reducing culture shock?

# Chapter 11

# Intercultural Competencies and Effectiveness

After completing this chapter, you should be able to

1. Define effectiveness and its dimensions

2. List factors of intercultural competency associated with intercultural effectiveness outcomes

3. Apply criteria from models of intercultural effectiveness toward intercultural selection

4. Identify effectiveness issues in a model

5. Develop steps for intercultural personnel selection

This chapter deals with the competencies necessary for effective intercultural communication outcomes. Our central text model stresses that in the context of the third culture C, we adapt to culture and develop communication accommodation strategies in ways that are functional leading to effective outcomes or dysfunctional leading to ineffective outcomes. The overall intercultural model along with the original models presented in this chapter linking competency to intercultural effectiveness will clarify this area of intercultural effectiveness research that previously lacked clear models, principles, and application for intercultural competency. The connection to personnel selection makes this material practical as well as theoretically insightful.

## What is Intercultural Communication Effectiveness?

The theme of the chapter is that intercultural competencies lead to intercultural communication effectiveness. Before learning what is involved in effective outcomes, we need to learn what is meant by intercultural communication effectiveness. Experts agree that some form of *outcome success* is expected. Not all agree exactly on the nature of the outcome, but the results of intercultural effectiveness fall into the general area of ability to function within a culture. Of course, how well you function is a matter of degree, but the critical question is what is central to outcomes. Once we have defined what is the expected outcome, then we are in a position to know how to get there.

Numerous articles, papers, and lectures are available on the topic of competency and effectiveness, although researchers and practioners sometimes mix these two concepts. A good review of issues surrounding effectiveness is extended by Hammer (1989), who reminds us of a central theme—communication competence is central to intercultural effectiveness. Intercultural competence factors are the skills and qualities associated with and leading to intercultural effectiveness. You have to know, do, or become something before successful outcomes occur.

In summary of a great deal of research, there are *three central outcomes for effectiveness: task performance, ability to adapt to the new culture, and the ability to establish healthy interpersonal relationships* (Hammer 1989; Hawes and Kealey 1981; Hammer 1987; Martin and Hammer 1989; Harris and Moran 1991; Gudykunst, Wiseman, and Hammer 1977; Kealey 1989).

First, task performance is doing well at your job. While significant, however, professional performance alone does not qualify for success. Second, successful adaptation to the culture is necessary (discussed in the last chapter). Third, successful interpersonal relationships are a sign of effectiveness outcomes. You cannot be defined as ultimately successful if you have no

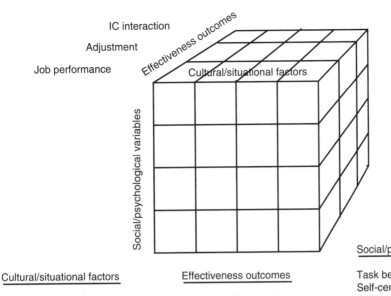

IC interaction
Adjustment
Job performance

Effectiveness outcomes

Cultural/situational factors

Social/psychological variables

Social/psychological variables

Cultural/situational factors

High/low context cultures
Societal values
Culture-specific characteristics

Effectiveness outcomes

Intercultural interaction
Personal/family adjustment
Professional effectiveness

Social/psychological variables

Task behavior
Self-centeredness
Judgmental behaviors
Interpersonal skills/flexibility
Acculturation

**Figure 11.1**
Cube model for intercultural effectiveness. (Kise, Phipps, and Sufferlein 1995, for this volume.)

friends, make enemies, do not interpersonally communicate well, and deal ineffectively with emotions in relationships. Overall, these three outcomes set the standards for expected intercultural outcomes. Fortunately, these are outcomes for which one can prepare. This trio of factors is not always accepted as a "package," as in some corporate cultures where task success is a primary measure.

I will resist the temptation to tell a hundred stories here from intercultural consulting experiences and briefly describe just one. Bill and Susan (not their real names) are an American expatriate couple working in an overseas environment. Their communication and psychological assessments revealed significant communication barriers between them as a couple as well as between them and their projected host culture. They were advised by their psychological consultant and by their communication consultant to avoid leaving until help was secured. They rejected the advice, only to experience severe difficulties not only in adjusting to the new culture, but in forming adequate relationships, and in getting the job done that the husband was hired to accomplish. All this and many more negative experiences occurred despite excelling in task-related professional training! In other words, one's professional competency can be obliterated by poor people skills and competencies. Within time they returned and suffered emotional and relationship problems and are now divorced.

When all these considerations are factored, creative research and insight has led several reseachers/trainers to conceive not only of effectiveness in a visually useful manner but to link competence-related qualities to show their leading to effectiveness outcomes. Figures 11.1, 11.2, and 11.3 reveal multiple intercultural

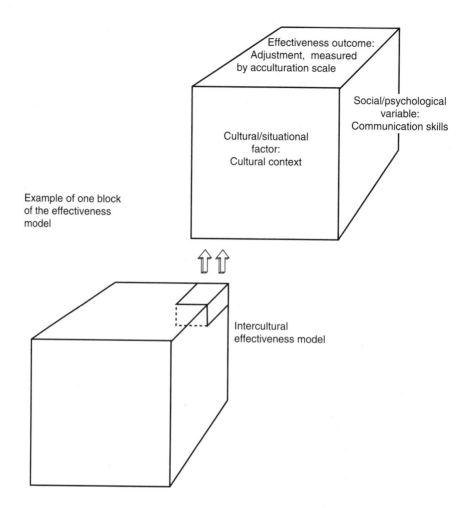

Effectiveness outcome:
Adjustment, measured
by acculturation scale

Social/psychological
variable:
Communication skills

Cultural/situational
factor:
Cultural context

Example of one block
of the effectiveness
model

Intercultural
effectiveness model

**Figure 11.2**
Enlarged example
of cube model.

aspects. The first model called the "cube model" demonstrates social/psychological competency predictors and cultural/situational competency predictors associated with the three effectiveness outcomes (Kise, Phipps, and Sufferlein 1995). This model is based on the behavioral categories indicated by Ruben (1977), and Hall's (1976) cultural factors.

The second model is called the E-Model, with the E standing for "effectiveness." The three outcomes defining effectiveness are pictured on the right as arms of the letter E, and the notion of intercultural competencies associated with effectiveness is pictured on the left as contributing to effectiveness (Walter, Choonjaroen, Bartosh, and Dodd 1995). Figure 11.3 portrays the model and identifies operational definitions of each effectiveness outcome. The model is

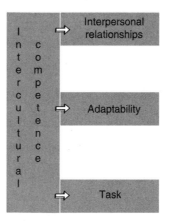

**Figure 11.3**
E-model of intercultural effectiveness. (Walter, Choonjaroen, Bartosh, and Dodd 1995, for this volume.)

## Task

- Technical and/or professional performance
- Resourcefulness
- Imagination/creativity
- Ability to innovate
- Performance evaluation
- Organizational communication
- Goal development
- Management of task

## Adaptability

- Flexibility
- Maturity
- Knowledge of host culture
- Language skills
- Nonjudgmental attitude
- Patience
- Respect for culture
- Open-mindedness
- Tolerance for ambiguity
- Appropriate social behavior

## Interpersonal relationships

- Friendship
- Emotional control
- Sense of humor
- Sensitivity towards others' needs
- Empathy
- Consideration towards others
- Trust others
- Leadership
- Positive relations with strangers
- Ability to get along with co-workers
- Family relations
- Lack of ethnocentrism/prejudice

**Figure 11.3 continued**
Operational outcomes of intercultural effectiveness categories for E-model.

built on research and papers primarily from Hammer and Clarke (1987), Harris and Moran (1991), Kealey and Ruben (1983), Tucker and Baier (1985). A scale was developed to accompany the E-model and is presented in the appendix.

## Competence in Cognitive Style and Social Variables Influencing Intercultural Effectiveness

What are the competencies that influence effectiveness? The models presented in this chapter underscore numerous competencies associated with and predictive of the three effectiveness outcomes. Next, an extensive set of cognitive style and social variables is shown to correlate with positive intercultural effectiveness outcomes. (Hammer 1989; Ruben 1977; Olebe and Koester 1989; Wiseman, Hammer, and Nishida 1989; Dinges and Lieberman 1989; Kealey 1989).

### Insistence on Task Behavior

Insistence on getting the job done can lead to ineffectiveness, at least for skills transfer and development (Ruben 1977). This role behavior is likely to become even more dysfunctional in cultures where occupational roles and expectations are at odds with cultural norms. A person who works for an organization that exhibits an intensive communication style is likely to experience failure within a culture that appreciates a more leisurely pace of work and task behavior.

### Self-Centered Behavior

Self-centered communication is less functional (Ruben 1977). Examples include calling attention to oneself, bragging, and showing disinterest in the ideas of the group. In Japan, making excuses for why something did not work out does not work as well as a simple apology. In general, excessive self-praise or self-blame usually are ineffective in intercultural interactions.

### Ethnocentrism

The deleterious effects of judgmental attitudes and a feeling of being superior to others from another cultural group are well documented. In a series of investigations correlating a scale to measure ethnocentrism (developed by Hood 1982) with culture stress, Dodd (1987) reported a significant correlation, indicating that highly ethnocentric individuals are less likely to adjust well during a transitional experience. Gudykunst and Kim (1984) explained that prejudice and ethnocentrism lead to less effectiveness in intercultural encounters. Furthermore, Tucker and Baier (1985) reported that the ability not to criticize or put down foreigners was significantly linked with intercultural adjustment.

### Tolerance for Ambiguity and Flexibility

The ability to react to new but ambiguous situations with little difficulty is a significant skill in intercultural effectiveness (Ruben 1977; Tucker and Baier 1985; Gudykunst and Kim 1984; *Overseas Diplomacy* 1973; Grove and Torbiorn 1985). In other words, if you can handle situations you do not immediately understand, then you probably have a high tolerance for ambiguity. Intercultural communication by nature poses ambiguities; other people, institutions, organizations, and even your attitude toward yourself just do not seem to make any sense. General confusion and disorientation may result just from being in another culture. Fluidity and flexibility are very important for building relationships in intercultural climates.

### Empathy

A number of researchers report that the ability to put ourselves in the shoes of others is a significant relationship skill. That same ability is helpful in intercultural effectiveness. To understand things from another's point of view is critical in a number of circumstances, including communicating innovative ideas (Rogers 1983) and performing up to our potential in intercultural communication (*Overseas Diplomacy* 1973). Active listening and accurate perceiving are significant extensions of empathy (Hammer 1989).

**Openness**

Observers like DeVito (1989) have noted how openness and flexibility in personal communication style are important for maximum interpersonal relationships to develop and to be maintained. Dogmatism has been significantly correlated with lack of adjustment by linking measures of flexibility with intercultural adjustment and performance (Tucker and Baier 1985). While it is good to share how we feel about things, we become obnoxious when we communicate in a way that puts people down or that leaves no room for disagreement or further dialogue.

**Cognitive Complexity**

Cognitive complexity refers to the ability of a person to perceive a wide variety of things about another person and to make finer interpersonal discriminations than cognitively simple individuals. Using a sample of Americans working in five countries of South America, Norton (1984) found that cognitively complex individuals scored significantly lower on measures of culture stress than cognitively simple individuals. Gudykunst and Kim (1984) later made the observation that category width, another way to describe cognitive complexity, makes for greater effectiveness. In general, cognitively complex individuals make better and more accurate judgments in developing impressions about others. They see more possibilities about people and situations.

**Interpersonal Comfort**

Research also shows that our ability to feel comfortable interpersonally is significantly correlated with maximum intercultural adjustment (Norton and Dodd 1984). Other research indicates that interpersonal trust, interpersonal interest, interpersonal harmony (Tucker and Baier 1985), and interaction (*Overseas Diplomacy* 1973) are correlated with effectiveness. Thus, if you do not feel comfortable with your interpersonal relationships in your home culture, you may not feel any more comfortable in a host culture.

**Personal Control in Communication World View**

The amount of immediate and personal control we sense about our communication environment has been significantly correlated with intercultural effectiveness. Researchers have identified a significant connection between personal control and intercultural adjustment and performance (Tucker and Baier 1985; Dodd 1987; Long, Javidi, and Pryately 1993). These findings suggest that taking charge of (but not dominating) your communication climate impacts adaptation in a new culture and your ultimate success in being interpersonally effective.

**Innovativeness**

Innovativeness refers to our ability to try new things, to engage in some social risk taking, particularly where new information and developing social relationships are concerned. Evidence suggests that our ability to try new things is linked with intercultural effectiveness (*Overseas Diplomacy* 1973). Being a risk taker does not mean advocating social deviancy or taboo-breaking behavior. On the contrary, innovativeness means the ability to make significant strides in developing and accepting new ideas within a context of social acceptance. A willingness to experiment with new approaches and especially a willingness to learn are highly linked with intercultural communication success.

## Self-Esteem/ Confidence

Clearly, our self-esteem predicts intercultural effectiveness. A negative self-esteem can shake the foundations of our personal outlook (Bennett 1977), thus inhibiting effectiveness. Also, self-confidence and initiative directly correlate with personal adjustment and performance (Tucker and Baier 1985; *Overseas Diplomacy* 1973).

Everyone has self-doubts once in a while, and even those occasional negatives can chip away at intercultural effectiveness. As Shakespeare said, "Our doubts are traitors and cause us to lose the good we oft might win by fearing to attempt." Fear can freeze our emotions and our spirits. At the root of some fear is low self-esteem. Beyond those momentary losses of confidence, however, most of us can really perform beyond our expectations.

One of the needs discovered in intercultural counseling is that some individuals need genuine, self-confidence-building programs before they go overseas. That need is also present for an entire family going together to an intercultural assignment.

## Communication Apprehension/ Assertiveness

Studies have revealed that our personal anxiety about communication affects intercultural adjustment and intercultural effectiveness. Research shows that the higher the communication apprehension, the lower the intercultural effectiveness (Dodd 1987). As expected, effectiveness is inhibited by lack of communication confidence (McCroskey 1982).

## Conversation Management

This area refers to social skills such as interpersonal harmony (Koester and Olebe 1986, 1987), responsiveness as part of communicator style (Myers 1990), and self-disclosure appropriate to the culture (Hammer and Nishida 1985). These imply turn-taking and the ability to adapt interaction goals and behaviors to others (Hammer and Nishida 1985). As Snyder (1980) indicated for interpersonal relationship management, self-monitoring enables a person to sense the appropriate amount of fitting into a new communication context, and obviously would be expected to be an important intercultural competency skill. Also role and status management (Yousef and Briggs 1975) as well as rule and procedure etiquette concerning formality (Sarbaugh 1979) are involved.

## Family Communication

Researchers and practioners realize that intercultural communication and cultural experiences touch everyone in a family. This system's approach stresses family life as a competency skill antecedent to successful overseas expatriation (Tucker and Baier 1982; Harris and Moran 1991).

Tucker and Baier (1985) remind us that trust in people is a part of intercultural success.

**Friendliness/ Outgoingness/ Trust in People**

Astute perception about the rhetorical rules and procedures in a culture can be significant as well as appropriate content material in speech and interaction (Koester and Holmberg 1983). This category could include media appropriateness where extremes have been linked to lack of adjustment and obsessive-compulsive behavior (Lewis, Dodd, and Tippens 1989).

**Rhetorical Competence/ Perception**

The desire to learn language and culture and adapt within a new culture is correlated with successful acculturation (Kim 1977, 1988).

**Acculturation Motivation**

Gudykunst and Kim (1984) identified the importance of closeness to the host culture as a predictor of successful outcomes. The amount of prior knowledge, experience, and familiarity with the potentially new culture is also important.

**Similarity- Difference and Familiarity with Culture**

All the positive personal and social characteristics imaginable do not lessen difficulty in a new culture if the host culture is hostile to outsiders or if the host culture is rigid (Gudykunst and Kim 1984).

**Rigidity of New Culture**

Intercultural training plays a vital role in developing competencies for effectiveness (Grove and Torbiorn 1985).

**Amount of Intercultural Training**

Briefly stated, administrators involved in personnel selection have a number of important considerations: personality, communication skills, family, professional competency, and so on. The decision maker must bear in mind that effectiveness is not a single but a multiple construct involving the major outcomes identified above: job performance, cultural adaptation, and interpersonal/ family/significant other relations.

**Selection for Intercultural Assignments**

How does one choose? The model in figure 11.4 provides a stepwise approach to making intercultural selection and allows us to put all this research into perspective.

1. Describe projected outcomes defining intercultural success. For example, job performance, interpersonal communication success, and positive adaptation.

2. Choose the most professionally competent person who is also the most relationally competent. Keep in mind who adjusted successfully in previous transfers. Interviews, peer reviews, and performance records are useful. The best should be chosen, for the consequences are severe otherwise. Entire overseas operations have been shut down because of poor selection. This

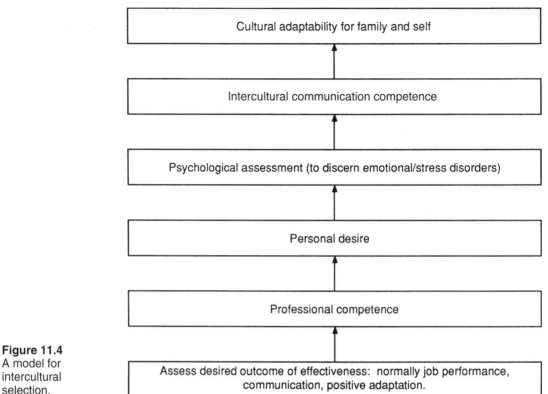

**Figure 11.4**
A model for
intercultural
selection.

| |
|---|
| Cultural adaptability for family and self |
| Intercultural communication competence |
| Psychological assessment (to discern emotional/stress disorders) |
| Personal desire |
| Professional competence |
| Assess desired outcome of effectiveness: normally job performance, communication, positive adaptation. |

Choosing for
intercultural
personnel
assignments
involves ability with
task, relationships,
and cultural
adaptation.
(Photo by Attitaya
Indrakanhang.)

first level examines technical and professional competence. (Can the person do the job expected? One AT&T human resources executive with an extensive training budget and himself a veteran of working in the Middle East once told me that job performance was the best predictor for overseas job performance.)

3. Choose a person who wants to go. Personal desire and motivation are highly significant building blocks.

4. Screen for psychological barriers or mental maladjustments that could prevent cultural adjustment or relationship building. Psychological testing (MMPI, 16 PF, Myers-Briggs, Taylor-Johnson Temperament Analysis, etc.) are used by many organizations to determine emotional disorders. This is not to suggest that a person cannot receive help and be prepared at a later time, but experienced practioners in this area insist that unresolved emotional disorders invite numerous problems connected with field work.

5. Does the candidate meet intercultural communication competencies noted earlier and in table 11.1? (See the previous list.)

6. Does the candidate's family relationship and motivation pose a barrier? Can training be developed for the family? Is the marriage experiencing difficulty?

Selection is complicated, but training must accompany intercultural deployment. Unfortunately, most training is minimal in many organizations, even though experts agree that expatriates should receive at least forty hours of intercultural training plus 150 hours of language training.

The broadest view of intercultural outcome is viewed in figure 11.5, which explores the broader picture among antecedent, process, and consequent conditions. Beyond merely exploring variables that predict intercultural effectiveness, we recognize the intercultural climates that intervene and affect the ultimate effectiveness outcomes.

In the long run, intercultural communication skills are not "push button" substitutes for understanding. Communication strategies are never mechanistic, artificial ways around loving, warm, personal involvement with people and the hard work required to make relationships work. Understanding what skills link with positive intercultural outcomes begins a positive journey. In that way, intercultural skills are really the application of an eclectic awareness of factors contributing to effectiveness and a personal motivation to make these work in our relationships.

**Table 11.1  Summary Predictors of Intercultural Communication Effectiveness**

| Effectiveness | Ineffectiveness |
| --- | --- |
| High people, less task emphasis | High task, less people emphasis |
| Few self-statements | Many self-statements |
| Low ethnocentrism | High ethnocentrism |
| High tolerance for ambiguity | Low tolerance for ambiguity |
| High empathy, good listening | Low empathy, poor listening |
| High openness, low dogmatism | Low openness, high dogmatism |
| Cognitive complexity | Cognitive simplicity |
| Comfort with interpersonal relations, trust | Discomfort with interpersonal relations, mistrust |
| High personal control, low fatalism | Low personal control, high fatalism |
| High innovativeness | Low innovativeness |
| High self-esteem | Low self-esteem |
| Low communication apprehension | High communication apprehension |
| Positive conversational management skills | Poor conversational management skills |
| Positive family communication | Negative family communication |
| Friendly, warm | Unfriendly, cold |
| Extroverted | Introverted |
| Rhetorical sensitivity | Lack of rhetorical sensitivity |
| High acculturation motivation | Low acculturation motivation |
| Familiarity and knowledge of host culture | Little knowledge of host culture |
| Openness to strangers of host culture | Rigidity of host culture |
| Great amount of intercultural training | Low amount of intercultural training |

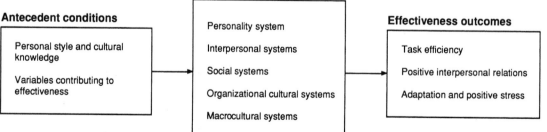

**Figure 11.5**
A model for
intercultural skills.

How can you perform better in intercultural contexts? Perhaps the strategies that follow will add more skills to your understanding of the principles already introduced in this chapter.

**Developing Skills in Building Intercultural Relationships**

1. *Work to emphasize areas of similarity with others.* To the extent you can underscore commonality, generally the better the interpersonal relationship.

2. *Try to accept differing opinions.* In this way, you can remain open and receptive. Dogmatism has a way of blocking intercultural communication.

3. *Make your verbal messages consistent with your nonverbal messages.* Listen to yourself, and try to see yourself talk. Discrepancies between the verbal and nonverbal send a mixed message that in the long run discredits you.

4. *Avoid dominating conversations.* Listen to how much time you spend communicating while in a group. You may be dominating others in the group, and it may not be long before they find you a bore. Listening to others, inviting their explanations, and showing genuine interest are communication suggestions.

5. *Avoid being submissive in conversations.* Although domination can prove to be harmful, if you are overly submissive, people may decide that you have nothing to contribute, a condition that leads to intercultural relationship demise.

6. *Be an affirmer.* You do not have to be a backslapper or act obsequiously to be confirming in your communication behavior. Your intercultural counterparts will appreciate your attempts at being understanding rather than critical.

---

This chapter highlights the settings of interpersonal communication, particularly focusing on the influence of intervening or mediating elements, including assumptions and variables related to the intercultural effectiveness process. The variables are numerous, but models for intercultural personnel selection and for viewing effectiveness are presented.

**This Chapter in Perspective**

**Exercises**

1. Observe children at play. List mediating variables that you observe in their communication, and give examples. Are racial differences noticed by children? If not, why not? Report these findings to your class and exchange observations with other class members. How do children reflect and foreshadow adult intercultural communication?

2. Do a field study in which you observe dyads, or pairs, of people. Keep records. Compare nonverbal communication between friends with nonverbal communication between strangers.

3. Read a news magazine account of an intercultural contact. After reading the story, list at least five ways in which most people display poor interpersonal-intercultural communication.

# Intercultural Communication and Conflict

After completing this chapter, you should be able to

**Objectives**

1. Identify the importance of interpersonal relationships in intercultural communication effectiveness and conflict

2. Understand and identify personality characteristics that mediate and influence intercultural communication conflict

3. Describe how perceived relationships and certain verbal behaviors, such as self-disclosure, affect communication conflict

4. Cope with interpersonal conflict and gain personal awareness of intrapersonal conflicts

5. Improve intercultural interaction skills

A mid-size city in the mid-southwestern portion of the United States received a number of Cambodian, Laotian, and Vietnamese refugees. Some of these people were once "boat people," and the community was sincerely interested in the refugees and their plight. Religious, civic, and governmental groups combined their efforts with the local mass media to encourage participation in various relocation efforts. Despite the encouragement and dedicated efforts of many people, a number of minor frustrations gradually arose among the townspeople. Finally, a seminar was conducted to assist not only community personnel, but educators and other interested persons. During the seminar, it became clear that one of the struggles in working with the refugee group was in the area of understanding the cultural differences involved. Other minor frustrations involved some basic needs to understand several personal as well as cultural factors—some people were ineffective and some suffered from lack of adaptation.

This particular situation is not unique, for it has been enacted thousands of times throughout the world, wherever people from two cultures meet. Beyond language, cultural and interpersonal differences, there are numerous conflict related factors that enter into intercultural relationships. This chapter explains the nature of intercultural conflict and offers concepts and orientations that should facilitate managing intercultural conflict.

Examples abound every day concerning intercultural conflict. A news story, for example, revealed that the Italian actress Sophia Loren was negotiating with legal advisors about staying in her home country. We also may learn that a Middle Eastern culture has heavy investments in land holdings in the midwestern section of the United States and that negotiations are underway for more property acquisition. A new international student may become a classmate. In the student center, we can observe and talk with other American students whose racial backgrounds differ from ours. Perhaps on Friday night, you have a date with a person from a different region of the country than your place of origin. The potential for intercultural conflict is almost certain—part of our understanding of intercultural communication involves exploring the reasons why intercultural conflict can occur in our relationships. In turn, how can we practice conflict management competencies facilitating intercultural success?

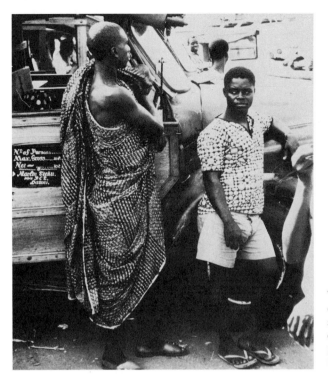

Without self-disclosure on some level, communication and personal growth remain static.

Conflict comes from a number of origins. Most experts agree with the fundamental principle that *misunderstanding cultural expectations* lies behind many conflict circumstances. By identifying cultural conflict areas, we can improve our awareness and skills for communication accommodation.

## Potential Sources of Intercultural Conflict

Self-disclosure is revealing personal information not normally conveyed. Self-disclosure is viewed as intimate and guarded information about oneself not obtained any other way (Jourard 1964). Research reveals a strong relationship between self-disclosure and trust, liking, and reciprocal self-disclosure, at least within some aspects of U.S. culture.

Two people who share or disclose at some level can set an important communication "stage" in preventing and managing conflict.

Self-disclosure varies interculturally. In high-context cultures information is gathered from means other than the message. Individuals, consequently, are thus expected to engage in more small talk and use indirect communication patterns (Gudykunst, Ting-Toomey, and Chua 1988). Comparison of cultural patterns shows that some macrocultures are more disclosive than others. When compared with Americans, British, Germans, Australians, Koreans, and Japanese disclose

### Self-Disclosure
### Relationships

less. Meyer and Salem's (1992) review of intercultural self-disclosure and friendship concluded that high- and low-context cultures account for differences: the high-context cultures are predicted to account for less disclosure.

For several reasons, understanding self-disclosure can help in meeting the demands involved in intercultural conflicts. First, when *reciprocity is not met,* expectations are not met. In intimacy, one usually is expected to match the other person. If you under-disclose in a culture that expects you to reveal more, violation of communication norms has occurred; similarly over-disclosure creates cultural conflict.

Second, when disclosure occurs with the *wrong person or at an inappropriate stage of relationship,* conflict occurs. Status and hierarchy are very important in many cultures, such as high power-distance cultures (chapter 6). Perhaps silence or small talk are more appropriate in some cultures with a high status person. Sometimes, too, a person is in a changing role relationship and mismatched with the stage of the relationship. For instance, an acquaintance now becomes a dating partner thus changing the amount of disclosure that can be expected in that relationship. Apparently, once a friendship reaches a certain stage, culture has less influence on communication patterns (Gudykunst 1985) and disclosiveness would likely follow that trend.

## Hierarchy Relationships

Another conflict source surrounds hierarchy in relationships. For instance, when talking with a close friend, what are your feelings? More than likely, the dominance-submission variable is not operating. How would you feel visiting a foreign ambassador in his or her office? Perhaps you would feel a bit more submissive. The same feeling can occur in various role relationships, such as employer-employee, officer-enlisted person, nurse-patient, parent-child, and teacher-student.

*Hierarchy and power.* In the case of intercultural communication, hierarchy and power are often products of group norms and expectations. The resultant communication in these cases is less culturally sensitive and often conflictual. Power-distance cultures, identified and discussed in chapter 6, remain potential sources of hierarchy leading to intercultural conflict. If person A from a high power-distance culture operates from cultural norms with person B from a low power-distance culture, we would expect differences in decision-making, rules, submission, cooperation, turn-taking, conversation equality, and a number of communication qualities important in building positive, healthy relationships.

*Hierarchy and roles.* Roles are behaviors performed because of attitudes or expectations of position. A person may communicate and behave in a certain way because his or her role demands such behavior. A law enforcement officer who seems hard and unbending in his or her work role may be highly sympathetic and jovial with family or friends.

*Hierarchy and status.* Status differences are potential sources of conflict related to hierarchy. For instance, a cultural role in the Middle East indicates that the higher status person pays the check in a restaurant. If you are the higher status person, you may be confused, especially if the other person dramatically insists on paying. However, this insistence is a way of saving face when the higher status person wins the battle of the check and pays—usually to the relief of the lower status person, who insisted in the first place to maintain his or her pride (Yousef and Briggs 1975).

In Asian, African, and Middle Eastern cultures, age is an indicator of status. Many cultures revere their elderly, showing honor and respect. If you were working as a manager in an international situation, you can imagine the personnel implications if you passed over an older employee for a younger worker.

Another potential intercultural conflict source occurs with misplaced formality in various relationships. With some people, little formality is necessary, while for other relationships, formality is expected. For instance, there is probably little formality between you and your roommate or between you and a good friend. Perhaps, however, your formality level increases with a professor or whenever you enter a situation where you cannot predict the degree of formality expected. **Formality in Relationships**

This concept of formality and informality is not merely a matter of etiquette, but a question of intercultural relationship. For example, you may approach a conversation informally, using first-person pronouns and using the other person's first name. The other person, approaching the relationship formally, may refer to titles and make frequent references to one's position in life. Naturally, this conflict over appropriateness of formality can cause embarrassment and extreme discomfort.

To his discussion of formality in relationships, Sarbaugh (1979) added that the more differences between two interacting parties—or heterogeneity, to use his term—the more difficult it is to predict the social roles and norms expected. This inability to sense what is expected creates a great deal of frustration. Thus, part of intercultural communication effectiveness involves some attempt to assess just what level of formality is expected. For instance, in the United States, if you are talking with an older person, what terms of address are appropriate? There are a number of older people who prefer formal methods of address and others who prefer that you call them by their first name. Before embarking on one level of formality or another, try to determine what the other person prefers; often, that person's conversation reveals a preference. In the same way, many cultural norms dictate formality—so, listen for any cues that can help you set the tone appropriate for a conversation.

Many of our perspectives on management and standard operating procedures cannot always be applied on the job in intercultural situations. Effective managers who work internationally often recognize the need to alter their organizational structure and their personal management styles because of cultural needs in several areas. Failure to adapt to the cultural differences in the workplace leads to conflict, as the following categories illustrate. **Interpersonal Work Relationships**

*Speed and efficiency.*   Some cultures work at slower rates than others. The job gets done in these cases, not because someone is insisting on speed and efficiency, but because workers respect others and try to build personal relationships. As Ruben (1977) emphasized, competence can be handled in such a way that people feel a part of the completed project and learn from the process. Adapting to a culture's time orientation is one of the simplest, yet most helpful, changes we can make when living in a second culture. For example, one U.S. firm waited two years in Japan for an important decision. The American executives were surprised to learn that that time was necessary for the indispensable preliminary of establishing relationships before negotiating.

*Cultural rules of employment.*   Because of status and equality norms, cultural rules toward employment differ. For example, in Iran, a worker who has become ill sends his brother in his place to work that day. In fact, loyalty is a very strong theme in many parts of Latin America and the Middle East, so much so that a worker who changes jobs too often is viewed as shiftless and disloyal. Ackermann (1976) told how a promotion of a manual laborer to foreman by a U.S. mining operation in the South Pacific led to his murder. In that culture, advancement above one's peers violates tribal rules of equality—hence, the death.

*Nonverbal communication.*   In parts of Africa, Latin America, Asia, North America, and the Middle East, an indication of "yes" can also mean "I hear you" but may not necessarily be an agreement. In Asia, pointing the soles of your feet or your toes is offensive, just as standing too close or too far can be offensive. In some cultures, a handshake implies welcome; in others, it implies distance.

*Work and friendship.*   In some cultures, work and friendship are distinct. In the U.S. work culture the standard is to work eight hours and then leave for some form of social life. In many cultures, such as Japan, the Middle East, and Latin America, work, play, and friendship are blended. A Japanese employee may work until 6:00 or 7:00 and then be expected to go to a restaurant or bar to engage socially with business associates. In these contexts, the after-hours work is a source of the company getting to know and trust someone. Also, many cultures expect several visits before doing business.

*Meaning of friendships.*   Friendships are long term in a number of cultures. The friendship opens commitments to hospitality, gift giving, and, in Latin America, godparenting. The North American concept of friendship is casual, with upward and social mobility overriding long friendships in favor of friendships that come and go. This difference makes a friendly North American vulnerable to being criticized as hypocritical because the person does not follow through with the friendship.

*Role expectations of a manager.*   Some cultures, expect managers to assume responsibility for the total life of the employee, including sickness, personal problems, and children's welfare (Yousef and Briggs 1975).

*Speaking in a straightforward manner.* Communication styles of directness or indirectness vary culturally. North Americans are expected to come to the point. Phrases like "get to the point" and "small talk before the main point" indicate that some U.S. Americans do not like wasting time, including time in their conversational and speech patterns. However, in parts of the Middle East and Latin America, people are considered rude if they come to the point too quickly, before appropriate timing and relationships are built. They talk around the point.

**Need for Acceptance and Empathy**

Most of us need to be accepted by others. That accounts for our seeking cultural and group identities. Some people, however, need more acceptance than others and may, in fact, be joiners. One study showed a correspondence between men who joined a fraternity and their simultaneous need for acceptance and their fear of rejection (Brady 1975). The individual who talks incessantly, may be expressing a deeper need for acceptance. Likewise, an extremely quiet person may be expressing a need for acceptance and a fear of rejection by his or her silence.

Consequently, not having acceptance needs met or not met in a culturally expected manner becomes a source of intercultural conflict. For instance, one's use of threatening messages or sarcasm can have a negative effect, especially from a contrast culture not accustomed to such treatment.

Empathy can build better relationships by heading off this problem of insufficient acceptance. Broome (1991) identifies the very heart of the model in this text by calling for relational empathy in the creation of a third culture. Rather than empathy being seen as a product, intercultural empathy involves a reproductive, creative approach where several things happen in creating a third culture: (1) shared meaning is developed; (2) process of developing understanding is open; (3) participants develop understanding during discourse approximating the other's point of view; (4) continual adjustment of the other's point of view during interaction. It is overall a growing, dynamic, change-sensitive approach to empathy rather than a static, recipe view of empathy.

**Communication Coping Style**

Have you noticed how some people seem able to stick with a point of discussion and solve problems while other people avoid working toward solutions? *Copers* are those individuals who generally work through problems or conflicts, while *avoiders* are those individuals who usually are either unable, or do not want, to seek solutions to issues. While everyone at times may choose to ignore problems and even flee various issues instead of maintaining an open line of communication, avoiders do so consistently. Getting angry, hiding behind a newspaper in the cafeteria, pretending not to see another, giving the silent treatment, or acting pompously and dictatorially are manifestations of avoidance behavior. An avoider can experience more frustration during various stages of culture shock.

Of course, cultural behaviors can include avoiding or coping. The Japanese man who sits silently or quietly exits during a confrontation may be responding culturally, not personally avoiding. He may choose another time or place to resolve a question. The American who seems intent on pressing for a contract with an Italian businessman may not be personally coping but insisting on a cultural pattern of efficiency or time management.

## Conflict Because of Imbalance and Disagreement in Communication

Inevitably, even our best efforts at establishing and maintaining intercultural relationships are sometimes shattered by our discovery that others like what we dislike or dislike what we like. The resulting communication and attitudes have implications for personal styles of resolving conflict.

In its extended form, the notion of balanced relationships suggests that if you and another person like the same thing and like each other, a balanced relationship exists. However, the relationship is unbalanced when people who like each other do not like the same thing or when two people who like the same thing do not like each other. The first component in this description of interpersonal relationships is A's orientation toward a topic X, which includes A's attitude toward Y (approach or avoidance) and various beliefs about X (cognitive attributes). The second component is A's orientation toward person B. A and B can have positive or negative attractions toward each other while holding favorable or unfavorable attitudes toward topic X. When there is an unbalanced state (A and B like each other, but A feels positively about topic X while B feels negatively about X), there is a tension to restore balance through communication (Heider 1958).

Balance can be restored in several ways. For example, suppose a Mexican American named Roberto (A) and an African American named Wes (B) like each other (they have been friends for two years and work as department heads in the same department store in San Antonio). Roberto likes a new accounting system recently installed (X), but Wes hates it and speaks negatively about the new system. In this obviously unbalanced situation (potentially producing some degree of conflict), several possibilities exist for change. To restore balance, (1) Roberto may convince Wes to change his attitude toward the new system (or Wes may convince Roberto); (2) Roberto may change his feelings about Wes or Wes about Roberto; (3) they may agree to tolerate the inconsistency and remain friends; or (4) each may work elsewhere.

These outcomes are augmented by some possible cultural differences. For example, both Roberto and Wes may unwittingly sift their perceptions of the other through some cultural stereotypes. Thus, Wes may think that Roberto is trying to win points with their store manager, also a Mexican American, and, for a moment, falls prey to the stereotype that Mexican Americans always stick together in groups. Roberto lets himself believe that Wes dislikes the system because Wes, according to Roberto's stereotype of other

Conflict can occur for a variety of reasons, including task or role misunderstandings. (Photo by Mike Moore, Kenya.)

African Americans, is not very innovative and prefers inefficiency to progress. Such misunderstandings occur frequently. By analyzing such topical likes or dislikes into their components, suggested by balance theorists, we can anticipate interpersonal outcomes.

What happens when interpersonal conflict develops between person A and person B, rather than topical conflict? For instance, Larry was a flight instructor who personally disliked his student Abdul from Iraq. Abdul assumed that he could bargain with Larry for free flight time and also waited to read the flight instruction manual until after several hours of Larry's personal instructions. Larry, however, had a set fee and expected Abdul to read the manual well in advance of any personal instruction. Thus, their topical disagreement was highlighted by Larry's personal dislike of Abdul, and, later, attempts to reconcile topical disagreements were thwarted by interpersonal conflict. Because Larry disliked Abdul, there was little motivation to work through their differences.

When the relationships between person A, person B, and a topic are variable, balance theory provides one way of analyzing and predicting interpersonal outcomes. By examining the personal attitudes between two or more people and their respective attitudes toward salient topics, we can better understand why we are motivated to change or why we choose to ignore development of some interpersonal relationships (see also table 12.1).

**Table 12.1**  Questions for Probing Intercultural Communication Conflict Management Skills

---

**Do You Check Contextual Variables?**

---

1. With whom are lines of communication (networks) open or closed in various groups?

2. Why are these networks open or closed? Are you turned off by someone's personality?

3. What is the frequency of communication among various group members? Do clique groups deny access to the group to others who could benefit from group participation?

4. Are hierarchical lines of communication within a formal group, such as an organization, open? How can those communication links be improved?

---

**What Intercultural Relationships Are Operating in Any Given Interpersonal Contact?**

---

1. Do you emphasize overlap of experience in communicating with others?

2. Do you emphasize areas that will build credibility?

3. Are you open in reception of information?

4. Is your verbal message consistent with your nonverbal message? Do your actions match your words?

5. Do you look for the what and the why of a message—what a person says and why that person is saying it?

6. Do you find yourself dominating most conversations? Do you only make statements, or do you periodically ask questions in conversation?

7. Do threatening or nonstatus quo messages that affect you cause you to screen out such messages?

---

**Are You Aware of the Listener as You Engage in Communication?**

---

1. Do you consider the knowledge, education, and background of the listener and speak in terms the listener understands? Do you use jargon and slang?

2. Is it easy for others to tell you what is on their minds? Why?

3. Do you work considerately with others who fear rejection? Do you provide reassuring and positive feedback in your communication?

4. Do you stay with problems and work toward solutions, or do you avoid working through problems?

5. Do you periodically compliment others? Do you separate an issue under consideration from the person?

---

**Conflict in Leadership Approach**

Communication and leadership style is another source of conflict in cultures and groups. One model useful to understand various leadership style options is presented by Quinn and McGrath (1985). An adaptation of their model in figure 12.1 reveals that styles of open versus authoritarian can be crossed with cooperative versus competitive styles. The resultant quadrants produce cultures that are inventive and risk-taking (I), directive and goal-oriented (II), conservative and

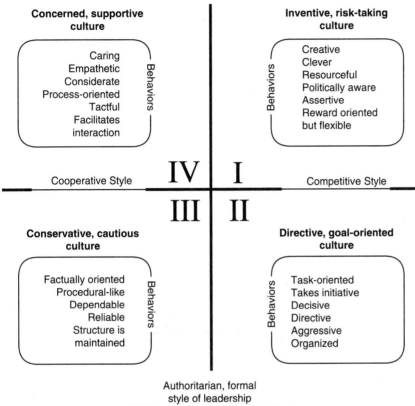

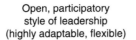

Figure 12.1
Leadership style
and potential
organizational
conflict. (Adapted
from Quinn and
McGrath 1985,
p. 324.)

cautious (III), and concerned and supportive (IV). This model illustrates the potential conflict because of differences in expectations and changes in organizational culture. Nadler, Nadler, and Broome (1985) use the Thomas-Kilmann conflict style model (resulting also in four quadrants: collaborating, competing, avoiding, and accommodating along with a middle style, compromising) to make a fundamental point (figure 12.2). Individual communication styles of conflict management along with the leadership or organization culture or both involved alters perceived topics such as decision making, time, trust, and power.

The movie "Gung Ho," a fictitious account of a Japanese car plant operating in the United States, reminds us of some realistic issues involved in conflict because of cultural differences and communication practices. The numerous reports of gung ho qualities in many Japanese plants abound in the United States. For example, the Sanyo plant in Forrest City, Arkansas, went through major

Conflict within
Intercultural
Organizational
Culture

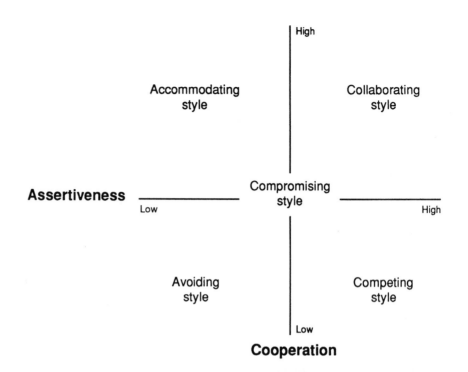

High

Accommodating
style

Collaborating
style

**Assertiveness** ———————   Compromising   ———————
  Low                                    style                                    High

Avoiding
style

Competing
style

Low

**Cooperation**

**Figure 12.2**
Thomas-Kilmann
conflict styles.

difficulty when American workers verbalized their frustration with what they considered a lack of information and other communication issues. How conflict is resolved in organizations, much less in organizational cultures where even international differences may be present, is a subject for an entire book. However, following are some key points that fit the brief discussion.

*Metaphors preventing intercultural conflict.* Ting-Toomey (1985) reminds us of fundamental metaphors in Japanese culture that describe the gentle nature of working through conflict. One of those is *nemawashi,* which means "root binding," or carefully binding the roots of a plant before pulling it out. The metaphor is rich, explaining to us the interpersonal smoothing process that occurs before actually taking actions concerning a decision within a system. Through the broadly based consultation approach, differences are worked out and a consensus is achieved. Disagreements are resolved privately before they become causes of public stress.

Another conflict-prevention strategy used in Japanese culture is the *ringi* system. This refers to the wide circulation of a document containing relevant proposals to which people up and down the organizational hierarchy affix their seals as a sign of approval. In this way, consensus is achieved and individuals feel ownership of the project. It has been said of the ringi system that it may take six months for a decision to be made, but once it is implemented, everybody is already on board. On the other hand, we have observed that while Americans make decisions quickly, implementation, involving standard operating procedures and acquainting the rest of the organization with an innovation, may take six months. So in the long run, there may not necessarily be any time advantage to one style over the other. Perhaps the Japanese would remind us politely that the ringi system achieves ultimate efficiency since agreement is reached before implementation.

Another conflict-prevention strategy is the *go-between* system. In this system, a neutral third party hears both sides of a disagreement or conflict. The person in this role works out differences between the two parties in ways that save face in the negotiation process (see also Nadler, Nadler, and Broome 1985). In fact, Cushman and King (1985) indicate the rituals and rules for resolving conflict in cultures are rooted in different values. For example, the group-harmony value of saving face in Japanese culture is illustrated by the word *wa,* or promoting group harmony. Also, the exchange of gifts, *oceiba,* and *ochugan,* favors, leads to trust and obligation. In fact, all of these interactions are supposed to take place in *kuuki,* a human atmosphere or a feeling of commonality.

Every cultural group has a different style. Clearly, two individuals exercise different styles, so when we put together the cultural differences and the personality differences, it is easy to see why people do not harmonize too well in their communication processes.

*Diversity in intercultural organizational values.*   Also linked with conflict are differences in organizational values. Clearly, attitudes and values are part of a systems model. When these are different, conflict within organizations often results. When individuals from different cultures come to work in the same organization, it is easy to see how culture clashes result. Consider, for example, the comparison of Japanese, American, and Yugoslavian cultures presented by Cushman and King (1985) and represented in table 12.2. When issues of merit, promotion, and work responsibility are brought up, it is not difficult to see why cultural differences intervene in many organizational settings.

Furthermore, organizational conflict can be said to have its roots in methods of decision making. Ed Stewart (1985) applies decision-making strategies within organizations to intercultural differences. His matrix assumes four types of decision making styles relevant for our discussion. In reality, the four major categories of decision-making styles are on a continuum: technical, logical, bureaucratic group, social-collective. For some decisions one style might be more appropriate than the other. Conflict comes when people do not understand the other person's use of style or they misuse a style. For example, a technical decision style, made with relevant skills and techniques appropriate to that decision, usually involves different approaches than a social-collective decision-making style, in which a person applies intuition, emotions, and holistic themes to the

**Table 12.2** Organizational Culture Values

| Japan | United States | Former Yugoslavia |
|---|---|---|
| lifelong employment | short-term employment | lifelong employment by state |
| slow evaluation and promotion | rapid evaluation and promotion | no evaluation/limited promotion |
| nonspecific job assignment | specialized career path | shifting job path |
| implicit control | explicit control | negotiated control |
| consensual decision making | individual decision making | intergroup decision making |
| collective responsibility | individual responsibility | individual and collaborative responsibility |
| collective concern | individual concern | diverse collective concern |

Source: Cushman and King 1985.

problem. The conflict emerges if one thinks the other style is wrong or irrelevant for the kind of problem. It is easy to see how the two could be missing each other in their communication. Each expects a different set of approaches to the process of resolving conflicts, but each misses the other person's diverse decision-making style. Also, Lea Stewart (1985) reminds us that a lot of conflict arises because of the clash between decision makers in an organization and the technical people in the organization, for instance, between management and scientists. Her analysis points to certain conflict when rules are made by nonprofessionals, without regard to front-line needs. Many times different goals as well as procedures are in conflict.

Kume (1985) also shows how decision-making styles can lie at the root of many of our conflicts (see table 12.3). Kume compares the communication function in decision making across cultural differences. For example, the locus of the decision for American style is the individual; that is, the leader is expected to take on much responsibility. However, for Japanese the locus of decision is in a group-collective format.

Kume (1985) reminds us how frustrating cultural procedures and styles can be. He presents these examples of Northern American managers' statements about working with Japanese:

Usually in American companies we have one strong man. There is a definite line of decision making, but it is not clear in the Japanese decision-making process. You are never exactly sure of whose decision it was.

Everybody's involved in everything. Everything is put on the table. Nothing is hidden. You may not understand the production aspects, but you listen and you learn certain things.

**Table 12.3** Comparisons of North American and Japanese Decision-Making Styles

| Communication Function for Decision Making | American Styles | Attendant American Cultural Factors | Japanese Styles | Attendant Japanese Cultural Factors |
|---|---|---|---|---|
| 1. Locus of decision | individual leader has capacity to direct and take personal responsibility | individualism independence control of events | group leader has capacity to facilitate and take shared responsibility | collectivism interdependence group orientation |
| 2. Initiation and coordination | top-down use of expert's information less frequent discussion | power competition self-reliance doing (get things done) | bottom (or middle) up prior consultation frequent discussion | subservience cooperation harmony being-in-becoming |
| 3. Temporal orientation | planning ahead quick decision slow implementation | future-oriented linear thinking sense of urgency individualism | adjusting to changing circumstances slow decision immediate implementation | present oriented circular thinking gradual buildup group loyalty |
| 4. Mode of reaching decision | individual decision majority decision split decision | choice among alternatives equal opportunity to express "matters of procedures" | consensus | acceptance of a given option conformity "tentativeness" |
| 5. Decision criterion | "rational" practical empiricism | analytical materialistic | "intuitive" group harmony | holistic spiritual commitment |
| 6. Communication style | direct confrontation | cognitive dichotomy | indirect agreement | affective "feeling around" |

Source: Kume 1985.

In most American companies, company policy is set by executives. And in this company I see that policy can come from me and many other employees. I think it is good and more appropriate for our company.

American meetings are generally more rapid—discussion, response, discussion, while Japanese meetings seem to go on and on.

There are examples of Japanese managers responding in some positive and some negative ways, too:

I really think American people work very individually. The quality control people in manufacturing departments seldom hold meetings. They don't think it necessary to hold cross-departmental meetings.

There may be a time when it is better to age a little bit. I think it is better not to make a snap judgment or a quick decision, but to think about it a little bit and get someone else involved.

Americans take it for granted that 2 percent or 3 percent of the total number of products will be defective, but the Japanese managers really try to make sure that not a single product will be defective. Of course, the Japanese way will take much more time.

So whether it is American or Japanese, Asian or Latin American, Middle Eastern or European cultures, the scenario can be the same. There are differences in communication style, organizational style, value differences, and methods of decision making that can lead to frustration or promise. Our understanding of those differences marks a major milestone in successful intercultural communication where organizational cultures are involved.

## Managing Conflict

Many strategies already have been explained as we presented the potential sources of conflict. Here, in this section, two fundamental strategies apply broadly to many intercultural contexts as well as many domestic, interpersonal situations.

### Relational Empathy

Relational empathy (Broome 1991) and active listening form the basis for beginning the conflict management process.

Listening involves the process of interpreting spoken messages through our communication filters, such as emotions, attitudes, and values. Unaltered, these become an obvious source of conflict. Listening involves a number of skills that usually need to be developed and managed. Studies indicate that we spend anywhere from 45 percent to 55 percent of our time listening each day. With such a large percentage of communication time devoted to listening, it is surprising how few people have any training in listening. Reasons that people are not good listeners include:

1. *Assuming listening is hearing.*   Listening is not the same as hearing. Most people have the ability to hear, a natural gift from birth. It is a fallacy, however, to assume that because we can hear, we also practice good listening skills. Billions of dollars are lost in industry every year because of poor listening

Conflict over intercultural, misunderstood listening or assertiveness accounts for much of the conflict between diverse cultures. (Photo by ACU student media.)

and communication habits. For instance, one international manufacturing executive lost several thousand dollars one day when he discovered that the machinists did not listen to instructions on making new valves.

2. *Prejudging messages.*   Sometimes we anticipate what the other person is going to say, mentally filling our minds with what we assume to be a completed message. Such prejudging is a silent interruption at best.

3. *Filtering messages.*   Another fault in listening is taking out message information that we find disagreeable or threatening. One tendency is to distort such messages. Another tendency is to take out the disquieting message altogether, screening it entirely from what we heard.

4. *Difference in thought and talk speed.*   Most people think at about 450 words per minute. Most people speak at about 150 to 175 words per minute. With such a large gap between talk and thought speed, listeners can wander off into mental excursions while another person is talking. Because of the ease of distraction, many people miss significant amounts of information from the person with whom they are interacting.

Consider the example of Kristina and Delores, two preprofessionals planning to work together and join a management team of six people. Their friendship was being subtly eroded through a number of small conflicts, until one week Kristina became furious with Delores. When Delores asked Kristina to come over to resolve the conflict, Kristina again erupted in anger. The wounds from the entire series of incidents surrounding this conflict took nearly a year to resolve and Delores and Kristina  needed counseling and intervention by trained experts to help them overcome their hostility. Several empathy and listening principles came to light as they were asked the following questions.

**Skills in Developing Effective Empathy and Listening**

1. *Do you assume your viewpoints are universal?* To think that others believe exactly as you do makes their eventual disagreement a shock. Their disagreement can be viewed as a personal attack, and listening is stifled. Generally, a person is better off to assume others do not share the same point of view and to actively listen for areas of agreement or points of difference. At least do not assume complete overlap of information. For instance, a major part of Kristina and Delores' breakdown was the assumption that they knew exactly what was in the other's mind. Delores particularly was not accustomed to clarifying her feelings with words.

2. *Do you interrupt?* Allowing the other person to finish completely is a basic listening skill. For whatever reason, it is rude not to allow another to finish his or her message. The relationship tends to suffer when one or both engage in interruptive behavior. Kristina and Delores, for example, not only prejudged the other's thoughts, they also consistently interrupted each other.

3. *Do you give positive feedback?* Good listening depends upon each person's providing encouraging, positive listening cues. Nodding your head, looking at the other person, smiling, and leaning forward are a few of the nonverbal cues that make you a good listener. Verbal signals include follow-up questions, reference to what the other just said, and reinforcing utterances such as "uh huh" and "mmm." In Kristina's case, she habitually looked down or put her head in her hands when Delores expressed ways to resolve their conflict.

4. *Do you ask for information?* Listening is not merely a process of nodding and smiling. Good, active listening involves follow-up comments that ask for clarification or generally for more information. That shows the other person you are interested in the topic. Examples include, "Hassan, the main point is clear, but I didn't get all your reasons," or "Tasha, here is an area where I feel lost; could you summarize the implications?"

5. *Is there freedom from ego threat?* Not only should you be free from being offended if others do not agree, a point made earlier, but you need to be sure you are not attacking the other person. Even in the guise of honest communication, many interactants blame, accuse, or attack. They may not even be aware of the negative perceptions held toward such behaviors, for they may sincerely see these communication behaviors as culturally or personally relevant. You may need to back up and look at your style of communication, asking if you come across harshly. Do you deal with people on a highly competitive basis? Do you seem demanding? Is there a need for instant closure to questions? These questions remind us to look at personal style.

6. *Do you paraphrase?* A great technique in active listening is to paraphrase what the person has just said. This gentle repetition clarifies understanding and strengthens the relationship emotionally, since the other person perceives that you really are being attentive to his or her needs.

Sometimes relationships are improved by the judicious application of assertiveness, where appropriate cultural norms and rules take precedence in defining assertiveness. As indicated earlier, some cultures are direct, some indirect; some low-context, some high-context.

Where western style assertiveness is appropriate, and from a U.S. dominant culture perspective, some of the following suggestions may be useful. Assertiveness is defined as the ability to state clearly what you expect or want and to work toward achieving that goal. Assertiveness differs from aggressiveness, which is an overpowering use of force, coercion, and physical or verbal abuse as a means of achieving personal goals. Assertiveness also differs from avoidance of conflict or statement of personal desires and goals. For instance, suppose you and a friend want to go for lunch. Contrast the different styles of these responses:

> Assertiveness: "There are two or three places I would really like to go, but I'm open to talking it over." Aggressiveness: "We are going to Pizza Jim's, or I'm not going." Nonassertiveness: "I'll go anywhere you want. Whatever you say." (Actually, the nonassertive person has some preferences.)

Assertiveness is simply having courage to speak up on what you think, while respecting the rights and opinions of others. Assertive people feel comfortable offering feelings and opinions of others, even when they know in advance others may disagree. In other words, assertive people are not guided by threats or fear of rejection, but neither are they obnoxious bullies who are careless of the feelings of others.

Individuals gain a number of advantages through assertive behavior, as this list by researcher and psychological trainer Dr. Clyde Austin suggests. Assertive behavior:

1. *Gives you energy.* There is something about assertiveness that makes you feel stronger, more confident in yourself and your relationships. Nonassertiveness has a way of discouraging you and literally making you feel more tired.

2. *Improves relationships.* Important issues are opened and discussed. With disagreement and resolution of issues, people feel a common task and feel a bond with one another.

3. *Becomes therapeutic.* Assertive people get their tensions and questions out in the open. Among other things, they feel better, getting issues off their minds. Also, assertive people deal constructively with ideas and listen actively to others. In the process, they feel emotionally satisfied.

4. *Achieves results.* When others around you know what you expect, and you know their needs, then creative systems can be developed to engage solutions. When people hide their feelings, no one knows what is needed or wanted, and little achievement occurs.

5. *Improves decision making.* Under assertiveness conditions, "half-baked" ideas are examined. Critiques allow for full discussion and create a condition for more input. Also, the loudest voice is not the only one heard.

## How Can One Gain Effective Assertiveness Skills?

These suggestions, some of which again come from Dr. Clyde Austin, represent a healthy summary of what you can do to improve your assertiveness skills. These simple and direct techniques have been useful to many skilled communicators.

1. *Avoid emotional presentations.* Adding emotion to your message usually does not bring the ultimate benefits that assertiveness can bring. Crying, pouting, using silence, and anger are common emotional strategies. Unfortunately, these emotions cloud communication.

2. *Deal with one issue at a time.* Too many of us bring up an issue and then raise unresolved questions from the past. Bringing up more than one issue at a time obscures the question for now. It is better to resolve one issue at a time.

3. *Do not insist on your own way.* This suggestion comes from the Corinthian letter in the New Testament and has been labeled steamrolling by some authors. Some people charge into an issue and intend to get exactly what they want by manipulating any way they can. Assertive individuals clearly state their position, but they are not domineering and do not use power to achieve those results. Rather, they use reason and perseverance and are willing to cooperate if they do not get their way.

4. *Be clear and direct.* Say what you mean. You are not being ugly or harsh to speak what you really think.

5. *Openly admit error.* When you are wrong, say so. Without vengeance, assertive persons are willing to seek for truth, not merely defend their positions.

6. *Have a coping outlook.* Assertive persons not only focus on clear analysis of a problem, but they are eager to move toward resolution of problems. They do not get stuck on problems only. In this sense, they are copers, looking for methods to resolve problems.

7. *Make "I" statements.* This technique of making "I" statements refers to owning your feelings. Rather than accusing another person ("You really don't care about me"), it is better to take responsibility for the feelings that are engendered by the other person's actions. In this case, you might say, "When you do

this, I'm left with a feeling that you do not care as much as I thought you did." The value of this strategy is that it takes the pressure off the other person to defend himself. If he feels responsible for the problem, there is a tendency to see this situation as an attack. If you take the responsibility for your own feelings, then the condition can become one of objective discussion, not one of blame resulting in personal defense. Of course in certain cultures "I" statements, no matter how well intended or skillfully applied, sound arrogant and offensive. In these cases, cultural rules should override this suggestion.

---

**This Chapter in Perspective**

This chapter deals with personal skills we can access for intercultural communication. One of the first aspects to change in improving one's interpersonal communication is to try to develop a healthy communication climate. Such a dyadic system can be improved by being supportive, nonjudgmental, spontaneous, and open-minded. Interpersonal communication effectiveness is also improved by developing self-disclosure and thus becoming more transparent and open. The advantages of self-disclosure center around self-awareness as well as the possibility for greater trust, liking, and mental health. Other skills involve our use of dominance and submission, formality, work relationships, need for acceptance, coping skills, and conflict management.

Using phatic communication, or rapport building, helps abruptness and builds trust. The chapter highlights listening skills as a major dimension of interpersonal communication improvement. By providing adequate nonverbal information and by developing skills at positive feedback, most people can increase their adequacy in listening. Finally, the chapter outlines the major dimensions of assertiveness skills. By saying what we really think and using appropriate techniques, we can heighten our ability to work with people, feel better, and accomplish more in culturally acceptable ways.

**Exercises**

1. Observe a business meeting. What variables from this chapter do you observe in the participants' communication? Give examples. Are differences rooted in culture observable?

2. Do a field study in a public setting. Compare communication effectiveness between friends with noncommunication between strangers.

3. Analyze news reports of some international conflict. What intercultural skills could have been employed?

**Chapter 12    Intercultural Communication and Conflict**                    261

**Chapter**

# 13

# Intercultural Communication and Mass Media as Cultural Influence

**Objectives**

After completing this chapter, you should be able to

1. Identify ways in which the mass media aid a nation's development

2. List the effects of mass media

3. Demonstrate the relationship between mass media and culture

4. Indicate and discuss how to use strategy involving media to adapt to a cultural audience

The mass media's role in intercultural communication is complex, ranging from association with national development to persuasion. This chapter surveys the role of the mass media in influencing culture and individuals. Tracing media influence begins with the role media traditionally have played in national and international development.

The role of the mass media in national development is well documented. Classic research by Lerner (1958) underscored the centrality of media, suggesting that urbanization produces individual participation. Schramm (1973) argued that the mass media serve as multipliers for information and learning and thus *accelerate the rate of development* within developing nations.

**Mass Media and National Development**

Concern over national development has caused a number of scholars to attempt to discover how the media facilitate a nation's economic and social development. Researchers generally agree that media is linked with national development, although the nature of the link is debated. For instance, Farace and Donohew (1965) analyzed forty-two variables in various combinations to establish a statistical link between media and national development with UNESCO data from 115 countries. They found the presence of communication infrastructure in a country corresponding with a rise in economic development indicators such as press freedom, newspaper circulation, cinema seats, radio receivers, literacy, and education.

In another example linking mass communication to national development, Frey (1973) reported that as literacy, income, industrialization, and media sources went up, so did gross national product per capita. It is not certain that economic increases have not caused media increases instead of the other way around. But this research along with others like Jeffres' (1975) research reinforces the theme that economic development and media coincide. Whatever the role of media in a nation's economic development, media use is rising worldwide. To that extent we would expect to see information opportunity, social and cultural awareness, and a tie to a nation's political process as outcomes of media presence in a country.

**Table 13.1** Correlations of Communication Variables with Gross National Product per Capita in Developing Nations

| Communication Variable | GNP/pc |
|---|---|
| Daily newspaper circulation (per 1,000) | .80 |
| Radios (per 1,000) | .85 |
| Television sets (per 1,000) | .75 |
| Cinema attendance per capita | .65 |
| Percent literate (fifteen years and older) | .80 |
| Domestic mail per capita | .89 |

Source: Frey 1973, p. 408.

## Mass Media Effects on Culture

Mass communication has enormous effects on culture today. The early models prior to the mid-1940s of an all-powerful mass media (the metaphor of a hypodermic needle was used) directly changing passive audiences (figure 13.1) have given way to complex outcomes of media effects. Media create plenty of effects, sometimes direct but often more indirect and mediated. Even though we speak of media institutions, people remain users and have some degree of choice in most cultures.

### Mass Media and Persuasion

From the 1940s forward, researchers have probed a number of other elements working jointly with media to explain persuasion and change. Media effects depend on a complex set of variables. As Gandy and Matabane (1989) stated, we must account for the variables that intervene in the theoretical path between exposure and effect, including:

1. Interpersonal networks;

2. Cultural norms, values, and world view;

3. Demographic categories (such as age, education, occupation, ethnicity, and so on) and group memberships;

4. Motivation, needs, and salient means of gratifying those needs;

5. Personality characteristics.

One example of how mediating effects work, at least from a U.S. perspective, comes from modern reports of television influence all the way back to the classic and massive Surgeon General's report in the 1970s concerning the effects of television violence on children. In general, the overall effects of mass media depend on a number of personality, intervening variables among audience

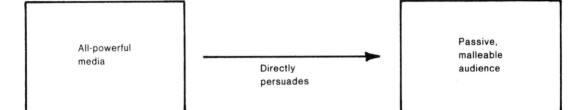

**Figure 13.1**
Hypodermic-needle theory of mass media influence. This early theory was replaced by a model of mediating variables of mass media influence.

viewers, and not just the media events themselves. Pointing to personality differences does not imply that the mass media have no effect; rather that the media effects often depend upon these personality and other intervening variables.*

What, then, are direct persuasive effects of the mass media? Research studies over four decades lead other researchers to believe the following general principles about media direct effects from a limited U.S. perspective (Klapper 1960; Patterson and McClure 1976; Caillouet 1978; Dodd 1979; Gandy and Matabane 1989; Lewis, Dodd, and Tippens 1989; Lewis, Dodd, and Tippens 1992; Rogers 1983):

1. The mass media serve an *awareness* function, creating interest in an event or an idea through direct information about its existence.

2. The dominant U.S. cultural faction of the mass media develop an *agenda;* that is, they call attention to what is salient. When news commentators say, "And that's the news," the subtle implication is that they have explained what is important and thereby call attention to that event exclusively. For the next few days, people then discuss that agenda. Unfortunately, such "agenda-setting" often omits cocultures who feel marginalized by the agenda omissions for their particular concerns.

3. The mass media serve as *accelerators for change*, creating a climate in which change can more easily occur. In another instance, the Solidarity movement in Poland captured worldwide media attention, likely speeding world-opinion change.

4. The mass media work in concert with and through *interpersonal sources*, depending upon the saliency, immediacy, and timing of the event. Special programs in India and Latin America, such as Telescuela, have enjoyed success in agricultural innovations when radio messages are listened to by an assembly of village family heads and leaders. Following the program a village worker leads a discussion, and the villagers return home, often to implement new ideas for productivity. It seems apparent from such examples that the mass media and interpersonal contacts have a simultaneous influence.

---

*This author wholeheartedly agrees with the deleterious effects on children of violence on television reported in a number of journals. The intended point here, though, is to introduce readers to the complex set of mediating variables that inevitably become other causes to the effects we observe. The exact blend and interaction of the media with other variables in producing some effect is a subject still under significant investigation.

Media have become a dominant feature of most cultures, influencing thought, behavior, and interpersonal relationships. (Photo by Keith Alwine.)

5. The mass media may *stimulate rumors*. The short nature of many electronic news broadcasts or advertisements means that, by necessity, some details are omitted. This screening sometimes leaves ambiguity or vagueness, features that can heighten the possibility of rumor formation. The rumor that the Wendy's restaurant chain was mixing worms with its hamburgers was traced to media: a story on worm farming in the United States was construed to be part of the Wendy's operation.

6. The mass media can become *addictive*, or an obsessive-compulsion. In a national study of 2,200 adolescents Lewis, Dodd, and Tippens (1989) reported a 5 percent rate of obsessive qualities toward movies and music videos. Although the rate is encouragingly low, the acting out level among this minority of media addicted teens was unusually high: 4 times higher alcohol use rate, 3 times higher drug use, 5 times higher sexual promiscuity rate, and generally valueless and more prone to violence.

7. The mass media can predispose some children toward *violence* and acting out. As indicated, violence, as one type of what therapists call acting out behavior, is an outcome of several factors. However, media can predispose some children to violence, something like turning up the heat for those so prone to respond. With exposure in the United States of over 15,000 hours of violence by age 18, many wonder why more violence does not exist.

**Mass Media as a Shaper of Cultural Thought and Logic**

Since the 1960s, a substantial amount of information has described the mass media as a direct institution of culture and an influential shaper of culture. "The Medium is the Message," or massage, as McLuhan (1967) so tersely put it, has become a media catch phrase. The clear implication is that a medium dominates our perceptions of an event, since it is precisely through some medium that we become aware of many events in our world. To put it loosely, we become the recipients of those scenes that the director selects, the reporter pens, and the gatekeeper for the news service allows to go through the wire. Should error exist, listeners have no way to check reality since the medium has, in a sense, become the reality.

However, media and culture intertwine, more on the cultural and cognitive level. Picking up on McLuhan's suggestion that cultures might be examined in stages, let us posit a relationship about how people in a culture think and communicate. This connection is illustrated in figure 13.2. This relationship is called the *linear-nonlinear* nature of culture. Type I is a culture we might term nonlinear. The thought framework (or how people think) in this society is configurational (nonlinear), which implies that it has multiple themes that are expressed in oral terms. Because of its configurational orientation, type I culture involves the simultaneous bombardment and processing of a variety of stimuli—so these people think in images, not just in words. Time orientation is less important than people and events, and time is not segmented.

Type II is a culture that has transformed auditory and oral communication into visual communication by means of written symbols, organized into linear thought patterns. This culture has beginnings and endings to its events, unitary themes throughout any one episode being described. It is object-centered rather than people- or event-centered, and it is empirical in its use of evidence. Furthermore, its speech patterns superimpose a visual (usually outlined) structure upon the auditory speech process. That is, these people think from left to right (or right to left in some cultures) in a linear fashion.

Type III is an electronic culture that is simultaneously configurational and linear. Events can be portrayed with several themes running simultaneously, although evidence is based on experiences of receivers who remain passive while viewing events through the media of the culture. Television and film illustrate communication in a type III culture where linear and nonlinear sensory stimuli are focused on the viewer simultaneously. Often, a single, organized theme undergirds the nonlinear collage of filmed scenes.

## Unintentional Effects of Mass Media

The mass media have an unintended influence that is sometimes subtle, sometimes obvious, but nevertheless real (Aronson 1980). The 1977 showing of Alex Haley's "Roots" on ABC television to over 130 million viewers, the largest television audience at that time to watch any one program in the United States, captured attention and inspired African Americans to take an increased pride in their heritage. The number of people in the United States to trace their genealogy increased, indicated by the genealogical inquiries after that showing. In 1978, NBC showed "Holocaust," a dramatization documenting Nazis' execution of millions of Jews. When the same program was telecast in West Germany, it was credited with providing the motivation for the passage of a law stiffening Nazi prosecution. The 1974 showing of the NBC television movie "Cry Rape,"

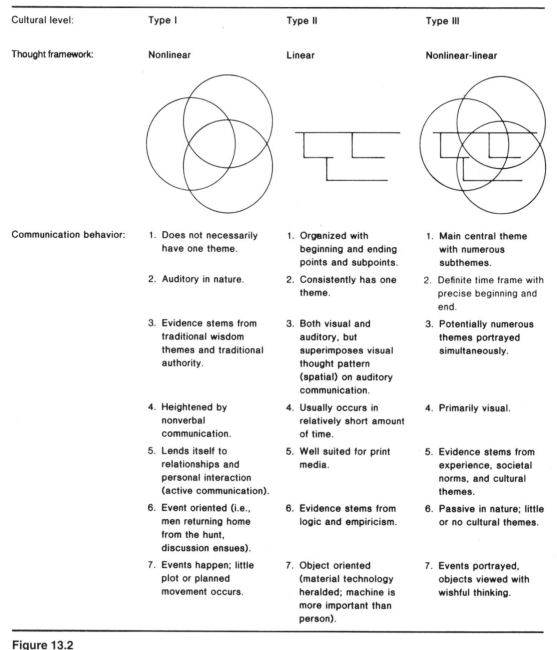

| Cultural level: | Type I | Type II | Type III |
|---|---|---|---|
| Thought framework: | Nonlinear | Linear | Nonlinear-linear |
| Communication behavior: | 1. Does not necessarily have one theme. | 1. Organized with beginning and ending points and subpoints. | 1. Main central theme with numerous subthemes. |
| | 2. Auditory in nature. | 2. Consistently has one theme. | 2. Definite time frame with precise beginning and end. |
| | 3. Evidence stems from traditional wisdom themes and traditional authority. | 3. Both visual and auditory, but superimposes visual thought pattern (spatial) on auditory communication. | 3. Potentially numerous themes portrayed simultaneously. |
| | 4. Heightened by nonverbal communication. | 4. Usually occurs in relatively short amount of time. | 4. Primarily visual. |
| | 5. Lends itself to relationships and personal interaction (active communication). | 5. Well suited for print media. | 5. Evidence stems from experience, societal norms, and cultural themes. |
| | 6. Event oriented (i.e., men returning home from the hunt, discussion ensues). | 6. Evidence stems from logic and empiricism. | 6. Passive in nature; little or no cultural themes. |
| | 7. Events happen; little plot or planned movement occurs. | 7. Object oriented (material technology heralded; machine is more important than person). | 7. Events portrayed, objects viewed with wishful thinking. |

**Figure 13.2**
The linear-nonlinear nature of culture through media: Type I, II, and III cultures.

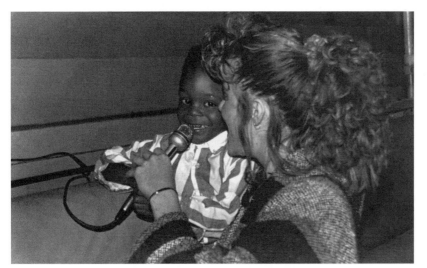

Media influences what a culture considers important. (Photo by Attitaya Indrakanhang.)

in which a rape victim went through more hassle in trying to press charges than the horror of the rape itself, may account for the decreased number of rapes reported to the police in the weeks that followed.

Mass media effects are mediated by a number of other effects, including social norms, the personalities of the viewers, the content of the mass media, and so on. What the examples in the previous paragraph suggest is that media presentations that are not intentionally trying to persuade us or even inform us may actually have a greater effect than some media messages with such intents. Perhaps the emotional appeal coupled with the vivid imagery of the cinema and television productions make a subtle impact on our conscious and subconscious minds. Thus, the media may be unwittingly influencing us in beliefs about things we see portrayed on the screen. If McDonald's restaurants advertise at intervals during a children's program that portrays violence, the child may unwittingly associate the positive image of Ronald McDonald with the violence. The reporter who selectively reports riots, murders, earthquakes, and international wars may inadvertently convey to viewers that all people behave violently and that the world is a pretty bad place.

## Mass Media and Social Learning

The mass media also create indirect effects of teaching and promoting social models. For instance, the negative stereotypes of African Americans, Hispanics, and Asians on television have harmed the images of those minorities. Efforts have been underway for years to eradicate sexism and negative male and female stereotypes from television and books. The opponents of media stereotyping generally object to the role models that the mass media, particularly television, inculcate by teaching through example. According to a news story released in

June of 1993 by George Gerbner and associates at the Annenberg School of Communication, after a ten-year study, these minority stereotypes and media usage of minorities have changed little. The exception is African Americans, who appear in the media 13 percent more now than ten years ago.

The media can inadvertently perpetuate stereotypes regarding childbirth, old age, adolescent behavior, sexuality, religion, war, parenthood, and a number of other topics. Serious news programs can help to erase misunderstandings on topics vulnerable to stereotypical perpetuation, but entertainment in movies, the theater, and television may inadvertently foster perceptual error. Fortunately, socially conscious network efforts are attempting to eliminate media stereotyping.

One television-specific application of social learning theory is the *cultivation hypothesis* (Gandy and Matabane 1989). Developed by George Gerbner and associates, this principle states that the more a person is exposed to a construction of reality, the more it is believed. For instance, can recurring patterns of violence with women and minorities as victims cultivate a belief that violence against them is okay? Through repeated exposure, television cultivates an indirect, cumulative set of beliefs and ideals. Not all experts agree, but few deny the power of myths conditioned or reinforced by television.

## Mass Media Uses and Gratification Theory

Another theory of mass media effects holds that the mass media solve needs and stimulate individual motivation to acquire solutions to needs. That is, the mass media content can solve audience needs, and sometimes the attention to the medium itself can be gratifying, as, for example, science fiction or mystery stories that provide escapism and emotional release. In fact, it can be argued that the mass media create a motivation to buy new technology and other consumer products; unfortunately, a person in an economically deprived state feels frustration that may erupt in social dissatisfaction.

The media, according to uses and gratification theory, may satisfy different social and emotional needs at different times in different ways. In fact, the media sometimes share in a division of labor. For instance, a person may want a radio on at work for entertainment, a newspaper for information, and a television for entertainment in the evening. A person who has interpersonal difficulties or problems with self-awareness may turn to various mass media sources (Katz, Blumer, and Gurevitch 1979). One is tempted to wonder, for instance, if some television talk shows and soap operas are not means of vicariously working out one's own problems or perhaps escaping from them. The rise in recent years of a number of magazines dealing with personal insight and self-help testify to audience needs met by media.

Some evidence suggests that media satisfaction may be connected to a culture's overall satisfaction with its vital information (Palmgreen and Rayburn 1985). Ultimately, we may discover that media consumption and satisfaction link with a culture's stress among its members.

From American media, only minor change has occurred in the last decade. However, media exposure can also facilitate and potentially influence ethnic identification, Gandy and Matabane (1989) conclude. First, they say media influence the very names or labels ethnic groups adopt. Second, similarity and identity operate simultaneously. For instance, African American viewing levels for programs with African American characters are higher than Anglo viewing. Further, African Americans evaluate the characters more positively than Anglos and are more likely to *identify* with them. Exposure ranging from "Roots" to "Cosby" to coverage of Jesse Jackson's campaign leads to a stimulus of sorts for African Americans to find identity, a point forcefully articulated by Betances (1987), himself a biracial sociologist and former talk-show host in Chicago.

Mass Media and Ethnic Identification

The international use of media has opened exciting new vistas of a global village. Television, satellite dishes, VCRs, computer use of gathering and disseminating news, faxes, fiber optic cable, and other technology open new borders around the world. Ironically, however, the technical sophistication of media scope and quality also functions to create several problems.

Mass Media and Trends in International Communication

First, technical innovation, McPhail (1989) argues, fractures the mass audience. We are living in a self-help generation, and media have become the way each one can participate in information to foster one's specialized interests. The result is fracture, not uniformity within countries.

Second, media communication has become a vehicle for globally relevant media events. This feature testifies to the overwhelming success of media, which allows the world to visualize simultaneously the same event: the Olympics, crises, famine, war, peace talks. This success in sending global information has been viewed as having a negative result—the same media that inform globally also dominate globally. This concern is so pervasive that it is called *Dallasization* of the world. McPhail continues by saying that corporations pay handsomely for the exporting of media messages and entertainment, and the networks commit upwards of $125 million for future marketing rights of events such as the Olympics.

Third, some observers see media as a support system for one culture to dominate another culture—a process called *hegemony* (Yaple and Korzenny 1989; Gandy and Matabane 1989). This idea implies that mass media colonize the thinking and values of a society. Even the global media events noted previously imply the dominant elite have control.

Developing nations, often the first ones to feel these effects, are not without blame. There is a thirst for media programming not quenched by local media systems. The result? They import foreign entertainment and programming. Once the system is created, the hungry rhinoceros has to be fed, and he has a big appetite, as Rogers (1989) put it. Cost limitations for domestic television production mean the hungry rhinoceros is fed with "Dynasty," "Diff'rent Strokes," and "Dallas."

Rogers laments these developments. They promote little development of the local cultures and create antidevelopment consequences such as *consumerism* and *overurbanization*. Incorrect attributions and stereotypes can be added to the list. Also, the information gap between developed and developing countries continues to widen—at least it is unbalanced (Nordenstreng and Kleinwachter 1989).

## Developing Skills in Understanding Media as Culture

Developing skills in understanding media as culture involves a set of cognitive skills. By looking for examples of how media and culture interrelate, you can understand the importance of media in the intercultural climate.

1. *Stay tuned to current events.* Knowledge of current events can assist all of your intercultural communication relationships.

2. *Try to be conscious of ways in which the media may have personally affected your perceptions of some group.* The media can portray positive stereotypes or negative stereotypes. Understanding the source of your personal feelings can be enlightening.

3. *Be aware of the positive value of the media.* The mass media can open us to new ideas, current events, and explanations of certain dynamics that we previously did not know. These positive learning effects can improve our understanding of culture.

4. *Use media as a tool for understanding one view of culture.* Media sources can highlight for us a culture's agenda—things that are considered important for that culture. For example, you might be surprised by how much you can learn about certain American values by browsing through a sales catalog. However, media sources also envision and produce erroneous stereotypes.

## This Chapter in Perspective

This chapter reminds readers of the important influence of media in shaping culture and individuals within a culture. Exploring these theories should assist in understanding social influence and the potential communication accommodation that shapes thoughts and action. This chapter initially focuses on the ways in which the mass media shape national development—and ultimately cultural change. While some scholars argue for the momentous impact of the mass media in precipitating positive changes in a nation (such as higher gross national product and so on), others quietly ponder the harmful effects such rapid introduction of mass media systems make upon the culture at large. Too, observers question the validity of a mass media system that often does not reach the illiterate masses because it favors programming that serves primarily elite, urban populations.

This chapter also focuses on mass media effects on culture. Typically, the mass media serve to make people aware of new information and to reinforce previously held opinions. While a large body of research shows that the media serve as influential initiators of information, another body of literature demonstrates that mass media influence is mediated by a large number of factors, including culture and personal influence. This section also highlights an increasing concern about the mass media as a shaper of culture—an institution and a process that influences culture and yet is also sensitive to culture's reciprocal influence. Finally, this section calls attention to some unintentional, yet pervasive, media effects, as well as to the ways in which the media gratify audience needs.

**Exercises**

1. Clip a number of newspaper articles dealing with current events. The same day watch the evening news on one of the national networks. How are the same stories treated? What effect do you think the treatment of each story has, in the long run, on your culture?

2. Try to pick out some item of news or some current rumor that is traceable to a mass medium and then ask twenty people or so three questions: (1) From whom or from what source did you first hear this information (that is, the news, rumor, etc.)? (2) If from a person, was this person a stranger, an acquaintance, a family member, or a close friend? (3) When did you *first* hear or discover the information? You can ask more questions if you want to, but these simple questions can provide abundant information about the comparison of mass media messages to interpersonal sources. How are the two the same? How do they differ?

3. Some claim that regionalism will overtake the place of the monolithic, centralized mass society in a process called demassification. Some authors predict that demassification will result in the death of the mass media as we know them. Do you agree or disagree? Why?

**Chapter** 14

# Intercultural Communication, Innovation, and Change

**Objectives**   After completing this chapter, you should be able to

1. Identify variables that influence the rapid spread of information among cultural members

2. Describe the decision-making process of individuals when confronted with information needs

3. Categorize early and late adopters of innovations by their personality characteristics

4. Develop strategies for effective intercultural efforts at social change and development

5. Summarize the factors that predispose a person or culture toward innovativeness

6. Understand factors related to group and organizational innovativeness

What would you do if you were asked to introduce a YMCA program in a predominantly Hispanic community? How would you involve elderly people in a community nutrition program? Working with a medical team as an intercultural communication specialist, how could you invite highland Indians in Ecuador to engage in different eating habits to correct a culture-wide nutritional deficiency? Suppose you were interested in a summer field trip to Guatemala to help in a reforestation project where woodland mountainsides have been stripped for firewood. What process of communication would initiate and sustain a reforestation effort among villagers? If you were working at a summer camp, how would you involve surrounding communities in a program of volunteerism to help you with large projects at the camp?

The principles stated throughout this book will assist you in being effective interpersonally and with groups. This chapter provides an answer to the question: How do you develop strategy for innovation and intercultural change? Two theory positions are stated. One is diffusion theory and its suggestions for strategic change (Rogers 1983), and the other is a summary of organizational development and change.

A few years ago, the Kenyan government offered herdsmen new land with low-interest loans near a new beef-producing location. The spread of this information, the decisions that were made, and the consequences that resulted are typical categories that social change researchers would investigate. Of course, the emphasis throughout this discussion of diffusion and social change is intercultural communication. In this case, the process of social influence is concentrated on.

**How Diffusion Studies Emerged**

The study of diffusion is traditionally linked with social and economic development in societies.* For example, the stone axes among the Yir Yoront of Australia (Sharp 1952) were symbols for masculinity and authority. Their replacement by steel axes led to the demise of that culture. Since values were undermined, prostitution, drunkenness, and other social breakdowns became rampant, and the culture lost its traditional structure. Early studies from 1940 to 1980 largely focused on change as a one-way process.

*In an anthropological sense, *diffusion* is the view that explains change in a society resulting from the introduction of innovations from another society. Kroeber (1937) noted that early diffusionists contributed primarily to calling the importance of diffusion to the attention of social scientists.

A number of social change efforts are aimed at the adoption of health innovations. By analyzing the communication-diffusion process, field workers facilitate their work.

Now, numerous research studies have used communication and cultural variables to analyze the social change process. The trend is to focus on how systems and people can be joint participants in exploring change. The early days of dominant development programs communicating change have given way to alternative paradigms involving participation, sharing knowledge, and equality among people (Rogers 1989).*

From that body of research come several important concepts of how information (particularly innovations) flows. This information flow affects people in cultures. This is called *diffusion theory*.

## Components of Diffusion

The basic components in the theory of diffusion and social change are: (1) the *innovation*, (2) which is communicated through certain *channels* (3) over *time* (4) among members of a *social system* (5) with certain *effects*. These categories stand as a type of model, highlighting major components. Everett Rogers and his various co-authors prolifically synthesized much of the diffusion research and theory. Close to three thousand diffusion studies have been conducted (Rogers 1973, 1983, 1989), with a number of aspects of diffusion applied to numerous intercultural situations.

## The Innovation as a Cultural Message

An innovation is an idea or product perceived as new. Since perception is a subjective measure of the innovation that does not make it objectively new or acceptable, then an innovation has two components: (1) an *idea* component

---

*The topics of social change communication efforts are varied, ranging from agricultural practices to family planning. Scholars continue to try to explain the social change process, including the nature of the innovation (Rogers 1973), the nature of the interpersonal relationships involved (Korzenny and Farace 1977), the nature of intercultural contact and attitude change (Gudykunst 1977), news diffusion (Greenberg 1964; Deutschmann and Danielson 1960), and other variables. For the rhetorical nature of social change, see Starosta (1974, 1975, 1976).

**Part 4  Cultural Adaptation and Communication Accommodation**

and (2) an *object* component, which is the physical referent of the idea. All innovations contain the first component, but not all innovations have a physical referent. For instance, adoption of improved farming methods is easily observable. Other innovations, however, such as political ideology, rumors, and new events, may not be as directly observable. Like any other persuasive message, an intercultural innovation message contains inherently motivating features.

The following five characteristics of innovations can make innovation messages innately motivating:

1. *Relative advantage* is the degree to which the innovation appears better than its predecessor. For instance, a government development officer must show how a village water system has advantages over the old method of carrying water from the river.

2. *Compatibility* represents the degree to which the innovation is congruent with existing beliefs, attitudes, values, experiences, and needs of the receiver. In intercultural efforts to persuade nationals to use a certain crop fertilizer, one obstacle sometimes facing change agents is cultural attitude and world view toward the earth. Among certain Central American Indians, for instance, the adding of fertilizer is considered sacrilegious. Consequently, a successful field worker must outline persuasive messages that demonstrate the cultural compatibility of the innovation. One solution for Central American Indians has been to describe the fertilizer as food for the earth.

3. *Complexity* is the extent to which the innovation appears difficult to understand and to use. As you might expect, simplicity is linked to adoption.

4. *Trialability* is the degree to which an innovation can be sampled or tried on a small-scale basis. For that reason, free samples constitute one reliable strategy for marketing new products in the United States.

5. *Observability* is the degree to which an innovation can be viewed and scrutinized before actual adoption. For instance, if a target population can see a comparison of a fertilized crop and an unfertilized crop, chances for adopting fertilizers are heightened.

These five factors must be carefully considered in message development for planned social change (Rogers 1983).

**Individual Choices about Innovations**

The time it takes for a message to spread throughout a social system is an important and distinct consideration in the diffusion process. However, personal choices depend not only on available information but also on the characteristics of the people making those choices.

When we face an especially important decision about a purchase, for example, or about engaging in some behavior, we almost always go through a period of awareness of the possibilities, talk with others if it is a major decision, and then continue a mental debate until a decision is made. Intercultural communication concerning some innovation also causes people to engage in a

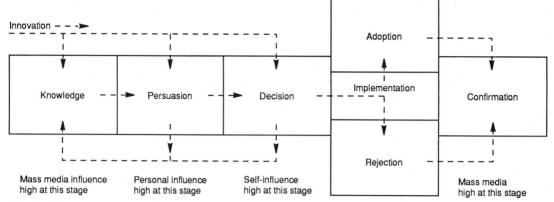

Knowledge — — → Persuasion — — → Decision — — — — Implementation → Adoption / Rejection → Confirmation

Innovation - - -→

Mass media influence high at this stage

Personal influence high at this stage

Self-influence high at this stage

Mass media high at this stage

**Figure 14.1**
Innovation-decision process and channels of influence at various stages.
(See Rogers 1983.)

decision-making process. Figure 14.1 presents a model to depict this process. In the *knowledge stage,* the individual becomes aware of the innovation and gains some understanding about it. The *persuasion stage* marks the person's evaluation of the innovation. During the *decision stage,* an individual may run a small-scale trial of the innovation. A potential adopter must mentally debate, choosing to adopt or reject the innovation. In some cases, a small-scale trial may constitute an important part of the decision to adopt. Many times, marketing firms apply this principle as they distribute free samples of everything from soap in the mail to sandwiches at the grocery store. After decision comes *implementation,* which involves adoption of the innovation into the existing system. At the *confirmation stage,* the person seeks reinforcement for the innovation-decision that has been made. The alternatives, of course, are continuance or discontinuance of the decision. The dotted lines in the figure indicate that these stages may be short-circuited, compressed, and even reversed.

The model underscores how different information sources can best serve as resources at different points along this time continuum. Media impact the decision-making process mostly at the knowledge and confirmation stages. Personal influence is highest at the persuasion stage, while people rely on self-influence at the decision stage (Rogers 1983; Dodd 1979).

**Characteristics of Individuals Choosing Innovations**

Whenever individuals choose an innovation, some people adopt early, and some people adopt late or not at all. The measure of time of adoption, called innovativeness, can be plotted mathematically. An average plotting across a number of studies results in a bell-shaped curve, illustrated in figure 14.2. The curve's significance lies in dividing the curve into mathematical segments (called standard deviations), which allow us to *categorize* people across these consistent units. Immediately, we observe that an entire sample can be divided

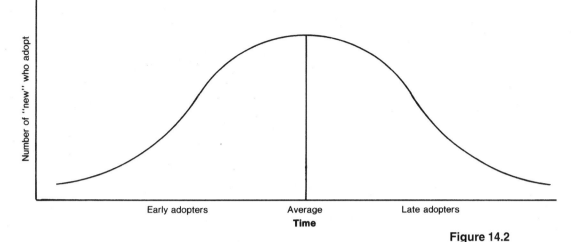

Early adopters      Average      Late adopters

**Time**

**Figure 14.2**
This bell-shaped curve shows the theoretical adoption of an innovation over time by the members of a social system. The curve develops when the number of new people adopting the innovation are plotted against time.

into those who are early and those who are late, simply by splitting the sample in half at the average time of adoption. The question that remains is whether some kind of systematic difference lies between the early people and the late people. The answer, from previous research studies, is unequivocally yes. In fact, investigations have taken the question a step further by analyzing not just the early and late adopters but also the percentages that fall under this bell-shaped curve within the early group and the late group. Furthermore, re-searchers have been able to detect personality differences among these categories (Rogers 1983).

1. *Innovators* make up the first 2.5 percent of the population who adopt under the bell curve. Their most salient characteristic is that they are *venturesome.* They are eager to try new ideas and usually can afford to take risks. For one thing, they are often deviant from their social system, meaning that they do not necessarily follow the norms of the locale where they live. In fact, other more normative members of the social system may think them very unusual. In addition, innovators are open to irrational adoption and consequently are subject to making many mistakes. Perhaps their irra-tionality is one reason why the majority of their social system do not nec-essarily look upon them with favor. However, as Marsh and Coleman (1954) pointed out, residents may go to innovators for information *if* the social system is highly innovative. Generally, however, innovators are not opinion leaders of society.

2. *Early adopters* compose the next 13.5 percent of the population who adopt an innovation. This group is best characterized by the word *respect.* As a whole, they are more innovative than the majority of the social system, but not so much as to be deviant. They are usually more local than innovators

This Masai tribal man has adopted social change by putting a film canister in place of a traditional ear decoration. (Photo by Mike Moore, Kenya.)

and adhere closely to community norms. In a sense, they are not too far ahead of other people in the culture, as the innovators are, but they are knowledgeable enough and respected enough to be a type of role model. The early adopter category is especially important in that it contains the highest number of opinion leaders.

3. The *early majority* are the 34 percent of the population who adopt an innovation just before the average person of the social system. Not many leaders stem from their ranks, but they serve as an important legitimizing link in the diffusion process. A key word for this category is *deliberate*.

4. The *late majority* are the 34 percent who adopt just after the average member of the social system. For the most part, adopters in this group are cautious, since they approach innovations with healthy skepticism. They may well see the value of an innovation but do not move to adopt it until public opinion favors the innovation or until peer group pressure is strong enough to motivate their adoption.

5. The *final adopters* are the final 16 percent of the population who are the last to adopt an innovation or who may never adopt at all. They are highly traditional, usually basing decisions on those of previous generations. Often quite suspicious of innovations, innovators, and change agents, this group is oriented toward local issues, and members of this group may function as negative opinion leaders.

People choose innovations not only because of the qualities outlined earlier, but also because of a cluster of factors. Why do some people adopt earlier than others in their social system? Why are some social systems resistant while others are open to change? These kinds of questions have led to research exploring *innovativeness.*

Sources of innovativeness or factors related to why people might adopt an innovation more quickly are:

1. *Communication sources.* Orientation outside the social system, media exposure, and interpersonal communication contribute to innovativeness.

2. *Attitudes toward change.* Some individuals who are initially responsive to change in one set of innovations are often receptive to additional innovations.

3. *Leadership status.* A person who perceives herself or himself as an opinion leader typically adopts early.

4. *Social and demographic variables.* Education, literacy, and previous experience predispose individuals to early adoption.

5. *Personality characteristics.* Cosmopolitanism, venturesomeness, empathy, desire to achieve, and levels of aspiration also contribute to early adoption.

6. *Economic factors.* Size of organization, high income, and loan ability are some of the economic factors that can intensify innovativeness.

7. *World view.* A personal or cultural outlook toward fate, family, or spiritual fortunes can restrain innovativeness.

8. *Social-system readiness.* Some cultures by nature embrace change; others reject change. Availability of funds or other support from government or private institutions also act as a catalyst for change.

9. *Cultural involvement.* Culturally interconnected and involved individuals typically display early adoption techniques.

10. *Cultural cohesion.* Cultures, or especially subcultures, that are highly cohesive tend to adopt as a unit. Their adoption time is influenced by the previous nine factors.

Increasingly, development planners and social-change experts consider all of these factors and the nature of the culture when they instigate planned change. The days of change programs without regard to personality, social, communication, and cultural factors are limited.* Instead, change efforts are relying upon a systems approach to form a holistic plan. Planners now know that change is

---

*Actually, little research has tested empirically the parameters of social-system innovativeness (see Davis 1968 and Saxena 1968). For that reason, most of the discussion in this section focuses on individual innovativeness (Rogers with Svenning 1969; Dodd 1976, 1978; Rogers 1983; Rogers 1989).

two-way; mutual growth is often a result. These elements in actual practice can be coupled with cultural and rhetorical sensitivity to accomplish goals mutually beneficial to all people.

## Organizational and Group Innovation and Change

The subject of innovation and change has been seriously investigated within organizations and groups, as well as in the traditional areas of intercultural change, community development, and national development. The innovation-and-change process within organizational culture is primarily a problem-solution orientation, by which managers and others attempt to assess organizational needs and then develop goals and plans to meet those needs, followed by strategies to reach the goals.

### Discovering the Need for Change

It is assumed that decision makers perceive the fundamental axiom for successful organizations: that change is inevitable. Without innovation and change, we become obsolete. Schmidt (1970, 1984) advances several conditions under which change opportunities appear. Change is needed when

1. *World economies and national competition* for goods and services call for clear directives to change or not exist.

2. *Obsolescence is apparent.* When equipment failures are frequent and complaints are high about equipment, facilities, work conditions, and tools, then it may be time to investigate and assess those claims.

3. *Productivity drops.* If task efficiency is low, innovation can stimulate growth. Changing systems, personnel, hardware, communication patterns, and so on can create a dramatic difference. The gap between actual performance and expected performance or between actual procedures and expected procedures, can activate a manager to consider new alternatives.

4. *There is a personnel shift.* When people leave or enter the organization, an opportune time exists to examine old procedures and goals to build new ones with the different human resources available.

5. *Morale and satisfaction are low.* When organizational satisfaction is consistently low, changes are needed. The obvious signs of dissatisfaction are tardiness, absenteeism, high employee turnover, and sabotage. The more subtle forms include higher than normal failure rates, emotional and psychological fatigue, lack of positive upward communication, a high number of rumors, frequent clique group interaction, and direct negative communication.

   Harris and Moran (1991) add still other change conditions. Change is needed after

6. *A new group leader is selected.* The opportunity to make corrections is needed and usually evident.

7. *Acquisition or relocation.*

8. *A consultant has completed the recommendations.*

9. *A structural or environmental change.*

10. *Significant failure.*

Rogers (1983) collected a number of variables that correlate with organizational acceptance of new practices and procedures. Organizational innovativeness tends to occur when

**Factors Associated with Organizational and Group Innovativeness**

1. The leader has a positive attitude toward change.

2. Decentralization prevails. Innovativeness is blocked when power and control remain in the hands of a relative few. Decentralization of at least information sharing and some decision making can enhance overall organizational performance.

3. Organization members possess complexity—that is, a range and high level of knowledge and expertise.

4. The organization de-emphasizes rules and procedures in members' performing their roles. Extreme formalization reduces innovativeness.

5. Organizational members experience high social interconnectedness. Interconnectedness is the degree to which people have a number of social communication networks. New ideas flow more rapidly, contributing to innovativeness.

Many plans and methodologies have proven helpful in introducing change in organizations. The diffusion approach, discussed in the first part of this chapter, offers valuable insights to the problems of organizational change. The strategies listed here for consideration with planned, organizational change are especially heuristic for organizational innovativeness (Schmidt 1984; Harris and Moran 1991; Peters and Waterman 1982; Peters 1992).

**Strategies for Innovation and Change**

*Get close to the market.* Staying close to the customer has been a traditional phrase of the Peters and Waterman (1982) material. In his book *Liberation Management* Tom Peters (1992) emphasizes that change is market oriented: "*The* innovation issue is learning that in a fashionable world we *must* create organizations that attempt, at least, to survive by getting close to the market, putting zanies in charge, and staying small enough to shift focus fast." (p. 14)

*The presence and communication of innovative information.* When organizations consistently emphasize development and innovation, members are obviously more inclined to accept change. Even if no norm for innovation is already established, decision makers can focus on and diffuse information about new processes. An up-to-date data base can stimulate the creativity of organizational members. The key is the communication and availability of new data.

*Social network method.* The social network methodology emphasizes the need to make contact with gatekeepers, opinion leaders, and liaisons in the informal communication networks that exist within the organization, as described in chapter 9. These are key people who are sufficiently influential in not only providing information to potential users, but in urging their acceptance of innovations.

*Outside pressure.* Obviously, organizations change in response to strikes, boycotts, demonstrations, pressure group demands, and legislation. Also, outside professional consultants can bring about change. The intervention strategy of consultancy can not only provide new data assessing needs for change, but the interventionist can often convince key leaders and top management of the structural, procedural, and economic methods that enhance performance.

*Change in top leaders.* Organizations change when the top management exercises personal and corporate change. During the economic recession of the 1980s, Lee Iacocca, president of Chrysler Corporation, accepted only a dollar a year for his otherwise extremely high salary. He then asked the auto union working with Chrysler to make a wage concession, which was accepted. As a result, Chrysler went from virtual bankruptcy to become a highly competitive automobile manufacturer in just a few short years and even paid off its federal loan early (which by obtaining presented the federal government with an innovative change).

*Job expectation technique.* The job expectation technique (JET) is used to clarify job expectations among managers, peers, and subordinates. The method allows individuals to write their job descriptions. Relevant management team members also contribute to the job description. By using this team-building approach, job productivity increases, role conflict and ambiguity are decreased, and quality-directed job effort results.

*Management by objectives.* Management by objectives (MBO) creates a system in which management and subordinates participate in setting goals for the subordinate. This method increases participatory style and communication and clarifies job expectations for a prescribed time period. The most common goals are set for six months or a year, after which evaluation is made and recommendations for the future are suggested.

*Job enrichment.* The job enrichment technique attempts to make the work more satisfying. The assumption here is that challenging and more satisfying jobs create more motivation. Job enrichment can include changes of title, structure, implementation, responsibilities, and growth potential in a job category.

*Team building.* The team-building strategy involves providing team members with an opportunity to discuss possibilities for change. Because team members discuss their ideas for improvement and make implementation suggestions, they tend to work more cohesively. Also, the ideas are generally useful, although not every idea can be implemented. The Japanese model of *quality circles,* a similar concept, has richly paid off for their corporate cultures and is being adopted by other nations.

*Organizational development.* Organizational development (OD) attempts to increase organizational effectiveness by connecting individual desires for growth with organizational goals (Harris and Moran 1991). OD is not so much technique in itself as it is a name for a total set of change strategies for the entire system over time. The heart of the planning really involves creating a support climate in which individuals can develop their methods for change (Schmidt 1970). By encouraging communication encounters among all levels of team management and employees, individual goals and organizational goals can be linked.

Terms related to OD include first order change and second order change. First order change offers changes in externals, such as colors, dress, new machines, and even procedure. Second order change implies changing the mission and purpose, the fundamental ways of thinking and doing, values, and world view. Most agree that second order change is more difficult but makes the biggest difference in the long run. First order change is necessary, but we should not be under the illusion that these changes necessarily cause a shift in fundamental outlooks and beliefs.

*Changing the root metaphor.* An excellent way of creating second order change is to change a group's root metaphor. Leaders in organizational theory and organizational change, such as Karl Weick, remind us that people operate on key assumptions that stem from their personal metaphors or the organization's most important metaphors about the organization. For instance, if the metaphor about a company is "family" then we could expect significant behaviors arising from that metaphor, assuming an individual accepts it and there are no intervening conditions preventing its potential actions. To change the root metaphor is to change fundamental assumptions about the way people look at their jobs, coworkers, and the organization as a whole.

The following are principles for a person seeking to engage in intercultural persuasion and social change. Although the list is not exhaustive, it does point to relevant considerations for the practitioner.

1. *Tailor a message to fit cultural values and past experiences.* As Rogers (1983) recorded, a Peruvian village failed to adopt a much needed innovation of boiling their drinking water because of their cultural value that only sickly people drank hot or warm things. Some years ago, a large

**Developing Skills in Intercultural Communication, Innovation, and Change**

drug-manufacturing firm in the United States developed a new headache pill to be taken without water. However, subsequent marketing revealed that the pill was unsuccessful. For a while, the manufacturers were baffled about the failure until finally they discovered that Americans simply had little faith in any headache medicine taken without water. Americans are more comfortable taking pills with water. The failure of a government attempt to install a water pump in a Zambian village is another example. The government reasoned that women could save time and improve efficiency by having water pumped from the river instead of walking the lengthy distance. The government project failed miserably, and the water pump fell into disuse for at least two reasons. One reason was that nobody had the mechanical skills necessary to keep the pump operational. A second and more important reason was that the trip to the river provided a means of conveying village news. Women also exchanged views on children, crops, and household matters during these river visits. These examples illustrate why a study of cultural values and a perusal of past experiences is vital to an understanding of effective change.

2. *Consider need before an innovation's introduction.* After an unsuccessful introduction of irrigation among the Papago Indians, Dobyns (1951) concluded that introduction of change will be successful to the degree that those who are affected by the change are brought into its planning and execution and thus made to feel that the innovation is their own. Margaret Mead has stated, "Experience has taught us that change can be best introduced, not through centralized planning, but after a study of local needs" (Mead 1955, p. 258). Those local needs must involve indigenous planning.

3. *As a communication planner, concentrate on opinion leaders.* One failure in intercultural communication may well stem from a preoccupation with innovators in a culture rather than opinion leaders. Characteristics of opinion leaders have already been documented. The key method is to discover respected members of a social system and work with those members. Numerous intercultural failures in social change occur from faulty planning and a disregard for cultural opinion leaders.

4. *Close the heterophily gap.* A *change agent* is a professional who works for adoption of an innovation within a social system. Usually, this person is heterophilous from most people with whom he or she is trying to bring about change. However, this person can close that heterophily gap by working with opinion leaders. Heterophily should be less of a barrier to opinion leaders than to their followers. In this way, information is introduced to the social system, and its dissemination is maximized.

5. *Anticipate and prevent undesirable social consequences of innovation adoption if possible.* The phenomenon of overadoption is not altogether uncommon. For example, after the introduction and diffusion of the weedkiller 2, 4-D, some farmers were so impressed with the results that they used it on their cornfields to excess and ultimate waste. Unsought overadoption occurred in the 1960s when some blacks pressed for strategies not planned or sought by many black leaders (Fotheringham 1966, p. 211).

6. *Perform demographic analysis of the target culture.* Understanding significant demographic variables and their importance can enhance a change movement. For instance, dominant involvement with youth in a culture that advocates decision making among and respect for older cultural members can result in a youth movement with little future potential or leadership. Targeting the message toward specific demographic categories has several additional advantages:
   a. The message is more easily tailored to fit existing conditions of various age groups, professions, and so on.
   b. The message has a chance of being spread by word of mouth among homogenous groups distinguished by their demography.
   c. The message can be aimed at "influentials" and informally respected persons in a village or other unit.

7. *Understand the use of the mass media.* Communication theory indicates that the mass media serve primarily to alert villagers to innovations, to reinforce villagers who already have adopted, and to develop a climate for change. Studies show, however, that the mass media do not influence adoption as directly as demographic, interpersonal, and cultural factors. Thus, the message must take on a grass roots, interpersonal dimension. If the media are used, the communication planner must understand their strengths and limitations. For instance, a strategy using a knowledge of demographic factors and interpersonal communication factors in conjunction with the mass media would be more effective than any one of these factors acting alone.

8. *Build bridges not walls.* The first people to adopt an innovation frequently are persons culturally disengaged from mainstream cultural life. Consequently, their rapid acceptance may produce a credibility gap for subsequent adopters who belong to the cultural mainstream. Therefore, work toward introducing the innovation to informal opinion leaders and to decision makers. Such a strategy need not ignore innovators, but direct contact with opinion leaders does provide a legitimizing effect that lends credence to the message. Consequently, opinion leaders' influence, through their existing communication networks, accelerates message flow and impact.

9. *Don't seek the cultural recluse.* This suggestion is related to the previous point. More rapid growth and acceptance occurs among people who are culturally involved in terms of group membership, attention to the mass media, and favorable attitudes toward others in their villages. Therefore, try to choose adopter prospects carefully, avoiding the disgruntled, disengaged, and reclusive individual. The cultural recluse may temporarily join the change agent's efforts but ultimately prevent long-range cultural penetration.

10. *Direct efforts toward members of existing homogeneous units.* People organize themselves into units that approach similarity in viewpoint, lifestyle, and so on. While the most obvious units are the tribe, clan, and village, do not overlook nuclear and extended family units and friendship relations. Data reported earlier in this chapter revealed that the more accelerated adoption rate was accompanied by consultation with friends. Inviting sociological networks of friendship units or other salient units to jointly hear an innovation message is one useful strategy.

11. *Practice empathy.* Numerous studies show that empathy is highly linked with change agent success. Listen rather than boss.

12. *Realize that some innovations may be harmful.* You may believe that some message or idea is necessary or important—not every culture agrees. If you are not wanted or are uninvited, then your effort may be futile. Cooperation is important. Remember that some innovations do not fit in a culture. Develop enough insight so that you do not give steel axes to a culture where such an innovation could bring harm.

---

**This Chapter in Perspective**

The theory of diffusion and social change provides insight into a grass roots movement of ideas from person to person within a culture. For instance, various characteristics describe early and late adopters of innovations. Understanding the decision-making process helps us to appreciate different sources of information at various stages of the decision process. This chapter also addresses the question of how individuals perceive innovations in terms of their relative advantage, compatibility, complexity, trialability, and observability. The variables that predispose a person or culture to innovativeness and social change are also examined. Finally, strategy considerations offer practical suggestions for intercultural communication efforts in persuasion.

Planners and communications-development people need to weigh the ethics of social change in their deliberations and to consider genuine needs and a systems approach. Change planners must invite all the input possible in making policies and implementing them. Inviting cultural members to help in the formulation and planning stages can ensure highly ethical decisions and principles. Organizational innovation and change is summarized here and is a function of several factors noted in the chapter.

1. Make an appointment to visit some organization that works on community **Exercises**
   development and social change. It may be some social or governmental
   organization in your town or city. During the meeting, ask how programs
   are developed, instituted, and communicated to the target populations.
   Find out what works well for this organization and what does not work
   well. How do their insights compare with the principles reported in this
   chapter? How could the principles in this chapter assist community agencies in communication?

2. Find current magazine articles, newspaper articles, and interviews dealing
   with some new idea or new technology. Gather as much factual reporting
   as you can from these sources and then compare what various people are
   saying about the innovation. Do people who seem more interested in the
   innovation do or say anything different from people who seem opposed to
   the innovation? Why or why not? Try to sketch a profile, from reading
   these interviews and articles, that characterizes early and late adopters of
   this innovation.

3. Choose some new idea or technology, perhaps the same one you chose for
   exercise 2. Interview five people, and ask each one to define what they like
   best and least about the innovation. Ask them what characteristics could be
   presented about the innovation that would motivate people toward persuasion. Do these characteristics add to the list of innovation characteristics
   given earlier in this chapter? What is it about persuasive messages that
   makes them compelling?

# Self-Report Assessment Applied to Intercultural Communication

(NOTE: See additional scales in chapters 6 and 9.)

# Monochronic-Polychronic Scale
## Charles Phipps J.D.

Please answer the following questions using this scale:

Strongly agree(SA) Agree(A) Neutral(N) Disagree(D) Strongly disagree(SD)

1. I usually feel frustrated after I choose to do a number of tasks when I could have chosen to do one at a time.    SA  A  N  D  SD

*2. When I talk with my friends in a group setting, I feel comfortable trying to hold two or three conversations at a time.    SA  A  N  D  SD

*3. When I work on a project around the house, it doesn't bother me to stop in the middle of one job to pick up on another job that needs to be done.    SA  A  N  D  SD

4. I like to finish one task before going on to another task.    SA  A  N  D  SD

*5. At church it wouldn't bother me to meet at the same time with several different people who all had different church matters to discuss.    SA  A  N  D  SD

6. I tend to concentrate on one idea before moving on to another task.    SA  A  N  D  SD

7. The easiest way for me to function is to organize my day to day activities with a schedule.    SA  A  N  D  SD

*8. If I were a teacher and had several students wishing to talk with me about assigned homework, I would meet with the whole group rather than one student at a time.    SA  A  N  D  SD

*9. I like doing several tasks at one time.    SA  A  N  D  SD

10. I am frustrated when I have to start on a task without first finishing a previous one.    SA  A  N  D  SD

*11. In trying to solve problems, I find it stimulating to think about several different problems at the same time.    SA  A  N  D  SD

12. I am mildly irritated when someone in a meeting wants to bring up a personal topic that is unrelated to the purpose of the meeting.    SA  A  N  D  SD

13. In school I prefer studying one subject to completion before going on to the next subject.    SA  A  N  D  SD

14. I'm hesitant to focus my attention on only one thing, because I may miss something equally important.    SA  A  N  D  SD

15. I usually need to pay attention to only one task at a time to finish it.    SA  A  N  D  SD

*Scoring:* Add the scores with SA = 1, A = 2, N = 3, D = 4, SD = 5. Reverse score (SA = 5, A = 4 etc.) for items marked with *. Scores of 30 and below indicated monochronic style; scores of 42 and above indicated polychronic style (reliability = .73).

# Ethnocentrism
## Kregg Hood Ed.D.

1. Visitors to America will naturally want to adopt our customs as soon as possible.    SA   A   N   D   SD

2. Generally speaking, the way we do things in my home town is the best way to do things in most other places as well.    SA   A   N   D   SD

3. Foreigners have a responsibility to learn our customs when they come to the United States.    SA   A   N   D   SD

4. Most people in the world really wish they could become American citizens.    SA   A   N   D   SD

5. In reality members of other cultures cannot adequately copy the characteristics of American culture.    SA   A   N   D   SD

6. It is wrong for visitors to our country to refuse to adapt to our customs when they come here.    SA   A   N   D   SD

7. The ceremonies in Africa that initiate a boy into manhood are barbaric.    SA   A   N   D   SD

8. Western cultures are more civilized than African cultures.    SA   A   N   D   SD

9. The rapid influx of immigrants into the USA will eventually ruin our country.    SA   A   N   D   SD

10. American usage of time in business is better than in Africa or South America.    SA   A   N   D   SD

11. The Asian practice of honoring the elderly is interesting but not very practical.    SA   A   N   D   SD

12. It would be better if English were spoken as a universal language.    SA   A   N   D   SD

13. No country has done more for the advancement of civilization than the USA.    SA   A   N   D   SD

14. It is unwise to trust a foreigner until you know him better.    SA   A   N   D   SD

15. South Americans are usually poor because they are lazy.    SA   A   N   D   SD

16. The native dress of an African tribesman looks silly.    SA   A   N   D   SD

17. Americans tend to be smarter than the Japanese.    SA   A   N   D   SD

This scale used with potential expatriates, generally surfaces extreme ethnocentrism.

*Scoring:* Add the scores with SA = 5, A = 4, N = 3, D = 2, SD = 1. Scores of 35 and below indicated low ethnocentrism, scores of 45 and above indicated high ethnocentrism. Norms: mean = 40, s.d. = 5; Reliability = .82.

## Cultural Reentry Stress
### Cynthia Roper, Ph.D.

Rate the following items according to the degree of adjustment of difficulty you have experienced during your last 4 months here. The responses range from 1 = no difficulty through 5 = severe difficulty.

| | | | | | | |
|---|---|---|---|---|---|---|
| 1. | Obtaining adequate funds for living/tuition expenses | 1 | 2 | 3 | 4 | 5 |
| 2. | Religious atmosphere of campus | 1 | 2 | 3 | 4 | 5 |
| 3. | Overall pace of life | 1 | 2 | 3 | 4 | 5 |
| 4. | Transportation needs | 1 | 2 | 3 | 4 | 5 |
| 5. | Clothing styles | 1 | 2 | 3 | 4 | 5 |
| 6. | Lack of friends | 1 | 2 | 3 | 4 | 5 |
| 7. | Maintaining spiritual adjustments | 1 | 2 | 3 | 4 | 5 |
| 8. | Religious attitudes of other students | 1 | 2 | 3 | 4 | 5 |
| 9. | Doubts about whether I should be here or not | 1 | 2 | 3 | 4 | 5 |
| 10. | Homesickness | 1 | 2 | 3 | 4 | 5 |
| 11. | Physical illness | 1 | 2 | 3 | 4 | 5 |
| 12. | Personal relationship with roommate | 1 | 2 | 3 | 4 | 5 |
| 13. | Life in the dorm | 1 | 2 | 3 | 4 | 5 |
| 14. | Nervousness | 1 | 2 | 3 | 4 | 5 |
| 15. | Trembling | 1 | 2 | 3 | 4 | 5 |
| 16. | Sleeplessness | 1 | 2 | 3 | 4 | 5 |
| 17. | Fearfulness | 1 | 2 | 3 | 4 | 5 |
| 18. | Dizziness | 1 | 2 | 3 | 4 | 5 |
| 19. | Tense or keyed up | 1 | 2 | 3 | 4 | 5 |
| 20. | Headache or backache | 1 | 2 | 3 | 4 | 5 |
| 21. | Worry/anxiety | 1 | 2 | 3 | 4 | 5 |
| 22. | Difficulty making simple decision | 1 | 2 | 3 | 4 | 5 |
| 23. | Fatigue/exhaustion | 1 | 2 | 3 | 4 | 5 |
| 24. | Easily discouraged | 1 | 2 | 3 | 4 | 5 |
| 25. | Depression | 1 | 2 | 3 | 4 | 5 |
| 26. | Excessive sleeping | 1 | 2 | 3 | 4 | 5 |
| 27. | Excessive emotionality | 1 | 2 | 3 | 4 | 5 |
| 28. | Overly sensitive | 1 | 2 | 3 | 4 | 5 |
| 29. | Criticalness | 1 | 2 | 3 | 4 | 5 |
| 30. | Ulcer, diarrhea, or stomach ache | 1 | 2 | 3 | 4 | 5 |

Used originally by Moore (1981) for repatriates, Roper (1986) adopted this scale for incoming freshmen.

*Scoring:* The greater the score, the higher the reentry stress. Scores of 50 and below indicated low stress; scores of 70 or above indicated high stress. Norms: mean = 60, s.d. = 10; Reliability = .85.

## Scale With E-MODEL for Intercultural Effectiveness
(Walter, Choonjaroen, Bartosh, and Dodd 1995)

Part I—The following scale asks for your personal views. Please answer as honestly as possible.

Circle the best answer

| Strongly agree (SA) | Agree (A) | Neutral (N) | Disagree (D) | Strongly disagree (SD) |
|---|---|---|---|---|

1.  I am a person of worth.     SA  A  N  D  SD
2.  I have a very deep level of understanding in most situations.     SA  A  N  D  SD
3.  Being around foreign people makes me nervous.     SA  A  N  D  SD
4.  I normally develop relationships easily.     SA  A  N  D  SD
5.  I don't always get the respect I deserve.     SA  A  N  D  SD
6.  My social life is great.     SA  A  N  D  SD
7.  I would like to visit other countries.     SA  A  N  D  SD
8.  I find it difficult to have meaningful conversations with others.     SA  A  N  D  SD
9.  When conflict arises between myself and a friend, I try to avoid the conflict.     SA  A  N  D  SD
10. People tend to not trust me until they get to know me.     SA  A  N  D  SD
11. I am very patient with other people.     SA  A  N  D  SD
12. There's no real need to ever learn a foreign language.     SA  A  N  D  SD
13. I always initiate conversation first.     SA  A  N  D  SD
14. I have several good qualities.     SA  A  N  D  SD
15. The English and Japanese drive their automobiles on the wrong side of the street.     SA  A  N  D  SD
16. I normally empathize with other peoples' problems.     SA  A  N  D  SD
17. I usually resist change to my lifestyle.     SA  A  N  D  SD
18. When I meet someone for the first time, my interpersonal effectiveness is good.     SA  A  N  D  SD
19. I get as much out of life as possible.     SA  A  N  D  SD
20. I am more than adequate intellectually.     SA  A  N  D  SD

(See next page for Part II and instructions.)

**Appendix: Self-Report Assessment Applied to Intercultural Communication**

Part II—Please answer as honestly as possible.
Circle the best answer.

| | |
|---|---|
| *1.Most people in the world wish they were Americans. | SA A N D SD |
| *2. Most people just don't know what's good for them. | SA A N D SD |
| *3. The influx of immigrants into the U.S. will ruin our country. | SA A N D SD |
| 4. I don't usually experience frustration at social functions. | SA A N D SD |
| *5. The native dress in Africa is ridiculous. | SA A N D SD |
| *6. Generally speaking, the best way to do things is how we do them here in America. | SA A N D SD |
| *7. There is a right way and a wrong way to do everything. | SA A N D SD |
| 8. Friendships with other people are important to me and last a long time. | SA A N D SD |
| *9. It disturbs me not to know someone's train of thought. | SA A N D SD |
| *10. It is usually unwise to trust a foreign person. | SA A N D SD |
| *11. It would be a better world if English were the only language spoken. | SA A N D SD |
| *12. American businessmen use time much better than Latin Americans and Africans. | SA A N D SD |
| 13. Problem solving is best accomplished through a systematic approach. | SA A N D SD |
| *14. Latin Americans and Africans are poor because they are lazy. | SA A N D SD |
| *15. Americans are more civilized than most other cultures. | SA A N D SD |
| 16. I usually handle stress very well. | SA A N D SD |
| *17. I don't feel comfortable around strangers. | SA A N D SD |
| *18. It disturbs me not to know how my actions affect others. | SA A N D SD |
| *19. I really dislike it when someone doesn't give me straight answers about themselves. | SA A N D SD |
| *20. I really don't care for all the stress and problems involved in traveling, I am better off right where I'm at. | SA A N D SD |

*Scoring:* Add the scores with SA = 5, A = 4, N = 3, D = 2, SD = 1. Reverse score (SA = 1, A = 4, etc.) for items marked with *. Add all points in Part I together, divide by four and apply to **INTERPERSONAL** arm of the big **E**. Add all points in Part II together, divide by four and apply to **ADAPTABILITY** arm of the big **E** (see chapter on effectiveness). The index is an initial screening for potential intercultural desirability only.

## Interpersonal Comfort
### Laurie Norton Diles, Ph.D.

1. At social functions, I experience frustrations, thinking I am not very effective in my communication.    SA  A  N  D  SD

2. In my conversations with people, I feel many people judge my communication effectiveness to be less than adequate.    SA  A  N  D  SD

*3. My interpersonal communication abilities seem to be fairly effective in working with persons of the middle class.    SA  A  N  D  SD

*4. I am comfortable communicating at a social event, even though it is a type of event I have not previously attended.    SA  A  N  D  SD

5. I find myself unable to say what I really feel when talking with people and this leaves me with a feeling of being ineffective in my interpersonal skills.    SA  A  N  D  SD

6. My interpersonal communication skills seem to be fairly ineffective when talking with higher class people.    SA  A  N  D  SD

7. In my interpersonal communication with people, I often walk away with a feeling that I have really said the wrong thing, or done something the wrong way, and thus was ineffective in my interpersonal communication.    SA  A  N  D  SD

*8. I find myself being more effective than the average person in my interpersonal communication with people with whom I interact on a business basis (store owners, bankers, post office clerks, etc.).    SA  A  N  D  SD

9. When I am not the leader in a given situation, I feel ineffective in my interpersonal communication.    SA  A  N  D  SD

*10. My interpersonal communication abilities seem to be fairly effective in talking with people from lower classes.    SA  A  N  D  SD

*11. When I meet somebody for the first time, I would judge my interpersonal effectiveness to be pretty good.    SA  A  N  D  SD

12. My interpersonal communication is effective but only in a limited sense; there is a point beyond which I cease to be effective.    SA  A  N  D  SD

13. When I express my ideas with a group of people, I often have the feeling that my words are "falling on deaf ears."    SA  A  N  D  SD

14. At those times when I sit down to visit with a businessman, I find we are speaking the same language, but I leave the conversation feeling that I have been virtually ineffective.    SA  A  N  D  SD

This scale presented in this text was modified from Norton (1984) and was used with expatriates in five Latin American countries to predict their level of communication comfort, especially with status.

*Scoring:* Add the scores with SA = 1, A = 2, N = 3, D = 4, SD = 5. Reverse score (SA = 5, A = 4 etc.) for items marked with *. Scores of 45 and below indicated low interpersonal comfort; scores of 55 or above indicated high interpersonal comfort. Norms: mean = 50, s.d. = 5; Reliability = .80.

## Self-Confidence
Joe Cardot, Ed.D.

| | | |
|---|---|---|
| 1. | I feel that I'm a person of worth, at least on an equal basis with others. | SA  A  N  D  SD |
| 2. | I feel that I have a number of good qualities. | SA  A  N  D  SD |
| *3. | All in all, I am inclined to feel that I am a failure. | SA  A  N  D  SD |
| 4. | I am able to do things as well as most other people. | SA  A  N  D  SD |
| 5. | I feel that I do not have much to be proud of. | SA  A  N  D  SD |
| 6. | I take a positive attitude toward myself. | SA  A  N  D  SD |
| 7. | On the whole, I am satisfied with myself. | SA  A  N  D  SD |
| *8. | I wish I could have more respect for myself. | SA  A  N  D  SD |
| *9. | I certainly feel useless at times. | SA  A  N  D  SD |
| *10. | At times I think I am no good at all. | SA  A  N  D  SD |

*Scoring:* Add the scores with SA = 5, A = 4, N = 3, D = 2, SD = 1. Reverse Score—SA = 1, A = 2, N = 3, D = 4, SD = 5—for items marked *. Scores of 30 and below indicated low confidence; scores of 40 and above indicated high confidence. Norms: mean = 35, s.d. = 5; Reliability = .80.

Scale adapted from Cardot (1980).

## Adapted Dogmatism/Rigidity
Joe Cardot, Ed.D.

| | | | | | | |
|---|---|---|---|---|---|---|
| 1. | In this complicated world of ours, the only way we can know what's going on is to rely on leaders and experts who can be trusted. | SA | A | N | D | SD |
| 2. | My blood boils whenever a person stubbornly refuses to admit he is wrong. | SA | A | N | D | SD |
| 3. | There are two kinds of people in this world: Those who are for the truth and those who are against the truth. | SA | A | N | D | SD |
| 4. | Most people just don't know what's good for them. | SA | A | N | D | SD |
| 5. | Of all the different philosophies which exist in this world, there is probably only one which is correct. | SA | A | N | D | SD |
| 6. | The main thing in life is for a person to want to do something important. | SA | A | N | D | SD |
| 7. | Most of the ideas which get printed nowadays aren't worth the paper they are printed on. | SA | A | N | D | SD |
| 8. | It is only when a person devotes himself to an idea or cause that life becomes meaningful. | SA | A | N | D | SD |
| 9. | It is often desirable to reserve judgment about what's going on until one has had a chance to hear the opinions of those one respects. | SA | A | N | D | SD |
| 10. | Most people really don't care about others. | SA | A | N | D | SD |

*Scoring:* Add the scores with SA = 5, A = 4, N = 3, D = 2, SD = 1. Scores of 24 and below indicated low rigidity; scores with 32 and above indicated high rigidity. Norms: mean = 28, s.d. = 4; Reliability = .79.

Scale adapted from Cardot (1980).

Abelson, Herbert I. *Persuasion.* New York: Springer, 1959.

Ackermann, Jean Marie. "Skill Training for Foreign Assignment: The Reluctant U.S. Case." In *Intercultural Communication: A Reader.* 2d ed., edited by Larry A. Samovar and Richard E. Porter. Belmont, Calif.: Wadsworth, 1976.

Adler, Peter S. "The Transitional Experience: An Alternative View of Culture Shock." *Journal of Humanistic Psychology* 15 (1975): 10–14.

Alpert, M.I., and W.T. Anderson. "Optimal Heterophily and Communication Effectiveness." *Journal of Communication* 23 (1973): 328–43.

Amir, Y. "Contact Hypothesis in Ethnic Relations." *Psychological Bulletin* 71 (1969): 319–41.

Applbaum, Ronald. *Fundamental Concepts in Human Communication.* San Francisco: Canfield, 1973.

Applbaum, Ronald, and Karl Anatol. "Factor Structure of Source Credibility as a Function of the Speaking Situation." *Speech Monographs* 39 (1972): 216–22.

Applegate, James, and Howard Sypher. "A Constructionist Theory of Communication and Culture." In *Theories in Intercultural Communication,* edited by Young Y. Kim and William B. Gudykunst. Newbury Park, Calif.: Sage, 1988.

Applegate, James, and Howard Sypher. "A Constructivist Outline." In *Intercultural Communication Theory: Current Perspectives,* edited by William B. Gudykunst. Beverly Hills, Calif.: Sage, 1983.

Arensberg, Conrad M., and Arthur H. Niehoff. *Introducing Social Change.* Chicago: Aldine, 1964.

Argyle, M., and J. Dean. "Eye Contact, Distance and Affiliation." *Sociometry* 28 (1965): 289–304.

Arnold, William E. "The Effect of Nonverbal Cues on Source Credibility." *Central States Speech Journal* 23 (1973): 227–30.

Aronson, Eliot. *The Social Animal.* 3d ed. San Francisco: W.H. Freeman, 1980.

Asante, Molefi Kete. "The Tradition of Advocacy in the Yoruba Courts." *The Southern Communication Journal* 55 (1990): 250–59.

Asante, Molefi Kete, and Alice Davis. "Encounters in the Interracial Workplace." In *Handbook of International and Intercultural Communication,* edited by Molefi Kete Asante and William B. Gudykunst. Newbury Park, Calif.: Sage, 1989.

Asante, Molefi, and William B. Gudykunst, eds. *Handbook of International and Intercultural Communication.* Newbury Park, Calif.: Sage, 1989.

Asch, Solomon E. "Effects of Group Pressures upon the Modification and Distortion of Judgments." In *Readings in Social Psychology,* edited by Eleanor E. Maccoby, Theodore M. Newcomb, and Eugene L. Hartley. New York: Henry Holt, 1958.

Atwood, L. Erwin, and Keith R. Sanders. "A Longitudinal Analysis of Information Sources, Source Credibility, and Gubernatorial Vote." Paper presented to International Communication Association, Chicago, April 1975.

Auletta, Gale. "Response to Driskill and Norton's Review of Research in Personal World View." Paper presented to the Speech Communication Association, San Francisco, November 1989.

Austin, Clyde N. "Cross-Cultural Reentry." In *Intercultural Skills for Multicultural Societies,* edited by Carley Dodd and Frank Montalvo. Washington, D.C.: SIETAR, 1987a.

Austin, Clyde N., ed. *Readings in Cross-Cultural Reentry.* Abilene, Texas: ACU Press, 1987b.

Back, Kurt. "Influence through Social Communication." In *Readings in Social Psychology,* edited by Eleanor E. Maccoby, Theodore M. Newcomb, and Eugene L. Hartley. New York: Henry Holt, 1958.

Baird, John E. "Some Nonverbal Elements of Leadership Emergence." *Southern Speech Communication Journal* 42 (1977): 352–61.

Baldassini, José G., and Vincent F. Flaherty. "Acculturation Process of Colombian Immigrants into the American Culture in Bergen County, New Jersey." *International Journal of Intercultural Relations* 6 (1982): 127–35.

Baldwin, John R. "Self-Monitoring, Cognitive Complexity, Stereotypes and Role Perception as Correlates of Communication Satisfaction in Intercultural Marriages." Master's thesis, Abilene Christian University, 1991.

Bandler, Richard. *Using Your Brain for a Change: Neurolinguistic Programming.* Moab, Utah: Real People Press, 1985.

Barnlund, Dean C. "A Consistency of Emergent Leadership in Groups with Changing Tasks and Members." *Speech Monographs* 29 (1962): 45–52.

Barnlund, Dean C., ed. *Interpersonal Communication: Surveys and Studies.* Boston: Houghton Mifflin, 1968.

Bates, Daniel G. "Normative and Alternative Systems of Marriage among the Yoruk of Southeastern Turkey." *Anthropological Quarterly* 47 (1974): 270–87.

Beals, Ralph L., and Harry Hoijer. *An Introduction to Anthropology.* New York: Macmillan, 1971.

Becker, F., and C. Mayo. "Delineating Personal Distance and Territory." *Environment and Behavior* 6 (1974): 212–32.

Becvar, R., and D. Becvar. *Systems Theory and Family Therapy.* New York: University Press of America, 1982.

Beebe, L.M., and Howard Giles. "Speech Accommodation Theories: Discussion of Terms of Second-Language Acquisition." *International Journal of the Sociology of Language* 46 (1984): 5–32.

Beebe, Steven A. "Eye Contact: A Nonverbal Determinant of Speaker Credibility." *Speech Teacher* 23 (1974): 21–25.

Beier, E.G., A.M. Rossi, and R.L. Garfield. "Similarity Plus Dissimilarity of Personality: Basis for Friendship?" *Psychological Reports* 8 (1961): 3–8.

Benedict, Ruth. *Patterns of Culture.* Boston: Houghton Mifflin, 1934.

Bennett, Janet. "Transition Shock: Putting Culture Shock into Perspective." *International and Intercultural Communication Annual* 4 (1977): 45–52.

Berelson, Bernard, and Gary A. Steiner. *Human Behavior: An Inventory of Scientific Findings.* New York: Harcourt, Brace & World, 1964.

Berelson, Bernard R., Paul F. Lazarsfeld, and William N. McPhee. *Voting.* Chicago: University of Chicago Press, 1954.

Berger, Charles R., and R.J. Calabrese. "Some Explorations in Initial Interactions and Beyond." *Human Communication Research* 1 (1975): 99–112.

Berger, Charles R., R.R. Gardner, Malcolm R. Parks, L. Shulman, and Gerald R. Miller. "Interpersonal Epistemology and Interpersonal Communication." In *Explorations in Interpersonal Communication,* edited by Gerald R. Miller. Beverly Hills, Calif.: Sage, 1976.

Berlo, David, James B. Lemert, and Robert J. Mertz. "Dimensions for Evaluating the Acceptability of Message Sources." *Public Opinion Quarterly* 33 (1966): 563–76.

Berlo, David K. *The Process of Communication: An Introduction to Theory and Practice.* New York: Holt, Rinehart and Winston, 1960.

Bernard, H. Russel, and Pertti Pelto. *Technology and Social Change.* New York: Macmillan, 1972.

Bernstein, Basil. "Elaborated and Restricted Codes: Their Social Origins and Some Consequences." In *Communication and Culture,* edited by Alfred G. Smith. New York: Holt, Rinehart and Winston, 1966.

Berscheid, Ellen. "Opinion Change and Communicator-Communicatee Similarity and Dissimilarity." *Journal of Personality and Social Psychology* 4 (1966): 670–80.

Berscheid, Ellen, and Elaine H. Walster. *Interpersonal Attraction.* Reading, Mass.: Addison-Wesley, 1969.

Betances, Samuel. "The Media and Multicultural Societies." In *Intercultural Skills for Multicultural Societies,* edited by Carley Dodd and Frank Montalvo. Washington, D.C.: SIETAR, 1987.

Bettinghaus, Erwin P. *Persuasive Communication.* 3d ed. New York: Holt, Rinehart and Winston, 1980.

Birdwhistell, Ray L. "Some Relations between American Kinesics and Spoken American English." In *Communication and Culture,* edited by Alfred G. Smith. New York: Holt, Rinehart and Winston, 1966.

Bizman, Aharon. "Perceived Causes and Compatability of Interethnic Marriage: An Attributional Analysis." *International Journal of Intercultural Relations* 9 (1987): 387–99.

Blackman, Bernard. "Toward A Grounded Theory." In *Intercultural Communication Theory: Current Perspectives,* edited by William B. Gudykunst. Beverly Hills, Calif.: Sage, 1983.

Blubaugh, Jon, and Dorothy Pennington. *Crossing Difference: Interracial Communication.* Columbus: Charles Merrill, 1976.

Boas, Franz. *Kwakiutl Ethnography.* Chicago: University of Chicago Press, 1966.

Bock, E. Hope, and James H. Pitts. "The Effects of Three Levels of Black Dialect on Perceived Speaker Image." *Speech Teacher* 24 (1975): 218–25.

Bock, Philip K. *Modern Cultural Anthropology.* New York: Alfred A. Knopf, 1969.

Boucher, Jerry D. "Culture and the Expression of Emotion." *International and Intercultural Communication Annual* 1 (1974): 82–86.

Boulding, Kenneth. *The Image.* Ann Arbor, Mich.: University of Michigan Press, 1972.

Brady, Robert M. "Predictive Correlates of Adoption Behavior in a Social Context: A Multiple Discriminant Analysis." Master's thesis, Western Kentucky University, 1975.

Brislin, Richard. "Intercultural Communication Training." In *Handbook of International and Intercultural Communication,* edited by Molefi Kete Asante and William B. Gudykunst. Newbury Park, Calif.: Sage, 1989.

Brislin, Richard. *Understanding Culture's Influence on Behavior.* Orlando: Harcourt Brace Jovanovich, 1993.

Brooks, William D., and Philip Emmert. *Interpersonal Communication.* Dubuque, Iowa: Wm. C. Brown Company Publishers, 1976.

Broome, Benjamin J. "Building Shared Meaning: Implications of a Relational Approach to Empathy for Teaching Intercultural Communication." *Communication Education* 40 (1991): 235–49.

Broome, Benjamin J. "Pavelome: Foundations of Struggle and Conflict in Greek Interpersonal Communication." *The Southern Communication Journal* 55 (1990): 260–75.

Brown, Dee. *Bury My Heart at Wounded Knee.* New York: Holt, Rinehart and Winston, 1970.

Burgoon, Michael, Stephen Jones, and Diane Stewart. "Toward a Message-Centered Theory of Persuasion." *Human Communication Research* 1 (1975): 240–56.

Burke, Jerry. "An Explanation and Evaluation of Cognitive Anthropology." *International and Intercultural Communication Annual* 1 (1974): 24–38.

Byrne, D. "Interpersonal Attraction and Attitude Similarity." *Journal of Abnormal and Social Psychology* 62 (1961): 713–15.

Caillouet, Larry. "Comparative Media Effectiveness in an Evangelistic Campaign." Ph.D. diss., University of Illinois, Urbana, 1978.

Capps, Randall, Carley H. Dodd, and Larry J. Winn. *Communication for the Business and Professional Speaker.* New York: Macmillan, 1981.

Carbaugh, Donald. "Cultural Communication and Organizing." In *Communication, Culture, and Organizational Processes,* edited by William B. Gudykunst, Lea P. Stewart, and Stella Ting-Toomey. Beverly Hills, Calif.: Sage, 1985.

Cardot, Joseph. "A Comparison of Communication Social Style and World View Between Administrators and Faculty Members of Higher Education." Ph.D. diss., Texas Tech University, 1990.

Carlos, Serge. "Religious Participation and the Urban-Suburban Continuum." *American Journal of Sociology* 75 (1970): 742.

Carter, William E. "Secular Reinforcement in Aymara Death Ritual." *American Anthropologist* 70 (1968): 238–61.

Casmir, Fred L. *Intercultural and International Communication.* Washington, D.C.: University Press of America, 1978.

Casmir, Fred L. "Introduction: Culture, Communication, and Education." *Communication Education* 40 (1991): 229–34.

Casmir, Fred L. "Stereotypes and Schemata." In *Communication, Culture, and Organizational Processes,* edited by William B. Gudykunst, Lea P. Stewart, and Stella Ting-Toomey. Newbury Park, Calif.: Sage, 1985.

Cattell, R. "New Concepts for Measuring Leadership, in Terms of Group Syntality." *Human Relations* 2 (1951): 161–84.

Chomsky, Noam. *Language and Mind.* New York: Harcourt and Brace, 1972.

Condon, E.C. "Cross-Cultural Interferences Affecting Teacher-Pupil Communication in American Schools." *International and Intercultural Communication Annual* 3 (1976): 108–20.

Condon, John C., and Fathi Yousef. *Introduction to Intercultural Communication.* New York: Bobbs-Merrill, 1975.

Cronen, Vernon, and Robert Shuter. "Forming Intercultural Bonds." In *Intercultural Communication Theory: Current Perspectives,* edited by William B. Gudykunst. Beverly Hills, Calif.: Sage, 1983.

Cronen, Vernon E., V. Chen, and W. Barnett Pearce. "Coordinated Management of Meaning." In *Theories in Intercultural Communication,* edited by Young Y. Kim and William B. Gudykunst. Newbury Park, Calif.: Sage, 1988.

Cushman, Donald P., and Sarah Sanderson King. "National and Organizational Cultures in Conflict Resolution: Japan, the United States, and Yugoslavia." In *Communication, Culture, and Organizational Processes,* edited by William B. Gudykunst, Lea P. Stewart, and Stella Ting-Toomey. Newbury Park, Calif.: Sage, 1985.

Dale, Philip S. *Language Development.* Hinsdale, Ill.: Dryden, 1972.

Daniel, Jack. "The Poor: Aliens in an Affluent Society." In *Intercultural Communication: A Reader.* 2d ed., edited by Larry Samovar and Richard Porter. Belmont, Calif.: Wadsworth, 1976.

Davis, B.E. "System Variables and Agricultural Innovativeness in Eastern Nigeria." Ph.D. diss., Michigan State University, 1968.

Davis, Cheryl. "The Relationship of Family and Peer Communication to Third Culture Kids." Master's thesis. Abilene Christian University, 1990.

DeFleur, Melvin L., and Sandra Ball-Rokeach. *Theories of Mass Communication.* 3d ed. New York: David McKay, 1976.

Delia, J.G. "Dialects and the Effects of Stereotypes on Interpersonal Attraction and Cognitive Processes in Impression Formation." *Quarterly Journal of Speech* 58 (1972): 285–97.

Delia, J.G. "Regional Dialect, Message Acceptance, and Perceptions of the Speaker." *Central States Speech Journal* 26 (1975): 188–94.

Deutschmann, Paul J., and Wayne A. Danielson. "Diffusion of Knowledge of the Major News Story." *Journalism Quarterly* 37 (1960): 345–55.

DeVito, Joseph. *The Human Communication Book.* 5th ed. New York: Harper and Row, 1989.

DeVito, Joseph A. *The Interpersonal Communication Book.* 5th ed. New York: Harper and Row, 1988.

Dimen-Schein, Muriel. *The Anthropological Imagination.* New York: McGraw-Hill, 1977.

Dinges, Norman, and Devorah Lieberman. "Intercultural Communication Competence: Coping with Stressful Work Conditions." *International Journal of Intercultural Relations* 13 (1989): 371–85.

Dobyns, Henry F. "Blunders with Bolsas: A Case Study of Diffusion of Closed-Basin Agriculture." *Human Organization* 10 (1951): 25–32.

Dodd, Carley H. "Early and Late Converts: Bridges to Scientific Missiological Insight." *Mission Strategy Bulletin* 6 (1984): 1–4.

Dodd, Carley H. "Homophily and Heterophily in Diffusion of Innovations: A Cross-Cultural Analysis in an African Setting." Paper presented at the Speech Communication Association Convention, New York, November 1973.

Dodd, Carley H. "Insights into Church Growth in Ghana." *Strategy* 5 (1978): 2–5.

Dodd, Carley H. "An Introduction to Intercultural Effectiveness Skills." In *Multicultural Skills for Multicultural Societies,* edited by Carley H. Dodd and Frank F. Montalvo. Washington, D.C.: SIETAR, 1987.

Dodd, Carley H. "Predicting Innovativeness in the Adoption of a Nontechnological Innovation in Africa." *International and Intercultural Communication Annual* 3 (1976): 100–10.

Dodd, Carley H. "Social Structure and Communication Behavior among the Children of God." Paper presented to the International Communication Association Convention, Chicago, April 1975.

Dodd, Carley H. "Sources of Communication in the Adoption and Rejection of Swine Flu Inoculation among the Elderly." Paper presented to the Southern Speech Communication Association, Biloxi, Mississippi, April 1979.

Dodd, Carley H., and Cecile W. Garmon. "The Measurement of Personal Report of World View." Paper presented to the Speech Communication Association, Boston, Massachusetts, November 1987.

Dodd, Carley H., and Cecile W. Garmon. "Scale for Measurement of Personal Communication World View." In *Dynamics of Intercultural Communication.* 3d ed., authored by Carley H. Dodd. Dubuque, Iowa: Wm. C. Brown Company Publishers, 1991.

Dodd, Carley H., and Michael L. Lewis. *Human Communication.* 2d. ed. Dubuque, Iowa: Kendall/Hunt, 1991.

Dodd, Carley H., and Kay E. Payne. "The Effects of Culture and Sex on Time Concepts between Black and White Children." Paper presented to the Southern Speech Communication Association, San Antonio, Texas, April 1976.

Doi, L. Takeo. "The Japanese Patterns of Communication and the Concept of Amae." In *Intercultural Communication: A Reader.* 2d ed., edited by Larry Samovar and Richard Porter. Belmont, Calif.: Wadsworth, 1976.

Dow, Thomas E. "The Theory of Charisma." In *Intercommunication among Nations and Peoples,* edited by Michael H. Prosser. New York: Harper and Row, 1973.

Driskill, Gerald, and Carley H. Dodd. "Opinion Leadership, Personal World View, and Communication Style in an Organizational Culture." Paper presented to the Speech Communication Association, Chicago, November 1988.

Driskill, Gerald W., and M. Laurie Norton. "Dodd and Garmon's Personal Communication World View: Past, Present, and Future Considerations." Paper presented to the Speech Communication Association, San Francisco, November 1989.

Ehrenhaus, Peter. "Culture and the Attribution Process: Barriers to Effective Communication." In *Intercultural Communication Theory: Current Perspectives,* edited by William B. Gudykunst. Beverly Hills, Calif.: Sage, 1983.

Eisenstadt, S.N. "Communication Processes among Immigrants in Israel." In *Communication and Culture,* edited by Alfred G. Smith. New York: Holt, Rinehart and Winston, 1966.

Ekman, Paul, and Wallace V. Friesen. "Hand Movements." *Journal of Communication* 22 (1972): 353–74.

Ellingsworth, Huber. "Adaptive Intercultural Communication." In *Intercultural Communication Theory: Current Perspectives,* edited by William B. Gudykunst. Beverly Hills, Calif.: Sage, 1983.

Ellsworth, Phoebe C., and Linda M. Ludwig. "Visual Behavior in Social Interaction." *Journal of Communication* 22 (1972): 379–81.

Emry, Robert and Richard Wiseman. "An Intercultural Understanding of Ablebodied and Disabled Persons' Communication." *International Journal of Intercultural Relations* 11 (1987): 7–27.

England, William. "The Stereotype of a Mexican American: Analysis by Semantic Differential Technique." Unpublished paper, Department of Anthropology, University of Texas, 1977.

Erbe, William. "Gregariousness, Group Membership, and the Flow of Information." *American Journal of Sociology* 67 (1962): 502–16.

Erickson, Frederick. "One Function of Proxemic Shifts in Face-to-Face Interaction." In *Organization of Behavior in Face-to-Face Interaction,* edited by Adam Kendon, Richard M. Harris, and Mary R. Key. Paris: Mouton, 1975.

Fagen, Richard R. "Charismatic Authority and the Leadership of Fidel Castro." In *Intercommunication among Nations and Peoples,* edited by Michael H. Prosser. New York: Harper and Row, 1973.

Faherty, Robert. "The American Indian: An Overview." In *Intercultural Communication: A Reader.* 2d ed., edited by Larry Samovar and Richard Porter. Belmont, Calif.: Wadsworth, 1976.

Farace, Vincent, "Identifying Regional Systems in National Development Research." *Journalism Quarterly* 43 (1966): 753–60.

Farace, Vincent, and Lewis Donohew. "Mass Communication in National Social Systems: A Study of 43 Variables in 115 Countries." *Journalism Quarterly* 42 (1965): 253–61.

Faron, Louis C. "On Ancestor Propitiation among the Mapuche of Central Chile." *American Anthropologist* 63 (1961): 824–49.

Faron, Louis C. "Symbolic Value and the Integration of Society among the Mapuche of Chile." *American Anthropologist* 64 (1962): 1151–63.

Flores, Nancy De La Zerda, and Robert Hopper. "Mexican Americans' Evaluations of Spoken Spanish and English." *Speech Monographs* 42 (1975): 91–98.

Foeman, Anita K. "Managing Multiracial Institutions: Goals and Approaches for Race-Relations Training." *Communication Training* 40 (1991): 255–65.

Fotheringham, Wallace. *Perspectives on Persuasion.* Boston: Allyn and Bacon, 1966.

Fox, Robin. *Kinship and Marriage.* Baltimore, Md.: Penguin, 1971.

French, J.R., and Bertram Raven. "The Bases of Power." In *Studies in Social Power,* edited by Darwin Cartwright. Ann Arbor: University of Michigan, 1959.

Frey, Frederick W. "Communication and Development." In *Handbook of Communication,* edited by Ithiel de Sola Pool. Chicago: Rand McNally, 1973.

Frost, Peter J., Larry F. Moore, Meryl R. Louis, Craig C. Lundberg, and Joanne Martin, eds. *Organizational Culture.* Beverly Hills, Calif.: Sage, 1985.

Furnham, A., and S. Bochner. *Culture Shock: Psychological Reactions to Unfamiliar Environments.* London: Methuen, 1986.

Furnham, A., and S. Bochner. "Social Difficulty in a Foreign Culture: An Empirical Analysis of Culture Shock." In *Cultures in Contact,* edited by S. Bochner. New York: Pergamon, 1982.

Gallois, C., A. Franklyn-Stokes, H. Giles, and N. Coupland. "Communication Accommodation in Intercultural Encounters." In *Theories in Intercultural Communication,* edited by Young Y. Kim and William B. Gudykunst. Newbury Park, Calif.: Sage, 1988.

Galvan, Kathleen M., and B.J. Brommel. *Family Communication: Cohesion and Change.* 2d ed. Glenview, Ill.: Scott, Foresman, 1986.

Gandy, Oscar H. Jr., and Paula W. Matabane. "Television and Social Perceptions Among African Americans and Hispanics." In *Handbook of International and Intercultural Communication,* edited by Molefi Kete Asante and William B. Gudykunst. Newbury Park, Calif.: Sage, 1989.

Garmon, Cecile W. "Correlates of World View." Master's thesis. Western Kentucky University, 1980.

Garmon, Cecile W. "World View Differences among College and University Administrations and Faculty in the South." Ph.D. diss., Vanderbilt University, 1984.

Garner, Pat. "Nonverbal Communication." In *Human Communication,* 2d ed., by Carley H. Dodd and Michael L. Lewis. Dubuque, Iowa: Kendall/Hunt, 1991.

Geertz, Clifford. *The Interpretation of Cultures.* New York: Basic Books, 1973.

Giles, Howard. "Communicative Effectiveness as a Function of Accented Speech." *Speech Monographs* 40 (1973): 330–31.

Giles, Howard, and Arlene Franklyn-Stokes. "Communication Characteristics." In *Handbook of International and Intercultural Communication,* edited by Molefi Kete Asante and William B. Gudykunst. Newbury Park, Calif.: Sage, 1989.

Giles, Howard, Richard Bourhis, Peter Trudgill, and Alan Lewis. "The Imposed Norm Hypothesis: A Validation." *Quarterly Journal of Speech* 60 (1974): 405–10.

Giles, Howard, and Richard Y. Bourhis. "Voice and Racial Categorization in Britain." *Communication Monographs* 43 (1976): 108–14.

Gleason, H.A. *An Introduction to Descriptive Linguistics.* New York: Holt, Rinehart and Winston, 1961.

Gonzalez, Alberto. "Mexican Otherness in the Rhetorical of Mexican Americans." *The Southern Communication Journal* 55 (1990): 276–91.

Goode, Erich. "Social Class and Church Participation." *American Journal of Sociology* 72 (1966): 102–11.

Goodenough, Ward. "Componential Analysis and the Study of Meaning." *Language* 35 (1956): 195–216.

Goodenough, Ward Hunt. *Property, Kin, and Community on Truk.* Hamden, Conn.: Archon Books, 1966.

Graham, Morris, Judith Moeai, and Lanette Shizuru. "Intercultural Marriages: An Intrareligious Perspective." *International Journal of Intercultural Relations* 9 (1985): 427–34.

Green, Margaret M. *Ibo Village Affairs.* New York: Frederick A. Praeger, 1964.

Greenberg, Bradley S. "Diffusion of News in the Kennedy Assassination." *Public Opinion Quarterly* 28 (1964): 225–32.

Greenberg, Joseph H. "The Linguistic Approach." In *Communication and Culture,* edited by Alfred G. Smith. New York: Holt, Rinehart and Winston, 1966.

Grove, Cornelius L., and Ingemar Torbiorn. "A New Conceptualization of Intercultural Adjustment and the Goals of Training." *International Journal of Intercultural Relations* 9 (1985): 205–33.

Gudykunst, William B. "An Exploratory Comparison of Close Intracultural and Intercultural Friendships." *Communication Quarterly* 33 (1985): 270–83.

Gudykunst, William B. "Intercultural Contact and Attitude Change: A Review of Literature and Suggestions for Future Research." *International and Intercultural Communication Annual* 4 (1977): 1–16.

Gudykunst, William B. "Uncertainty and Anxiety." In *Theories in Intercultural Communication,* edited by Young Y. Kim and William B. Gudykunst. Newbury Park, Calif.: Sage, 1988.

Gudykunst, William B., and Lauren I. Gumbs. "Social Cognition and Intergroup Communication." In *Handbook of International and Intercultural Communication,* edited by Molefi Kete Asante and William B. Gudykunst. Newbury Park, Calif.: Sage, 1989.

Gudykunst, William B., and Mitchell Hammer. "Strangers and Hosts: An Uncertainty Reduction Theory of Intercultural Adaptation." In *Cross-Cultural Adaptation: Current Approaches,* edited by Young Y. Kim and William B. Gudykunst. Newbury Park, Calif.: Sage, 1988.

Gudykunst, William B., and Young Yun Kim. *Communicating with Strangers.* New York: Random House, 1984.

Gudykunst, William B., and Tsukasa Nishida. "Theoretical Perspectives for Studying Intercultural Communication." In *Handbook of International and Intercultural Communication,* edited by Molefi Kete Asante and William B. Gudykunst. Newbury Park, Calif.: Sage, 1989.

Gudykunst, William B., Lea P. Stewart, and Stella Ting-Toomey, eds. *Communication, Culture, and Organizational Processes.* Beverly Hills, Calif.: Sage, 1985.

Gudykunst, William B., Stella Ting-Toomey, and E. Chua. *Culture and Interpersonal Communication.* Newbury Park, Calif.: Sage, 1988.

Gudykunst, William B., Stella Ting-Toomey, Bradford J. Hall, and Karen L. Schmidt. "Language and Intergroup Communication." In *Handbook of International and Intercultural Communication,* edited by Molefi Kete Asante and William B. Gudykunst. Newbury Park, Calif.: Sage, 1989.

Gudykunst, William B., Richard I. Wiseman, and Mitch R. Hammer. "Determinants of a Sojourner's Attitudinal Satisfaction." In *Communication Yearbook* 1, edited by Brent Ruben. New Brunswick, N.J.: Transaction, 1977.

Gumpert, Gary, and Robert Cathcart. *Interpersonal Communication in a Media World.* New York: Oxford University Press, 1979.

Hall, E.T. *Beyond Culture.* Garden City, N.Y.: Anchor, 1976.

Hall, E.T., "Environmental Communication." In *Behavior and Environment: The Use of Space by Animals and Men,* edited by A.H. Esser. New York: Plenum, 1971.

Hall, E.T. *The Hidden Dimension.* Garden City, N.Y.: Doubleday, 1966.

Hall, E.T. "Proxemics." *Current Anthropology* 9 (1969): 83–108.

Hall, E.T. *The Silent Language.* Garden City, N.Y.: Anchor, 1973.

Hammer, Mitchell R. "Behavioral Dimensions of Intercultural Effectiveness: A Replication and Extension." *International Journal of Intercultural Relations* 11 (1987): 65–88.

Hammer, Mitchell R. "Intercultural Communication Competence." In *Handbook of International and Intercultural Communication,* edited by Molefi Kete Asante and William B. Gudykunst. Newbury Park, Calif.: Sage, 1989.

Hammer, Mitch R., and Clifford Clarke. "Predictors of Japanese and American Manager's Job Success, Personal Adjustment, and Intercultural Effectiveness." Paper presented to SIETAR Annual Congress, Montreal, Canada, May 1987.

Hammer, Mitch R., William B. Gudykunst, and Richard L. Wiseman. "Dimensions of Intercultural Effectiveness." *International Journal of Intercultural Relations* 2 (1978): 382–93.

Hammond, Peter B. *Cultural and Social Anthropology.* New York: Macmillan, 1970.

Harms, L.S. *Intercultural Communication.* New York: Harper and Row, 1973.

Harms, L.S. "Listener Judgments of Status Cues in Speech." *Quarterly Journal of Speech* 47 (1961): 164–68.

Harner, Michael J. "Jivaro Souls." *American Anthropologist* 64 (1962): 258–71.

Harris, Marvin. *Cows, Pigs, Wars and Witches.* New York: Random House, 1974.

Harris, Marvin. *Cultural Anthropology.* New York: Harper and Row, 1983.

Harris, Marvin. *Culture, People, Nature: An Introduction to General Anthropology.* New York: Harper and Row, 1975.

Harris, Marvin. *The Rise of Anthropological Theory.* New York: Thomas Crowell, 1968.

Harris, Philip R., and Robert T. Moran. *Managing Cultural Differences.* 3d ed. Houston: Gulf, 1991.

Havelock, Ronald. *Planning for Innovation.* Ann Arbor, Mich.: Institute for Social Research, University of Michigan, 1973.

Hawes, F., and Daniel Kealey. "An Empirical Study of Canadian Technical Assistance." *International Journal of Intercultural Relations* 5 (1981): 239–56.

Hecht, Michael L., Peter A. Andersen, and Sidney A. Ribeau. "The Cultural Dimensions of Nonverbal Communication." In *Handbook of International and Intercultural Communication,* edited by Molefi Kete Asante and William B. Gudykunst. Newbury Park, Calif.: Sage, 1989.

Heider, Fritz. *The Psychology of Interpersonal Relations.* New York: Wiley, 1958.

Henderson, Richard N. *The King in Every Man: Evolutionary Trends in Onitsha Ibo Society and Culture.* New Haven: Yale University Press, 1972.

Heston, Judee K. "Effects of Personal Space Invasion and Anomic or Anxiety, Nonperson Orientation and Source Credibility." *Central States Speech Journal* 25 (1974): 19–27.

Hickson, Mark, and Don Stacks. *Nonverbal Communication Studies and Applications.* Dubuque, Iowa: Wm. C. Brown Publishers, 1985.

Hiebert, Paul G. *Cultural Anthropology.* Philadelphia: J.B. Lippincott, 1976.

Hill, L. Brooks, and Philip Lujan. "Rhetoric of Self Identity: The Case of the Mississippi Choctaw." Paper presented to the Rhetoric of the Contemporary South Conference, New Orleans, June 1978.

Hirsch, Kenneth W. "Diffusion and Consistency of Media Source: The News of Lyndon Baines Johnson and Martin Luther King." Paper presented to the International Communication Association, April 1975.

Ho, Yung Chang. "Homophily in Interaction Patterns in the Diffusion of Innovations in Colombian Villages." Master's thesis, Michigan State University, 1969.

Hockett, C.F. *Man's Place in Nature.* New York: McGraw-Hill, 1973.

Hoebel, E. Adamson, and Everett L. Frost. *Cultural and Social Anthropology.* New York: McGraw-Hill, 1976.

Hofstede, Geert. *Culture's Consequences.* Beverly Hills, Calif.: Sage, 1984.

Hoijer, Harry. "The Sapir-Whorf Hypothesis." In *Intercultural Communication: A Reader.* 2d ed., edited by Larry A. Samovar and Richard E. Porter. Belmont, Calif.: Wadsworth, 1976.

Holleman, Bonnie B. "Marital Communication Satisfaction Among Female Compulsive Overeaters." Master's thesis, Abilene Christian University, 1993.

Hong, Nguyen Kim. "Vietnamese Themes." Paper presented to the Regional Indochinese Task Force Workshop for the New York City Board of Education, New York, January 1976.

Hood, Kregg. "Correlation of Ethnocentrism and World View." Manuscript, Abilene Christian University, Abilene, Texas, 1982.

Hoopes, David S., ed. *Readings in Intercultural Communication,* vols. 1–5. Washington, D.C.: SIETAR, n.d.

Hopper, Robert, and Frederick Williams. "Speech Characteristics and Employability." *Communication Monographs* 40 (1973): 296–302.

Horton, John. "Time and Cool People." In *Intercultural Communication: A Reader.* 2d ed., edited by Larry A. Samovar and Richard E. Porter. Belmont, Calif.: Wadsworth, 1976.

Inglis, Margaret, and William B. Gudykunst. "Institutional Completeness and Communication-Acculturation." *International Journal of Intercultural Relations* 6 (1982): 251–72.

Jeffres, Leo W. "Factors Affecting the Print Media: Media as Dependent Variables." Paper presented to the International Communication Association, Chicago, April 1975.

Jimenez, Robert. "Mythology of Life and Mexican-American Acculturation." In *Intercultural Skills for Multicultural Societies,* edited by Carley Dodd and Frank Montalvo. Washington, D.C.: SIETAR, 1987.

Johnson, Kenneth R. "Black Kinesics: Some Non-Verbal Communication Patterns in the Black Culture." In *Intercultural Communication: A Reader.* 2d ed., edited by Larry A. Samovar and Richard E. Porter. Belmont, Calif.: Wadsworth, 1976.

Jourard, Sidney. *The Transparent Self.* Princeton, N.J.: Van Nostrand Reinhold, 1964.

Junghare, Y.N. "Factors Influencing the Adoption of Farm Practices." *Indian Journal of Social Work* 23 (1962): 291–96.

Kahn, A., and T. McGaughey. "Distance and Liking: When Moving Close Produces Increased Liking." *Sociometry* 40 (1977): 138–44.

Kalbfleisch, Pamela J., and Andrea B. Davies. "Minorities and Mentoring: Managing the Multicultural Institution." *Communication Education* 40 (1991): 266–71.

Katz, Elihu. "The Diffusion of New Ideas and Practices." In *The Science of Human Communication,* edited by Wilbur Schramm. New York: Basic Books, 1963.

Katz, Elihu, Jay Blumer, and Michael Gurevitch. "Utilization of Mass Communication by the Individual." In *Inter/Media,* edited by Gary Gumpert and Robert Cathcart. New York: Oxford University Press, 1979.

Kealey, Daniel. "A Study of Cross-Cultural Effectiveness: Theoretical Issues, Practical Applications." *International Journal of Intercultural Relations* 13 (1989): 387–428.

Kealey, Daniel, and Brent Ruben. "Cross-Cultural Personnel Selection Criteria, Issues, and Methods." In *Handbook for Intercultural Training,* edited by Dan Landis and Richard Brislin. New York: Pergamon, 1983.

Kennan, William, and L. Brooks Hill. "Mythmaking as Social Process: Directions for Myth Analysis and Cross-Cultural Communication Research." Paper presented to SIETAR Conference, Phoenix, February 1978.

Kim, Jin K. "Explaining Acculturation in a Communication Framework: An Empirical Test." *Communication Monographs* 47 (1980): 155–79.

Kim, Min-Sun, William F. Sharkey, and Theodore Singelis. "Explaining Individualist and Collectivist Communication—Focusing on the Perceived Importance of Interactive Constraints." Paper presented to the Speech Communication Association, Chicago, October 1992.

Kim, Young Y. *Communication and Cross-Cultural Adaptation: An Integrative Theory.* Avon, England: Multilingual Matters, 1988.

Kim, Young Y. "Searching for Creative Integration." In *Methods for Intercultural Communication Research,* edited by William B. Gudykunst and Young Yun Kim. Beverly Hills, Calif.: Sage, 1984.

Kim, Young Yun. "Intercultural Adaptation." In *Handbook of International and Intercultural Communication,* edited by Molefi Kete Asante and William B. Gudykunst. Newbury Park, Calif.: Sage, 1989.

Kim, Young Yun. "Inter-Ethnic and Intra-Ethnic Communication: A Study of Korean Immigrants in Chicago." *International and Intercultural Communication Annual* (1977): 53–68.

Kim, Young Yun. "Toward an Interactive Theory of Communication—Acculturation." *Communication Yearbook* 3 (1979): 436–53.

Kim, Young Y., and William B. Gudykunst, eds. *Theories in Intercultural Communication.* Newbury Park, Calif.: Sage, 1988.

Kise, Kaoru, Charles Phipps, and Terry Sufferlein. "Cube Model for Intercultural Effectiveness." Presented originally for this text, Department of Communication, Abilene Christian University, 1995.

Klapper, Joseph T. *The Effects of Mass Communication.* New York: Free Press, 1960.

Klopf, Donald W. *The Fundamentals of Intercultural Communication.* 2nd ed. Englewood, Colorado: Morton, 1991.

Kluckhohn, Clyde. "The Gift of Tongues." In *Intercultural Communication: A Reader,* edited by Larry A. Samovar and Richard E. Porter. Belmont, Calif.: Wadsworth, 1972.

Kluckhohn, Florence, and Fred Strodtbeck. *Variations in Value Orientations.* Evanston, Ill.: Row and Petersen, 1961.

Knapp, Mark L. *Essentials of Nonverbal Communication.* New York: Holt, Rinehart and Winston, 1980.

Knapp, Mark L., Roderick P. Hart, Gustav W. Friedrich, and Gary M. Shulmen. "The Rhetoric of Goodbye: Verbal and Nonverbal Correlates of Human Leave Taking." *Speech Monographs* 40 (1973): 198.

Koester, Jolene, and Carl Holmberg. "Returning to Rhetoric." In *Intercultural Communication Theory: Current Perspectives,* edited by William B. Gudykunst. Beverly Hills, Calif.: Sage, 1983.

Koester, Jolene, and Myron W. Lustig. "Communication Curricula in the Multicultural University." *Communication Education* 40 (1991): 250–54.

Korinek, John. "Perceived Evaluation of Speech Characteristics of Jimmy Carter." Unpublished paper, Department of Communication and Theatre, Western Kentucky University, 1976.

Korzenny, Felipe, and Richard Farace. "Communication Networks and Social Change in Developing Countries." *International and Intercultural Communication Annual* 4 (1977): 69–94.

Krail, K., and G. Leventhal. "The Sex Variable in the Instruction of Personal Space." *Sociometry* 39 (1976): 170–73.

Kroeber, A.L. *Anthropology.* New York: Harcourt, Brace and World, 1948.

Kroeber, A.L. "Diffusion." In *The Encyclopedia of the Social Sciences,* II, edited by Edwin Seligan and Alvin Johnson. New York: Macmillan, 1937.

Kume, Teruyuki. "Managerial Attitudes Toward Decision-Making: North America and Japan." In *Communication, Culture, and Organizational Processes,* edited by William B. Gudykunst, Lea P. Stewart, and Stella Ting-Toomey. Newbury Park, Calif.: Sage, 1985.

LaBarre, Weston. "Paralinguistics, Kinesics, and Cultural Anthropology." In *Intercultural Communication: A Reader.* 2d ed., edited by Larry A. Samovar and Richard E. Porter. Belmont, Calif.: Wadsworth, 1976.

Labov, William. *The Social Stratification of English in New York City.* Washington, D.C.: Center for Applied Linguistics, 1966.

Lakey, Paul. "Communication/Social Difficulty of Thai Students in the Process of Cultural Adaptation." Ph.D. diss., University of Oklahoma, 1988.

Lazarsfeld, Paul F., Bernard Berelson, and Hazel Gaudet. *The People's Choice.* 3d ed. New York: Columbia University Press, 1968.

Leathers, D.G. *Successful Nonverbal Communication: Principles and Applications.* New York: Macmillan, 1986.

Lee, Richard R. "Preliminaries to Language Intervention." *Quarterly Journal of Speech* 56 (1970): 270–76.

Leeds-Hurwitz, Wendy. "Notes in the History of Intercultural Communication: The Foreign Service Institute and the Mandate for Intercultural Training." *The Quarterly Journal of Speech* 76 (1990): 262–81.

Leighton, Alexander, and Dorothea Leighton. *The Navajo Door.* New York: Russell and Russell, 1944.

Lerner, Daniel. *The Passing of Traditional Society.* New York: Free Press, 1958.

Lewis, David, Carley Dodd, and Darryl Tippens. *Dying to Tell: The Hidden Meaning of Adolescent Substance Abuse.* Abilene, Texas: Abilene Christian University Press, 1992.

Lewis, David, Carley Dodd, and Darryl Tippens. *Shattering the Silence.* Nashville: Christian Communications, 1989.

Long, Larry W., Manoocher Javidi, and Margaret Pryately. "Motives for Moves: A Cross-Cultural Examination of Communication Motives and Style Among Americans, Japanese, and Ukranians." Paper presented to the Southern and Central Communication Associations, Lexington, Ky., April 1993.

McAulay, J.D. "What Understandings Do Second-Grade Children Have of Time Relationships?" *Journal of Educational Research* 54 (1961): 312–14.

McCroskey, James C. *Introduction in Rhetorical Communication.* Englewood Cliffs, N.J.: Prentice-Hall, 1972.

McCroskey, James C. "Oral Communication Apprehension: A Reconceptualization." Paper presented to the Speech Communication Association, Louisville, Ky., November 1982.

McCroskey, James C. "Scales for the Measurement of Ethos." *Speech Monographs* 33 (1966): 65–72.

McCroskey, James C., and Thomas McCain. "The Measurement of Interpersonal Attraction." *Speech Monographs* 41 (1974): 261–66.

McCroskey, James C., and Lawrence Wheeless. *Introduction to Human Communication.* Boston: Allyn and Bacon, 1976.

McCroskey, James C., Virginia P. Richmond, and John A. Daly. "The Development of a Measure of Perceived Homophily in Interpersonal Communication." *Human Communication Research* 1 (1975): 323–32.

McDonald, Gordon. *Ordering your Private World.* Nashville: Thomas Nelson, 1985.

McLuhan, Marshall. *The Medium is the Message.* New York: Bantam, 1967.

McLuhan, Marshall. *Understanding Media: The Extensions of Man.* New York: McGraw-Hill, 1966.

McLuhan, T.C., ed. *Touch the Earth.* New York: Pocket Books, 1972.

McPhail, Thomas L. "Inquiry in Intercultural Communication." In *Handbook of International and Intercultural Communication,* edited by Molefi Kete Asante and William B. Gudykunst. Newbury Park, Calif.: Sage, 1989.

McPhee, Robert D., and Phillip K. Tompkins, eds. *Organizational Communication.* Beverly Hills, Calif.: Sage, 1985.

Malandro, Loretta A., and Larry Barker. *Nonverbal Communication.* New York: Random House, 1983.

Malinowski, Bronislaw. *A Scientific Theory of Culture.* New York: Oxford University Press, 1960.

Malinowski, Bronislaw. *A Scientific Theory of Culture and Other Essays.* Chapel Hill, N.C.: University of North Carolina Press, 1944.

Markoff, R. "Intercultural Marriage: Problem Areas." In *Adjustment in Intercultural Marriage,* edited by W.S. Tseng, J.K. McDermott, and T. Maretski. Honolulu: University of Hawaii Press, 1977.

Marsella, Anthony J., Michael D. Murray, and Charles Golden. "Ethnic Variations in the Phenomenology of Emotions." In *Intercultural Communication: A Reader.* 2d ed., edited by Larry Samovar and Richard Porter. Belmont, Calif.: Wadsworth, 1976.

Marsh, C. Paul, and A. Lee Coleman. "Farmers' Practice-Adoption Rates in Relation to Adoption Rates of Leaders." *Rural Sociology* 19 (1954): 180–81.

Martin, Judith, and Mitchell Hammer. "Behavioral Categories of Intercultural Communication Competence: Everyday Communicators' Perceptions." *International Journal of Intercultural Relations* 13 (1989): 303–32.

Matsumoto, David, Harald G. Wallbott, and Klaus R. Scherer. "Emotions in Intercultural Communication." In *Handbook of International and Intercultural Communication,* edited by Molefi Kete Asante and William B. Gudykunst. Newbury Park, Calif.: Sage, 1989.

Mead, Margaret. *Cultural Patterns and Technical Change.* New York: New American Library, 1955.

Mehrabian, Albert. "Relationship of Attitude to Seated Posture, Orientation and Distance." *Journal of Personality and Social Psychology* 10 (1968): 26–31.

Mehrabian, Albert. "Significance of Posture and Position in the Communication of Attitude and Status Relationship." *Psychological Bulletin* 71 (1969): 359–72.

Mehrabian, Albert. *Silent Messages.* 2d ed. Belmont, Calif.: Wadsworth, 1981.

Mehrabian, Albert, and J.T. Friar. "Encoding of Attitudes by a Seated Communicator via Posture and Position Cues." *Journal of Consulting and Clinical Psychology* 33 (1969): 339–46.

Menzel, Herbert, and Elihu Katz. "Social Relations and Innovation in the Medical Profession: The Epidemiology of a New Drug." *Public Opinion Quarterly* 19 (1955): 337–52.

Metge, Joan. *The Maoris of New Zealand: Rautahi.* London: Routledge and Kegan Paul Ltd., 1976.

Meyer, Christine M., and Philip Salem. "Reciprocal Self-Disclosure in Intercultural Friendships." Paper presented to the Southern States Communication Association, San Antonio, April 1992.

Miller, Dale T. "The Effect of Dialect and Ethnicity on Communicator Effectiveness." *Speech Monographs* 42 (1975): 69–74.

Miller, Jack. "Black American Speech Patterns: Origins, Evidence, and Implications." Paper presented to Southern Speech Communication Association, Atlanta, April 1978.

Minnick, Wayne. *Public Speaking.* Boston: Houghton Mifflin, 1979.

Monfils, Barbara. "The Critical Perspective in Intercultural Communication." Paper presented to the Speech Communication Association, New York, November, 1980.

Montagu, M.F.A. *Touching: The Human Significance of Skin.* New York: Columbia University Press, 1971.

Moore, Leslie. "A Study of Reentry Stress of Returned Missionaries from Churches of Christ." Master's thesis, Abilene Christian University, Abilene, Texas, 1981.

Moran, Robert, and Philip Harris. *Managing Cultural Differences.* 3d ed. Houston: Gulf, 1991.

Mulac, Anthony, and Mary Jo Rudd. "Effects of Selected American Regional Dialects upon Regional Audience Members." *Communication Monographs* 44 (1977): 185–95.

Myers, Byron. "Predictions of Intercultural Effectiveness." Master's thesis, Abilene Christian University, 1990.

Nadler, Lawrence B., Margorie Keeshan Nadler, and Benjamin J. Broome. "Culture and the Management of Conflict Situations." In *Communication, Culture, and Organizational Processes,* edited by William B. Gudykunst, Lea P. Stewart, and Stella Ting-Toomey. Newbury Park, Calif.: Sage, 1985.

Nanda, Serena. *Cultural Anthropology.* New York: Van Nostrand, 1980.

Naravane, V.S. *The Elephant and the Lotus.* London: Asia Publishing House, 1965.

Newmark, Eileen, and Molefi Asante. "Perceptions of Self and Others: An Approach to Intercultural Communication." *International and Intercultural Communication Annual* 2 (1975): 54–62.

Nordenstreng, Kaarle, and Wolfgang Kleinwachter. "The New International Information and Communication Order." In *Handbook of International and Intercultural Communication,* edited by Molefi Kete Asante and William B. Gudykunst. Newbury Park, Calif.: Sage, 1989.

Norton, M. Laurie. "Adaptation Among the Elderly as a Subculture." Ph.D. diss., University of Oklahoma, 1990.

Norton, M. Laurie. "The Effects of Communication Effectiveness and Cognitive Complexity on Culture Shock." Master's thesis, Abilene Christian University, Abilene, Texas, 1984.

Norton, M. Laurie, and Carley H. Dodd. "The Relationship of Self-Report Communication Effectiveness to Culture Shock." Paper presented to the Speech Communication Association, Chicago, November 1984.

Norton, R.W. "Foundation of a Communication Style Construct." *Human Communication Research* 4 (1978): 99–111.

Oberg, Calvero. "Cultural Shock: Adjustment to New Cultural Environments." *Practical Anthropology* 7 (1960): 170–79.

Olebe, Margaret, and Jolene Koester. "Exploring the Cross-Cultural Equivalence of the Behavioral Assessment Scale for Intercultural Perceptions." *International Journal of Intercultural Relations* 13 (1989): 333–47.

Olson, D.H. *Treating Relationships.* Lake Mills, Iowa: Graphic, 1976.

Ong, Walter J. *In the Human Grain.* New York: Macmillan, 1967.

Ong, Walter J. "World as View and World as Event." In *Intercommunication among Nations and Peoples,* edited by Michael H. Prosser. New York: Harper and Row, 1973.

Ouchi, W.G. and A.M. Jaeger. "Made in America Under Japanese Management." *Harvard Business Review* 52 (1974): 61–69.

*Overseas Diplomacy.* U.S. Navy, Bureau of Navy Personnel, 1973.

Palmgreen, Philip, and J.D. Rayburn. "A Comparison of Gratification Models of Media Satisfaction." *Communication Monographs* 52 (1985): 334–46.

Parrish, Camille. "Observations from Department Human Services Client Load." Interview by author. Abilene, Texas, 18 June 1993.

Patterson, Thomas E., and Robert D. McClure. "Political Campaigns: TV Power Is a Myth." *Psychology Today* 10 (1976): 61–64f.

Pearce, W. Barnett, and K.W. Kang. "Acculturation and Communication Competence." In *Communication Theory from Eastern and Western Perspectives,* edited by D.L. Kincaid. New York: Academic Press, 1987.

Pearce, W. Barnett, and Richard Wiseman. "Rules Theories: Varieties, Limitations, and Potentials." In *Intercultural Communication Theory: Current Perspectives,* edited by William B. Gudykunst. Beverly Hills, Calif.: Sage, 1983.

Pearson, Judy. *Communication in the Family.* New York: Harper and Row, 1989.

Pennington, Dorthy L. "Interpersonal Power and Influence in Intercultural Communication." In *Handbook of International and Intercultural Communication,* edited by Molefi Kete Asante and William B. Gudykunst. Newbury Park, Calif.: Sage, 1989.

Perrin, L.J. *Second Person Rural.* New York: Doubleday, 1980.

Peters, Thomas J. *Liberation Management.* New York: Knopf, 1992.

Peters, Thomas J., and Robert H. Waterman. *In Search of Excellence.* New York: Harper and Row, 1982.

Phipps, Charles A. "The Measurement of Monochronic and Polychronic Cognitions Among Hispanics and Anglos." Senior Honors thesis, Abilene Christian University, 1987.

Piche, Gene L., Michael Michlin, Donald Rubin, and Allan Sullivan. "Effects of Dialect-Ethnicity, Social Class, and Quality of Written Compositions on Teachers' Subjective Evaluations of Children." *Communication Monographs* 44 (1977): 60–62.

Porter, Richard. "An Overview of Intercultural Communication." In *Intercultural Communication: A Reader,* edited by Larry A. Samovar and Richard E. Porter. Belmont, Calif.: Wadsworth, 1972.

Prosser, Michael H. *The Cultural Dialogue.* Boston: Houghton Mifflin, 1978.

Prosser, Michael H., ed. *Intercommunication among Nations and Peoples.* New York: Harper and Row, 1973.

Putnam, Linda L., and Michael E. Pacanowsky, eds. *Communication and Organizations: An Interpretive Approach.* Beverly Hills, Calif.: Sage, 1983.

Quinn, Robert E., and Michael R. McGrath. "The Transformation of Organizational Cultures: A Competing Values Perspective." In *Organizational Culture,* edited by Peter J. Frost. Beverly Hills, Calif.: Sage, 1985.

Remland, Martin S., Tricia S. Jones, and Heidi Brinkman. "Interpersonal Distance, Body Orientation, and Touch in the Dyadic Interactions of Northern and Southern Europeans." Paper presented to the Speech Communication Association, Chicago, October 1992.

Rich, Andrea. *Interracial Communication.* New York: Harper and Row, 1974.

Richmond, Virginia. "Monomorphic and Polymorphic Opinion Leadership within a Relatively Closed Communication System." *Human Communication Research* 6 (1980): 111–16.

Rodgers, Raymond. "Folklore Analysis and Subcultural Communication Research: Another View of World View." Paper presented to the Society for Intercultural Education, Training, and Research, Phoenix, February 1978.

Rogers, Everett M. *Communication Strategies for Family Planning.* New York: Free Press, 1973.

Rogers, Everett M. *Diffusion of Innovations.* New York: Free Press, 1983.

Rogers, Everett M. "Elements in the Subculture of Traditionalism." Paper presented to the Society for Applied Anthropology, Mexico City, April 1969.

Rogers, Everett M. "Inquiry in Development Communication." In *Handbook of International and Intercultural Communication,* edited by Molefi Kete Asante and William B. Gudykunst. Newbury Park, Calif.: Sage, 1989.

Rogers, Everett M., and D.K. Bhowmik. "Homophily-Heterophily: Relational Concepts for Communication Research." *Public Opinion Quarterly* 34 (1971): 523–37.

Rogers, Everett M., and Nemi C. Jain. "Needed Research on Diffusion within Educational Organizations." Paper presented at the National Conference on the Diffusion of Educational Ideas, East Lansing, Michigan, March 1968.

Rogers, Everett M., and D. Lawrence Kincaid. *Communication Networks: Toward a Paradigm for Research.* New York: Free Press, 1981.

Rogers, Everett M., and F. Floyd Shoemaker. *Communication of Innovations: A Cross-Cultural Approach.* New York: Free Press, 1971.

Rogers, Everett M., with Lynne Svenning. *Modernization among Peasants: The Impact of Communication.* New York: Holt, Rinehart and Winston, 1969.

Rohrlich, Beulah. "Dual-Culture Marriage and Communication." *International Journal of Intercultural Relations* 12 (1988): 35–44.

Rokeach, Milton. *Beliefs, Attitudes, and Values.* San Francisco: Jossey-Bass, 1968.

Rokeach, Milton. *The Open and Closed Mind.* New York: Basic Books, 1960.

Roper, Cynthia S. "The Effects of Communication Apprehension, World View, Innovativeness, and Communication Style on Culture Shock." Master's thesis, Abilene Christian University, Abilene, Texas, 1986.

Rosegrant, Teresa J., and James C. McCroskey. "The Effects of Race and Sex on Proxemic Behavior in an Interview Setting." *Southern Speech Communication Journal* 40 (1975): 408–20.

Rosenfeld, H.M. "Effect of an Approval-Seeking Induction on Interpersonal Proximity." *Psychological Reports* 17 (1965): 120–22.

Ruben, Brent, "A System-Theoretic View." In *Intercultural Communication Theory: Current Perspectives,* edited by William B. Gudykunst. Beverly Hills, Calif.: Sage, 1983.

Ruben, Brent D. "Human Communication and Cross-Cultural Effectiveness." *International and Intercultural Communication Annual* 4 (1977): 95–105.

Rubin, D.L. "Nobody Play by the Rule He Know: Interethnic Interference in Classroom Questioning Events." In *Interethnic Communication: Recent Research,* edited by Young Y. Kim. Newbury Park, Calif.: Sage, 1986.

Rubin, R.B., E.M. Perse, and C.A. Barbato. "Conceptualization and Measurement of Interpersonal Communication Motives." *Human Communication Research* 14 (1988): 602–628.

Ruhly, Sharon. *Orientations to Intercultural Communication.* Chicago: SRA, 1976.

Ryan, Bryce, and Neal C. Gross. "The Diffusion of Hybrid Seed Corn in Two Iowa Communities." *Rural Sociology* 8 (1943): 15–24.

St. Martin, Gail M. "Intercultural Differential Decoding of Nonverbal Affective Communication." *International and Intercultural Communication Annual* 3 (1976): 44–57.

Samovar, Larry, Richard Porter, and Nemi Jain. *Understanding Intercultural Communication.* Belmont, Calif.: Wadsworth, 1981.

Samovar, Larry A., and Richard E. Porter. *Intercultural Communication: A Reader.* 4th ed. Belmont, Calif.: Wadsworth, 1985.

Sanders, Irwin T., ed. *Societies Around the World.* New York: Dryden Press, 1953.

Sarbaugh, Larry. *Intercultural Communication.* Rochelle Park, N.J.: Hayden, 1979.

Saxena, Anant P. "System Effects on Innovativeness among Indian Farmers." Ph.D. diss., Michigan State University, 1968.

Schaeffer, Francis. *The God Who Is There.* Downers Grove, Ill.: Inter-Varsity, 1968.

Schiller, Herbert I. *Communication and Cultural Domination.* White Plains, N.Y.: International Arts and Sciences Press, 1976.

Schmidt, W.H. "Communication, Change, and Innovation: A Selective View of Current Theory and Research." Paper presented at the American Business Communication Association International Conference, 1984.

Schmidt, W.H. *Organizational Frontiers and Human Values.* Belmont, Calif.: Wadsworth, 1970.

Schmidt, Wallace. Letter to author, 1986.

Schramm, Wilbur. *Men, Messages, and Media.* New York: Harper and Row, 1973.

Seelye, H. Ned. *Teaching Culture.* 3rd ed. Lincolnwood, Illinois: National Textbook, 1993.

Sharp, Lauriston. "Steel Axes for Stone Age Australians." In *Human Problems in Technological Change,* edited by Edward H. Spicer. New York: Russell Sage Foundation, 1952.

Shaw, Marvin E. *Group Dynamics: The Psychology of Small Group Behavior.* 2d ed. New York: McGraw-Hill, 1976.

Sheflen, Albert E. *Body Language and Social Order.* Englewood Cliffs, N.J.: Prentice-Hall, 1972.

Sheflen, Albert E. "The Significance of Posture in Communication Systems." *Psychiatry* 27 (1964): 27–36.

Sherif, Carolyn W., and Muzafer Sherif, eds. *Attitude, Ego-Involvement, and Change.* New York: John Wiley & Sons, 1967.

Sherif, Carolyn W., Muzafer Sherif, and Roger E. Nebergall. *Attitude and Attitude Change.* Philadelphia: Saunders, 1965.

Sherif, M., C. Sherif, and R. Nebergall. *Attitude and Attitude Change: The Social Judgment-Involvement Approach.* Philadelphia: Saunders, 1965.

Shuter, Robert. "The Centrality of Culture." *The Southern Communication Journal* 55 (1990): 237–49.

Shuter, Robert. "A Field Study of Nonverbal Communication in Germany, Italy, and the United States." *Communication Monographs* 44 (1977): 298–305.

Shuy, Roger. "The Sociolinguist and Urban Language Problems." In *Language and Poverty: Perspectives on a Theme,* edited by Frederick Williams. Chicago: Markham, 1970.

Shuy, Roger, et. al. "Linguistic Correlates of Social Stratification in Detroit Speech." U.S.O.E. project 6–1347, Michigan State University, 1967.

Singer, Marshall R. *Intercultural Communication: A Perceptual Approach.* Englewood Cliffs, New Jersey: Prentice-Hall, 1987.

Sitaram, K.S., and Roy T. Cogdell. *Foundations of Intercultural Communications.* Columbus, Ohio: Charles Merrill, 1976.

Smith, Alfred F. *Communication and Culture.* New York: Holt, Rinehart and Winston, 1966.

Smith, Arthur L. *Transracial Communication.* Englewood Cliffs, N.J.: Prentice-Hall, 1973.

Smith, Brewster M., Jerome S. Bruner, and Robert White. *Opinions and Personality.* New York: John Wiley & Sons, 1956.

Smutkupt, Suriya, and La Ray Barna. "Impact of Nonverbal Communication in an Intercultural Setting: Thailand." *International and Intercultural Communication Annual* 3 (1976): 130–38.

Snyder, Mark. "The Many Me's of the Self-Monitor." *Psychology Today* 13 (1980): 10–15.

Sohns, Helen. "Training Mataco Indian Birth Attendants." *Missiology* 3 (1975): 307–16.

Sommer, R. "Sociofugal Space." *American Journal of Sociology* 72 (1967): 654–60.

Spiro, Melford E. *Context and Meanings in Cultural Domination.* New York: Free Press, 1965.

Starosta, William J. "Critical Review of Recent Literature." *International and Intercultural Communication Annual* 2 (1975): 108–15.

Starosta, William J. "Toward the Use of Traditional Entertainment Forms to Stimulate Social Change." *Quarterly Journal of Speech* 60 (1974): 306–12.

Starosta, William J. "The Village Worker as Rhetorician: An Adaptation of Diffusion Theory." *Central States Speech Journal* 27 (1976): 144–50.

Steen, William U. "Outstanding Contact and the Cultural Stability in a Peruvian Highland Village." In *A Reader in Culture Change,* edited by Ivan A. Brady and Barry L. Isaac. Cambridge, Mass.: Schenkman, 1975.

Steinfatt, Thomas M., Walter Gantz, David R. Siebold, and Larry Miller. "News Diffusion of the George Wallace Shooting: The Apparent Lack of Interpersonal Communication as an Artifact of Delayed Measurement." *Quarterly Journal of Speech* 59 (1973): 401–12.

Stewart, Edward. *Outline of International Communication.* Washington, D.C.: The BCIU Institute: American University, 1973.

Stewart, Edward C. "The Survival Stage of Intercultural Communication." *International and Intercultural Communication Annual* 4 (1977): 17–31.

Stewart, Lea P. "Subjective Culture and Organizational Decision-Making." In *Communication, Culture, and Organizational Processes,* edited by William B. Gudykunst, Lea P. Stewart, and Stella Ting-Toomey. Newbury Park, Calif.: Sage, 1985.

Storm, Hyemeyohsts. *Seven Arrows.* New York: Ballantine Books, 1972.

Stross, Brian. "Tzetal Marriage by Capture." *Anthropological Quarterly* 47 (1974): 328–46.

Sudweeks, Sandra. "Taking Cultural Theory into the Classroom: A Review Essay." *Communication Education* 40 (1991): 294–302.

Sypher, Beverly D., James L. Applegate, and Howard E. Sypher. "Culture and Communication in Organizational Contexts." In *Communication, Culture, and Organizational Processes,* edited by William B. Gudykunst, Lea P. Stewart, and Stella Ting-Toomey. Beverly Hills, Calif.: Sage, 1985.

Szalay, Lorand B. "Adapting Communication Research to the Needs of International and Intercultural Communication." *International and Intercultural Communication Annual* 1 (1974): 1–16.

Tafoya, Dennis, "The Roots of Conflict: A Theory and Typology." In *Intercultural Communication Theory: Current Perspectives,* edited by William B. Gudykunst. Beverly Hills, Calif.: Sage, 1983.

Taylor, Harvey M. "Non-Verbal Communication and Cross-Cultural Communication Problems." *ESL Papers,* 1976–1977.

Thibaut, J.W., and H.H. Kelley. *The Social Psychology of Groups.* New York: Wiley, 1959.

Tichenor, Charla J. "An Examination of Cognitive Complexity and Its Relationship with Urban-Rural Locality." Master's thesis, Western Kentucky University, 1981.

Ting-Toomey, Stella. "Identity and Interpersonal Bonding." In *Handbook of International and Intercultural Communication,* edited by Molefi Kete Asante and William B. Gudykunst. Newbury Park, Calif.: Sage, 1989.

Ting-Toomey, Stella. "Intercultural Conflict Styles: A Face Negotiation Theory." In *Theories in Intercultural Communication.* Newbury Park, Calif.: Sage, 1988.

Ting-Toomey, Stella, "Perceived Decision-Making Power and Marital Adjustment." *Communication Research Reports* 1 (1984): 15–20.

Ting-Toomey, Stella. "Toward a Theory of Conflict and Culture." In *Communication, Culture, and Organizational Processes,* edited by William B. Gudykunst, Lea P. Stewart, and Stella Ting-Toomey. Newbury Park, Calif.: Sage, 1985.

Tippett, Alan. "A Mexican Flashback." *Missiology* 3 (1975): 259–64.

Toffler, Alvin. *Future Shock.* New York: Random House, 1970.

Tomlinson, Delorese. "Bi-Dilectism: Solution for American Minority Members." *Speech Teacher* 24 (1975): 232–36.

Triandis, Harry. "Cross-Cultural Psychology as the Scientific Foundation of Cross-Cultural Training." In *Intercultural Skills for Multicultural Societies,* edited by Carley H. Dodd and Frank F. Montalvo. Washington, D.C.: SIETAR, 1987.

Triandis, Harry. "Individualism-Collectivism: Implications for Intercultural Communication." Paper presented to the Intercultural and International Communication Conference, Fullerton, Calif., March 1990.

Tseng, W.S., J.K. McDermott, and J. Maretzki, eds. *Adjustment in Intercultural Marriages.* Honolulu: University of Hawaii Press, 1977.

Tucker, Michael F., and Vicki E. Baier. "Research Background for the Overseas Assignment Inventory." Paper presented to the SIETAR International Conference, San Antonio, Texas, May 1985.

Tuppen, Christopher. "Dimensions of Communicator Credibility: An Oblique Solution." *Speech Monographs* 41 (1974): 253–66.

Van den Ban, A.W. "Interpersonal Communication and the Diffusion of Innovations." In *Intercommunication among Nations and Peoples,* edited by Michael H. Prosser. New York: Harper & Row, 1973.

Walter, Michael, Nanmanas Choonjaroen, Kimberly Bartosh, and Carley Dodd. "E-Model of Intercultural Communication Effectiveness." Presented originally in this text, 1995.

Watson, Michael. "Conflicts and Directions in Proxemic Research." *Journal of Communication* 22 (1972): 442–43.

Watzlawick, Paul, Janet H. Beavin, and Don D. Jackson. *Pragmatics of Human Communication.* New York: Norton, 1967.

Weimann, Gabriel. "Social Networks and Communication." In *Handbook of International and Intercultural Communication,* edited by Molefi Kete Asante and William B. Gudykunst. Newbury Park, Calif.: Sage, 1989.

Wheeler, Christopher, Judith Wilson, and Carol Tarantola. "An Investigation of Children's Social Perception of Child Speakers with Reference to Verbal Style." *Central States Speech Journal* 27 (1976): 31–35.

Wheeless, Lawrence R., and Janis Grotz. "Self-Disclosure and Trust: Conceptualization, Measurement, and Inter-relationships." Paper presented to the International Communication Association Convention, Chicago, April 1975.

Whitehead, Jack L., Frederick Williams, Jean Civikly, and Judith Algino. "Latitude of Attitude in Ratings of Dialect Variations." *Communication Monographs* 41 (1974): 387–407.

Whitsett, Gavin. "An Examination of Eye Contact, Body Orientation, and Proxemics in Black-White Interviews." Paper, Western Kentucky University, 1974.

Whorf, Benjamin Lee. *Language, Thought, and Reality: Selected Writings of Benjamin Lee Whorf,* edited by John B. Carroll. New York: Wiley, 1956.

Williams, Frederick. *Language and Speech.* Englewood Cliffs, N.J.: Prentice-Hall, 1972.

Williams, Frederick. "Psychological Correlates of Speech Characteristics: On Sounding 'Disadvantaged.' " *Journal of Speech and Hearing Research* 13 (1970): 472–88.

Williams, Frederick, and Rita C. Naremore. "Language Attitudes: An Analysis of Teacher Differences." *Communication Monographs* 41 (1974): 391–96.

Williams, Frederick, Jack L. Whitehead, and Leslie M. Miller. "Ethnic Stereotyping and Judgments of Children's Speech." *Speech Monographs* 38 (1971): 166–70.

Williams, M. Lee. "Cases in Organizational Culture." Paper presented to the Southern Communication Association, San Antonio, Texas, April 1992.

Windt, Theodore Otto. "The Rhetoric of Peaceful Coexistence: Khrushchev in America, 1959." In *Intercommunication among Nations and Peoples,* edited by Michael H. Prosser. New York: Harper and Row, 1973.

Winn, Larry James. "Jimmy Carter and the American Political Image." Paper presented at the Southern Speech Communication Association, Atlanta, April 1978.

Wiseman, Richard, and H. Abe. "Finding and Exploring Differences: A Reply to Gudykunst and Hammer." *International Journal of Intercultural Relations* 8 (1984): 185–99.

Wiseman, Richard, Mitchell Hammer, and Hiroko Nishida. "Predictors of Intercultural Communication Competence." *International Journal of Intercultural Relations* 13 (1989): 349–70.

Wolff, Peter, and Joyce Gustein. "Effects of Induced Motor Gestures on Vocal Output." *Journal of Communication* 22 (1972): 227.

Yaple, Peter, and Felipe Korzenny. "Electronic Mass Media Effects Across Cultures." In *Handbook of International and Intercultural Communication,* edited by Molefi Kete Asante and William B. Gudykunst. Newbury Park, Calif.: Sage, 1989.

Yousef, Fathi. "Nonverbal Communication: Some Intricate and Diverse Dimensions in Intercultural Communication." In *Intercultural Communication: A Reader.* 2d ed., edited by Larry A. Samovar and Richard E. Porter. Belmont, Calif.: Wadsworth, 1976.

Yousef, Fathi, and Nancy Briggs. "The Multinational Business Organization: A Schema for the Training of Overseas Personnel in Communication." *International and Intercultural Communication Annual* 2 (1975): 74–85.

# Subject Index

Dissonance, 248
Diversity, 27, 32–128
Dogmatism, 232, 235, 238
Dominance, 234, 238
Dynamism, 194. *See also* Intercultural communication credibility
Dysfunction, 7

Early adopters, 279
Early majority, 280
Ecological theory, 55
Economics and culture, 49, 282
Education, 53
Effects of mass communication. *See* Mass media effects
Elderly. *See* Age
Electronic culture, 268
Elites, 188
Emotions, 121
Empathy, 88, 232, 247, 256, 288
Employability and language, 145
Endogamy, 49
Ethics, 121
Ethnicity, 61–69, 218, 223, 271
Ethnocentrism, 46, 69, 232
Ethnolinguistic identity, 63, 146
Ethnolinguistic variation, 136, 140, 145
Ethnolinguistic vitality, 65, 146
Exogamy, 49
Extended family, 49

Facial expression, 162
Familism, 86
Family, 49, 117, 234
    culture, 14
    extended, 49
    nuclear, 49
Fatalism, 87, 111
Filtering, 215
Final adopters, 280
Fixed features of space, 163–64
Formality in culture, 51, 170, 245
Frame of reference. *See* Perception
Friendship, 43, 223, 246
Functional culture, 7
Functionalism, 57

Gatekeeper, 203–4
Gender, 13, 43
Gestures, 159
GNP, 264
Gratification, 87, 270
Greeting, 161
Group membership, 79
Groups
    affiliation needs, 81
    cohesiveness, 80
    contact, 80
    context, 81

homogeneity, 81
individuals in, 80–82
in-group/out-group, 22, 62–65, 68, 120
issues, 81
norms, 81, 255
reference, 79–82
salience, 81
size, 80
Guilt, 106

Haley, Alex, 38
Haptics, 171–73
Harmony, 119
Health management, 52
Hegemony, 271
Heritage, 60–72
Heterophily, 178–86
High-context culture, 92, 99–102
Homogeneity, 81. *See also* Homophily
Homophily, 19, 178–86
Human relations theory, 38
Hypodermic needle theory, 197, 265

Idiocentric. *See* Individualism-collectivism
Immediacy, 174
Implicit personality theory, 22
Individualism-collectivism, 74, 102–3, 122
Informality. *See* Formality in culture
Information seeking, 40
Information sharing, 202–5
Information theory, 9
Innovativeness, 45, 87, 233, 277–85
Innovators, 279
Institutions, 49–53
Interaction, 44
Interconnectedness, 204
Intercultural communication
    axioms, 18–24
    change, 45
    competence, 8, 198, 228–38
    credibility (*see* Credibility)
    defined, 3, 9
    effectiveness, 6, 24
    history, 24–28
    model, 6, 229–31
Intercultural marriage, 72–76
International communication, 24–27
Interpersonal communication, 178ff
Interracial, 69
Isolates, 203–4

Job selection. *See* Personnel selection

Kinesics, 155–63
    kine, 157
    micro-kinesics, 157
    pre-kinesics, 157
    social kinesics, 157

Kinship, 49–51

Land as value, 123
Language, 44, 74
Late majority, 280
Leadership, 250–51, 284
Learning theory, 269
Liaison, 204
Life cycle, 111
Limited good, 86
Linear culture, 255, 267–68
Linguistic community, 131ff
Linguistic convergence, 147
Linguistic determinism, 132
Linguistic relativity, 132
Linguistics, 131–50
Link, 203–4
Listening, 250, 257, 258
Low-context culture, 92, 99–102

Macroculture, 10
Mana, 111
Management. *See* Organizational culture
Masculine-Feminine cultures, 103
Mass media, 220–22, 263–71
Mass media effects, 254, 269, 276
Mass media exposure, 266
Mass media growth, 264
Material culture, 40–42, 125
Matriarchy, 49
Matrilineal, 51
Metacommunication, 174
Microculture, 11–14, 60–77
Minorities. *See* Ethnicity
MMPI, 237
Monochronic time, 96–116
Monogamy, 49
Monomorphic opinion leaders, 200
Motivation, 87
Multi-step flow of information, 199
Myers-Briggs, 237

National development, 263
Native American, 122–26
Needs gratification theory, 270
Negotiation style, 251
Nemawashi, 252
Networks, 178–204, 265–66, 284
Node, 204
Nonverbal communication, 46–47, 152–75, 246. *See also* Chronemics, Haptics, Kinesics, Oculesics, Paralinguistics, Proxemics, Sensorics
Nonverbal functions, 153–55, 174
Norms, 138
Nuclear family, 49

Observability, 277
Occupation, 43
Oculesics, 160
Openness, 233
Opinion leaders, 286
Opinion leadership, 195–206
  characteristics of, 198–200
  defined, 195–96
  function, 198–200
  measurement of, 200
Optimal heterophily, 183
Organizational culture, 13, 88–92,
  251–56, 282
Organizational development, 285

Paralinguistics, 173–74
Patriarchy, 49
Patrilineal, 51
Perception, 132, 143–45
Personal Communication World View
  (PCWV), 112–16
Personality, 180
Personal space, 166–69
Personnel selection, 235–38
Persuasion, 264–66
PF-16, 237
Political system, 51
Polyandry, 49
Polychronic time, 96–99, 169
Polygamy, 49
Polygyny, 49
Polymorphic opinion leaders, 200
Posture, 159
Poverty culture, 86
Power, 43, 174, 188, 255
Power distance, 76, 104
Prejudice. *See* Racism
Primary groups, 79–82
Proxemics, 46, 159, 163–69
Putnam-Wilson Organizational
  Communication Conflict
  Instrument (OCCI), 251ff
Pygmalion effect, 144

Race, 61ff
Racism, 71, 233
Receptivity. *See* Innovativeness

Reentry, 216, 222–24
Reference groups. *See* Groups
Region, 13, 82
Reincarnation, 111
Relationship, 6, 24, 106, 228–34,
  256–57
Relative advantage, 277
Religious systems, 53
Reward, 47
Rhetorical communication, 234
Rhetorical Theory, 9
Ringi, 252
Ritual, 34, 49
Roles, 42–43, 63–64, 196, 244, 246
Rules, 34–36, 48
Rumor transmission. *See* Networks
Rurality, 13, 83

Sacred culture, 107
Secular culture, 107
Self-disclosure, 243
Self-esteem, 117, 122, 233, 234
Semi-fixed features of space, 165–66
Sense ratio, 171
Sensorics, 170–71
Sex differences. *See* Gender
Shamanism, 112
Shame, 106, 118
Similarity. *See* Homophily
Smell, 170
Sociability. *See* Credibility
Social categorization, 7, 62–65
Social change. *See* Intercultural
  communication change
Social class, 13, 85, 140
Social cognition. *See* Social
  categorization
Social control, 51
Social identity, 79
Socialization, 4, 34
Social style. *See* Communication style
Social system. *See* Systems
Society. *See* Systems
Socioeconomic cultures, 199
Sociofugal space, 165
Sociolinguistics. *See* Ethnolinguistics

Sociometric choice, 201
Sociopetal, 165
Spatial relationships. *See* Proxemics
Status, 174, 244
Stereotyping, 66–67, 69
"Stranger," 4
Stress. *See* Cultural stress
Stress-Adaptation-Growth Dynamic,
  219
Success, 122
Symbiosis, 56, 88
Symbols, 91, 195
Synchrony in culture, 169
Systems, 32, 37, 49–53, 120, 276, 281

Task, 6, 24, 106, 228, 232
Taylor-Johnson Temperament
  Analysis, 237
Team building, 284
Territoriality. *See* Proxemics
Themes of culture, 55
Theory X and Y, 110
Thomas-Kilman Conflict Model, 251
Thought, 40
Time. *See* Chronemics
Tolerance of ambiguity. *See*
  Uncertainty avoidance
Touch. *See* Haptics
Tradition, 122
Trialability, 277
Trust, 188. *See also* Credibility

Uncertainty avoidance, 104–5, 232,
  238
Uncertainty reduction, 4, 7, 21, 65
United Nations, 25
Urban, 13, 85, 272
USIA, 26

Values, 116–26, 179, 253–56

W-Curve, 216
Whorf hypothesis, 131–34
Work values, 121, 245
World view, 40, 233, 281
  cultural, 105–12
  personal, 112–16
World War II, 24–26, 158, 196